EARLY FATHERS FROM
THE PHILOKALIA

Uniform with this volume

*

Writings from the Philokalia
on Prayer of the Heart

Unseen Warfare
being The Spiritual Combat *and* Path to Paradise
of Lorenzo Scupoli

EARLY FATHERS
FROM THE PHILOKALIA

together with some writings of
St. Abba Dorotheus, St. Isaac of Syria and
St. Gregory Palamas

Selected and translated from the Russian text

DOBROTOLUBIYE

✝

by

E. KADLOUBOVSKY

and

G. E. H. PALMER

FABER AND FABER LIMITED
London

First published in 1954
by Faber and Faber Limited
24 Russell Square London W.C.1
Second impression 1959
Third impression 1963
Fourth impression 1969
Printed in Great Britain by
John Dickens & Co Ltd Northampton
All rights reserved

SBN 571 03794 1

To

OUR SPIRITUAL HELPERS

CONTENTS

* The volume numbers refer to the edition of the Dobrotolubiye published in Moscow, 1896–1901.

CONTENTS

INTRODUCTION

'Christians are mercifully given the most blessed, bright possibilities to have access to the Eternal Absolute, if only they follow with purity of heart, sincerity, abnegation and perseverance the Divine Teachings and leadership of our Redeemer, God and Saviour Jesus Christ, Son of God.'

These few words written to us by a friend from Mt. Athos serve as a fitting introduction to the Philokalia, for they clearly reflect the outlook and the level of attainment of the fathers, whose writings it comprises.

When, in the eighteenth century, Macarius of Corinth and Nicodemus of the Holy Mountain compiled their great selection from the holy fathers and called it the Philokalia,[1] they had precisely the aim of presenting a complete picture of the traditional way of Christian spirituality as it had been practised throughout the centuries from the earliest times of Christianity.

The original Greek Philokalia, published in Venice in A.D. 1792, contained 1,207 in-folio pages. The first translation to appear in Russia was an abridged version made by Paissy Velichkovsky in Slavonic and was published very soon afterwards. It was this version that was carried by the Pilgrim in *The Way of a Pilgrim*.[2] The Russian version, the Dobrotolubiye, being a translation made in the latter part of the nineteenth century by Theophan the Recluse, was considerably longer than the original; its five volumes contain almost 3,000 pages in all. Some omissions as well as additions were made by Theophan. It is from this text that our translations have been made. We include a list of the writers in all three versions in an appendix.

[1] See *La Prière de Jésus*, par un Moine de l'Église d'Orient. Collection Irénikon, Éditions de Chevetogne, Belgium. This little book gives an excellent historical account of the Jesus Prayer, as also of the Philokalia.
[2] *The Way of a Pilgrim*. Trans. by R. M. French, 1930. S.P.C.K., 1941.

INTRODUCTION

It is evident that to select from this quantity of material is not an easy task; and we must give some account of the considerations that determined our choice. In the first place, we had not this time the same great advantage that we enjoyed in relation to the previous volume,3 because in that case we had been given, by a contemporary monk of Mt. Athos, a selection and arrangement that has been used traditionally by those who are engaged in following this way; this fact naturally gave a special value to that selection. In this case, however, we must accept responsibility for the selection ourselves. Our object has been to confine the choice to writings of the fathers of the third to the seventh centuries of the Christian era, except that we have added (in an appendix) two short writings of St. Gregory Palamas, for reasons that will be explained later. The first task was to exclude certain fathers on the grounds that they were already to a greater or less extent available in English. This consideration excluded the famous Life of St. Antony the Great, and the writings of St. Macarius the Great, St. Ephraim of Syria, and St. John Cassian. In addition we omitted Diadoch on the grounds that there has been a recent French translation of his Century on Spiritual Perfection in the Sources Chrétiennes series4; finally we omitted St. John of the Ladder, as we understand that there are two English translations from the Greek in course of preparation.

This process still left us with some obvious great names: St. Antony the Great, St. Mark the Ascetic, Evagrius, St. Nilus of Sinai, St. Abba Dorotheus, St. Isaac of Syria (or Nineveh) and St. Maximus the Confessor. Despite the existence of an English translation of some writings of St. Isaac, we decided to include him, both for the depth of his understanding and the peculiar power of his style. In the case of St. Maximus we were aware of the translation of his Four Centuries on Love in the Sources Chrétiennes series,5 but could not resist the temptation of including here what must be one of the most profound and beautiful works in all

3 *Writings from the Philokalia on Prayer of the Heart*. Trans. by E. Kadloubovsky and G. E. H. Palmer, Faber & Faber, 1951.

4 *Diadoque de Photice. Cent Chapitres sur la Perfection Spirituelle*. Sources Chrétiennes—Éditions du Cerf, Paris, 1943.

5 *St. Maxime le Confesseur. Centuries sur la Charité*. Sources Chrétiennes—Éditions du Cerf, Paris, 1943.

Christian writing. To these names we have added that of Theodore, whose identity seems uncertain, but whose short Theoretikon has the qualities of comprehensive view and short exact expression, which make it a most fitting coda.

All the fathers so far mentioned lived early enough to belong to the common heritage of East and West, before the schism of the eleventh century. After consideration, it seemed useful to add some writings of St. Gregory Palamas (fourteenth century) for the reason that the West is turning to a study of Eastern spirituality, and these two short texts of his show how Palamas himself was in line with its great tradition, and they give the substance of his reply to some of the attacks that were made on him, attacks which widened still further the divergence between Eastern and Western spirituality. If this divergence is now gradually giving way to a desire in the West for a better understanding of the Eastern point of view, it may be that the inclusion of these two texts in company with some of the great fathers of the common heritage will be helpful to such understanding.

Finally we have included, as an appendix, some closing passages apparently written by Macarius of Corinth or Nicodemus the Hagiorite, which terminate both the Greek Philokalia and the last volume of the Dobrotolubiye. The purpose of including these was to show that the practice of ceaseless prayer, far from being confined to priests and monks, was considered in their day, as in earlier times, proper for all Christians. Such an idea may seem unfamiliar to many today; and in view of current conditions it is necessary to balance it by quoting a short passage from the Foreword to our previous volume, in which a monk of Mt. Athos wrote: 'Like all attempts to reach a certain spiritual level the practices described require a man's care, attention and constant watchfulness, to evade the very real and unsuspected dangers of trying anything *in his own way. . . .*'

It may be important to emphasise the scope of the themes that Macarius and Nicodemus considered it necessary to embrace in their selection. This traditional way of Christian spirituality is indeed all-embracing in the realm of doctrine as in the realms of theory and practical method. There will be found therefore in the Philokalia the fathers' treatment of the sublime themes of the relationship of God to His creation, and the relationship of man to both; a profound understanding of man's real nature; his actual, unnatural position; the means whereby he can not only recover what is his by nature, but transcend this to achieve. by grace, his highest potentiality, union with his Creator; in other words, the theme of man's unique role in the creation as the 'image and likeness' of God, the theme of sonship and deification.

Against such a background of doctrine, these writings describe the obstacles in man; his normal and subnormal psychology, his supranatural possibilities; the means whereby he can be purified, illumined and made perfect, pass from the darkness of ignorance to the light of knowledge (the Kingdom of Heaven); the essential role of the Sacraments; the stages whereby man must unify the three powers of his soul; must make single his tripartite nature; must overcome passions and acquire virtues to reach the final state of passionlessness, the fruit of which is love—in short the means and the stages whereby he learns to withdraw from the passionate, the sensory and even the intelligible worlds, to reach the perfect stillness and silence wherein he may be granted the final knowledge of God by union in love between knower and Known.

Together with all this, permeating and vivifying it all, there is much precious instruction as to fulfilling St. Paul's injunction to 'pray without ceasing'; and in particular as to the practice of constant invocation of Jesus, not only as a powerful aid in the processes of purification and illumination, but also as the supreme means by which the man, who has finally attained virtues, passionlessness and inner silence, may be raised by the Divine Name in his heart to know the Truth that makes men free.

There is one comment that we think should be made on these writings: namely, that they vary widely in respect of the spiritual levels to which they relate, while at the same time there are no indications in the texts to show to which level a particular passage is appropriate. This follows naturally from the fact that such writers would in those days assume that there would be personal direction normally available to readers who were making use of such texts. Today the position is quite different; hence it is important to grasp the difficulty, because it is by no means only a question of intelligence which determines whether a particular passage can be understood or applied in practice by a particular person; quite the contrary, it depends on his general degree of spiritual development, integration, understanding, discipline, being.

God is Immutable; and man does not change in his fundamental relationship, as a human creature, with his Creator. So despite the contrast of conditions, attitudes, habits of thought and sentiment between those centuries and today, these writings remain relevant for those who are seeking the true themes and principles of the authentic original Christian tradition; and we offer these translations, though we know that they must be imperfect, in the hope that they may prove of real value to some who have that aim. This work, in fact, is not meant as a contribution either to history or scholarship, but is based on the belief that it may meet some practical needs of the day.

Thus we have tried to make a selection which is representative of the most authoritative fathers, and which also presents the principal themes in the vast field covered by their teachings; no doubt our choice is to some extent arbitrary; others might well have made another and better choice; indeed no selection of this length can do full justice to the whole of the material.[6] The only final solution to the problem of making the treasures contained in the Philokalia available to the West in a form as rich and as wisely balanced as the original is for someone with the necessary qualities of scholarship, understanding and endurance, to undertake to translate the whole from the original Greek itself. We can only hope that this work will one day be achieved; it might well be one of the greatest single contributions to perpetuating in the West what is highest in the Christian tradition.

Meanwhile we hope that this volume will bring blessings to its readers. 'Whosoever shall confess me before men, him shall the son of man also confess before the angels of God.' (Luke xii. 8.)

E. KADLOUBOVSKY
July, 1953   G. E. H. PALMER

[6] There has recently appeared in France an interesting anthology, *La Petite Philocalie*, translated from the Greek by Jean Gouillard. Cahiers du Sud, 1953.

TRANSLATORS' NOTE

The Old Testament quotations (including the references to chapter and verse) are taken from the English version of the Septuagint[7]; for the New Testament, the Authorised Version was used.

The numbering of the paragraphs is as in the Russian version throughout (with one exception, specifically noted, in the extracts from Evagrius).

No parenthetical clauses have been inserted by the translators; those occurring in the English text are translated from the Russian; the majority were probably introduced by Theophan. Some of those in the Russian text have been omitted.

We are aware that some of the biographical details and some of the attributions of authorship (e.g. notably, as between Evagrius and St. Nilus of Sinai) are questionable according to modern scholarship. But since we do not possess the authority to make final pronouncements on these questions, and since to argue them would in any case distract attention from the main purpose of this book, we have judged it better to leave such questions to scholarly authority, and have confined ourselves to reproducing the biographical notes (sometimes abridged) and the attributions of authorship given in the Russian version.

The Four Centuries on Love of St. Maximus, and the Theoretikon of Theodore, are given in full; the texts of St. Nilus of Sinai, St. Isaac of Syria and St. Gregory Palamas are slightly abridged from the Russian version; the remaining writings consist of selections made by the translators.

To avoid footnotes, we give here some explanations about the use of a few words:

7 *The Septuagint Version of the Old Testament with an English translation and with various readings and critical notes.* S. Bagster & Sons Ltd., London.

TRANSLATORS' NOTE

(*a*) In the former volume we introduced the word 'prelest' (прелесть), and after due consideration have decided to retain it in a few cases where no English term seemed adequate for the context. The nearest equivalent seems to be 'beguilement' (cf. 'the serpent beguiled[8] me, and I did eat' [Gen. iii. 13]). But the meaning of prelest is both wider and more technical; unlike beguilement it is a state rather than the result of a particular action. Прелесть in general translates the Greek πλάνη; the latter literally means 'wandering' or 'going astray' (cf. πλάνος, deceiver, impostor). Prelest is the resulting state in the soul which wanders away from Truth.

If we may paraphrase Bishop Ignatiy Brianchaninov (d. 1867), we could define prelest as the corruption of human nature through the acceptance by man of mirages mistaken for truth; we are all in prelest.

(*b*) The word 'mind' (generally translating the Russian умъ and the Greek νοῦς) has been used comprehensively in these texts; that is to say that it comprises a range of meanings including discursive reasoning and the faculty of direct knowledge or intellectual apprehension of Truth. In each case the reader has to discriminate the sense from the context. The adjective 'mental' is to be understood as including a corresponding range of meanings. Man's nature is tripartite, comprising body, soul and spirit; mind is in some contexts taken as equivalent to this last; the soul also is tripartite, comprising the thinking, excitable and desiring powers. There are many passages in this volume which clarify these points; see, for example, St. Antony's 170 Texts on Saintly Life, paras. 93–8, 106, 118–19 and 126–31.

The word 'spiritual' is used throughout only as the adjective of spirit, never as meaning 'of the soul', which would be quite inadmissible.

(*c*) 'Theology' in these texts does not mean, as in the West, systematic theoretical knowledge relating to God. It means a gift of the Spirit, the gift of speaking about God with deep insight and with powerful and winning words. It is given only to those who have also received the high gift of 'wisdom' and have risen to 'contemplation'; hence it is sometimes spoken of as if it were

8 A.V. The Septuagint has 'deceived'.

identical with these. In the Orthodox tradition the title of 'Theologos' is given only to three writers: St. John the Evangelist, St. Gregory of Nazianzus and St. Simeon the New Theologian.

(*d*) The Russian word Искушеніе means both 'trial' and 'temptation'; it is impossible to avoid choosing one or another sense in translating, but there are many cases in which both meanings are implied by the context.

(*e*) The word 'ascetic' has been used occasionally, e.g. St. Mark the Ascetic. But it has been avoided as far as possible since modern western usage tends both to reduce and to distort its original meaning by laying the emphasis on bodily self-mortification, sometimes implying a kind of morbid excess which makes of physical suffering not a means but an end in itself.

The original Greek ἀσκητής implied primarily a man who *trained* for something, whether in the field of a trade or an art, of athletics or spiritual endeavour. The Russian word Подвижникъ has the same implication, but is limited to the field of spiritual endeavours. It will be obvious from these texts that this training (ασκησις, подвигъ) consists primarily of efforts to attain sobriety of mind and its spiritual fruits, whilst the mastery of the body and of the passions are subordinate and proportionate to this aim. We have found no single words which are equivalent in English.

Finally, though we take full responsibility for the translation ourselves, we wish to express our thanks to Prof. H. A. Hodges for the useful comments he was good enough to make about certain passages.

ST. ANTONY THE GREAT

ST. ANTONY THE GREAT[9]

1. 170 texts on Saintly Life

1. People are generally called intelligent through a wrong use of this word. The intelligent are not those who have studied the sayings and writings of the wise men of old, but those whose soul is intelligent, who can judge what is good and what evil; they avoid what is evil and harms the soul and intelligently care for and practise what is good and profits the soul, greatly thanking God. It is these alone who should properly be called intelligent.

2. A truly intelligent man has only one care—wholeheartedly to obey Almighty God and to please Him. The one and only thing he teaches his soul is how best to do things agreeable to God, thanking Him for His merciful Providence in whatever may happen in his life. For just as it would be unseemly not to thank physicians for curing our body, even when they give us bitter and unpleasant remedies, so too would it be to remain ungrateful to God for things that appear to us painful, failing to understand that everything happens through His Providence for our good. In this understanding and this faith in God lie salvation and peace of soul.

3. Restraint, meekness, chastity, steadfastness, patience and similar great virtues are given us by God for weapons to resist and oppose the tribulations we meet with, and to help us when they occur. So if we train ourselves in the use of these powers and keep them always ready, then nothing that may befall us will ever be hard, grievous, destructive or unbearable, for all would be overcome by the virtues we possess. Those whose soul is not intelligent never think of this, for they do not believe that all happens

9 Lived A.D. 250–350. The Life of St. Antony the Great by Athanasius is available in English in vol. i of the *Paradise of the Fathers*, Wallis Budge. (Translator's note.)

for our good, in order that our virtues should shine forth and that we should be crowned by God for them.

4. If you consider riches and their full enjoyment to be merely a short-lived illusory vanity, if you know that a virtuous life pleasing to God is better than riches, you will hold fast to this conviction and keep it in memory; then you will not sigh, complain or reproach anyone, but will thank God for everything, when you see that men worse than you are praised for eloquence or erudition and wealth. Insatiable desire of riches and pleasures, love of fame and vainglory, coupled with ignorance of truth, are the worst passions of the soul.

5. When an intelligent man examines himself he sees what he should do and what is useful to him, what is akin to his soul and leads to salvation and what is foreign and leads to perdition. In this way he avoids what harms the soul, as something foreign to it.

6. The more a man uses moderation in his life, the more he is at peace, for he is not full of cares for many things—servants, hired labourers and acquisition of cattle. But when we cling to such things, we become liable to vexations arising from them and are led to murmur against God. Thus our self-willed desire (for many things) fills us with turmoil and we wander in the darkness of a sinful life, not knowing ourselves.

7. We should say not that it is impossible for a man to lead a virtuous life, but that it is not easy. Indeed, it is not attainable for everyone in equal measure, for only those attain to virtuous life who are devout and who have a God-loving mind. The ordinary mind is worldly and unstable; it produces both good and bad thoughts, is changeable and leans towards material things. But a God-loving mind is an executioner of the evil which comes to men as a result of their self-willed carelessness.

8. Simple and uneducated men laugh at sciences and refuse to hear anything about them, for knowledge shows up their ignorance—and they want everyone to be like them. In the same way, men of unrestrained life and character greatly desire all others to be worse than themselves, thinking to find themselves excused by the fact that the wicked are many. . . .

13. He alone should be called a man who is intelligent (in the sense of the first text), or who has set about correcting himself.

An uncorrected person should not be called a man; for this quality (that is, incorrigibility) is not that of a man. Such men should be avoided. Those who live contentedly with evil will never be among the immortals (that is, gain blessed immortality).

14. Only by its actual use does the intelligence that qualifies us (according to the first text) make us worthy of being called men. Lacking such intelligence we differ from dumb animals only by the arrangement of our limbs and the gift of speech. So, let an intelligent man know that he is immortal, and let him hate all the shameful lusts which are for men the cause of death

15. Just as an artist shows his art by giving a beautiful form to the material he uses—one wood, another brass, another gold and silver—so too must we show that we are men not by the way our bodies are fashioned but by being truly intelligent in our souls— by the fact that we obey the law of good life, that is, a life that is virtuous and acceptable to God. A truly intelligent and God-loving soul knows how all things should be in life, lovingly inclines God to mercy, gives sincere thanks to Him and strives towards Him with all its desire and all its thought.

17. As helmsmen and charioteers acquire skill in their work through judgment and diligence, so those who seek a truly virtuous life must use attentive judgment and take care to live as they ought and as is acceptable to God. For a man who desires it, and is convinced that it is possible for him to attain his desire, does by faith attain incorruptibility (pure life).

18. Regard as free not those who are free by their status, but those who are free in their life and disposition. For example, one should not call truly free people who are illustrious and rich when they are wicked and intemperate, for such men are the slaves of sensual passions. Freedom and blessedness of the soul are the result of true purity and contempt of temporal things.

19. Remind yourself that you must constantly show your intelligence, but show it by a good life and by your actions themselves. In the same way, those who are sick consider and acknowledge physicians to be their saviours and benefactors not by the physicians' words but by their deeds.

20. That a soul is truly intelligent and virtuous is shown in a

man's look, walk, voice, smile, conversation and manner. In such a soul all has been transformed and has taken on its fairest aspect. Its God-loving mind, like a watchful doorkeeper, bars the entrance to evil and shameful thoughts.

23. Those whose life is passed in small and modest efforts become free of dangers and have no need of special precautions. By always conquering desires, they readily find the way leading to God.

24. Intelligent men should not listen to all kinds of conversation, but only to those which are profitable and lead to the understanding of God's will; for His will is the way by which men return once more to life and eternal light.

25. Those who strive to lead a virtuous and God-loving life should relinquish self-esteem and all false and empty glory, and should strive to reform their life and heart. A God-loving and steadfast mind is a guide and a way to God.

26. There is no profit in studying sciences if the soul has no good life pleasing to God. And the cause of all evils is delusion, prelest and ignorance of God.

27. Profound reflection on good life and care of the soul produce good and God-loving men. He who seeks God, finds Him by overcoming all desires through unceasing prayer to Him. Such a man does not fear the demons.

28. Those who are beguiled by earthly blessings, while knowing to the last word all that should be done to lead a good life, resemble those who have acquired remedies and medical appliances, but do not know how to use them and do not even trouble about it. Therefore let us not lay the blame for the sins we have committed either on our birth or on anyone else, but only on ourselves. For if our soul voluntarily surrenders to laziness, it cannot avoid being conquered.

29. A man who does not know how to discriminate between good and evil has no right to judge who is good and who evil among men. A man who knows God, is good; when a man is not good, it means that he does not know (God) and will never be known (by Him): for the only means to know God is goodness.

30. Good and God-loving men accuse people of something bad

when they are present, but when they are absent they not only refrain from accusing them, but do not permit others to do so when they attempt to speak of them.

31. No coarseness should be allowed in conversations; for modesty and chastity are usually attributes of the intelligent even more than of virgins. A God-loving mind is the light which illumines the soul as the sun does the body.

32. At the uprising of each of the passions of your soul, remember that those who think rightly and wish to put what concerns them (their lot) on a right and firm foundation, count as delight not the acquiring of perishable riches, but true glory (in heaven). It is this that makes them blessed. Riches can be stolen or taken away by those who are more powerful, but virtue of the soul is alone a safe possession, which cannot be taken away; moreover it is such as saves its owners after death. Those who reason in this way are not enticed by the illusory glitter of riches and other delights.

33. People who are inconstant and unskilled should not attempt to subject intelligent men to questioning. He alone is intelligent who tries to please God and is mostly silent, or, if he speaks, speaks little—and says only what is necessary and pleasing to God.

34. Men who strive after a virtuous and God-loving life are zealous for virtues of the soul, as a possession which is inalienably their own and brings eternal comfort. They use temporal things only as much as is necessary and as God wishes and provides, using them with gladness and all gratitude, even if they be very moderate. For a rich table feeds bodies, as being material, whereas knowledge of God, self-mastery, goodness, doing good to others, piety and meekness—deify the soul.

36. Those who count as a misfortune the loss of money, or children, or slaves, or some other possessions, should know, first, that we ought to be satisfied with what God provides; and then, when required, we ought to be ready to give this back with equanimity, not tormenting ourselves with grief at its loss, or rather at giving it back; like those who, for a time, use what is not theirs, and then return it.

40. It is impossible to become good and wise suddenly; but it

is achieved by careful deliberation, training, practice, long work and (above all) a strong desire of good. A good man who loves God and truly knows Him gives himself no peace in doing all without exception that is pleasing to Him. But such men are rarely met with.

41. People who have no natural inclination to good must not be discouraged and give way to despair. They must not cease striving after a virtuous life pleasing to God, however inaccessible and unattainable it is to them. They too must take thought and have a care for themselves as best they can. For, although they may not reach the summit of virtue and perfection, by taking thought and caring for themselves in every possible way they will either become better or, at least, not worse—and this is no small profit to the soul.

42. Through his mind man comes into contact with the ineffable Divine power, while in his body he is akin to animals. But those men are few who as real, that is intelligent, men strive to turn their thought to God and the Saviour, and to gain kinship with Him, and who prove this by deeds and a virtuous life. The majority, whose souls lack good sense, disregard this Divine and immortal sonship and incline towards dead, beggarly and short-lived kinship with bodies. Thinking only of physical things and inflamed by lust, like dumb animals, they cut themselves off from God of their own action and bring their souls down from heaven into the abyss of carnal desires.

43. An intelligent man, who thinks about communion and life with God, will never cling to anything low and earthly, but will direct his mind towards the heavenly and the eternal, knowing that God's will—this cause of all good and source of all blessings for men—is that men should be saved.

44. When you meet a man who loves to argue and he starts a dispute with you against what is true and self-evident, break off this dispute and withdraw from him, since his mind is completely turned to stone. For as putrid water makes even the best wines undrinkable, so evil conversations corrupt men who are virtuous in life and disposition.

45. If we use all means and all efforts to avoid death of the body, how much more must we seek to avoid death of the soul.

For there is no obstacle for a man wishing to be saved, except negligence and laziness of soul.

46. One can say of those who are not keen to learn what is useful for them and what should be considered good, that they are not in good health. Of those who, having learnt the truth, shamelessly argue against it, one can say that their good sense has been killed; their disposition has become animal, they do not know God and their soul is not illumined by light.

47. By His Word, God called into being various kinds of animals for our use—some to be used as food, others for our service. But man God created to be a witness and grateful interpreter of His works. This is what men should strive for, lest they die as dumb animals, without having seen or understood God and His works. Man should know that God can do all things. No one can resist Him Who can do all things. Just as by His word He brought all things into being from non-being, according to His will, so (now) He does all for the salvation of men.

48. Heavenly beings are immortal owing to the goodness which is in them. Earthly beings have become mortal owing to the self-willed evil in them, which increases in the unintelligent through laziness and ignorance of God.

49. Death, for those who understand it, is immortality; but for simpletons, who do not understand it, it is death. It is not this death that should be feared, but the perdition of the soul, which is ignorance of God. This is what is terrible for the soul!

50. Sin has found support in the material, and the body has become its seat. But an intelligent soul, having understood this, throws off the burden of materiality and, arising from under this weight, apprehends the Almighty God, carefully watching the body and mistrusting it as an enemy and an adversary. In this way, having conquered evil passions and matter, the soul is crowned by God.

51. When sin is understood by the soul, it is hated by it like a foul-smelling beast. But when it is not understood, it is loved by him who does not understand it and, enslaving its lover, keeps him in captivity. And the poor miserable man does not see what can save him, and does not even think about it; but thinking that sin adorns him, he welcomes it gladly.

52. A pure soul, for its fine quality, is sanctified and illumined by God; then the mind thinks of what is good and gives birth to godly intentions and actions. But when the soul is defiled by sin, God turns away from it, or rather, the soul itself falls away from God, and evil demons, entering its thought, suggest to it unseemly things: adultery, murder, plunder and other similar devilish evil deeds.

53. Those who know God are filled with all kinds of good thoughts and, desiring the heavenly, despise the earthly. But such men are seldom pleasing to others; so that many of the foolish not only hate them but also deride and abuse them. They are ready to endure dire poverty, for they know that what seems an evil to many is good for them. He who thinks of heavenly things believes in God and knows that all creatures are the work of His will; but those who do not think of it, never believe that the world is the work of God and created for the salvation of man.

54. Those who are full of sin and intoxicated by ignorance do not know God, for they are not sober in soul. But God is apprehensible to mind (that is, can be known only by a sober mind). Although He is invisible, yet is He very clearly manifest in the visible, like the soul in the body. As the body cannot live without the soul, so nothing visible and existing can stand without God.

55. What is man created for? In order that, through the knowledge of God's creatures, he should see God Himself and should glorify Him, Who has created them for man. A mind cleaving to God by love (a God-loving and God-beloved mind) is an invisible blessing, given by God to the worthy for their good life.

56. He is free who is not a slave of pleasures (sensory pleasures), but rules over the body by means of good judgment and chastity, and who is content with what God provides, however moderate, with wholehearted gratitude. When God-loving mind and soul come to an understanding with one another, the body is docile, however unwillingly, for then by the action of the mind the soul extinguishes every animal stirring.

57. Those who are not satisfied with what they have to sustain life, but who seek for more, make themselves slaves of passions, which trouble the soul and introduce into it ever worse thoughts

and fantasies—that everything is bad and, therefore, that new and better things must be acquired. As excessively long garments hinder travellers in their walking, so desire for excessive possessions does not allow the soul to make efforts and be saved.

58. Whatever a man finds himself in against his will and inclination is for him prison and torture. So be content with what you have; otherwise, if you endure (your condition) without gratitude (reluctantly, with discontent), you will be your own tyrant, without being aware of it. But there is only one way—scorn of worldly blessings.

62. When you close the door of your dwelling and are left alone, know that there is with you an Angel, allotted by God to every man, whom the Hellenes call the spirit of the home. He never sleeps and being always with you, sees everything. He cannot be deceived, and darkness hides nothing from him. And be aware that, besides him, God is present everywhere. For there is no place or substance where God is not present. He is greater than all and holds all in His hand.

67. If you wish, you can be a slave of passions, and if you wish, you can remain free and not submit to their yoke; for God has created you with that power. A man who overcomes passions of the flesh is crowned with incorruptibility. If there were no passions there would be no virtues, and no crowns given by God to those who are worthy.

68. Those who do not see what is profitable for them and do not know what is good, have an unseeing soul and their reason has gone blind. One must not look to them, lest perforce we should inadvertently suffer as do the blind.

72. Know that bodily ills are natural to the body, since it is material and corruptible. Therefore, if any such ill befalls, a soul instructed (in good) should thankfully show courage and patience, instead of reproaching God for having created the body.

73. Those who take part in Olympic games are crowned not after defeating one, or another, or a third opponent, but after defeating them all. In the same way every man who wishes to be crowned by God must teach his soul chastity, not only in relation to bodily passions, but also when he is tempted by greed of gain, by desire to seize what does not belong to him, by envy, love of

pleasures, vainglory, or tried by accusations, mortal dangers and the like.

74. Let us strive after a good and God-loving life not for the sake of human praise, but let us choose it for the sake of saving our soul. For death is every day before our eyes, and all that is human is insecure.

80. Some of those who stop in inns are given beds, while others having no beds stretch themselves on the floor and sleep as soundly as those in beds. In the morning, when night is over, all alike get up and leave the inn, carrying away with them only their own belongings. It is the same with those who tread the path of this life: both those who have lived in modest circumstances, and those who had wealth and fame, leave this life like an inn, taking with them no worldly comforts or riches, but only what they have done in this life, whether it be good or bad.

82. It is impossible by any means to escape death. Knowing this, truly intelligent men, experienced in virtues and God-loving thoughts, meet death without groanings, fear or tears, for they bear in mind the thought that on the one hand it is inevitable, while on the other it frees us of the ills to which we are subject in this life.

84. Do not talk with everyone about piety and good life. I say this, not out of jealousy, but because I think that in the eyes of a foolish man you will appear ridiculous. Like accords with like, and listeners for such conversations are few, or rather very rare. So it is better not to speak, for it is not this that God wishes for man's salvation.

85. The soul suffers with the body, but the body does not suffer with the soul. Thus, when the body is being mutilated, the soul suffers with it, and when the body is strong and healthy, the senses of the soul take pleasure in it. But when the soul reflects anew (repents), the body does not reflect (repent) with it, but remains detached, unmoving. For reflecting anew (repentance) is a painful feeling of the soul. In the same way ignorance, pride, unbelief, covetousness, hatred, envy, anger, cowardice, vainglory, ambition, discord, insensitiveness to good and the like are produced by the soul.

86. When you think about God, be pious, free from envy,

good, chaste, meek, as generous as you can, friendly, not argumentative and so on. For to please God by all this is that wealth of the soul, which cannot be taken away. In addition, you must not condemn anyone or say of anyone that he is not good, that he has sinned. It is better to search out one's own evil deeds and examine one's own life alone with oneself, to find whether it is pleasing to God. What business is it of ours if someone is not good?

87. A real man strives to be pious. That man is pious who desires nothing alien to him. What is alien to man is everything created. So, disdain all things, as befits the image of God. Man is an image of God when he leads a right life pleasing to God, and this is impossible unless he renounces all that is passionate. He whose mind loves God is skilful in all things salutary to the soul, and in every act of devotion required of him. A God-loving man blames no one else, for he knows that he too sins—and this is a sign of a soul on the way to salvation.

90. A man leading a pious life does not let evil enter the soul; and when the soul is free of evil, it is safe and sound. Over such men neither the evil demon, nor chance happenings have power. God delivers them from evil and they live invisibly protected as God-like beings. If anyone should praise such a man, he would smile inwardly at those who praise him; if anyone defames him, he does not defend himself against those who abuse him and is not indignant at what they say of him.

91. Evil clings ᴛo our nature like rust to iron, or dirt to the body. But as rust is not produced by the iron-worker nor dirt by the parents, so also evil is not produced by God. He gave man conscience and reason to avoid evil, knowing that it is harmful and prepares torment for him. So pay strict attention and when you meet some man possessed of power and wealth, be in no way beguiled by the demon to pander to him. But let death immediately stand before your eyes; and you will never desire anything bad or worldly.

93. Life is union and junction of mind (spirit), soul and body; death is not the destruction of these parts, but the disruption of their union; God preserves it all even after this disruption.

94. Mind is not soul, but a gift of God which saves the soul. A

mind pleasing to God flows ahead of the soul and counsels it to scorn the temporal, material and corruptible, and to love blessings that are eternal, incorruptible and immaterial, so that, while living in the body, man should, with his mind, apprehend and contemplate the heavenly and the divine. In this way a God-loving mind is a benefactor and saviour of the human soul.

96. Souls not bridled by reason and not governed by mind which restrains, steadies and directs (correctly) their passions—i.e. pleasure and pain—perish like dumb beasts, for their reason is swept along by passions, like a driver by runaway horses.

97. The most grievous disease of the soul, the worst calamity and disaster, is not to know God, Who has created all for man and has given him mind and word, by which, rising on high, he can enter into communion with God, contemplating and glorifying Him.

98. In the body is the soul, in soul is mind, and in mind is word. God, contemplated and praised by these, gives immortality to the soul, granting it incorruptibility and eternal bliss. For God has granted being to all that exists solely through His goodness.

100. Man receives good from God, since He is good. But man subjects himself to evil from himself, from the evil, lust and insensitiveness which are in him.

102. God is good but man is evil. There is no evil in heaven, and there is no true good on earth. But an intelligent man chooses the best: he learns to know the Almighty God, thanks and praises Him; he disdains the body even before death and does not allow its evil feelings (demands, desires) to be fulfilled, for he knows their harmfulness and their evil action.

103. A man who loves sin loves many possessions; he neglects righteousness and does not think of the uncertainty, instability and brevity of life, and does not remember the inevitability of death, which cannot be bribed. If a man shows such shamelessness and lack of sense even in old age, he is like a rotten tree and is no use for anything.

105. Word is servant to mind. What mind wishes, word expresses.

106. The mind sees all things, even those in heaven, and

nothing darkens it, save sin. But a pure mind finds nothing too hard to understand, and its word—nothing too hard to express.

107. In his body man is mortal, but in his mind and word immortal. In silence you use your mind, and in using your mind you speak inwardly in yourself; for in silence mind gives birth to word. And a grateful word offered to God is salvation to man.

108. He who speaks foolishly has no mind, for he speaks with no thought at all. But examine what is useful for you to do for the salvation of your soul.

109. An intelligent word, that profits the soul, is a gift of God; but an empty word, that seeks to determine the measure of heaven and earth, their distance apart, and the size of the sun and the stars, is an invention of men who labour in vain and through empty vainglory seek things which bring them no profit, as though trying to draw water with a sieve. For men cannot discover these things.

110. No one sees heaven or can know what is there except a man striving after a virtuous life, who knows and glorifies Him Who created it for the salvation and life of man. Such a God-loving man knows beyond doubt that nothing exists without God, that He is everywhere and in all things, for He is God, by nothing limited.

111. As man leaves his mother's womb naked, so does the soul leave the body; one soul emerges pure and bright, another is stained by downfalls, yet another is blackened by many sins. Therefore an intelligent and God-loving soul, remembering and reflecting on the trials and extremities that follow death, lives righteously, lest it be condemned and subjected to them. But unbelievers have no feeling, and so they sin, disdaining what awaits them there.

112. Just as when you leave the womb you do not remember what happened in the womb, so when you leave the body you do not remember what happened in the body.

113. As on leaving the womb you became better and larger in body, so on leaving the body pure and unpolluted you will become better and incorruptible in heaven.

114. As the body must be born after completing its development in the womb, so a soul, when it has reached the limit of life in the body allotted it by God, must leave the body.

115. Just as you treat the soul while it is in the body, so it will treat you on leaving the body. A man who indulges his body in this life, providing it with all kinds of comforts, serves himself ill for after death, for in his foolishness he has brought his soul to condemnation.

116. Just as the body cannot live if it comes out of the womb imperfect, so the soul cannot be saved or be in communion with God upon leaving the body, if it has not attained to vision of God through good life.

117. Uniting with the soul the body emerges into light from the darkness of the womb; but the soul, uniting with the body, becomes confined in the darkness of the body. Therefore we should not pity the body, but curb it as an enemy and adversary of the soul. For indulgence in good eating evokes evil passions, whereas an abstemious stomach stills the passions and saves the soul.

118. The body's organ of sight is the eyes, and the soul's organ of sight is the mind. As the body without eyes is blind, does not see the sun, which illumines the whole earth and sea, and cannot enjoy its light, so too a soul is blind when it lacks its proper mind and righteous life. It has no knowledge of God, does not glorify the Creator and Benefactor of all creatures, and cannot enter into His joy through being incorruptible and eternally blessed.

119. Ignorance of God springs from insensitivity and mindless-ness of soul; and this ignorance gives birth to evil. Conversely, knowledge of God brings good to men and saves the soul. So, if you remain in a state of sobriety and knowledge of God and try not to fulfil your own desires, your mind is turned towards virtue. But if, intoxicated by ignorance of God, you take pleasure in fulfilling your own evil desires, you will perish like a dumb animal, forgetful of the trials awaiting you after death.

124. A *man* is he who has understood what the body is, namely, that it is corruptible and short-lived. Such a man also has understanding of the soul, namely that it is divine and immortal and, being the breath of God, is joined to the body to be proved and to ascend to the likeness of God. A man who has rightly understood the soul, leads a righteous life pleasing to God, not trusting nor indulging his body. Contemplating God with his

mind, he also sees mentally the eternal blessings which God grants to the soul.

125. Being good and ungrudging (bountiful), God gave man freedom in relation to good and evil, by endowing him with reason, in order that man should see the world and all things in it and, through this, apprehend Him, Who has created every kind of thing for man. But an unrighteous man may desire and yet not understand this; to his misfortune he may not believe and may think contrary to truth. Such is man's freedom in relation to good and evil!

126. God decreed that as the body grows the soul should be filled with mind, so that man should choose out of good and evil what is pleasing to mind. A soul which does not choose good has no mind. So, although all bodies have souls, one cannot say that every soul has mind. A God-loving mind is found among the chaste, the just, the righteous, the good and pure, the merciful and devout. The presence of mind is the support of man in his relationship with God.

127. Only one thing is impossible for man—to avoid death. To have communion with God is possible for him, if he understands how it is possible. For if he so wishes and understands (how it is to be done), through faith and love, testified by a good life, a man can commune with God.

128. The eye sees the visible, mind apprehends the invisible. A God-loving mind is the light of the soul. He whose mind loves God is enlightened in heart and sees God with his mind.

131. As body without soul is dead, so soul without mind is inactive (barren) and cannot inherit God.

132. Only to man does God listen; to man alone does God reveal Himself; for God loves men, and wherever man may be, there too is God. Man alone is worthy to worship God; for man's sake God transforms Himself.

134. Good is invisible, as things in heaven are invisible. But evil is visible, as things on earth are visible. Good is outside comparison; and man, possessed of mind, chooses the best. Man alone is capable of apprehending God and His creatures.

135. In the soul it is mind that acts, but in the body—nature. Mind makes the soul divine, whilst nature decomposes the body.

Nature acts in every body, but not every soul has mind—and so not every soul is saved.

136. The soul is in the world, since it is born; but mind is above the world, since it is not born. A soul, which understands what the world is and wishes to be saved, has a rigid rule—to think every hour within itself 'Here comes the trial (of death), and the inquisition (of deeds), where you will not be able to endure (the glance of) the Judge, and the soul is about to perish.' Thinking thus, it preserves itself from worthless and shameful pleasures.

138. The mortal is subordinate to the immortal and serves it, that is, the elements serve man, through the loving-kindness and essential goodness of God the Creator.

140. Through the loving-kindness of our Creator, there are very many ways to salvation, which convert souls and lead them to heaven. Human souls receive rewards for virtue and punishment for sins.

141. The Son is in the Father, the Spirit is in the Son, the Father in Both. Through faith man apprehends all that is invisible and apprehensible by the mind. Faith is a free conviction of the soul as to the truth of what is proclaimed from God.

142. If people, who through some necessity or circumstances are forced to cross wide rivers, are sober, they preserve their life; for, even if the waters are turbulent and their boat ships water, they save themselves by clinging to something on the banks. If they are drunk, they may make numberless attempts to swim to the bank, but are overcome by wine, sink in the waves and leave the circle of the living. It is the same with the soul: if, having fallen into the turbulent waters and swirling currents of life, it does not by its own efforts rise above love of flesh and does not learn to know itself—namely, that it is divine and immortal, and is joined to a material body, mortal, full of passions and without faith, merely as a test; and if it allows itself to be enticed by carnal passions to its own perdition—then, negligent of itself, intoxicated by ignorance and disdaining its own good, it perishes and is left outside the circle of the saved. For like a river, the body often sweeps us towards worthless pleasures.

150. God is good, and passionless and immutable. If a man

accepts it as right and true that God does not change, yet is puzzled how (being such) He rejoices at the good, turns away from the wicked, is angered with sinners and shows them mercy when they repent, the answer to this is that God does not rejoice and is not angered, for joy and anger are passions. It is absurd to think that the Deity could be helped or harmed by human deeds. God is good and does only good; He harms no one and remains always the same. As to ourselves, when we are good we enter into communion with God through our likeness to Him, and when we become evil, we cut ourselves off from God, through our un-likeness to Him. When we live virtuously we are God's own, and when we become wicked, we fall away from Him. This does not mean that He is angry with us, but that our sins do not let God shine in us, and that they link us with the tormentors—the demons. If later, through prayers and good deeds, we obtain absolution of our sins, it does not mean that we have propitiated God and changed Him, but that through such actions and our turning to God we have cured the evil in ourselves and have again become able to partake of God's goodness. Thus, to say that God turns away from the wicked is the same as to say that the sun hides itself from those who lose their sight.

154. The mind which lives in a pure God-loving soul, truly sees God—non-begotten, invisible, ineffable—Him Who Alone is Pure for pure hearts.

156. The world is maintained through God's providence and there is no place which this providence does not touch. Providence is the self-fulfilling Word of God, the Giver of form to the substance constituting this world, the Architect and Artist of all that is. It is utterly impossible for matter to assume beautifully ordered form without the sagacious power of the Word, Which is the image, mind, wisdom and providence of God.

160. To a man who believes and desires, it is in no way difficult to apprehend God. But if you wish also to see Him, look at the perfect order and providence for all things, which have been and are through His Word.—And all this is for man.

161. He is called a saint who is pure from evil and sin. So the greatest perfection of the soul, a state most pleasing to God is—absence of evil in man.

166. I have written the present paragraph for the information of those who are simple, against men who assert that plants and grasses have a soul. Plants have physical life, but have no soul. Man is called a rational animal, because he is endowed with mind and capable of acquiring knowledge. Other animals—those on the ground and in the air who possess voice—breathe and have a soul. All things that grow and decrease can be called alive because they live and grow, but it cannot be said that all such things have soul. There are four kinds of living beings:—some of them are immortal and have souls, such as angels; others have mind, soul and breath, such as men; yet others have soul and breath, such as animals; and others only have life, such as plants. Life in plants is maintained without soul or breathing, without mind or immortality. But all the rest, too, cannot be without life. Every human soul is very changeable.

170. When you lie down on your bed, remember with thanksgiving the blessings and providence of God. Thereupon, filled with this good thought, you will rejoice in spirit and the sleep of your body will mean sobriety of the soul; the closing of your eyes—a true knowledge of God, and your silence, brimming with the feeling of good, will wholeheartedly and with all its strength glorify the Almighty God, giving Him from the heart praises that rise on high. For when there is no evil in man, then even thanksgiving alone is more pleasing to God than costly sacrifices. To Him be glory for ages of ages. Amen.

ST. ANTONY THE GREAT

2. Directions of our Holy Father Antony the Great on Life in Christ, derived from his Twenty Epistles

16. In my opinion the grace of the Holy Spirit most readily fills those who undertake spiritual work wholeheartedly and determine from the very beginning to stand firm and never to give ground to the enemy in no matter what battle, until they conquer him. However, the Holy Spirit, Who has called them, at first makes all things easy for them, in order thus to sweeten the beginning of the work of repentance, and only later shows them its ways in their full truth (arduousness). Helping them in all things, He impresses on them what works of repentance they should undertake, and lays down the form and limits both as regards the body and the soul, until He brings them to complete conversion to God, their Creator. For this purpose He constantly urges them to give exertion to body and soul in order that both alike, being equally sanctified, should equally become worthy heirs of eternal life; to exert the body in constant fasting, work and frequent vigils, and the soul, in spiritual exercises and diligence in all forms of service (and obediences) performed through the body. This (to do nothing carelessly, but always with care and the fear of God) should be zealously observed in all work done with the body, if we wish it to bear fruit. (Epistle I.)

17. Leading the repentant man to undertake spiritual work, the Holy Spirit, Who called him to repentance, also grants him His comforts and teaches him not to turn back nor be attached to anything of this world. To this end, He opens the eyes of the soul and gives her to see the beauty of the purity reached through the

works of repentance. In this way He kindles in it zeal for complete purification both of itself and of the body, that the two may be one in purity. For this is the aim of the teaching and guidance of the Holy Spirit—to purify them completely and bring them back to their original state, in which they were before the Fall, by destroying in them all adulterations introduced by the devil's envy, so that nothing of the enemy should remain therein. Then the body will become obedient to the dictates of the mind in all things, and the mind will masterfully determine its food and drink, its sleep and its every other action, constantly learning from the Holy Spirit to 'keep under' the 'body, and bring it into subjection' (1 Cor. ix. 27) as did Apostle Paul. (Ibid.)

18. It is known that the body has three kinds of carnal movements. The first is a natural movement, inherent in it, which does not produce anything (sinful, burdening the conscience) without the consent of the soul and merely lets it be known that it exists in the body. The second kind of movement in the body is produced by too abundant food and drink, when the resulting heat in the blood stimulates the body to fight against the soul and urges it towards impure lusts. Wherefore the Apostle says: 'be not drunk with wine, wherein is excess' (Eph. v. 18). In the same way the Lord commands His disciples in the Gospels: 'take heed to yourselves, lest at any time your hearts be overcharged with surfeiting, and drunkenness' (Luke xxi. 34). And those who are monks, and are zealous to achieve the full measure of sanctity and purity, should take particular care always to keep themselves such that they can say with the Apostle, 'I keep under my body, and bring it into subjection' (1 Cor. ix. 27). The third movement comes from the evil spirits, who thus tempt us out of envy and try to weaken those who have found purity (who are already monks), or to lead astray from the path those who wish to enter into the door of purity (that is, those who are as yet on the threshold of monkhood). (Ibid.)

19. However, if a man arms himself with patience and an unswerving faithfulness to the commandments of God, the Holy Spirit will teach his mind how to purify his soul and body from such movements. But if at any time he weakens in his feeling and permits himself to neglect the commandments and ordinances he

has heard, the evil spirits will begin to overpower him, will press upon all parts of the body and will befoul it by this movement, until the tormented soul will not know where to turn, in its despair seeing nowhere whence help could come. Only when, sobered, it returns again to the commandments and, shouldering their yoke (or realising the strength of its obligations), commits itself to the Holy Spirit, it regains a salutary disposition. Then it understands that it should seek peace solely in God, and that only thus is peace possible. (Ibid.)

20. Striving to attain perfect purity, it is needful to bear the labours of repentance both in soul and body, harmoniously and in equal measure. When the mind is granted such grace that it can enter upon its struggle against passions without self-pity or self-indulgence, it receives suggestions, directions and comforts of the Spirit, with Whose help it can successfully repulse from the soul all impure impacts that come from the lusts of the heart. Combining with the mind or the spirit of man, this Spirit helps a man in his decision strictly to fulfil the commandments he has learnt, by directing him to repulse from the soul all passions, both those which mix with it from the side of the body and those of its own, which exist in it independently of the body. He teaches a man to keep the body in order—the whole of it, from head to foot; eyes—to look with purity; ears—to listen in peace (or to peaceful things) and not to take pleasure in gossip, slander and criticism; tongue—to say only what is good, weighing every word, and allowing nothing impure or passionate to become mixed with its speech; hands—to be moved primarily for lifting in prayer and for acts of mercy and generosity; stomach—to be kept within suitable bounds in food and drink, allowing only as much as is needful to support the body, not letting lust and gluttony lead it beyond that measure; feet—to walk righteously, according to the will of God, aiming at the service of good deeds. In this way the whole of the body becomes accustomed to every good and, submitting to the power of the Holy Spirit, gradually changes, so that in the end it begins to participate, in a certain measure, in the qualities of the spiritual body, which it is to receive at the resurrection of the just. (Ibid.)

22. In His goodness, God the Father 'spared not his own'

only-begotten 'Son, but delivered him up' (Rom. viii. 32) to free us of our sins and wrongdoings. And the Son of God, humbling Himself for our sakes, cured us of the ills of our soul and provided salvation from our sins. I exhort you in the name of our Lord Jesus Christ, always to keep in mind and be aware of this great Divine Dispensation, that is, that for our sake God the Word became like us in all things save sin. It behoves those who have the gift of reason, to use it for this knowledge, and to strive to become free (from sins) in actual deed, by virtue of the Lord coming to us. Those who make use of this Dispensation as they should are His servants. But this status is not yet perfection. Perfection leads to sonship—and is a consecration, which comes in its own time. Thus when our Lord Jesus Christ saw that His disciples had already come near to sonship and, being taught by the Holy Spirit, had recognised Him, He said to them: 'Henceforth I call you not servants; . . . but I have called you friends; for all things that I have heard of my Father I have made known unto you' (John xv. 15). And those who understood what they had become in Christ Jesus, raised their voices saying: we 'have not received the spirit of bondage again to fear; but' we 'have received the Spirit of adoption, whereby we cry, Abba, Father' (Rom. viii. 15). If a man fails to show a full and zealous readiness to arise (from sin), let him be aware that the coming of our Lord and Saviour will be to his condemnation. Thus even in the beginning Simeon said, 'Behold, this child is set for the fall and rising again of many in Israel; and for a sign which shall be spoken against' (Luke ii. 34). And later the Apostles also said, 'To the one we are the savour of death unto death; and to the other the savour of life unto life' (2 Cor. ii. 16). (Epistle 2.)

23. It is not unknown to you that the enemies of truth never cease to strive to destroy truth. But God at all times, from the very beginning of the creation of the world, has visited His creation and taught those who approached their Creator with all their heart how they must worship Him. But through the passionate nature of the flesh and the malice of the enemies who fight us, the good tendencies of the soul lost their power; and men could not even grasp what was proper to them according to their nature and designation, let alone free themselves of sins to

regain their original state; then God showed them mercy and taught them true worship through written law. But when even this failed, God, seeing that the wound grows wider and demands drastic treatment, determined to send down His only-begotten Son, Who is our only Physician. (Epistle 3.)

24. When, overcome by love for Jesus Christ, I look at our times, I feel now joy, now grief and mourning. Very many of our race have put on the habit of devotion (monkhood). But of these only some have done this with their whole heart and been granted the deliverance brought by the coming of our Lord Jesus. These are they of whom I rejoice. Others, neglecting the strength (of their vow), obey the will of the flesh and the dictates of their heart—through which the coming of the Lord denounces them. These are they of whom I grieve. Finally, others have lost heart at the thought of the length of their labours; so they have taken off the habit of piety and become, as it were, dumb animals. These are they for whom I mourn, for the coming of our Lord Jesus Christ has condemned them. (Ibid.)

25. With all my strength I pray God for you, that He may send into your hearts that fire, which our Lord Jesus Christ has come to send on the earth (Luke xii. 49), that you may have power to govern rightly your intentions and senses and to distinguish good from evil. (Ibid.)

26. When the wind blows steadily, every sailor can think highly of himself and boast of his skill; but only a sudden change of wind reveals the skill of experienced helmsmen. (Ibid.)

28. God guides all by the action of His grace. Therefore do not be lazy or lose heart, but call to God day and night to entreat God the Father in His loving-kindness to send you help from above to teach you what to do. Do not give sleep to your eyes, nor slumber to your eyelids (Ps. cxxxi. 4) in your zeal to bring yourself to God as a pure offering, in order to see Him; for without holiness no one can see God, as the Apostle says (Heb. xii. 14). (Epistle 5.)

30. He who does not with his whole heart conceive hatred of all that belongs to the material and earthly flesh and to all its movements and actions, and who does not lift his mind on high to the Father of all, cannot receive salvation. But a man who does

this will move our Lord to mercy by his labours and will be given an invisible transubstantial fire, which will burn up all the passions in him and completely purify his mind. Then the Spirit of our Lord Jesus Christ will come to dwell in him and will abide there, teaching him to worship the Father aright. But as long as we take pleasure in our material flesh we shall be enemies of God, His angels and all the saints. I beseech you in the name of our Lord Jesus Christ, do not neglect your life and your salvation, do not let this short moment of time rob you of eternity which has no end, nor this material body deprive you of the kingdom of light, which has no bounds and which no words can describe. Truly my soul is troubled and my spirit freezes at the fact that, although we are given freedom to choose and do the deeds of the saints, we are intoxicated by passions, as though drunk with wine, and do not want to lift our minds on high and seek higher glory, do not want to imitate the deeds of the saints nor follow in their footsteps, to become heirs of their works and receive with them an eternal heritage. (Ibid.)

32. How many myriads there are of evil demons and how numberless are their varied wiles! . . . They urge us to speak evil of one another, or, speaking sweet words, to conceal bitterness in our hearts, to criticise the outer aspect of our brother, while we harbour a wild beast in ourselves, to quarrel among ourselves and oppose one another, wishing to have our own way and appear as the most upright. Every man who enjoys sinful thoughts falls willingly when he welcomes (is in sympathy with) the suggestions of the enemies and when he expects to justify himself solely by his visible deeds, while within he is the abode of the spirit of wickedness, who teaches him every evil. The body of such a man will be full of shameful uncleanness—for he becomes a prey to devilish passions, which he does not repulse from himself. Demons are not visible bodies, but we become their bodies when our souls accept dark thoughts from them. For, having accepted these thoughts, we accept the demons themselves and make them bodily manifest. (Epistle 6.)

33. Intelligent and immortal nature is hidden in our perishable body, that in and through this body it may reveal its actions. So, having made of this body an altar for the burning of incense, put

upon it all your thoughts and your bad counsels and, placing them before the face of the Lord, lift your mind and heart to Him, begging Him to send you from on high His transubstantial fire, to burn all that lies on that altar and purify it. And your adversaries, the priests of Baal, will be filled with fear and will perish at your hands as they did at the hands of the Prophet Elijah (1 Kings xviii. 25 et seq.). Then you will see a Man emerging from the Divine waters, who will cause spiritual rain to fall upon you, that is, the Holy Comforter. (Ibid.)

34. Having fallen from his heavenly rank through pride, the devil constantly strives to bring down also all those who whole-heartedly wish to approach the Lord; and he uses the same means which caused his own downfall, that is pride and love of vain-glory. These and similar things are the means by which the demons fight us and hope to separate us from God. Moreover, knowing that he who loves his brother loves also God, they put into our hearts hatred of one another—and this to such degree that at times a man cannot bear to see his brother or say a word to him. Many have performed truly great labours of virtue, but have ruined themselves through folly. It would not be surprising if the same thing were to happen to you too; if, for example, having cooled towards active work, you begin to imagine that you already possess virtues. For there you have already fallen into that devilish disease (high opinion of yourself), thinking that you are close to God and are in the light, whereas in actual fact you are in darkness. What made our Lord Jesus Christ lay aside his garments, gird himself with a towel, and, pouring water into a basin, begin to wash the feet of those who were below Him (John xiii. 4 et seq.), if not to teach us humility? For it was humility He showed us by the example of what He then did. And indeed those who want to be accepted into the foremost rank cannot achieve this otherwise than through humility; for in the beginning the thing that caused downfall from heaven was a movement of pride. So, if a man lacks extreme humility, if he is not humble with all his heart, all his mind, all his spirit, all his soul and body—he will not inherit the kingdom of God. (Ibid.)

38. I have prayed for you, that you too may be granted that great Spirit of fire, Whom I have received. If you wish to receive

Him, so that He dwells in you, first offer physical labours and humility of heart and, lifting your thoughts to heaven day and night, seek this Spirit of fire with a righteous heart—and He will be given unto you. In this way Elijah the Tishbite, Elisha and other prophets received Him. He who tills himself thus (as I have described) is granted this Spirit for ever and for ages of ages. Remain in prayer, seeking most arduously with your whole heart —and you will be given. For this Spirit resides in righteous hearts. And when He is received, He will reveal to you the highest mysteries, will banish from you the fear of man or beast, and heavenly joy will be yours day and night, so that you will be, in this body, like those who are already in the kingdom. (Epistle 8.)

39. If a man wishes to attain to love of God, he must have fear of God. Fear gives birth to mourning, and mourning to courage. When all this has ripened in the soul, it begins to bear fruit in all things. And, seeing these beautiful fruits in the soul, God draws it to Himself, like choice incense, takes joy in it with His Angels for all time, fills it with rejoicing, and protects it in all its ways, to let it reach its place of rest without harm. Then, seeing the Most High Guardian encompassing it, the devil no longer attacks it; indeed he fears to come near it owing to this great power. Obtain this power that the demons may fear you, your labours be light and Divine things a sweet joy. This sweetness of Divine love is far sweeter than honey. Many monks and virgins, living in communities, having had no taste of this Divine sweetness nor received Divine power, have thought that they had it already. But, since they had made no effort to gain it, God did not give it to them, He who strives to obtain it will surely gain it through God's mercy; for God is no respecter of persons. When a man wishes to have in himself the light of God and His power, and so disregards both the abuse and the honours of this world, hates all things of the world and ease of the body, and purifies his heart of all bad thoughts, when he unceasingly brings to God fasting and tears day and night, as well as pure prayers, then God enriches him with that power. Strive to obtain this power—and you will do all your works with calm and ease, will receive a great daring towards God and He will grant all that you ask. (Epistle 9).

41. Pray that God may give you grace to see and understand

all things clearly, so that you can discriminate correctly between good and evil. It is written by Apostle Paul that 'strong meat belongeth to them that are of full age' (Heb. v. 14). These are men, who by long and diligent work have their senses and intentions trained to discern both good and evil, who have become sons of the kingdom and are enrolled for Divine sonship. God has given them wisdom and good judgment in all their works, so that neither man nor devil can seduce them. You must know that the enemy tempts the faithful under the guise of good and succeeds in seducing many because they have neither wisdom nor good judgment. Therefore when Apostle Paul had learnt the riches of understanding, which are destined for the faithful, and whose greatness has no bounds, he wrote to the Ephesians, 'That the God of our Lord Jesus Christ, the Father of glory, may give unto you the spirit of wisdom and revelation in the knowledge of him: the eyes of your understanding being enlightened; that ye may know what is the hope of his calling, and what the riches of the glory of his inheritance in the saints' (Eph. i. 17, 18). He wrote this from his exceeding great love for them, knowing that if they attain it they will find hardship in nothing, no fear will touch them; but the joy of the Lord will comfort them day and night and their labours will be sweet for them at all times. Many of the monks and virgins living in communities do not attain to this measure. And you, if you wish to attain to this measure, in which is the height of perfection, should withdraw from all those who while they bear such names, that is, monkhood and virginity, yet lack this clear vision and good judgment. For, if you become connected with them, they will not let you make progress, and may even cool your ardour, because they themselves have no ardour but only coldness, since they follow their own desires. So, if they come to you and begin worldly conversations, according to their own desires, do not consent to it. For Apostle Paul writes, 'Quench not the Spirit. Despise not prophesyings' (1 Thess. v. 19, 20). Know that nothing quenches the Spirit more than idle talk. (Epistle 11.)

42. All rational beings, whether they be men or women, have an organ of love, by which they can embrace both the Divine and the human. Men of God love what is of God; men of the flesh love

what is of the flesh. Men who love what is of God, purify their hearts from all impurities and the affairs of this transient world, hate the world and their own souls and, bearing their cross, follow the Lord, doing His will in all things. Therefore God comes to dwell in them and gives them joy and sweetness, which feeds their souls, nourishes them and makes them grow. Just as trees cannot grow, if they have no natural water, so too with a soul, unless it receives heavenly sweetness. Only those souls grow, which have received the Spirit and are watered by heavenly sweetness. (Epistle 13.)

47. When the reign of sin comes to an end in man, God appears to the soul and purifies it together with the body. But if the kingdom of sin still lives in the body, man cannot see God; for his soul is in the body and there is no place in the soul for the light, which is seeing God. David says, 'In thy light we shall see light' (Ps. xxxv. 9). What is this light, in which man sees light? It is the light of which our Lord Jesus Christ speaks in the Gospels, 'If thy whole body therefore be full of light, having no part dark, the whole shall be full of light' (Luke xi. 36). The Lord also said, 'Neither knoweth any man the Father, save the Son, and he to whomsoever the Son will reveal him' (Matt. xi. 27). And the Son does not reveal His Father to sons of darkness, but to those who dwell in light and are sons of light, the eyes of whose hearts He has illumined by knowledge of the commandments. (Epistle 17.)

49. As the body, while the soul is in it, goes through three phases: youth, maturity and old age, so the soul, concealed in the body, also goes through three phases, namely: the beginning of faith, progress in it and perfection. In the first, when the soul begins to have faith, it is born in Christ, as is said in the Gospels. St. John the Apostle gave us signs of this new birth, of the middle state and of perfection, when he said; 'I write unto you, little children . . . I write unto you, fathers . . . I write unto you, young men . . .' (1 John ii. 12–14). He wrote thus not to his carnal friends but to those who have faith, depicting the three states, through which those who seek the realm of the spirit have to pass to attain perfection and to be endowed with fullness of grace. (Ibid.)

51. Every man whose effort is to become truly spiritual must try to hold himself aloof from noisy crowds and not go near them, so as to be outside the vortex and turmoil of men in body, heart and mind; for where there are men, there is turmoil. Our Lord showed us an example of withdrawal from people and solitude, when He used to go alone up into a mountain to pray. In the wilderness too He conquered the devil, who dared to wrestle with Him. Naturally He was not powerless to conquer him even among the multitude; but He acted thus to teach us that we can more easily overcome the enemy and reach perfection in silence and solitude. Neither did the Lord show His glory to the disciples in the midst of people, but led them up into a mountain and there showed them His glory. John the Forerunner also dwelt in the wilderness until he appeared to Israel. In the world it is easier for the enemy to press upon us with his weapons, both inner and outer; attracting some men as helpers and assistants obedient to him, he there wages war against the faithful. Some shameless woman may serve as a very strong weapon to him, spreading wide her ensnaring nets. When Ezekiel saw four living creatures, each with four faces, all showing the glory of the Lord, he was not in a city or a village but outside in a plain; for God said to him, 'Arise, and go forth into the plain, and there shalt thou be spoken to' (Ezek. iii. 22). In general such visions and revelations were given to the saints only in mountains and wilderness. Prophet Jeremiah, knowing how much solitude pleases God, also said, 'It is good for a man when he bears a yoke in his youth. He will sit alone, and be silent' (Lam. iii. 27–8). Again, knowing well how much harm human talk brings to those who want to please God, he could not refrain from saying, 'Who would give me a most distant lodge in the wilderness, that I might leave my people, and depart from them?' (Jer. ix. 2). Also Prophet Elijah received food from the angels, and this not among a crowd of people, not in a city or a village, but in the wilderness. All these and similar things, which occurred to the saints, were written to persuade us to imitate those who loved retirement, for it can lead us too to the Lord. So try to be well grounded in it, that you may be led to the vision of God, which is the most spiritual contemplation. (Epistle 17.)

52. I wish to tell you, too, what is the likeness of a soul when the fire of God has come to dwell in it. It is like a winged bird, soaring on high in the air of heaven. Of all creatures birds alone have wings, as their special feature. The wings of a soul obeying God are the leapings of Divine fire, which give it power to rise on high to heaven. If it is stripped of these wings it will be powerless to soar upwards, as lacking this fire, which lifts on high; and it becomes like a bird stripped of wings, which can no longer fly. Moreover, a man's soul is like a bird in this too: warmth is the cause of a bird's birth into the world; for if a bird does not warm the eggs it sits on, no living fledglings would come out of them, for they can come to life only through warmth. So too God, by encompassing and warming the souls that obey Him, rouses them to spiritual life. When you have realised that a soul that is obedient to God and cleaves to Him is like a bird whose source of life is warmth, never let yourselves be deprived of the power of this fire. Know that because of this fire, which God gives you, the devil has prepared many onslaughts to deprive you of it; for he well knows that while you have this fire in you, he has no means to overcome you. (Epistle 18.)

53. Oppose the devil and try to discern his wiles. He usually hides his gall under an appearance of sweetness, so as to avoid detection, and he fabricates various illusions, beautiful to look at —which in reality are not at all what they seem—to seduce your hearts by a cunning imitation of truth, which is rightly attractive. All his art is directed to this end—to oppose by all possible means every soul working well for God. Many and varied are the passions he introduces into the soul to quench the Divine fire, in which all strength lies; but above all he overcomes it by the inertia of the body and all that is connected with it. None the less, when he sees at last that some men guard themselves from all this and accept nothing from him and show no promise of ever obeying him—he withdraws from them with shame. Then the Spirit of God comes to dwell in them. And when the Spirit of God comes to dwell in them, He brings them rest, or lets them enjoy rest in all their activities, and makes the yoke of the Lord sweet for them, as it is written in the Gospels 'and ye shall find rest unto your souls' (Matt. xi. 29), although they have taken His yoke upon them-

selves and are bearing it. Then they become indefatigable, both in the practice of virtue and in carrying out obediences and night vigils. They feel no anger at human calumny and have no fear, whether of man, beast or spirit; for the joy of the Lord stays with them day and night, gives life to their reason and is their food. Through this joy the soul grows and becomes apt for all things or perfect; and through this joy it ascends to heaven. (Ibid.)

54. We see that a child grows, taking first the milk of the mother, then some other food and finally all kinds of food that men usually eat. Thus he grows strong, becomes mature and his heart valiantly meets enemies, if they attack him. But if he catches some disease in childhood, his feeding and gaining strength go less well; he grows up weak and any foe overcomes and vanquishes him. To regain his health and acquire the strength to overcome his enemies, he must have the help and care of an experienced physician. It is the same with the human soul: if it lacks Divine joy it is weak and suffers many wounds. If it tries to find a man, a servant of God skilled in spiritual healing, and attaches itself to him, he will first cure it of passions, and then will resurrect it and teach it how, with God's help, to obtain that joy which is its food. Then it will resist its enemies, which are evil spirits, will overcome them, will trample underfoot their counsels and will be filled with the most perfect joy. (Ibid.)

55. Beware of the counsels of the evil one, if he should come in the guise of one professing truth to beguile you and lead you into deceit. Even if he should come to you as an angel of light, do not believe him or obey him: for he is apt to fascinate the faithful by the attractive semblance of truth. Those who are not perfect do not know these wiles of the devil and are not aware of what he is constantly putting into them; but the perfect know, as the Apostle says, 'But strong meat belongeth to them that are of full age, even those who by reason of use have their senses exercised to discern both good and evil' (Heb. v. 14). These the devil cannot seduce; but he easily fascinates those faithful, who keep scant attention on themselves, by a bait which appears sweet, and he catches them as a fisherman catches fish with a hook hidden in the bait . . . as Solomon says, 'There are ways that seem to be right to a man, but the end of them looks to the depth of hell'

(Prov. xvi. 25). These things happen to them because in their self-reliance they always follow the inclinations of their heart and fulfil their own desires, not listening to their fathers or asking their advice. So the devil shows them visions and illusions, and puffs up their hearts with pride. Sometimes he sends them dreams at night, which he fulfils in the daytime, thus to plunge them into greater prelest. More than that, he at times shows them light at night, so that the place where they are becomes bright; and he does many other things mistaken for true signs. He does all this to set their mind at rest as regards himself and make them accept him for an angel. As soon as they have accepted him as such, he hurls them down from their height, through the spirit of pride which takes possession of them. He strives to keep them in the conviction that they have become greater and more glorious in spirit than many others and have no need to turn to their fathers and listen to them. But they, according to the Scriptures, are in reality clusters of grapes, shiny but bitter and unripe. Directions of the fathers are onerous for them, for they are convinced that they know everything already. (Ibid.)

57. I shall indicate to you the practice, which alone makes a man firm in the good and keeps him such from beginning to end: and this is—love God with all your soul, all your heart and all your mind, and work for Him alone. Then God will give you great strength and joy, and all godly works will become for you as sweet as honey, and all physical labours, mental occupations and vigils, generally the whole yoke of God, will be sweet and light for you. However, from His love for men the Lord at times sends them adversities, that they should not exalt themselves but continue striving; and, instead of courage, they feel heaviness and weakness; instead of joy—sadness; instead of peace and quiet they feel agitation; instead of sweetness—bitterness; and many other similar things happen to those who love God. But, by struggling and prevailing, they gradually become stronger and stronger. When they finally overcome it all, then the Holy Spirit abides with them in all things and they fear evil no more. (Ibid.)

58. The fragrance of the Holy Spirit is ever pleasing, most sweet, ineffable for human tongue. But who knows this pleasantness and sweetness of the Spirit, save those in whom He has come

to dwell? The Holy Spirit comes to dwell in the souls of penitents only after many labours. We see many similar things even in this world; for example, precious stones are obtained only with great labour. Having sought this Spirit, the saints have obtained Him, and He is that precious pearl of which the Gospel speaks in the parable of a merchant man, seeking goodly pearls, who, when he had found one pearl of great price, went and sold all that he had, and bought it (Matt. xiii. 45–6). The same is in the parable of a 'treasure hid in a field; the which when a man hath found, he hideth, and for joy thereof goeth and selleth all that he hath, and buyeth that field' (Matt. xiii. 44). Temptations assail no one more than those who have received the Holy Spirit. Our Lord too, when in baptism the Holy Spirit descended on Him like a dove, being led by the Spirit into the wilderness, was tempted by the devil, who tried Him with all his temptations, but in no way succeeded against Him; as it is written in the Gospel of St. Luke: 'And when the devil had ended all the temptation, he departed from him for a season' (Luke iv. 13). The Lord Jesus then returned to Galilee in the strength of the Spirit. So, too, the Holy Spirit fortifies also all those who have received Him, who fight and overcome, and He gives them strength to conquer all temptations. (Epistle 19.)

60. Purity, everlasting and unchanging peace, fullness of mercy and other beautiful virtues, crowned by blessing, are God's commandments. Strive to fulfil these commands of the Spirit, which will give life to your souls and through which you will receive the Lord into yourselves—they are the safe way. Without purity of heart and body no one can be perfect before God; therefore it is said in the Gospels, 'Blessed are the pure in heart: for they shall see God' (Matt. v. 8). Perfection is born of purity of heart. The heart contains good naturally and evil unnaturally. Evil gives birth to passions of the soul, such as condemnation, hatred, vainglory and the like. The good gives birth to knowledge of God and sanctity or purity of soul from all passions. If a man decides to mend his ways and begins to avoid all evil, arming himself against it by his efforts—mourning, contrition, sighings, fasting, vigils, poverty and many prayers to God—the Lord by His grace will help him and will free him also of all passions of the

soul. Many who have long been monks and virgins have not learnt to master this science of purity, because, disdaining the directions of their fathers, they have followed the desires of their own hearts. For this reason evil soul-destroying spirits have taken possession of them, wounding them day and night with invisible arrows and giving them no peace in any place, so that their hearts were occupied now by pride, now by vanity, now by impious envy, now by censure, now by anger and rage, now by quarrels and many other passions. Their lot will be with the five foolish virgins, because they senselessly waste all their time—do not curb their tongues, do not keep their eyes pure, do not protect their bodies from lusts and their hearts from impurities and other things, lamentable for their uncleanness—and they are satisfied simply with a linen garment, which is a mere token of virginity. So they are deprived of the heavenly oil for lighting their lamps, and the bridegroom will not one day open to them the doors of his chamber but will say to them, as he said to the foolish virgins: 'Verily I say unto you, I know you not' (Matt. xxv. 12). I am writing this because I wish you to be saved—to become free and true, and a pure bride for Christ, Who is the Bridegroom of all souls, as Apostle Paul says: 'I have espoused you to one husband, that I may present you as a chaste virgin to Christ' (2 Cor. xi. 2). (Epistle 20.)

64. Let us awake from sleep, while we are still in the body, let us sigh over ourselves and mourn over ourselves from our whole heart day and night, to be delivered from the terrible torment, groaning, weeping and anguish which will have no end. Let us beware of the wide gate and the broad way leading to destruction, although a great many go in thereat; but let us go in at the strait gate and the narrow way which lead unto life, and few there are which go through it. Those who follow the latter way are real doers, who receive the reward of their labours with joy and inherit the kingdom. As to those who are not yet quite ready to approach it, I implore them not to be negligent while there is time, lest in the hour of need they find themselves without oil and with no one who would agree to sell it. For this happened to the five foolish virgins who found no one from whom to buy it. Then they cried, weeping, 'Lord, Lord, open to us.

But he answered and said, Verily I say unto you, I know you not'
(Matt. xxv. 11, 12). And this happened to them for no other
reason than laziness. Later they woke up and began to busy themselves, but it was of no avail, for the Master of the house got up
and closed the door, as it is written. (Ibid.)

ST. MARK THE ASCETIC

ST. MARK THE ASCETIC
Short Biographical Note

St. Mark the Ascetic is amongst the most famous Egyptian Fathers. But little is known of the circumstances of his life. Palladius,[10] who had met him personally, says that his quiet and meek disposition was beyond compare, and that from his youth he was fond of studying the Holy Scriptures and knew them so well that he learnt by heart both the Old and the New Testaments.[11]

His strict life and purity of heart raised him to a high degree of spiritual perfection. St. Macarius of Alexandria testifies to a special manifestation of Divine grace towards him during communion, which shows the great strength of St. Mark's faith, the fire of his love for the Lord and his extreme humility.

St. Mark lived for more than a hundred years and died probably at the beginning of the fifth century. But he lived at a time which enabled him to meet the first successors of St. Antony's life and teaching, and perhaps even St. Antony himself.

Divine grace, experience of life and study of the word of God gave him a profound knowledge of the mysteries of spiritual life. He did not hide this talent and taught and wrote much, but only a few of his writings have reached us.

[10] *Paradise of the Fathers*, vol. I, bk. II, 1. (Translators' note.)
[11] Sosomen records the same. *History of the Church*, vol. VI, ch. 29. (Note in the Dobrotolubiye.)

ST. MARK THE ASCETIC

1. Epistle to the Monk Nicholas

Beloved Son Nicholas . . .

10. A man must, above all, strive after knowledge and reason, if he wants to take up his cross and follow Christ, constantly examining his thoughts, taking every care to gain salvation and adhering to God with all his strength. He should also question other servants of God, who are of the same mind and soul and who are doing the same work, in order to know how and where to direct his steps and not walk in the dark without a bright lamp. For a self-reliant man, walking without the knowledge and guidance of the Gospels, often stumbles and falls into many pitfalls and nets of the evil one, frequently goes astray and is subject to many calamities, not knowing where he will arrive in the end. Many have gone through great feats of self-mortification and endured much labour and sweat for the sake of God; but their self-will, lack of good judgment and the fact that they did not deem it necessary to seek salutary advice from their brethren, made these labours useless and vain.

22. If you wish, my son, to acquire and possess within yourself your own lamp of mental light and spiritual knowledge, that you may walk without stumbling in the deepest night of this age and have your steps ordered by the Lord (Ps. cxviii. 133), according to the words of the Prophet, you must greatly desire the path of the Gospels, that is, to practise the most perfect Gospel commandments with ardent faith and become a participant in the passion of Christ through desire and prayer; then I will show you a wonderful method to achieve this, consisting of an inner state of the spirit, which demands no physical work or effort, but the most painful labour of the soul, mastery of the mind (over all

things within) and attentive thought, together with the fear and love of God. By this state you can easily turn to flight enemy hordes, as did the blessed David who, having slain one alien giant with faith and trust in God, by this very fact put to flight the hordes of the enemies with their peoples.

23. I speak of the three strong and powerful alien giants, on whom are founded all the hostile forces of the mental Holophernes. If they are cast down and slain, all the forces of the evil spirits will be finally defeated. These three giants of the evil one, who seem to be strong are *ignorance,* mother of all ills, *forgetfulness,* her sister, aider and abettor, and *laziness* (indifference) which out of darkness weaves a dusky garment and cloak in the soul. This latter strengthens and affirms the former two, gives them substance and makes evil take firm root in a negligent soul and become an essential part of it. For through indifference (laziness), forgetfulness and ignorance the props of all other passions grow and strengthen. Since they mutually help one another and cannot exist independently of one another, they (in their totality) are powerful forces of the enemy and chief generals of the evil one. With their help the hordes of evil spirits fashion their snares in the soul and succeed in carrying out their plans.

24. If you wish to gain victory over passions and easily put to flight the hordes of mental aliens, collect yourself inwardly with God's help by prayer and, descending into the depths of your heart, find there those three strong giants of the devil—I mean forgetfulness, indifference or laziness, and ignorance, the food on which all other passions feed and act, live and grow strong in self-indulgent hearts and unpunished souls. With strict attention to yourself and a sober mind, and with help from above, you will certainly find these evil passions, unknown and not even suspected by others, yet more pernicious than the rest; you will find them by the weapons of righteousness which are their contrary. These weapons are memory of the good, the source of all blessings, enlightened knowledge, by which a soul kept in sobriety chases away the darkness of ignorance, and a lively zeal, which rouses the soul and leads it to salvation. Thereupon, armed with these weapons of virtue, accompanied by every prayer and supplication, you will manfully and valiantly conquer (completely chase

away) these three giants of mental aliens by the power of the Holy Spirit. That is to say, with the help of an excellent godly memory always reflecting on 'whatsoever things are true, whatsoever things are honest, whatsoever things are just, whatsoever things are pure, whatsoever things are lovely, whatsoever things are of good report; if there be any virtue, and if there be any praise' (Phil. iv. 8), you will chase away wicked forgetfulness; by enlightened heavenly knowledge you will destroy the pernicious darkness of ignorance; and by a lively zeal, ready for every good action, you will drive away godless indifference (laziness), through which evil becomes firmly rooted in the soul. You acquire these virtues not merely by your own will alone, but by the power of God and with the help of the Holy Spirit, with much attention and prayer. Having thus acquired them you will be able, through them, to free yourself from the said three strong giants of the evil one. When through the power of active grace there is formed and carefully preserved in the soul a (tripartite) alliance of true knowledge, memory of the words of God and righteous zeal, then every trace of forgetfulness, ignorance and indifference will vanish from the soul. They will be resolved into nothing, and at last there will reign in the soul the grace of Christ Jesus, our Lord, to Whom be power and glory for ever and ever, Amen.*

* Cf. St. Gregory of Sinai, paras. 122–3, *Writings from the Philokalia*, pp. 66–7.

ST. MARK THE ASCETIC

2. Directions of St. Mark extracted from his other discourses

1. Faith consists not only in being baptised into Christ, but in fulfilling His commandments. Holy baptism is perfect and offers us perfection, but does not perfect a man who fails to fulfil the commandments.

3. Of his own will a man remains there where is his love, even if he has been baptised, for the freedom of his will is not constrained. When the Scriptures say that 'the kingdom of heaven suffereth violence' (Matt. xi. 12), they are speaking of one's own will, so that each one of us should urge himself, after baptism, not to turn towards evil but to abide in good. Those who have received the power to fulfil the commandments, the Lord commands, as being faithful, to be diligent in them, that they may not turn back.

4. Spiritual training is not something separate from commandments. It is the commandments. Show me works which are not commandments. If you speak of prayer—this is a commandment; if of casting down imaginations—this is a commandment (be sober and watch); if of fasting and vigil, this too is a commandment; if you consider self-mortification, this is a commandment (renounce yourselves). Whatever act of ascetic virtue you may mention—each one is a commandment.

5. Holy baptism gives us complete liberation; but to shackle oneself once more by passionate attachment or to remain liberated through doing the commandments lies within our own free will. If thought is firmly caught in some sinful pleasure, it is through our own wilful attachment and is not something that

happens against our will. According to the Scriptures, we have the power of 'casting down imaginations' (2 Cor. x. 5). An evil thought, for those who cast it down in themselves, is a sign of their love of God, and not of sin; for not the impact of the thought is sin, but friendly converse of the mind with it. If we have no fondness for it, why do we linger in it? It is impossible that anything we hate whole-heartedly should have long converse with our heart, unless we are wickedly parties to it.

6. When after holy baptism, being endowed with power to fulfil the commandments, we do not do so, we become possessed by sin even unwillingly, until we move God to mercy by repentance, striving to do all His commandments, and He abolishes the sin of our self-will.

7. You have put on Christ through baptism (Gal. iii. 27) and have the power and the weapon to cast down imaginations (2 Cor. x. 5). But if, having power over them, you do not cast them down at the first suggestion, it is obvious that you are pleasure-loving through unbelief; that you consent to them and make friends with them. So you are yourself guilty in such behaviour.

8. At times some bad thought we hate suddenly attacks us without our consent like a robber, and forcibly imprisons our mind. Yet know for certain that even this thought arose from ourselves; for either we have been surrendering to this bad thought since baptism, although not acting upon it; or we voluntarily keep within ourselves some seeds of evil, which give the evil one strength to dwell in us; and having power in us through these evil seeds, he will not leave us until we discard them. As to an evil thought which remains in us through our doing evil, it will be driven away when we bring to God works worthy of repentance. So you are yourself guilty of an involuntary thought which troubles you, for having the power to drive it away and cleanse your mind of it at the start of its first suggestion, you have not done so, but have willingly conversed with it, although not carrying it into action. (It comes to a place kept warm, as to an old friend or comrade.)

9. When you see in your heart help coming to you, know for certain that this grace has not come to you from outside, but that the grace mysteriously given you at baptism has now become

active in you, in the measure that you have hated a thought and turned away from it.

11. As though linked in evil kinship, our lusts and impacts of thoughts act in consort with one another. Each thought, taking root in the man who has welcomed it, passes him on to its next of kin, so that the man, strongly drawn by habit to the first, is carried away by the second, even against his will. For who can escape pride if he is full of vainglory? Or who, having slept his fill and abandoned himself to pleasure, will not be overcome by lustful imaginings? Or who, having given himself up to extortion, will not fall captive to mercilessness? And how can those who enjoy all this avoid irritability and anger?

12. Even after receiving grace, it is in our will to walk according to the flesh or according to the spirit. But to walk according to the spirit is impossible for a man, who loves human praise and indulging his body; and to live according to the flesh is impossible for those who have inwardly chosen to give preference to the future life over the present. Therefore we should hate human praise and indulgence of the body, through which evil thoughts are born in us even without our will, and should say sincerely to the Lord, 'I have hated them with perfect hatred; they were counted my enemies' (Ps. cxxxviii. 22).

13. To those baptised in the Church baptism mysteriously gives grace, which dwells in them secretly; later, as they practise the commandments and keep hope in their minds, grace reveals itself in the believer according to the words of the Lord: 'He that believeth on me . . . out of his belly shall flow rivers of living water. (But this spake he of the Spirit, which they that believe on him should receive.)' (John vii. 38, 39).

16. Thus, if any of the faithful, living according to the commandments, has correspondingly acquired a certain spiritual doing, he should believe that he had already received the power for this; for he received at baptism the grace of the Holy Spirit— the cause of all good, of virtues not only secret and spiritual, but also visible. Let no virtuous man suppose that he can do anything good by his own powers alone, for 'a good man out of the good treasure of the heart bringeth forth good things' (Matt. xii. 35),

and not out of himself, meaning by the treasure, the Holy Spirit concealed in the hearts of the faithful.

17. A man who has convinced himself that, according to the words of the Apostle, he has Christ concealed in him from baptism, renounces all things of the world and remains in his heart, keeping it with the utmost care (Prov. iv. 23). 'For it is God which worketh in you both to will and to do of his[12] good pleasure' (Phil. ii. 13). By the words 'of good pleasure' the Apostle shows that to have good pleasure in virtues depends on our free will, but to practise them or to uproot sins without God is impossible. The words 'without me ye can do nothing' (John xv. 5) have the same meaning. But in all things there is too our own participation.

18. The sovereign mind of every man first receives, from out the secret temple of the heart, good and blessed counsels from Christ dwelling within; (thereupon) he puts these counsels into practice by virtuous living, which he offers back to Christ, Who gave him counsel through good thoughts.

19. The blessings that the righteous will receive on resurrection are on high; but betrothals to these blessings and their first-fruits are even now acting spiritually in the hearts of believers, so that, possessing testimony of the future, we should renounce all the present and should love God unto death. Therefore the Apostle said, not you are to come, but 'ye are come unto mount Sion, and unto the city of the living God, the heavenly Jerusalem' (Heb. xii. 22), for we were all given this possibility upon baptism, but only those of firm faith are granted it, those who die daily for love of Christ, that is, those who have risen above all thought of the present life and think of nothing but how to attain to perfect love of Christ. Seeking this above all else St. Paul said, 'I follow after, if that I may apprehend that for which also I am apprehended of Christ Jesus' (Phil. iii. 12), that is, that I may love as I am beloved of Christ. And when he reached this love, he no longer wished to think of aught else—neither of afflictions of the body, nor of the marvels of creation, but he abandoned all visible things and said, 'Who shall separate us from the love of

[12] The word 'his' appears italicised in the A.V. Mark interprets the passage without it. (Translators' note.)

Christ?' (Rom. viii. 35). So he no longer wanted to think of anything, but only to dwell there (in the heart, in the love of Christ).

20. The Apostle said that we have in ourselves the firstfruits of the Spirit (Rom. viii. 23), thus showing the measure of our capacity; for we cannot contain the total effect of the Spirit except by perfection in the commandments. Just as the sun, being perfect, pours out upon all a perfect, single and equal blessing, but each man receives its light so far as his eye is clear; so too the Holy Spirit has made those who believe in Him able from baptism to receive all His effects and gifts; yet His gifts do not act in all people in equal measure, but to each they are given in the measure of his practice of the commandments, that is, to the degree that he has testified by good deeds and has shown the measure of his faith in Christ.

21. A suggestion of Satan is a purely mental imagining of some wicked thing (or action); it is only our lack of faith which allows it the possibility of even coming near our mind. For when, after receiving the commandment to lay aside all troubles and to keep our heart with the utmost care (Prov. iv. 23) and to seek the kingdom of heaven which is within us, the mind falls away from the heart and from this seeking, it immediately gives room to the devil's suggestions and becomes accessible to evil counsel. But even then the devil has no power to move our thoughts, for otherwise he would show us no mercy, but would force every kind of evil thought upon us and allow us none that are good. His power is limited to suggesting the false only at the first onset of a thought, to test which way our inner disposition will incline, towards his counsel or towards God's commandment, for they are opposed to one another.

22. When the impact of some hateful thought lingers inside and becomes established there, this is due not to our new disposition but to what we have previously received. Such an impact stands arrested as a single thought. Resentment of the heart prevents its passing into multiplicity of thought and passion. A single (bare) thought, hated by a man who pays heed to himself, has no power to entice the mind into multiplicity of thoughts. This can happen only when the heart has a sympathy for it. Therefore, if we completely renounce all sympathy, the appearance (in the

mind) of previously received images will always remain merely a bare thought and will no longer have the power to harm us or offend our conscience.

23. When the mind understands the uselessness of its struggle against images (impressions) received previously and confesses its former guilt to God, this temptation itself is withdrawn and the mind regains its power to take heed of the heart and to keep it with the utmost care by prayer, striving to enter into the most inner and safe chambers of the heart, where there are no longer tempestuous winds of evil thoughts to drive both soul and body into the rapids of lust and the torrent of uncleanness; nor is there there the broad and roomy way, paved with words and images of worldly sophistry, which beguiles those who follow it, however wise they may be. For the innermost pure chambers of the soul and the house of Christ admit our mind, when it is stripped bare and brings with it nothing of this world, whether justified by reason or not, except 'these three,' designated by the Apostle, 'Faith, hope, charity' (1 Cor. xiii. 13). So, if a man loves truth and wants to guard his heart, then, as was said above, he can stop being enticed away even by the impressions he has previously received, but can pay heed to his heart, make progress (in attainment) towards the innermost and draw nearer to God, provided he does not neglect the work of prayer and living (according to God). For a man cannot help working in his heart if he heedfully abstains every day not only externally, but also internally, from distractions of the mind and carnal pleasures.

24. Not to experience impacts of evil belongs only to the Immutable—but not to human nature. Adam too was accessible to suggestions of Satan. But he had the power either to listen to them or not. The impact of a thought is neither sinful nor righteous— it is a test of our free will. This is why it is allowed to impinge upon us, so that those who incline towards the commandment should be rewarded for their faithfulness with crowns (of victory), and those who incline towards self-indulgence, be shown as worthy of condemnation for their faithlessness. But even here we must know that it is not immediately after every change of ours that we are judged as to whether we have proved skilful or worthy of reprobation. But when we have been tried all our life with

suggestions, conquering and being conquered, falling and rising
again, straying and being directed to the right way, then only, on
the day of departure, will all be counted and we shall be judged
or praised accordingly. So it is not suggestion that is sin. Not at
all! For although it involuntarily (without our consent) offers us
things in a bare thought, we have received from the Lord the
power of spiritual doing and it is within our will, at the first onset
of a thought, to discriminate the harmful and the useful, and to
reject or accept thoughts, which multiply not through necessity,
but through the soul's disposition.

25. Since our soul, darkened by lustfulness and vainglory, has
sunk into the depths of foolishness, it listens neither to the commandments of the Scriptures nor to natural reason, nor to explanations by the experienced, but follows only its own fancies.
Therefore, since it keeps these causes of evil in itself, neither can
it be free from corresponding actions. To the extent that each
man believes the Lord concerning future blessings and despises
human glory and pleasures, he will have corresponding power to
control his thoughts and to be more at peace than a man who loves
pleasures; therefore we differ from one another both in thoughts
and in life.

26. Know for certain that the Lord sees into the hearts of all
men; and, as He promised, He immediately protects those who
hate the first appearance of evil thoughts, and does not allow them
to multiply and, in rising, to defile the mind and conscience.
But those who do not by faith and hope in God repulse the first
inception of thoughts, but take pleasure in them, He leaves
without help, as unfaithful ones, to be overcome by subsequent
thoughts, which He does not drive away, for He sees that we love
their first impact and do not hate them at their first appearance.

27. No power impels us forcibly either to good or to evil.
But for whomever we work of our own free will, be it God or
devil, he later incites us to whatever things constitute his realm.

28. The beginnings of action are two suggestions of thoughts,
unnoticed by the mind: human praise and indulgence to the body;
when they impinge upon us involuntarily, before our will con-
sents to them, they constitute neither virtue nor vice, but merely
disclose the inclination of our will. . . .

33. Those who have sinned must not despair. Let that never be. For we are condemned not for the multitude of evils but because we do not want to repent and learn the miracles of Christ, as Truth Himself says, speaking of the Galilæans, whose blood Pilate had mingled with their sacrifices, 'Suppose ye', said the Lord, 'that these Galilæans were sinners above all the Galilæans, because they suffered such things? I tell you, Nay: but, except ye repent, ye shall all likewise perish. Or those eighteen, upon whom the tower in Siloam fell, and slew them, think ye that they were sinners above all men that dwelt in Jerusalem? I tell you, Nay: but, except ye repent, ye shall all likewise perish' (Luke xiii; 1–5). So do you see, we are condemned for not having repentance.

34. Repentance, as I understand it, is not limited by time or any deeds, but is accomplished by means of Christ's commandments, and is measured by them. Some of the commandments are more general and include many particular ones, thus cutting off at one stroke many aspects of evil. For instance, it is said in the Scriptures, 'Give to every man that asketh of thee; and of him that taketh away thy goods ask them not again' (Luke vi. 30) 'and from him that would borrow of thee turn not thou away' (Matt. v. 42). These are particular commandments. The general commandment, which includes them in itself, is 'Sell that thou hast, and give to the poor' (Matt. xix. 21) and, let him 'take up his cross, and follow me' (Matt. xvi. 24), meaning by cross, endurance of our afflictions. For a man who has given all he has to the poor and has taken up his cross has fulfilled at one stroke all the foregoing commandments. The same applies when the Apostle says, 'I will therefore that men pray everywhere, lifting up holy hands' (1 Tim. ii. 8); and the general commandment is the words of the Lord, 'But thou, when thou prayest, enter into thy closet, and . . . pray to thy Father, which is in secret' (Matt. vi. 6) and also 'Pray without ceasing' (1. Thess. v. 17). He who has entered his closet and prays without ceasing has included in this all prayer offered everywhere. It is said also 'Thou shalt not kill, Thou shalt not commit adultery, Thou shalt not steal' and so forth. But the general form of this is, 'Casting down imaginations, and every high thing that exalteth itself against the

knowledge of God' (2 Cor. x. 5). He who casts down imaginations has made a barrier against all these vices. This is why God-loving people of firm faith urge themselves to fulfil general commandments, not neglecting the particular ones when the occasion arises. Therefore, in my opinion, the work of repentance is accomplished by the following three virtues: purification of thoughts, unceasing prayer and endurance of the afflictions which come upon us. And all this must be done not only outwardly, but also practised in inner doing, so that those who have worked at it for a long time should thereby become passionless. And, since the work of repentance cannot be accomplished without these three virtues, I think that repentance is proper at all times and for all who want to be saved, whether righteous men or sinners. For there is no such summit of perfection as would not require the practice of these virtues: through them beginners are introduced to piety, those on the way are given progress in it and the perfect are confirmed in it.

35. The Lord commands all men to repent (Matt. iv. 17), so that even the spiritual and those making progress should not neglect this injunction and fail to give attention to the smallest and most subtle errors. For it is said, 'He that contemneth small things shall fall by little and little' (Ecclesiasticus. xix. 1). And do not say: How can a spiritual man fall? If he remains such, he will not fall; but when he admits something contrary, however small, and lets it stay in him without repenting, then this small thing, taking root and growing, can no longer bear to be apart from him, but urges him to link on to itself as with a chain, forcibly attracting him by long-established attachment. If a man fights this (evil) by means of prayer and repulses it, he will preserve the measure of his spiritual stature. But if finally the increasing force of what possesses him succeeds in bringing him down (from his usual degree) by diminishing his struggle and his work of prayer, then he will inevitably be beguiled also by other passions. Thus, being gradually led astray by each passion, according to the measure of his straying, he becomes deprived of Divine help; and finally he is led to large offences, at times even against his will, through the urge of what had previously possessed him. But you will say, could he not, at the start of the evil, pray God not to let him

succumb to final evil? And I will tell you, yes, he could, but having disregarded a small thing and taken it in of his own free will as something insignificant, he no longer prays about it, unaware of the fact that this small thing can be the beginning and cause of something big; thus is it with both good and evil! But when passion has gained strength and has found a place in him with the help of his own will, it begins to attack him forcibly, against his will. Then, realising his plight, he prays to God, as he struggles with the enemy, whom previously he had defended through ignorance and for whom he had disputed with others. Sometimes however he does not receive help, even if he is heard by the Lord, for help comes not as man thinks, but as God disposes for our benefit. For He, knowing our instability and heedlessness, often helps us by sorrows and afflictions, lest, having been freed without pain, we begin diligently to practise the same trespasses. Therefore we affirm that we must endure whatever befalls us and should properly keep ourselves in (a state of) repentance.

46. The blessed Paul, desiring that we should be by no means neglectful of prayer says, 'Pray without ceasing' (1 Thess. v. 17). Moreover, referring to collectedness of mind, he says, 'Be not conformed to this world: but be ye transformed by the renewing of your mind, that ye may prove what is that good, and acceptable, and perfect, will of God' (Rom. xii. 2). Since God, through our weakness and lack of faith, has given us different commandments, so that each man, in the measure of his efforts, should escape torment and be granted salvation, the Apostle directs us to the perfect will of God, desirous that we should altogether escape judgment. And knowing that prayer helps the fulfilment of all commandments, he never ceases to enjoin it in many different ways, saying, 'Praying always with all prayer and supplication in the Spirit, and watching thereunto with all perseverance' (Eph. vi. 18).

47. Prayer can vary: for it is one thing to pray to God with undistracted thought, and another for the body to stand at prayer, while the thought is distracted. Again, it is one thing to choose one's time and pray when worldly conversations and occupations are done; and another, as far as is possible, to prefer prayer to all

worldly cares and to give it first place; according to the words of the Apostle, 'The Lord is at hand. Be careful for nothing; but in everything by prayer and supplication with thanksgiving let your requests be made known unto God' (Phil. iv. 5, 6). And the blessed Peter says, 'Be ye therefore sober, and watch unto prayer. . . . Casting all your care upon him; for he careth for you' (1 Peter iv. 7 and v. 7). And before them, the Lord Himself, knowing that all things are established by prayer, said, 'Therefore take no thought, saying, What shall we eat? or, What shall we drink? or, Wherewithal shall we be clothed? . . . But seek ye first the kingdom of God, and his righteousness; and all these things shall be added unto you' (Matt. vi. 31, 33). But it may be that through this the Lord calls us also to greater faith: for who, having relinquished all care for temporal things and yet suffering no want, will not trust in God also concerning eternal blessings? Speaking of this the Lord said, 'He that is faithful in that which is least is faithful also in much' (Luke xvi. 10).

48. The Lord, knowing that daily care of the body is inevitable for us, did not repudiate it, but, having allowed us to take care of today, very fittingly, becomingly and with loving-kindness commands us not to care for tomorrow. For men clothed in the flesh cannot completely relinquish what concerns the life of the body. Through prayer and self-mastery, much can be reduced to little, but completely to renounce all (relating to the body) is impossible. So a man who wishes to come, according to the Scriptures, 'unto the measure of the stature of the fulness of Christ' (Eph. iv. 13) must not prefer various occupations to prayer and undertake them without need as they chance. On the other hand, he must not avoid those that occur through some necessity and by God's ordinance, nor repudiate them on the pretext of prayer; but he (must) learn to discern the difference (between prayer and other occupations) and to obey God's ordinance without question. Who thinks differently does not believe that, according to the Scriptures, one commandment can be higher and more important than another, and does not wish, in the words of the Prophet, to direct himself according to all commandments. (Ps. cxviii. 128.)

49. Occupations that are necessary and result from God's

ordinance are inevitable, but untimely occupations should be rejected, and preference given to prayer; especially should we reject those which involve us in great expenditure and acquiring superfluous possessions. For in so far as a man limits them for the Lord's sake and cuts off their superfluous substance, he restrains his thought from distraction. And in so far as he restrains his thought, he gives room to pure prayer and shows sincere faith in Christ. But if someone cannot do this through lack of faith or from some other weakness, let him at least know the truth and press forward as much as is in his power, accusing himself of infancy.

50. Let us try to banish all worldly cares by prayer and hope. But if we cannot do so to perfection, let us confess to God our shortcomings and on no account abandon diligence in prayer. For it is better to be blamed for frequent omissions than for complete neglect. In all we have said about prayer and necessary occupations, we greatly need that God should teach us good judgment, so that we may know what kind of occupation to prefer to prayer and when. For each man, practising the occupation he loves, thinks he renders a necessary service, not knowing that all our occupations should be directed to pleasing God rather than oneself. It is still more difficult to discern that even these necessary and unavoidable ordinances are not always the same and that in its own time one of them should be preferred to another. For every service is performed not at all times but in its proper time, whereas the service of prayer is ordained to be unceasing. So we must prefer it to other occupations, which are not unavoidably necessary. And all the Apostles, teaching about this discernment to the multitude, who sought to divert them to service, said 'It is not reason that we should leave the word of God, and serve tables. Wherefore, brethren, look ye out among you seven men of honest report, full of the Holy Ghost and wisdom, whom we may appoint over this business. But we will give ourselves continually to prayer, and to the ministry of the word. And the saying pleased the whole multitude' (Acts vi. 2–5). What do we learn from this? That for those who cannot remain in prayer it is good to be in service, lest we lose both the one and the other; but for those who can—it is better not to neglect the better.

51. So let us begin the work of prayer and, gradually making

progress, we shall find that not only hope in God but also firm faith and unfeigned love, absence of rancour, love for one's brethren, self-mastery, patience, the innermost knowledge, deliverance from temptations, gifts of grace, heartfelt profession of faith and fervent tears are given to the faithful through prayer. And not these gifts alone, but also endurance of afflictions, a pure love of one's neighbour, knowledge of spiritual law, acquisition of God's righteousness, infusion of the Holy Spirit, the gift of spiritual treasures and all that God has promised to give the faithful here and in the future life—(all this they receive through prayer). In short, it is impossible to re-establish the image of God in oneself otherwise than by the Divine grace and faith, granted to a man who with great humility remains with his mind in undistracted prayer.

52. There are three kinds of piety: the first, to avoid sin, the second, having sinned to endure the sorrows that come to pass, and the third, when unable to bear the sorrows, to mourn one's lack of endurance. For what is not justified here by appropriate means of reconciliation (with God), necessarily makes us incur judgment there, unless God, seeing us humbled and mourning, wipes away our sins as He Alone knows how by His all-powerful grace.

53. Oh how insinuating and imperceptible is the passion of pleasing men: it possesses even the wise! For the effects of other passions are easily seen by those who obey them and so bring those they possess to humility and mourning. But the effort to please men clothes itself in the words and appearances of piety, so that men whom it beguiles find it hard to detect its various aspects.

55. What are the aspects of pleasing men? The first, their mother, is lack of faith, and its offspring which follow after are: envy, hatred, flattery, jealousy, quarrelling, hypocrisy, partiality, doing service only for show, calumny, lies, an air of false not true piety and other such dark passions which are difficult to detect. But the worst thing is that some people praise all this with artful words as something good, and the harm it contains they conceal.

59. The cause of every distressing event is the thoughts of each one of us. I could have said words and deeds as well; but since

they do not occur before thought, I ascribe all to thoughts. A thought comes first, and then, through words and deeds, communication is established between us (and our neighbours). Communication can be of two kinds: one comes from malice, the other from love. Through communication we take one another upon ourselves, even those we do not know; and taking (a neighbour) upon oneself is inevitably followed by tribulations, as the Divine Scriptures say, 'If thou become surety for thy friend, thou shalt deliver thine hand to an enemy' (Prov. vi. 1). Thus every man has to bear what befalls not only for himself but also for his neighbour, inasmuch as he has taken him upon himself.

60. The taking of one's neighbour upon oneself from malice is involuntary. And it happens thus: a man who deprives (his neighbour) of something, takes upon himself the trials of him he has deprived, even though he does not wish it; similarly the slanderer—the trials of the slandered, the defrauder—those of the defrauded, the oppressor—those of the oppressed, the blamer—those of the blamed, the despiser—those of the despised; the liar takes upon himself the trials of the man about whom he lied and, not to enumerate it all in detail, I shall say briefly—every man who offends his neighbour correspondingly takes upon himself the trials of the man he offends. The Divine Scriptures testify to this, saying, 'He that digs a pit for his neighbour shall fall into it: and he that rolls a stone, rolls it upon himself' (Prov. xxvi. 27), and 'All evils come upon the ungodly into their bosoms; but all righteous things come of the Lord' (Prov. xvi. 33), and 'Is God unrighteous who taketh vengeance?' (Rom. iii. 5) not only upon those who are taught sense by afflictions but also upon those who senselessly revolt against these afflictions.

61. Taking a neighbour upon oneself through love was repeatedly shown to us by the Lord Jesus, first by healing the ills of our souls, and then 'healing all manner of sickness and all manner of disease' (Matt. iv. 23), taking away the sin of the world, renewing those who firmly believed in Him and purifying their nature; liberating them from death; bequeathing to men the worship of God, teaching them piety, showing that for the sake of love we must suffer even unto death. Moreover He gave us patience with the help of the Spirit, and future blessings which

'eye hath not seen, nor ear heard, neither have entered into the heart of man' (1 Cor. ii. 9). And so He takes upon Himself trials for our sakes, endures abuse, insults, is bound and betrayed, smitten on the cheeks, given vinegar and gall to drink, nailed to the cross, pierced by a lance. Thus becoming one with us in flesh and in spirit and suffering for us, He transmitted this law also to the holy Apostles and disciples, prophets, fathers, patriarchs, instructing some first through the Holy Spirit and to others showing it through His Most Pure Body. While thus showing this taking of the neighbour upon Himself, He said, 'Greater love hath no man than this, that a man lay down his life for his friends' (John xv. 13). Therefore St. Paul, imitating the Lord, also says, 'Who now rejoice in my sufferings for you, and fill up that which is behind of the afflictions of Christ in my flesh for his body's sake, which is the church' (Col. i. 24), pointing to the taking upon oneself from love.

71. He who fulfils the law in his outer life and conduct is free only of the results of an evil disposition, sacrificing to God the senseless actions of the passions. Such a man is content with this method (of action) for his salvation, because of his spiritual infancy.

72. A man who truly loves to live according to the Gospels has destroyed the beginning and the end of his evil disposition, and practises every virtue by word and deed, bringing as an offering praise and profession of faith. He is liberated from all disturbance caused by the action of passions; and his mind, being free from this struggle, is possessed by the hope of future blessings and knows nothing but insatiable delight, which feeds his soul.

73. The fear of gehenna encourages beginners (in the practice of virtues) to avoid evil disposition; and desire of good reward gives those who make progress zeal to accomplish what is good. But the mystery of love exalts the mind above all created things, blinding it to all that is not God. For only to those who have become blind to all that is below God, does the Lord give wisdom (Ps. cxlv. 8), showing them the most Divine.

74. 'The kingdom of heaven is like unto leaven, which a woman took, and hid in three measures of meal, till the whole was leavened' (Matt. xiii. 33). This means that the mind, having

received the word of the Lord, hid it in the tripartite being, composed, according to the Apostle, of body, spirit and soul; and it has gathered together into one leaven of faith all their fineness, spread through thoughts like flour diffusely scattered, in the expectation of thus becoming in all things like the word acting in it.[13] In the same way, the Lord likened the word of truth to a mustard seed which, being small, penetrates the heart of those who hear, but thereupon growing through conformable efforts becomes like a great tree standing on raised ground, so that, according to the Scriptures, approaching thoughts come and lodge in it.

78. A heart is clean (Ps. l. 10) when it presents to God a memory completely free of forms (impressions) or images, and ready to receive nothing but Divine imprints, which fill it with light.

79. He who through Divine desire has overcome the leaning of his soul towards the body, becomes free from limit even while remaining in the body. For God, Who attracts his desire, is incomparably higher than all things and does not allow the man to attach his desire to anything below God. So let us desire God with all the strength of our desire and let nothing belonging to the body hold captive our free choice. Let us place ourselves by the disposition of our soul truly above all sensory and mental things. If we do this, our will will suffer no harm from natural life in respect of dwelling with God, Whose nature passes all understanding.

80. The great Moses, having pitched his tabernacle without the camp (Ex. xxxiii. 7), that is, firmly pitching his thought and mind outside the visible, begins to worship God (Ex. xxxiv. 8), and going into the darkness (Ex. xx. 21), the invisible and intangible place of knowledge, abides there, initiated into the most sacred mysteries.

81. So long as we have not completely abandoned in mind our customary clinging to our own substance and to what is below God, we shall not win constancy in virtue. But when, through love, we attain this degree, we shall experience the force of God's

---

[13] This passage is obscure. (Translators' note.)

promise. For the worthy should believe that nothing can be shaken there, where the mind has first established its power through love. For the mind cannot be freed from the changeability (innate) in all things, unless it goes out of itself and of all objects of thought, and establishes itself in silence which is above thinking.

82. Those who sit 'for fear of the Jews' in Galilee in a room whose 'doors are shut' (John xx. 19), that is, those who for fear of evil spirits live safely in the country of revelation on the height of Divine contemplation, having shut their senses like doors, receive the Word of God; coming in an unknown manner, It appears to them without the action of the senses; announcing peace, It gives them passionlessness; breathing on them, It gives the varied gifts of the Holy Ghost and power over evil spirits, and shows them the signs (John xx. 20) of the mysteries of the Lord.

83. He who spends the sixth day in accordance with the Gospels, having previously slain the first movements of sin, attains through the virtues to the state of passionlessness, pure of all evil, keeping the sabbath (Ex. xvi. 29, 30) in his mind even from the most subtle representation of passions in the imagination —and he who has passed over Jordan (Gen. xxxii. 10, 22) is translated into the country of knowledge in which the mind, mysteriously fashioned by peace, becomes the dwelling place of God in spirit.

84. The Sabbath of Sabbaths (Lev. xvi. 31) is the rest of a wise soul, which has withdrawn the mind away even from all Divine 'words' mysteriously concealed in creatures, and, in the ecstasy of love, has wholly clothed it in God alone; so that through mysterious knowledge of Him, the soul has made the mind wholly inseparable from God.

ST. MARK THE ASCETIC

3. Two Centuries on Spiritual Law

1. Since you have repeatedly expressed the desire to learn in what way, according to the Apostle, 'the law is spiritual' (Rom. vii. 14), and what is the ordering of mind and the activity of those, who endeavour to obey it, we shall tell you of this, as far as we can.

2. First of all, as we know, God is the beginning, the middle and the end of every good. But the good[14] cannot become active or be believed in otherwise than in Jesus Christ and the Holy Spirit.

3. Every good is given us by the Lord discerningly (with a particular intention). Who believes this will not ruin it.

4. Firm faith is a strong tower. For a believer, Christ is all.

5. Let the Master of all good be Master of every undertaking of yours, so that it is according to God.

6. A humble and spiritually active man, when he reads the Holy Scriptures, will refer everything to himself and not to another.

7. Call to God to open the eyes of your heart that you may see the usefulness of prayer and of reading, understood in experience.

8. A man who has some spiritual gift and who commiserates with those who have not got it, by this compassion keeps his gift. But the vainglorious one will lose it, beaten down by boastful thoughts.

15. Do not puff yourself up for shedding tears in your prayer, for it is Christ Who has touched your eyes and has given you inner sight.

---

[14] What is meant here is not human good deeds, but blessings coming from God. (Footnote in the Dobrotolubiye.)

16. Only he who, like the blind man, casts away his garment and approaches the Lord, becomes His (true) follower and a preacher of the most perfect doctrines (Mark x. 50, 51).

17. Evil (sin) revolved in thoughts (with enjoyment) coarsens the heart (hardens it), whereas self-mastery with hope destroys evil and softens the heart (grinds it into powder).

18. There is a right and useful grinding of the heart, which touches it deeply; and there is another grinding, disorderly and harmful, which leads only to defeat.[15]

19. Vigilance, prayer and endurance of afflictions (sorrows, misfortunes, distress) is a grinding which does not merely inflict wounds but is also useful to the heart, provided we do not interfere with the dissolving process by attachment.[16] He who continues in these will be helped in other things also. But a man who neglects and divides them (separates them one from another) will suffer unbearably in his departure.[17]

20. A pleasure-loving heart at the moment of departure is a prison and shackles for the soul. And a diligent heart is an open door.

21. 'The iron gate that leadeth unto the city' (Acts xii. 10) is a hard heart.[18] To a man who suffers and is contrite the gate will open 'of his own accord' as to Peter.

54. Do nothing and think nothing without an aim which is in accordance with God; for he who journeys aimlessly labours in vain.

56. To an intelligent man an affliction brings remembrance of

15 Whether a man wearies himself senselessly or is treated severely by his spiritual father, the heart only suffers wounds. He is struck—it hurts—but no good comes of it. It is like a sick man who is given a wrong medicine. (Footnote in the Dobrotolubiye.)

16 Dissolving process—the mixing of different ingredients, for instance, of water and wine. The three virtues mentioned above should always interpenetrate one another. Attachment prevents their mixing. (Footnote in the Dobrotolubiye.)

17 He will realise then how wrong he was to be neglectful. (Footnote in the Dobrotolubiye.)

18 Not merciless, but stone-like, suffering from insensibility. A spiritual interpretation is given here of the opening of closed gates before St. Peter. Suffering is self-mortification by external privations, and contrition—grinding— is the mind beating on the heart by presenting truths that bring contrition. Both these roll away the stone from the heart. (Footnote in the Dobrotolubiye.)

God; but if a man forgets God, he is correspondingly saddened by it.

57. Let every accidental affliction teach you this remembrance, and the impulse to repentance will never be wanting in you.

58. In itself forgetfulness has no power; it is sustained by our negligence and corresponds to it.

59. Do not say, What can I do? I do not want it (forgetfulness) and yet it comes. This is so because you have neglected what was necessary when you remembered.

60. Do the good you remember; then the good you do not remember will also reveal itself to you. And do not foolishly give your thought up to forgetfulness.

61. The Scriptures say, 'Hell and destruction are manifest to the Lord' (Prov. xv. 11). This is said of ignorance and forgetfulness of the heart.

62. Hell is ignorance; for both are dark. Destruction is forgetfulness; for in both something that was, is lost.

65. Suffering in God is an inherent attribute of piety; for true love is tested by adversities.

66. Do not think to acquire virtue without suffering: such virtue is insecure by reason of its ease.

67. Look to the end of every involuntary suffering, and you will find in it removal of sins.

71. Man does as much as he can according to his own will; but God determines the outcome of his actions according to justice.

74. When a man does good to another by word or deed, let both recognise in it the grace of God. He who does not understand this will have him who understands it as master.

77. The result of love of pleasures is negligence; and negligence gives birth to forgetfulness. For God has given every man knowledge of what is good for him.

81. A man who belittles knowledge and boasts of his lack of education is ignorant not only in word, but also in his reason.

84. Do not say: I do not know what is right and am therefore not guilty if I do not do it. If you did the good you know, then gradually all the rest would be revealed to you, since one is understood by means of the other. . . . It is not profitable for you before you fulfil the former, to know the latter. For 'knowledge

puffeth up,' owing to inaction, 'but charity edifieth' for it 'endureth all things' (1 Cor. viii. 1; xiii. 7).

85. Read the words of the Holy Scriptures by means of deeds; and do not be expansive in words, puffing yourself up with bare theoretical ideas.

86. He who neglects deeds and is satisfied with knowledge alone holds not a double-edged sword, but a staff of reed, which, according to the Scriptures, will go into his hand in battle, and pierce it (Isaiah xxxvi. 6), pouring into it, quicker than the enemy, the poison of arrogance.

94. The devil presents small sins to us as insignificant in our eyes, for otherwise he cannot lead us to great sins.

96. There is no profit for a man to renounce the world and to lead a pleasure-loving life. For what he used to do before through possessions, he now does possessing nothing.

110. He who is ignorant of truth cannot have true faith. For, by its nature, knowledge precedes faith.

117. Wilfully sowing evil and reaping it against our will, we should marvel at God's justice.

118. There is a certain interval between sowing and reaping. Therefore we must not lose belief in the reward.

119. Having sinned, blame your thought and not your body; for if your mind had not run ahead, the body would not have followed.

138. When we have repudiated every voluntary sin, be it only in the mind, then we shall begin real warfare with the impacts of the passions which fill us.

139. An impact is an involuntary memory of past sins. He who still struggles (with passions) strives not to allow (such a thought) to come to passion; but he who has already conquered passions, drives away the first suggestion itself.

140. A suggestion is an involuntary movement of the heart, not accompanied by images.[19] It is like a key (which opens the door of the heart to sin); therefore the experienced try to catch it right at the start.

141. Where images of thoughts linger, there coupling has

19 A paraphrase owing to the conciseness of the Greek sentence. (Footnote in the Dobrotolubiye.)

taken place: for that movement which is a guiltless (involuntary) suggestion is not accompanied by images. One man shoots out of them like a brand from the fire; while another does not repulse them until the fire is alight.

147. Without remembrance of God, knowledge cannot be true. Without the first, the second is counterfeit.

163. Abide with your mind in the heart and you will not be troubled by temptations; but if you go out from there, suffer what befalls you.

164. Pray that temptation may not come upon you, but when it does come, accept it as something not alien but your own.

168. He who is carried away by thoughts is blinded by them; he sees the effects of sin, but their causes he cannot see.

176. Some call men of good sense those who are clever in dealing with material things. But true men of sense are those who are masters of their desires.

177. Before you have destroyed evil (passions) do not listen to your heart. For whatever has been put into it, that it demands.

178. As some snakes are found in woods, while others secretly slither about in houses, so, too, is it with passions; some are imagined in the mind, while others are expressed in action. It happens, however, that each kind is transformed into the other.

179. When you see that what is within you has come into violent movement and urges the silent mind to passion, know that at some past time the mind has itself been occupied with it, brought it to action and put it into the heart.

180. No cloud is formed without the breath of wind; no passion is born without (a movement) of thoughts.

181. If we no longer fulfil the wills of the flesh, in accordance with the Scriptures, then, with the Lord's help, what was instilled into us before (passions of the soul and wrong habits) will readily cease to trouble us.

182. Images which are rooted in the substance of the mind are worse and more powerful than purely mental images; but these latter precede the former and are their cause.

183. There is evil which proceeds out of the heart and takes possession of us through old suggestions and through the heart's

conjunction with them; and there is evil which mentally attacks us through everyday occurrences.

184. God values deeds according to their intention. 'Grant thee according to thy heart' (Ps. xix. 4).

186. Conscience is a natural book (of God's ordinances); he who reads it actively gains experience of Divine intercession.

190. The Lord is concealed in His commandments and those who seek Him find Him in proportion (to fulfilling them).

191. Do not say: I have fulfilled the commandments but have not found the Lord. All those who seek Him rightly, will find peace.

192. Peace is liberation from passions, which cannot be attained without the action of the Holy Spirit.

193. Fulfilling a commandment is one thing, and virtue is another, although they mutually borrow from one another occasions for good.

194. Fulfilling a commandment means performing what was commanded; when what is done is truly pleasing to God, that is virtue.

198. Good conscience is attained through prayer, and pure prayer through conscience. By their nature they have need of one another.

ST. MARK THE ASCETIC

4. 226 texts entitled: To those who think to be justified by deeds

1. In these chapters the poverty of faith of those who lead a righteous life merely outwardly is exposed by those whose faith is exact and who know real truth.

2. Wishing to show that, although every commandment is obligatory, none the less it is by His blood that sonship is granted to men, the Lord says: 'When ye shall have done all those things which are commanded you, say, We are unprofitable servants: we have done that which was our duty to do' (Luke xvii. 10). Thus the kingdom of heaven is not a reward for deeds, but a gift of the Lord prepared for faithful servants.

3. The servant does not demand freedom as a reward, but tries to give satisfaction as a debtor and awaits freedom as a grace.

4. 'Christ died for our sins according to the scriptures' (1 Cor. xv. 3), and He grants freedom to those who serve Him well. For He says: 'Well done, good and faithful servant; thou hast been faithful over a few things, I will make thee ruler over many things: enter thou into the joy of thy lord' (Matt. xxv. 23).

5. He is not yet a faithful servant who bases himself on bare knowledge alone; a faithful servant is he who professes his faith by obedience to Christ, Who gave the commandments.

6. He who reveres the Lord does what is commanded, and if he commits some sin or disobeys Him, endures whatever he has to suffer for this as being his desert.

7. If you love knowledge, love also work, for bare knowledge puffs a man up.

12. Knowledge without corresponding practice is still insecure, even if it is true. All is made firm by practice.

13. Often neglect of practice obscures also the knowledge (relating to it). For if practices are completely neglected, even memory of them will gradually vanish.

16. He who wants to do something and cannot is, in the eyes of God Who sees our hearts, as though he has done it. This should be understood as being so in relation to good and evil alike.

17. The mind does much good and much evil even without the body; but the body can do nothing without the mind; for free decisions precede actions.

18. Some think they believe rightly, while not practising the commandments; others, while practising them, expect the kingdom as a just reward. Both sin against truth.

19. To reward the servants is not an obligation on the master. On the other hand, those who do not serve well do not receive freedom.

20. If Christ died for our sake, and 'they which live should not henceforth live unto themselves, but unto him which died for them, and rose again' (2 Cor. v. 15), it is clear that we are under an obligation to serve Him unto death. So how can we regard sonship as a just reward?

22. When you hear the words of the Scriptures that the Lord will 'recompense every one according to his works' (Ps. lxi. 12), do not think that works (in themselves) are worthy of gehenna or of the kingdom, but that Christ will recompense every man according to the works of his faith or lack of faith in Him, as being God our Creator and Redeemer, and not as being the Measurer of things (that is, works and rewards).

23. We who have been granted the bath of eternal life do good works not for the sake of reward, but to preserve the purity which was given us.

24. Every good deed we perform by our own natural powers, although it removes us further from the (evil deed) opposed to it, cannot make us holy without grace.

25. The abstinent withdraws from gluttony, the uncovetous from covetousness, the silent from wordiness, the pure from attachment to sensory pleasures, the chaste from fornication, he who is content with what he has from love of money, the meek from agitation (anger), the humble from vanity, the obedient

from objection, he who is honest with himself from hypocrisy; equally, he who prays withdraws from despair, the willing pauper from acquisitiveness, he who professes his faith from denying it, the martyr from idolatry—so you see that each virtue, performed even unto death, is nothing but withdrawal from sin; and withdrawal from sin is a natural action, not an action which could be rewarded by the kingdom.

26. Man can barely preserve what is natural to him; but Christ gives sonship by the cross.

28. There is an action of grace, imperceptible to the child (in spiritual stature) and there is an action of malice (of the enemy) which resembles truth; it is good not to become too engrossed[20] in looking at such actions lest one be deceived, and not to damn them, lest there be truth in them; but to bring all to God with hope, for He knows the profit of each alike.

29. He who wants to cross the mental sea is longsuffering, humble, vigilant and abstinent. If he attempts to do it without these four virtues, he will only torture his heart, but will not cross the sea.

30. Silence is the cutting off of all evil. If it, and those four virtues are joined to prayer, there is no greater help nor shorter way to passionlessness than this.

31. The mind cannot become silent without the body, nor can the wall between them be destroyed without silence and prayer.

33. Prayer is not perfect without mental invocation. A mind calling to God without distraction is heard by the Lord.

34. When the mind prays without distraction, the heart is contrite. 'A broken and humbled heart God will not despise' (Ps. l. 17).

48. The sign of undissembled love is forgiveness of offences. So the Lord loved the world.

49. It is impossible to forgive someone else's offences wholeheartedly without true knowledge; for this knowledge shows to every man that what befalls him belongs to himself.

50. You will lose nothing of what you have renounced for the Lord, for in its own time it will return to you manifold.

[20] The Greek word implied the idea of admiring one's smartness in a mirror. (Footnote in the Dobrotolubiye.)

51. When the mind forgets the purpose of piety, then visible works of virtue become useless.

52. If evil counsel (not that of others, but absence of one's own good judgment) is harmful to any man, it is more so to those who have undertaken a strict life.

57. He who does good and seeks a reward works not for God but for his own desire.

59. Some say that we can do nothing good until we actively receive the grace of the Holy Spirit. (This is not true.)

60. Those whose will always inclines to self-indulgence refuse to do even what is in their power under the pretext that they have no help from above.

61. To him who has been baptised into Christ grace has been mysteriously given already. But it acts in proportion to his fulfilment of commandments. Although this grace never ceases to help us in secret, it lies in our power to do or not to do good according to our own will.

62. In the first place, it fittingly arouses conscience, through which even evil-doers have been accepted by God when they repented.

63. Again, it may be concealed in the advice of a brother. Sometimes it follows thought during reading and teaches its truth to the mind by means of a natural deduction (from that thought). Thus, if we do not bury this talent bestowed upon us on these and similar occasions, we shall in truth enter into the joy of the Lord.

66. If you will keep in mind that, according to the Scriptures, the Lord's 'judgments are in all the earth' (Ps. civ. 7), then every event will teach you knowledge of God.

67. Each man meets with his deserts according to his inner state; but the exact relationship of external happenings (to the inner state) are known to God alone.

80. The mole burrowing in the earth cannot see the stars, for it is blind; so a man who does not believe in God concerning the temporal, equally cannot believe concerning the eternal.

83. The mind that has forgotten true knowledge wages war with people for things that are harmful to it, as though they were profitable.

86. We are fond of the causes of involuntary thoughts, and that

is why they come. In the case of voluntary thoughts we are obviously fond also of their subjects themselves.

90. There exist three regions of the mind, and as it enters them the mind undergoes an inner change: they are the natural, the supranatural and the contranatural. When it enters its natural region it finds itself to be the cause of evil thoughts and of passions; and it confesses its sins to God. When it is in the contranatural region, it forgets God's justice and fights with people, thinking their treatment unfair. And when it rises to the supranatural region, it finds in itself the fruits of the Holy Spirit, which the Apostle showed forth, 'love, joy, peace' and the like (Gal. v. 22). The mind then knows that if it prefers the cares of the body it cannot stay there and, leaving this place, it will fall into sin and its ensuing tribulations, perhaps not at once but in its own time, as God's justice deems it necessary.

104. If, according to the Scriptures, the cause of all that is involuntary lies in what is voluntary, no one is a man's greater enemy than himself.

132. Do not say that a passionless man cannot grieve; for if not about himself, he must do so about his brother.

144. Knowledge of actions is one thing and knowledge of truth, another. As the sun is more excellent than the moon, so is the latter more profitable than the former.

145. Knowledge of actions increases in proportion to fulfilling commandments; knowledge of truth—in proportion to hope in Christ.

146. If you wish to be saved and to come to the knowledge of truth, always urge yourself to rise above sensory things and to cling with hope to God alone. Thus compelling yourself to turn inwards, you will meet principalities and powers, which wage war against you by suggestions in thoughts. If you overcome them by prayer and remain in good hope, you will receive Divine grace, which will free you from the wrath to come.

147. He who understands the mysterious saying of St. Paul that 'we wrestle . . . against spiritual wickedness' (Eph. vi. 12), will understand also the Lord's parable, which He gave to this end, 'that men ought always to pray, and not to faint' (Luke xviii. 1).

148. The law figuratively commands us to labour for six days and in the seventh to rest from labours. The labour of the soul consists in the right use of its possessions, that is, deeds. Its freedom from labours or rest consists in selling all one has, according to the words of the Lord, and giving it to the poor and, being at peace through this detachment from possessions, to remain inactive in inner hope. St. Paul too urges us to enter with all diligence into this rest, saying, 'Let us labour therefore to enter into that rest' (Heb. iv. 11).

151. When past sins are remembered in appearance (in detail) they harm a man of good hope. For if they again arise in the soul accompanied by grief, they repel hope; and if they are visualised without grief, they again introduce the old defilement within.

152. When, through self-denial, the mind receives hope free from doubt, then, under the pretext of confession, the enemy shows him, as in a picture, the sins he has previously committed, that he may set fire to passions already forgotten by the grace of God, and thus may secretly harm a man. For in this case even an illumined (mind), which hates passions, becomes necessarily obscured, perturbed by what has been done. But if it is still enveloped in fog and feels sympathy for passions, it will linger and begin to converse passionately with their impacts, so that this remembrance will be not confession but passionate suggestion.

153. If you wish to bring a blameless confession to God, do not recollect your past faults in appearance (in detail), but suffer their results with courage.

155. A man of experience who has learnt the truth, confesses to God not by recollection of what he has done, but by enduring what befalls him.

156. Having repudiated heartfelt grief for sins and ignominy, do not vow to do penitence by means of other virtues, for vanity and insensitiveness frequently serve sin, even by means of right things.

157. As virtues are usually born from painful afflictions and ignominy—so are sins from vanity and indulgences.

196. Actions pleasing to God are assisted by all creation; but actions from which God turns away are opposed by all creation.

204. Every tribulation reveals the state of our will, whether it

inclines to the right or to the left. An unexpected tribulation is called temptation, because it subjects a man to a test of his secret dispositions.

212. The current events of life are like a market. He who is a good merchant makes a profit, he who is not suffers loss.

223. Every word of Christ shows Divine mercy, righteousness and wisdom and, through the ear, brings its force into the souls of those who hear it willingly. This is why the unmerciful and unrighteous men, who heard it unwillingly, could not only not understand the Divine wisdom, but crucified Him Who taught it. So we too must see whether we hear Him willingly. For He said, 'If ye love me, keep my commandments. . . . He that hath my commandments, and keepeth them, he it is that loveth me: and he that loveth me shall be loved of my Father, and I will love him, and will manifest myself to him' (John xiv. 15, 21). So do you see how He concealed His manifestation in the commandments? And the most all-embracing commandment is love of God and of neighbour, which is born after renunciation of all material things and in stillness of thoughts.

224. Knowing this the Lord commands us saying, 'Take therefore no thought for the morrow' (Matt. vi. 34). And this we should do. For how can a man be freed from wrong thoughts if he has not renounced material things and his cares for them? And how can a man enveloped in thoughts see the essential sin concealed behind them, which is the fog and darkness of the soul? Here all wrong thoughts and desires have their beginning, when the devil, tempting with a suggestion that is not compelling, points to a sin, and man, urged by vanity and self-indulgence, combines with it. Even if in his reasoning he did not decide to commit it, yet he enjoyed its movement and coupled himself with it. But if he does not know this chief sin, how and when can he pray about it and be cleansed of it? And not being cleansed, how will he find the sanctuary of purity of being? (Ezek. xxxvii. 27). And not having found it, how shall he see the inner dwelling place of Christ?—if we are the abode of God according to the words of the prophets, the Gospels and the Apostles (Zech. ii. 10; John xiv. 23; 1 Cor. iii. 16).

225. Thus we must take care to find this dwelling place in the

order described above and, remaining in prayer, to go on knocking at the door (Matt. vii. 7), that the Lord may open it to us either here or at the time of our departure, and that He may not say, for our negligence, 'I know you not whence ye are' (Luke xiii. 25). We must not only ask and be given, but also preserve what we are given; for some who have received have later lost. A bare knowledge of the foregoing things and an occasional experience may be possible even for those who have started their training late and for the young. But a constant patient practice of these things is preserved with difficulty even by devout and experienced old men, who have repeatedly lost it through inattention and then sought and attained it again by deliberate efforts. So let us do the same until we acquire this doing and it becomes a part of us that we can never lose.

ABBA EVAGRIUS THE MONK

ABBA EVAGRIUS THE MONK
Short Biographical Note

It is known of Evagrius, a monk of Sketis and an abba, that he was born about the middle of the fourth century near the Pontus Euxinus. His birth (he was a priest's son) or his capacities attracted to him the attention of the great contemporary teachers Basil the Great, Gregory of Nyssa and Gregory the Theologian. Under their guidance he grew and developed in spirit and knowledge of faith and life in our Lord Jesus Christ. Basil the Great appointed him reader and Gregory of Nyssa ordained him as deacon and took him with him to Constantinople to the second Oecumenical Council. He left him there, but a circumstance which threatened his chastity made him leave Constantinople after a while and go to Jerusalem. There he took monastic vows and a short time later went to Egypt, where he lived for two years in Nitria and later in so-called cells and finally in Sketis. . . . In Egypt he met the two Macarii—of Egypt and of Alexandria—under whose guidance he became a philosopher, not only in words but also in his life. He died in A.D. 399. The blessed Jeronimus, quoted in Patrologia, wrote that 'books by Evagrius are being read not only by the Greeks throughout the East, but also in the West by the Latins, translated by Rufinus, his disciple.'

ABBA EVAGRIUS THE MONK
Directions on Spiritual Training
1. To Anatolius: Texts on Active Life

1. Christianity is the law (δόγμα) of our Saviour Jesus Christ, comprising what refers to life, knowledge of things and knowledge of God.

2. The kingdom of heaven is the passionless state of the soul with true knowledge of the One Who Is.

3. The kingdom of God is knowledge of the Holy Trinity, extending as far as the state of one's mind permits, and filling it with an endlessly blessed life.

4. What a man loves that he certainly desires, and what he desires that he strives to obtain. Every enjoyment is preceded by desire, and desire is born of feeling. What has no part in feeling is free also of passion.

6. A wandering mind is made stable by reading, vigil and prayer. Flaming lust is extinguished by hunger, labour and solitude. Stirrings of anger are calmed by psalmody, magnanimity and mercifulness. All this has its effect when used at its proper time and in due measure. Everything untimely or without proper measure is short-lived; and short-lived things are more harmful than useful.

7. When the soul lusts for various foods, let us confine it to bread and water, to make it grateful even for a thin slice of bread. For satiety desires varied foods, but hunger regards it as bliss to be satisfied even with bread.

10. He who flees worldly pleasures is a tower inaccessible to the demon of discontent. For discontent comes of being deprived of a pleasure, whether actual or expected. We cannot overcome this enemy so long as we are attached to something earthly. He

spreads his nets to provoke discontent wherever he sees us most attached.

11. Anger and hatred increase the excitation of the heart, and mercy and meekness extinguish it.

13. When for some reason the excitable part of our soul becomes agitated, the demons offer us solitude as something good, in order that, while removing the causes of distress, we should not be freed from our proneness to disturbance.[21] But when lust becomes inflamed, they strive to fill us with love for men (to keep us among men), calling us cruel and barbarous if we retreat from them, in order that, lusting for bodies, we should meet with bodies. We should not believe these demons, but strive all the more to do the opposite.

15. Anger is by nature designed for waging war with the demons and for struggling with every kind of sinful pleasure. Therefore angels, arousing spiritual pleasure in us and giving us to taste its blessedness, incline us to direct our anger against the demons. But the demons, enticing us towards worldly lusts, make us use anger to fight with men, which is against nature, so that the mind, thus stupefied and darkened, should become a traitor to virtues.

18. When we are attacked by the demon of despondency let us divide our soul into two, and, making one half the comforter and the other the one to be comforted, let us sow seeds of good hope in ourselves, singing the following verses of David, 'Wherefore art thou very sad, O my soul? and wherefore dost thou trouble me? hope in God; for I will give thanks to him; he is the salvation of my countenance' (Ps. xli. 5).

19. In time of temptations do not leave your cell, inventing some well-sounding excuses; but sit within and endure, courageously meeting all the assailants, especially the demon of despondency, who indeed is the most grievous of all, but who, more than all, makes the soul experienced. If you flee or avoid the struggle, your mind will remain inexperienced, timid and easily turned to flight.

[21] In order that, in overcoming distress we should not blunt our excitability and propensity to anger when living among others. (Footnote in the Dobrotolubiye.)

20. It is hard to escape the thought of vainglory, for whatever you do to banish it serves as a start for a new impulse of vainglory. Besides, the demons do not oppose every right thought that we have; these evil creatures encourage some of them in the hope of deceiving us.

21. He who has touched knowledge and has tasted its sweetness, will no longer trust the demon of vainglory, even if he offers him all the pleasures of the world. For what can he promise greater than spiritual contemplation? But while we have not as yet tasted knowledge, let us zealously lead a life of action, testifying to God our aim of doing everything for the sake of knowledge of Him.

23. Anything, of which we preserve a passionate memory, was formerly in fact accepted by us with passion; and again, what we receive with passion in actual fact, of that we shall later have a passionate memory. To those who have conquered the demons inciting passions, the things through which they incite them are of no account; for the immaterial foe is more bitter than the material.

24. Passions of the soul receive their impulse from people, and those of the body from the body. The movement of bodily passions is arrested by self-mastery, and of those of the soul by spiritual love.

25. The demons arousing passions of the soul stand by persistently and disturb the soul till death; but the demons arousing bodily passions withdraw more easily. Moreover some demons, like the rising or setting sun, touch only one or another part of the soul, while the noon-day demon usually envelops the whole soul and drowns the mind. This is why seclusion is sweet when the passions have been overcome; for then what is left of them is only bare memories. As to warfare, it is then not so much active warfare, as contemplating it.

26. It is worth considering whether thought brings passions into motion, or passions thought. Some think the first is true, others the second. It is usual for passions to be set into motion by the senses; but when a man has love and self-mastery they do not move, and when he has not, they move. Anger needs more drastic remedies than lust; and love is called great because it curbs anger.

28. It is not always possible to fulfil the usual rules; one must take circumstances into account and try to fulfil what they make possible, as far as one can. The demons themselves are not unmindful of this law. So, being in constant enmity with us, they prevent us from doing what is possible and urge us to do what is impossible. Thus they turn the sick away from thanking God for their afflictions and from bearing with good heart those who serve them. Also they urge the feeble to practise the strictest abstinence, and those weighed down (by years or labours) to practise psalmody standing on their feet.

31. A man who wishes to test the evil demons and to gain experience in discrimination of their wiles must observe his thoughts and notice on what they lay emphasis and what they let pass, which of them and in what circumstances is particularly active, which follows which, and which of them do not come together; and he must seek from Christ Jesus to be delivered of it all. The demons are very wroth with those who actively practise virtues with understanding (bringing all things to light), for they wish 'to shoot privily at the upright in heart' (Ps. x. 3).

33. To separate the body from the soul is possible only for Him, Who has combined them; but to separate the soul from the body is possible for him who strives after virtue (in seclusion). For our fathers mean by seclusion, memory of death and fleeing from the body.

34. Those who feed their body too lavishly and make provision for it, 'to fulfil the lusts thereof' (Rom. xiii. 14), should later blame not their body but themselves. But those who have acquired passionlessness of soul through this very body and are diligent in contemplating the One Who Is, as far as is in their power (again with the help of the body), profess the bounty of the Creator (who has given us the body).

35. When the mind begins to pray without distraction, then the whole day and night struggle reduces itself to struggle with the excitable part of the soul.

36. The sign of passionlessness is when the mind begins to see its own light, when it is untroubled by dreams in sleep and easily (and rightly) understands things.

37. When during prayer the mind imagines nothing worldly, that means it has become strong.

38. When, with God's help, the mind has concluded the course of active life and has reached knowledge (contemplation), it is very little, or not at all sensitive to movements of the irrational part of the soul. Knowledge (contemplation) raises it on high and separates it from all sensory things.

39. The soul is passionless not when it is no longer captivated by things, but when it remains undisturbed even by their memories.

40. It is not right to say of a perfect man that he abstains, and of a passionless man that he endures; for endurance belongs to him who suffers, and abstinence to him who is drawn by desire.

41. It is a great thing to pray without distraction; but to psalmodise without distraction is still greater.

42. He who has established virtues in himself and is entirely possessed by them, no longer remembers the law, or the commandments, or punishment, but says and does what the excellent disposition established in him suggests.

45. Wisdom consorts with repose, and good judgment with work. Wisdom cannot be gained without struggle, nor success in struggle without good judgment. It is the task of good judgment to oppose anger provoked by demons and to force the powers of the soul to act as they should, according to their nature, thus paving the way to wisdom.

46. Temptation for a monk is a thought which enters through the passionate part of the soul and obscures the mind.

47. Sin for a monk is the consent of thought to a forbidden sinful passion.

49. Virtues do not stop demons attacking us, but keep us unscathed by them.

50. Active life (practice of virtue) is the spiritual method for purifying the passionate part of the soul.

51. For a complete healing of the powers of the soul the salutary effect of commandments is not enough, unless in addition the mind holds corresponding contemplations.

53. The offspring of passionlessness is love; and passionlessness is the flower of active life, which in its turn consists of practice of

commandments. The guardian of this practice of commandments is fear of God, which is the fruit of right belief. Belief is the inner good of the soul, which is frequent even in those who have not yet come to faith in God.[22]

54. As the soul, acting through the body, senses which members are weak, so the mind, in using its own activity, learns its powers and noticing which of them hinder it, seeks the right commandment for healing them.

55. A mind which wages passionate war does not see the plans of the adversary; for then it is like a warrior fighting at night (in the dark). But after gaining passionlessness, it easily discerns the wiles of the enemies.

56. The ultimate end of active life is love, and the end of knowledge is theology. The beginning of them both is faith and contemplation of things. The demons who attack the passionate part of the soul are called the adversaries of active life; while those who attack the power of the mind itself are called the enemies of all truth and adversaries of contemplation.

58. The intelligent soul acts in accordance with its nature; when its desiring part strives after virtue, its excitable part works for it, and its mental part applies itself to contemplation of what is.

59. He who progresses in active life diminishes passions; and he who progresses in contemplation diminishes ignorance. Of passions it is said that in time they will be wholly destroyed, but of ignorance it is said that in part it will have an end, and in part not.

60. The good and the bad that we meet with in life can aid both virtues and vices. It is the task of good judgment to use them to further the first and to frustrate the second.

61. According to our wise teacher (St. Gregory of Nyssa) the soul is tripartite. When virtue is in the mental part it is called circumspection ($\phi\rho\acute{o}\nu\eta\sigma\iota\varsigma$), sagacity ($\sigma\acute{v}\nu\epsilon\sigma\iota\varsigma$) and wisdom ($\sigma o\phi\acute{\iota}a$). When it is in the desiring part it is called chastity, love and self-mastery. When it is in the excitable part it is called courage and patience. When it is in the whole soul it is called righteousness. The task of circumspection is to fight forces hostile

[22] This sentence is obscure. (Translators' note.)

to us, to protect virtues, to drive away vices and to manage neutral (indifferent) things according to the moment. The task of sagacity is to organise rightly everything which assists our aim; and the task of wisdom is to contemplate corporeal and incorporeal beings in all their aspects. The task of chastity is to look at things without passion, especially the foolish dreams and desires which agitate us. The task of love is to show itself towards every person, bearing God's image, almost as it does towards the Prototype, even though the demons strive to degrade someone in our eyes. The task of self-mastery is to refuse with joy all that pleases the palate. The work of patience and courage is not to fear the enemies and willingly to endure all afflictions. The task of righteousness is to keep all the parts of the soul in harmony and concord.

65. Three thoughts oppose thought coming from the demons and cut it off when it lingers in the mind: angelic thought; our own thought coming from our will when it is directed towards the better; and another thought of ours, which comes from human nature, moved by which even the heathens love their children, for example, and respect their parents. But a good thought is opposed by only two thoughts: the thought which comes from the demons and our own, resulting from our own will when it turns towards the worse. For our natural being engenders no bad thoughts; in the beginning we were not evil, because the Lord sowed good seed in His field. There was a time when evil did not exist, and the time will come when it will exist no more. The seeds of virtues are ineffaceable. I am convinced of that by the rich man of the Gospels who, even when condemned to hell, thought mercifully of his brethren; and mercy is the best seed of virtue.

69. Our intelligent nature, deadened by sin, Christ awakes (to repentance) by the contemplation of all the ages (what was, what is and what will be); and His Father resurrects through knowledge of God this soul, which then dies by the death of Christ, death to sin. This is the meaning of the words of the Apostle, 'For if we be dead with him, we shall also live with him' (2 Tim. ii. 11).

70. When the mind discards the old Adam and becomes clothed in the new man, who is of grace, he sees his state during

prayer like a sapphire or the colour of the firmament—what in the Holy Scriptures is called the place of God, as the elders saw it on Mount Sinai (Ex. xxiv. 10).

71. The mind will not see the place of God in itself, unless it rises above all thoughts of material and created things; and it cannot rise above them unless it becomes free of the passions binding it to sensory objects and inciting thoughts about them. It will free itself of passions by means of virtues, and of simple thoughts by means of spiritual contemplation; but it will discard even this when there appears to it that light which, during prayer, marks the place of God.

ABBA EVAGRIUS THE MONK

2. Century on Active Life

29. Our holy and most experienced teacher used to say: a monk should be attuned in himself, as if he had to die tomorrow; and he should deal with his body as though he had to live many years. For, as he said, the first stops despondent thoughts and makes a monk more zealous, and the second keeps the body healthy and makes it always preserve an even temperance.

43. It is necessary to distinguish the differences between demons and to note their times. From thoughts we learn which demons are rare but grievous, which are constant but lighter, which jump on one suddenly and entice the mind to blasphemy. It is also important to observe when thoughts begin to bring forward their objects, so that, before quitting our usual state, we may have time to say something against them and to notice who is in them. For in this way we shall succeed with God's help and shall force them to turn away from us with vexation, marvelling at us.

44. When the demons become exhausted in their struggle with monks, they withdraw a little and watch which virtue will be neglected during that interval; then, suddenly attacking this side they pillage the poor soul.

48. With laymen the demons fight rather by means of actual things, but with monks mostly by means of thoughts; for in the wilderness they have no things. But as it is easier and quicker to sin in thought than in deed, so mental warfare is more arduous than that waged by means of things. The mind is something extremely mobile and unrestrainable, susceptible to sinful fantasies.

49. We are not commanded to work, keep vigil and fast unceasingly; but we are commanded to pray without ceasing. For

the former efforts, directed towards healing the lustful part of the soul, have need of the body for their action; and the body cannot exist in constant work and privations without support. Prayer, however, purifies and renders strong in battle the mind, which is created to pray even without this body, and to fight the demons for the protection of all the powers of the soul.

56. Let us discern the signs of passionlessness during daytime by means of thoughts, and at night by means of dreams. Let us call passionlessness the health of the soul, and knowledge its food; because it alone unites us with the holy powers, since union with the incorporeal beings is possible only when our state corresponds to theirs.

57. There are two peaceable states of the soul: one comes of the weakening and drying up of natural juices, the other is due to withdrawal of the demons. The first is accompanied by humility with contrition of heart—tears and a measureless desire of the Divine; the second is followed by vainglory and pride, which take possession of a monk when other demons have withdrawn. He who protects the realm of the first state can more easily discern the attacks and wiles of the demons.

58. The demon of vainglory is opposed to the demon of fornication; it is not feasible for the two to attack the soul together, for one promises honours and the other casts into dishonour. Therefore if one of them approaches and begins to disturb you, bring to your mind the thoughts of the opposing demon. If you succeed, as the saying goes, in driving out one nail with another, know that you are close to the realm of passionlessness; for your mind has proved able to drive away the demon's suggestions by human thoughts. But of course, to banish the thought of vainglory by humility, or the thought of fornication by chastity, would be a sign of the deepest passionlessness. Try to act thus in relation to all demons and their opposites. Doing this you will also learn what passion was filling you. Yet beg God with all your strength to teach you and help you to drive away the enemies by the second method.

59. The further the soul progresses, the more powerful are the enemies who attack it. I do not think that the demons who surround it are always the same. This is known best to those who

watch sharply the temptations which attack them, and see that
their customary passionlessness is being shaken more violently
than before by new demons, successors of the old.

60. Perfect passionlessness comes to the soul when all the
demons who oppose active life are overcome. Passionlessness is
called imperfect when the soul still wages war as much as it can
with the demon who attacks it, without, however, giving ground.

61. The mind will not pass through, will not complete safely
this passionate way (of trials) and will not enter the realm of the
incorporeal, unless it sets right what is within. Domestic disorder is bound to turn it back to things it has left behind.

62. Both virtues and vices make the mind blind: with the first
it does not see vices, and with the second, virtues.

ABBA EVAGRIUS THE MONK

3. Miscellaneous Sayings from Various Texts[23]

1. Hell is the darkness of ignorance, which envelops sentient creatures, when they have lost the contemplation of God.

2. It is unseemly for the man who seeks honours to shirk the efforts for which honours are given.

3. Do you wish to know God? Learn first to know yourself.

4. It is inconsistent to think highly of oneself, while one's actions are base.

5. In every man self-opinion prevents self-knowledge.

6. He is pious who is not at variance with himself.

7. A soul pure in God is God.

8. If you wish to be free from discontent, strive to please God.

9. If you wish to know who you are, do not look at what you have been, but at what you were originally created.

10. A proud soul is a den of robbers; it cannot bear the voice of knowledge.

11. Without temptations no one would be saved.

12. Pray without ceasing and remember Christ, Who has regenerated you.

[23] The numbering of the paragraphs in this section is consecutive and does not follow the Russian version. (Translators' note.)

ABBA EVAGRIUS THE MONK

4. To Anatolius : On Eight Thoughts

1. There are eight principal thoughts, from which all other thoughts stem. The first thought is of gluttony; the second, of fornication; the third, of love of money; the fourth, of discontent; the fifth, of anger; the sixth, of despondency; the seventh, of vainglory; the eighth, of pride. Whether these thoughts disturb the soul or not does not depend on us; but whether they linger in us or not and set passions in motion or not—does depend on us.

2. The thought of gluttony suggests to a monk that he make haste to give up his ascetic life, depicting to him diseases of the stomach, liver or bile, dropsy or some other long illness, the lack of medical remedies and the absence of physicians. Moreover, it brings to his memory brethren who actually contracted such diseases. At times the enemy urges brethren, who have suffered such diseases, to visit monks who are fasting and to relate what has happened to them, adding that this was due to too strict an abstinence.

3. The demon of fornication excites carnal lust, and insidiously attacks abstainers, striving to make them abandon their abstinence, thinking that it brings them no profit. Polluting the soul, it urges it also towards such actions and makes them say and hear certain words, as though the act itself were before their eyes.

4. Love of money conjectures a long old age, inability to work with one's hands, hunger, illness, the hardships of want and the grievousness of accepting from others the wherewithal for bodily needs.

5. Discontent is sometimes caused by the loss of what is desirable, and sometimes accompanies anger. When caused by the loss of what is desirable it happens thus. Certain thoughts come first

and bring to the soul memories of home, relatives and the old way of life. When they see that the soul does not oppose them but goes with them and mentally spreads itself in enjoying them, they seize it and immerse it in discontent, both because the objects of their thoughts are absent, and because by the statutes of a monk's life he cannot have them. So the more eagerly the poor soul spreads itself in the initial thoughts, the more it is stricken and grieved by the sequel.

6. Anger is the quickest passion of all. It is aroused and inflamed against a man who has done, or seems to have done one an injury. It hardens the soul ever more and more; it particularly captures the mind during prayer, vividly bringing up the face of an offender. At times, lingering in the soul and passing into enmity, it causes nightmares, depicting physical tortures, the horrors of death, attacks of poisonous snakes and beasts. These four phenomena accompanying the birth of enmity, bring with them many thoughts, as every observer will find for himself.

7. The demon of despondency, which is also called the noonday demon (Ps. xc. 6), is more grievous than all others. It attacks a monk in about the fourth hour (about ten in the morning) and whirls the soul round and round till about the eighth hour (two o'clock in the afternoon). It begins by making a man notice dejectedly how slowly the sun moves, or does not move at all, and that the day seems to have become fifty hours long. Then it urges the man to look frequently out of the window or even to go out of his cell to look at the sun and see how long it is till the ninth hour, at the same time making him glance hither and thither to see if some of the brethren are about. Then it arouses in him vexation against the place and his mode of life itself and his work, adding that there is no more love among the brethren and no one to comfort him. If in these days someone has offended him, the demon reminds him of it to increase his vexation. Then it provokes in him a longing for other places, where it would be easier to find the wherewithal to satisfy his needs by adopting some craft which is less strenuous and more profitable. He adds that to please God does not depend on the place; God can be worshipped everywhere. He connects with this thought memories of relatives and former well-being; and prophesies here a long life with the

hardships of asceticism, and uses every wile to make the monk end by leaving his cell and taking flight from his career. This demon is followed by another, but not at once. However if a monk fights and conquers, this struggle is followed by a peaceful state, and the soul becomes filled with ineffable joy.

8. The thought of vainglory is the most subtle of all. It comes to those who lead a righteous life, and begins to extol their efforts and collect praise from men, making them imagine the cries of demons being cast out, the healing of women, crowds pressing round a man to touch his garments. Finally it predicts his consecration into priesthood, brings to his doors men to seek him who, on his refusal, bind him and lead him forcibly away against his will. Having thus kindled idle hopes in him, the demon withdraws, leaving the field for further temptations either by the demon of pride or the demon of discontent, who at once suggests to him thoughts opposed to these hopes. At times he even surrenders to the demon of fornication, this man who, only a short time before, saw himself as a holy and venerable priest.

9. The demon of pride is the cause of the most grievous fall of the soul. It counsels the soul not to profess God as its helper, but to ascribe to itself its righteousness and to puff itself up before its brethren, considering them to be ignorant because not all of them think so highly of it. Pride is followed by anger and discontent and by the final evil—going out of one's mind, frenzy and visions of many demons in the air.

ABBA EVAGRIUS THE MONK

5. Reflections on the Eight Thoughts

1. There are five occupations which help to gain God's benevolence. The first is pure prayer; the second, psalmody; the third, reading the Holy Scriptures; the fourth, contrite remembrance of one's sins, of death and the terrible judgment; the fifth, work with one's hands.

2. If while still in your body you wish to serve God like the incorporeal beings, strive to have in your heart a secret unceasing prayer. For in this way your soul will come near to resembling the angels even before death.

3. As our body becomes dead and full of stench when the soul leaves it, so a soul in which prayer is not active is dead and stenches. That to be deprived of prayer should be counted worse than death is clearly shown us by Prophet Daniel, who was ready to die rather than be deprived of prayer at any hour. One should remember God more often than one breathes.

4. Join to every breath a sober invocation of the name of Jesus [24] and the thought of death with humility. Both these practices bring great profit to the soul.

5. Do you wish to be known by God? Try as much as possible to be less known to men. If you will always remember that God is the Seer of all you do with soul or body, you will not sin in any action, and will have God as your Companion.

6. Nothing so makes a man resemble God as doing good to others. But in doing good to them, one should take great care not to transform these good deeds into a thought.

[24] The constant invocation of the Divine Name of Jesus, either as a single word or as part of a short prayer, derives, according to tradition, from apostolic times; this would seem to be one of the earliest specific mentions of this practice in patristic writings. Cf. St. John Chrysostom in *Writings from the Philokalia*, pp. 193–4. (Translators' note.)

7. In the end you will become worthy of God by the fact that you do nothing unworthy of Him.

8. You will pay glorious homage to God if, through virtues, you imprint His likeness on your soul.

9. Men become better as they come nearer to God.

10. A wise man who offers to God honour and worship is known by Him. So he is in no way troubled if he remains unknown to all men. The task of good judgment is to incite the part of the soul where anger lies to the waging of inner warfare. The task of wisdom is to urge the mind to constant attentive watchfulness. The task of righteousness is to direct the part, in which lies lust, towards virtue and towards God. Finally, the task of courage is to govern the five senses and not let our inner man, that is the spirit, or our outer man, that is the body, be defiled through them.

11. The soul is a living substance, simple, incorporeal, invisible to the physical eye, immortal and endowed with mind and reason. What the eye is to the body, that the mind is to the soul.

13. Evil is not an actual substance, but absence of good; just as darkness is nothing but absence of light.

20. Occupy yourself with reading with a calm spirit, so that your mind may be constantly raised up to contemplation of the wondrous acts of God, lifted, as it were, by some hand outstretched to it.

22. Every soul, by the grace of the Holy Spirit and by its own work and diligence, can conjoin and combine in itself the following qualities: word with mind, action with contemplation, virtue with science, faith with knowledge free of all forgetfulness, in such a way, moreover, that none of these qualities would be greater or less than another. For then it will be united with God, Who is good and true, and with Him alone.

ABBA EVAGRIUS THE MONK

6. Instructions to Cenobites and others

2. Faith is the beginning of love; the end of love is knowledge of God.

4. Man's patience gives birth to hope; good hope will glorify him.

5. He who keeps his flesh in strict subjection will reach passionlessness. He who feeds it will suffer from it.

7. Solitude with love purifies the heart. Withdrawal from others with anger agitates it.

8. It is better to be among thousands with love, than to hide alone in caves with hatred.

18. He dishonours God who transgresses His law. But he who obeys it glorifies his Creator.

20. Where sin enters, there too enters ignorance; but the hearts of the righteous are filled with knowledge.

21. Better poverty with knowledge than riches with ignorance.

22. The highest adornment of the head is the crown; the highest adornment of the heart is knowledge of God.

25. He who prays often will escape temptation; but thoughts will trouble the heart of the careless.

43. If the spirit of despondency attacks you, do not leave your cell, and do not turn aside in time of discontent. For as silver is purified (by friction), so will your heart be made bright if you stand firm.

44. The spirit of despondency takes away tears, and the spirit of discontent stifles prayer.

51. Love is preceded by passionlessness; knowledge is preceded by love.

75. Honour God and you will know the incorporeal; serve Him and He will show you the understanding of the ages.

76. The body of Christ is active virtues; he who tastes them will be free from passions.

77. The blood of Christ is discrimination of actions; he who drinks it will be illumined.

78. The bosom of the Lord is knowledge of God; he who rests therein will be a theologian.

79. When he who is filled with knowledge and he who practises good meet one another, the Lord is between them.

ABBA EVAGRIUS THE MONK

7. On Various Evil Thoughts

1. Amongst the demons who work against active life, those who stand in the forefront in battle are demons entrusted with lusts, or the appetites of gluttony, those who implant in us love of money and those who provoke us to seek human glory. All the rest follow behind and receive the wounded, whom these three pass down to them. For it is impossible to fall into the hands of adultery, unless a man has fallen because of gluttony; it is impossible to be agitated by anger, unless one covets and fights for food, or money, or fame; it is impossible to avoid the demon of discontent, unless a man has suffered some privation in all this; impossible to escape pride, this first offspring of the devil, unless a man has uprooted 'the love of money . . . the root of all evil' (1 Tim. vi. 10), since, according to the wise Solomon, 'Poverty brings a man low' (Prov. x. 4). In short, it is impossible for a man to fall under the power of any demon, unless he is first wounded by the three foremost. This is why the devil suggested those three thoughts to the Lord: the first, when he asked that stones should be made bread; the second, when he promised all the kingdoms of the world, if the Lord would fall down and worship him; and the third, when he asserted that if the Lord would listen to him, He would be glorified and suffer no harm in casting Himself down from a pinnacle of the temple. But the Lord Who was above all this, ordered the devil to get thence, thus showing us that it is impossible to banish the devil, unless we scorn these three thoughts.

2. All thoughts coming from the demons introduce into the soul images of sensory objects, and the mind, having received their imprint, revolves them in itself. So we can learn from the

subject of the thought, which demon has approached us. For instance, if an image of someone who has done me harm or who has insulted me comes into my mind, it shows that the demon of resentment has drawn near; again, if I remember money or fame, it is impossible not to know by their subject matter who is troubling us. It is the same with other thoughts. I do not mean that all memories of such things come from demons, for it is usual for the mind itself, when a man brings it into motion, to reproduce images of past events. But only those memories come from the demons which unnaturally evoke excitation or desires. Owing to the disturbance of these powers, the mind commits mental adultery or quarrels, and is no longer able to keep in itself the thought of God, its Lawgiver; for such luminosity (that is, untroubled thought of God) appears in the sovereign mind only on condition that thoughts turning among things during prayer are cut off.

5. The intentions of the demons and all their cunning devices are greatly helped by our excitability, when it comes into motion in a way not intended by nature. Therefore none of them refuses a chance to arouse it day and night. But when they see that it is shackled by meekness, they try to unshackle it beforehand by some seemingly right pretext, so that, once aroused, it should become suitable for provoking their bestial thoughts. For this reason we should never let it be aroused, whether for right or wrong purposes, lest we put a dangerous sword into the hands of those who incite us to evil. Yet I know that many do this for the most paltry reasons, by becoming inflamed more than is expedient. Why is it, will you tell me, that you so quickly assume a combative attitude, if you have renounced food, money and fame? Why do you feed the dog, if you have vowed to possess nothing? If it barks and attacks people it is clear that you have something within that you want to preserve. Such a man, I am sure, is far from pure prayer, for he knows that anger kills such prayer. I am surprised, moreover, that he has forgotten the saints: David, who cries, 'Cease from anger, and forsake wrath' (Ps. xxxvi. 8); and the Apostle who commands everywhere to lift up 'holy hands, without wrath and doubting' (1 Tim. ii. 8). The old custom of driving dogs out of the house in time of prayer teaches us allegorically the

same thing, for it means that men who pray should be free from anger. Even one of the pagan sages asserted that the gods do not eat gall and thigh-bones. I do not suppose he understood himself what he was saying; but in my opinion gall is the symbol of anger and thigh-bones of animal lust.

7. Through long observation we have found that the difference between thoughts which are of the angels, those of men and those which come from the demons is as follows: those of the angels seek to discover the nature of things and their spiritual meaning: for instance, for what purpose gold is created and why it is dispersed like sand in the earth's valleys and is found with much effort and labour? How, when found, it is washed in water, put in the fire and then comes into the hands of artists, who make out of it for the house of God a candlestick, a censer, bowls (2 Chron. iv. 19–21) from which by the grace of God, the Babylonian king no longer drinks (Dan. v. 3). But a Cleopas brings a heart burning with these mysteries (Luke xxiv. 32). The thought of the demons does not know or understand this, but shamelessly suggests only the acquisition of physical gold, predicting the pleasure and glory to be had from it. And human thought neither seeks to possess it nor is curious about what gold symbolises; it merely introduces into the mind a bare image of gold, without passion or cupidity. If a man exercises his mind in accordance with this example he will find that the same reasoning applies also to other objects.

8. There is a thought which can suitably be called the wanderer. It mostly comes to the brethren towards the end of the night and leads the mind from town to town, from village to village, from house to house. At first the mind conducts simple conversations but later, drawn into long talks with some old acquaintances, it lets its state be corrupted according to the qualities of those it meets. Thus, little by little, it falls away from consciousness of God and virtue, and forgets its calling and its vow. Therefore a hermit must watch this demon, observing whence he comes and what he touches, for it is not for nothing that he makes such a wide circuit. He does this to disturb the hermit's state in order that the mind, inflamed by it all and intoxicated by many conversations, should at once fall under the

demon of fornication, or anger, or discontent, which are the most injurious to its light. But if we wish to know better the wiles of this demon, we should not immediately oppose it, and should not at once reveal (to the fathers) how he builds up mental conversations in us and by what means he gradually drives the mind to the realm of death, for then he will at once run away, unable to bear anyone seeing how he does all this; and we shall thus learn nothing of what we wished to learn. But let us rather allow him to bring his drama to a conclusion on the next or the third day, so as to learn all his cunning methods and thus later be able to put him to flight by a single word of denunciation. But since during temptation the mind is often troubled and fails to see clearly what takes place in us, when the demon has withdrawn you should act as follows. Sit down alone with yourself and recollect what happened to you; where you started from and whither you wandered, at what place you were seized by the spirit of fornication, or discontent, or anger, and how all that followed came about. Study all this and commit it to memory, so that you can expose him when he comes again. Note also the very place which he kept concealed, and you will no longer follow him again. After this, if you wish to enrage him, expose him as soon as he presents himself, and name verbally the first place you had entered (mentally, in the first wanderings), then the second and the third; for he cannot bear disgrace and will be greatly vexed. The flight of the thought from you will be proof of the usefulness of dealing with him in this way, for he cannot stand such open exposure. Such a conquest of the demon is followed by great sleepiness, deadening of the eyelids, a feeling of coldness, excessive yawning and drooping shoulders; but with diligent prayer the Holy Spirit disperses it all.

16. The Lord entrusted the thoughts of this age to man, as sheep to a good shepherd, giving him as his helpers desire and wrath; that with wrath he might put to flight the thoughts of wolves (those of the demons), and with desire wholeheartedly love the sheep (good thoughts) and feed them, suffering frequent attacks of rain and winds that knock a man off his feet. Moreover He gave him the law of how to tend sheep, and green grass and the water of rest (Ps. xxii. 2), the psalter and the harp, the rod

and the staff, so that from this flock (and grass) he should get food and garments and gather the mountain hay (Prov. xxvii. 25). For He says, 'Who feedeth a flock, and eateth not of the milk of the flock?' (1 Cor. ix. 7). Therefore a hermit must guard this flock day and night, so that no lamb should be stolen by beasts or fall into the hands of robbers. Should this happen in some wild place, he must at once draw the spoil out of the mouth of the lion or the she-bear (1 Kings xvii. 34, 35). Beasts of prey are—thought of a brother, if it feeds in us with hatred; thought of a woman, if it turns in us with shameful lust; thought of silver and gold, if it comes to dwell in us with cupidity; even thoughts of holy gifts, if they feed in the mind with vainglory. The same should be said of other thoughts if they are ravished by passions. We must guard (our flock) not only by day, but must protect it watchfully also by night. For it happens that a man dreaming shameful and treacherous dreams loses what is his own. This is the meaning of the words of Jacob: 'That which was taken of beasts I brought not to thee; I made good of myself the thefts of the day, and the thefts of the night. I was parched with heat by day, and chilled with frost by night, and my sleep departed from my eyes' (Gen. xxxi. 39, 40). If, exhausted by work, we fall into despondency, let us hasten to the rock of knowledge and converse with the psalter, plucking with virtues at the strings of the harp of knowledge. Let us keep our sheep again under Mount Sinai, that the God of our fathers may call to us too out of the burning bush (Ex. iii. 1–4) and give us the power of signs and miracles.

19. Some of the unclean demons tempt a man as man, while others disturb him as a dumb animal. The first introduce into us thoughts of vainglory, or pride, or envy, or condemnation which do not affect any dumb animal. The second arouse anger, or lust that are not according to nature. For these passions are common to us and to dumb animals and are concealed in us beneath rational nature. Therefore the Holy Spirit, having regard for thoughts which come to men as men, says, 'I have said, Ye are gods; and all of you children of the Most High. But ye die as men, and fall as one of the princes' (Ps. lxxxi. 6, 7). And having regard for thoughts which move in man as a dumb animal, what does He say? 'Be ye not as horse and mule, which have no understanding:

but thou must constrain their jaws with bit and curb, lest they should come nigh to thee' (Ps. xxxi. 9).

20. When an enemy comes and wounds you and you wish, according to the Scriptures, that his sword may enter into his own heart (Ps. xxxvi. 15), do as we tell you. Analyse in yourself the thought introduced by him, what it is, of what it is composed and what in it affects the mind. For instance, suppose a thought of love of money has been suggested to you. Separate it by analysis into the mind which has received it, the thought of gold, gold itself and the money-loving passion. Finally ask, which of all these is sin? Is it the mind? But how can it be, if it is the image of God? The thought of gold then? But what man who has a mind can say even that? Is then gold itself a sin? But why was it created? Thus it remains to refer sin to the fourth (that is the money-loving passion) which is neither a concrete independent thing, nor an apprehension of a thing, but an inhuman lust, born of free will and urging the mind to misuse God's creations, which lust the Divine law commands us to cut off. If you examine it all, the thought will vanish when thus analysed into its component parts, and the demon will run away, as soon as your thought rises on high on the wings of this knowledge.

If you do not wish that his sword may enter into his own heart, but desire first to strike him with your sling, take a stone out of your shepherd's bag and consider the following: How is it that angels and demons affect our world, whereas we do not affect theirs? For we cannot bring the angels nearer to God, neither will it ever enter our head to make the demons more unclean. Ponder also over the following: 'How has Lucifer, that rose in the morning, fallen from heaven!' (Isaiah xiv. 12). 'He makes the deep boil like a brazen caldron; and he regards the sea as a pot of ointment, and the lowest part of the deep as a captive: he reckons the deep as his range' (Job xli. 22, 23), disturbing all by his malice and wishing to be master of all. Pondering over these things greatly wounds the demon and turns to flight his whole army. But to act thus is possible only for those who have achieved a degree of purification and have a certain insight into the causes of the event. Impure men do not know how to ponder over these questions, and, even if taught by others how to put a spell on the enemy, will not be heard, since in time of battle all inside them is turmoil and clouds of dust raised by passions. For certainly it is essential for all the alien hosts to stand still, so that only Goliath should come forward against our David. Thus with other unclean thoughts too, let us use the (aforementioned) method of analysis, and also this (second) method of warfare.

21. When some unclean thoughts desist too readily, let us seek the cause of their flight, whether the enemy could not harm us because of the improbability of the suggestion, that is, the difficulty of attaining it, or because of our passionlessness. For instance, if a hermit should imagine that the spiritual guidance of a capital city has been entrusted to him, and he does not linger on those fantasies, it is obviously due to the first reason. But if a thought occurs to someone that he is to become a ruler of a certain city (which is quite possible) and treats this thought in the same manner (with disdain), this would mean that he is blessed with passionlessness. If we use this method of investigation we shall discover with other thoughts too (why they fled from us so quickly). We should know this to enliven our zeal and efforts, for by this means we shall discover whether we have already crossed Jordan and are close to the city of palm-trees (Deut. xxxiv. 3), or are still in the wilderness and being attacked by aliens.

22. All unclean thoughts take root in us because of the passions which cast the mind into ruin and perdition. For as the thought of bread lingers in a hungry man because of his hunger, and the thought of water in a thirsty man because of his thirst, so thoughts of money and shameful thoughts, born of rich and plentiful food, also linger in us owing to (corresponding) passions. The same applies to thoughts of vainglory and others like them. But it is impossible for a mind, oppressed by such thoughts, to appear before God and be adorned by the crown of righteousness. It is by these thoughts that the thrice-accursed mind was occupied when, according to the Gospel parable, it excused itself from the supper of knowledge of God (Luke xiv. 18–20). Similarly the man who was bound hand and foot and cast into outer darkness had a garment woven from such thoughts, which his Host judged unworthy of the wedding feast (Matt. xxii. 11–13). The wedding garment

is the passionlessness of the intelligent soul, which has discarded worldly lusts.

27. The demons do not know our hearts, as some people think, for only He Who understandeth 'the mind of men' (Job vii. 20) and 'who fashioned their hearts alone' (Ps. xxxii. 15), knows men's hearts. But either from words which are uttered, or from some movements of the body, they recognise many of the movements occurring in the heart. Suppose that in conversation we have denounced those who have spoken evil of us; from these words, the demons conclude that we have a hostile attitude towards those people, and they use it as a chance to introduce into us evil thoughts against them; having accepted these, we fall under the yoke of the demon of resentment, who thereupon constantly incites us to vengeful thoughts against them. Therefore the Holy Spirit rightly denounces us, saying: 'Thou didst sit and speak against thy brother, and didst scandalise thy mother's son' (Ps. xlix. 20), that is, you opened the door to thoughts of resentment, and confused your mind during prayer, constantly imagining the face of your enemy, and thus having him as a god; for what the mind constantly looks upon during prayer should rightly be acknowledged as its god. So let us avoid this disease of malicious talk, let us have no evil memory against anyone, nor make faces at the memory of a brother. For evil demons eagerly watch our every movement and leave nothing unexplored that could be used against us, whether our sitting, or our getting up, our standing, our walk, our words or our look. They are always curious, devising 'deceits all the day' (Ps. xxxvii. 12) in order, during prayer, to put to shame the humble mind and to extinguish its blessed light.

ST. NILUS OF SINAI

ST. NILUS OF SINAI
Short Biographical Note

The blessed Nilus belonged to a wealthy and illustrious family and was probably already a pupil of St. John Chrysostom when the latter was preaching in Antioch. His noble birth and personal gifts raised him to the rank of prefect of the capital. But his spiritual aspirations conflicted with the occupations imposed by his office and the social life of the capital. Therefore, having come to an agreement with his wife, from whom he already had two children, he renounced the world in order better to follow the path of salvation in solitude. He took with him his son Theodul and settled on Mount Sinai, while his wife and daughter entered one of the Egyptian convents.

His life in the wilderness of Sinai was very austere; with the help of his son, he dug out a cave with his own hands, and the two settled there, having for food not even bread but only bitter wild plants. They spent all their time in prayer, study of the Scriptures, meditation and labours.

But though he had left the world St. Nilus did not renounce communication with his fellow men. People of all kinds from far and wide appealed to him for help in their spiritual needs, and no one was ever left without the direction and advice that they needed. The Emperor also wrote to him, begging for his prayers, and he wrote to the Emperor, reproaching him for his injustice towards St. John Chrysostom. His other writings are mostly of a moral and ascetic character. All of them show clearly the breadth and depth of his knowledge and his untiring labours in this work.

To test his love of God he was sent a special trial. Sinai and the surrounding countryside were invaded by wild barbarians from Arabia, who pillaged everything, slaughtered many and led others away into captivity. Among the latter was Theodul, his son. This calamity was exceedingly painful for the saint and he could find no rest, especially when, two or three days after the raid, he heard the news that the barbarians had decided to sacrifice his son as an offering to Venus, the morning star. The message did not say whether or not this decision had been executed. But God did not leave the father's heart too long in painful uncertainty. He soon heard that the sacrifice did not take place and the captives were sold into Christian countries. Enquiries found him later in the town of Elusius, whose bishop had bought him from the barbarians, together with other captives, and was preparing him for the service of the Church. When the father arrived there to fetch him back, the bishop tried to persuade him to enter the same service. Love of solitude prevented them from agreeing to this course; so the bishop ordained them both into priesthood and, after blessing them, let them return to their beloved Sinai, where they remained to the end of their lives.

St. Nilus left the world in A.D. 390; he spent 60 years in the Sinai wilderness and died in about A.D. 450. His memory is celebrated on November 12th and January 14th. In the reign of Justin the Younger his remains were transported to Constantinople and laid in the church of the Holy Apostles.

ST. NILUS OF SINAI

153 Texts on Prayer[25]

1. If one should wish to prepare an aromatic oil, one should, according to the law, take an equal weight of stacte, onycha, sweet galbanum and transparent frankincense (Ex. xxx. 34). These are the four virtues.[26] When they all exist in the soul in equal force and full perfection, the mind will not be betrayed (by some inner traitor).

2. Purified by the fullness of virtue[27] the soul renders the mind steadfast, able to acquire the structure needed (for prayer).

3. Prayer is the speaking of mind to God. What structure does the mind need so that, not looking back (nor hither and thither), it may rise to the Lord and converse with Him, with no intermediary?[28]

4. If Moses was forbidden to approach the earthly burning bush until he had loosed his sandals from off his feet (Ex. iii. 5), how can you not cast away from yourself every passionate thought when you wish to see Him, Who is above all feeling and thought, and to converse with Him?

5. Before all else pray to be given tears, that weeping may soften the hardness (ἀγριότητα) which is in your soul, and having acknowledged your sin unto the Lord (Ps. xxxi. 5), you may receive from Him the remission of sins.

---

[25] 'Simon Peter . . . drew the net to land full of great fishes, an hundred and fifty and three' (John xxi. 11).

[26] Self-mastery, courage, wisdom, righteousness. (Footnote in the Dobrotolubiye.)

[27] In the Greek and Slavonic Philokalia 'by the fulfilment of commandments'. (Footnote in the Dobrotolubiye.)

[28] The Slavonic 'nothing being in between' may be better. (Footnote in the Dobrotolubiye.)

6. Use tears as a weapon for the obtaining of every request; for the Almighty rejoices exceedingly when you pray with tears.

7. When you shed floods of tears during prayer, do not exalt yourself for this, as though you were above many others. It is that your prayer has received help from above, so that, having zealously confessed your sins, you may incline the Almighty to mercy by your tears.

8. So do not make a passion of the remedy against passions, lest you anger still more Him Who granted you this blessing (that is, tears). In shedding tears for their sins many people forget the purpose of tears and, getting into a frenzy, go astray.

9. Stand patiently and pray steadfastly, brushing off the impacts of worldly cares and all thoughts; for they distract and worry you in order to disturb the impetus of your prayer.

10. When the demons see that someone has the zeal and diligence to pray as he ought, then they suggest to him thoughts about something, supposedly important (and then draw away); but a little later they again call up the memory of this thing, urging his mind to examine it (if it is a problem—to solve it; if it is a thing—to acquire it); and he, not finding what he seeks, feels vexed and grieved. Then, when he stands up to pray, the demons remind him of what he had thought of and sought for, so that his mind should once more be moved to enquiry and his prayer become barren.

11. Strive to render your mind deaf and dumb during prayer: then you will be able to pray as you ought.

12. When you meet with temptation, or are irritated by someone's disagreement, so that you are filled with anger against the man who has disagreed with you, or even say some unseemly word, remember prayer and the judgment (of your conscience before the face of God) during it, and the unseemly movement will at once be stilled in you.

13. Anything you may do to revenge yourself upon a brother who has done you an injustice will offend you during prayer.

14. Prayer is a branch (of the tree) of meekness, and freedom from anger.

15. Prayer is an expression of joy and thankfulness.

16. Prayer is a remedy against sorrow and depression.

17. 'Go and sell that thou hast, and give to the poor' (Matt. xix. 21), and, taking up thy cross, deny thyself (Matt. xvi. 24), that you may be able to pray without distraction.

21. 'Leave there thy gift before the altar,' says the Lord, 'and go thy way; first be reconciled to thy brother' (Matt. v. 24), and then, when you return, you will pray without disturbance; for rancour obscures the sovereign mind of a man at prayer, and envelops his prayer in darkness.

22. Those who collect in themselves distress and resentment and who practise prayer in this state are like people pouring water into a leaky bucket.

24. When you pray as you ought, there may come into your mind things about which it seems right to be angry with your brother. There is absolutely no anger against your brother which could be justified. If you look, you will find that the question can be settled quite well without anger. Therefore do your best not to be moved to anger.

25. Beware, lest in thinking to cure another, you remain yourself unhealed and hinder your prayer.

28. In praying do not limit yourself to external movements and postures, but raise your mind, with great fear, to the feeling of spiritual prayer.

29. At times you have but to stand up to pray, and you pray well; at others, however hard you try, you fail to reach that desired aim; (this is allowed) so that you should seek (prayer) the more eagerly and, having received it, should have your prayer perfectly right and safe from being robbed.

30. When an Angel comes near us, all (the demons) around us withdraw at once; then the mind is in a state of great joy and prays soundly. At times, however, under pressure of the customary warfare, the mind struggles in fighting and is not given to rise (to right thought and feeling). This is because it has previously fallen under the power of various passions (has been captivated by them, has tasted them). However, if it goes on seeking, it will find, and if it persists in knocking, the door will be opened unto it.

31. Do not pray that things may be according to your desires, for they are not always in keeping with the will of God. Better pray as you were taught, saying: 'Thy will be done' on me

Matt. vi. 10). And ask thus about all things, for He always desires what is good and profitable for your soul, whereas you do not always seek it.

32. How many times have I prayed for what seemed a good thing for me, and persisted with my petition, foolishly importuning God's will, and not leaving it to God to do what, as He knows best, is useful for me. But, having obtained (what I had asked for) I found myself in great distress, and precisely because I had not asked for it to be, rather, according to God's will; for the thing proved not what I thought it to be.

33. What is good, except God? So let us leave to Him all that concerns us, and good will come to us; for He Who is Good is certainly also the Giver of good gifts.

34. Do not grieve if you do not at once receive from God that which you ask. He wishes to benefit you still more by making you persist longer in your patient prayer before Him. For what can be higher than to address one's converse to God and be in communion with Him?

35. Undistracted prayer is the highest doing of the mind.

36. Prayer is the ascent of mind to God.

37. If you desire true prayer, renounce all to inherit all.

38. Pray firstly to be purified of passions, secondly to be freed from ignorance and forgetfulness, and thirdly to be delivered from all temptation and forsaking.

39. Seek in your prayer only righteousness and the kingdom, that is, virtue and knowledge—and all the rest 'shall be added unto you' (Matt. vi. 33).

40. It is right to pray not only for one's own purification, but for the purification of every man, imitating the angelic order.

41. Watch, to see whether you are truly standing before God in your prayer, or are swayed by a desire for human praise and are trying to attract it, covering this (wrong desire by fair-seeming) length of prayer.

42. Whether you pray with the brethren or alone, try not merely to obey the rule, but to pray with feeling.

43. There belong to prayer (with feeling) going deep into oneself with reverence, touching of the heart, and contrition of the soul when with inaudible sighs it confesses its trespasses.

44. If during prayer the mind is being robbed (is looking hither and thither or around) a man does not pray like a monk, but is still a layman, adorning the outer tabernacle.

45. When you pray, guard your memory with all your strength, lest it offer you something of its own. Lift yourself up in every possible way to the consciousness of standing before God. For during prayer the mind is often greatly robbed by memory.

46. During prayer memory brings to your mind either pictures of past events, or new cares, or the face of some man who has offended you.

47. The demon is greatly envious of a man who prays, and uses many wiles to disturb his intention; so he does not cease to provoke, through memory, thoughts of various things, while through the body he sets all the passions in movement; his one aim is somehow to spoil the excellence of the man's progress and his ascent (by attention) to God.

48. When the sly demon, after using many devices, fails to hinder the prayer of the diligent, he desists a little; but when the man has finished his prayer, he takes his revenge. He either fires his anger and thus destroys the fair state produced by prayer, or excites an impulse towards some animal pleasure and thus mocks his mind.

49. Having prayed as is fitting, expect what is unfitting, and stand firm, protecting your fruit. This has been your task from the very beginning—to cultivate and keep (Gen. ii. 15). Therefore having cultivated (having prayed as you ought), do not leave unprotected the fruits of your labour, or no profit will be left you from your prayer.

50. The whole warfare between us and the unclean spirits is for the sake of spiritual prayer; for to them it is most harmful and unbearable and to us salutary and favourable.

51. Why do demons wish to excite in us gluttony, fornication, greed, anger, rancour and other passions? So that the mind, under their weight, should be unable to pray as it ought; for when the passions of our irrational part begin to act, they prevent the mind from acting rationally.

53. The state of prayer is a passionless state, in which supreme love transports on high a wisdom-loving, spiritual mind.

54. Not only must a man, who wishes truly to pray, be master of anger and lust, he must be a stranger to all passionate thought.

55. He who loves God is always in converse with Him as with his Father, turning away from all passionate thought.

56. Not every man who has achieved passionlessness has as yet true prayer; for he may still be occupied with simple thoughts (with no stirring of passions) and distracted by their stories and thus be far from God. (There are no passionate movements, but the mind dreams.)

57. Even when the mind does not linger on simple thoughts about things, it does not mean that it has as yet reached the place of prayer; for it can be occupied by speculations concerning these things and ponder over their causal relationships. Although all these are abstractions, since they are speculations about things, they imprint their images on the mind and lead it far from God. (Passions are not in motion, but the mind philosophises, instead of praying—the state of savants.)

58. But supposing the mind is above speculations concerning material nature it does not yet follow that it has discovered the true place of God; for it may be occupied with enquiry about the immaterial creation (the world of angels), and thus diversified (filled with varied thoughts and ideas about them).

59. If you wish to pray as you ought, you have need of God, Who gives prayer to him who prays. So call to Him in prayer, saying, 'Hallowed be Thy name. Thy kingdom come ' (Matt. vi. 9, 10), that is, the Holy Spirit and Thy only-begotten Son. For thus did the Lord Himself teach us, saying, 'God is a Spirit: and they that worship him must worship him in spirit and in truth' (John iv. 24).

60. He who prays in spirit and in truth does not borrow from creatures thoughts to glorify the Creator, but draws from the Creator Himself contemplations for His praise.

61. If you are a theologian, you will pray in truth; and if you pray in truth, you are a theologian.

62. When your mind, inflamed by longing for God, little by little divests itself of flesh, as it were, and turns away from all thoughts engendered by sensory impressions, or from memory, being at the same time full of adoration and rejoicing, then

you may conclude that it has approached the boundaries of prayer.

63. The Holy Spirit, in compassion for our weakness, comes to us even when we are still impure; and if only He finds our mind sincerely praying to Him, descends upon it and disperses all the swarm of thoughts and images which surrounds it, thus disposing it towards desire for spiritual prayer.

64. Other (spirits, both good and evil) by acting on the body introduce into the mind thoughts, representations and fantasies. But the Lord acts inversely: by influencing the mind itself, He instils what knowledge He pleases—and through the mind tames the unrestraint of the body.

65. He is worthy of all blame, who loves true prayer and yet is angry or resentful; for he is like a man who wants to see clearly, yet fills his eyes with dust.

66. If you wish to pray as you ought, do nothing that is opposed to prayer, in order that God may draw near and descend to you.

67. When you pray, do not invest the Deity with any form and do not let your mind be transformed into any image; but approach the immaterial in an immaterial manner—and you will come together with it.

68. Beware of the snares of the enemy; for it may sometimes be that while you are praying purely and serenely, suddenly some strange and alien image comes before you. This is the work of the enemies to lead you into conceit, suggesting the thought that here is the Deity; and further, to make you believe that, like this sudden apparition, the Deity too is quantitative (occupies space, has dimensions, parts), whereas the Deity has neither quantity nor form.

69. When the envious demon has failed to bring memory into motion, he acts on the blood and the juices, in order through them to produce in the mind some alien fantasies and to fill it with images. Thanks to its habit of turning among thoughts, the mind is easily led astray by this and, thinking that it is going towards immaterial formless knowledge, is deceived and takes smoke for light.

70. Stand on guard during prayer, protecting your mind from thoughts and trying to be in a state of peace, in order that He

'Who can have compassion on the ignorant' (Heb. v. 2), should come to you and grant you the most glorious gift of prayer.

71. It is impossible for you to have pure prayer while entangled in material affairs and agitated by constant cares; for prayer means laying thoughts aside.

72. A man who is tied cannot run; nor can a mind which serves some passion see the place of spiritual prayer; moreover, it is constantly caught and drawn hither and thither by passionate thoughts and has no steadiness.

73. When in the end the mind begins to pray purely and without passion, the demons attack it not from the left but from the right: they offer it an appearance as if of God's glory and some image agreeable to the senses, so that it imagines it has already attained the perfect end of prayer. In the words of a certain wise man,[29] this is due to the passion of vainglory, and also to the devil touching a certain place in the brain, and to a disturbance (inflammation) of its tracts.

74. I think that, in touching this spot, the demon transforms, as he wills, the light which is round the mind; hence vainglory overruns thought and urges the mind foolishly to attribute Divine and essential knowledge to itself.[30] Since it is not troubled by impure carnal passions and its prayer is pure, it never imagines this to be an action of the enemy, and becomes convinced that it is truly a Divine apparition, whereas it comes from the demon. Using extreme cunning, the latter, as we have said, changes through the brain the light connected with the mind and offers an image to the mind itself (or makes it imagine this or that).

75. If an angel of God appears, with one word he stops the enemy action in us and causes the light of the mind to work without illusion.

76. The words of the Revelation about the angel bringing a golden censer with 'much incense, that he should offer it with the prayers of all saints' (Rev. viii. 3) refer, in my opinion, to this grace, which acts through an angel and gives the ability to pray in

[29] Evagrius, in 'Γνωστικός. Something similar is also to be found in Cassian. (Footnote in the Dobrotolubiye.)

[30] This place is very obscure. A paraphrase. (Footnote in the Dobrotolubiye.)

truth, so that, in the end, the mind prays without a turmoil of thoughts, without despondency or faintness of heart.

77. As is there said, the vials full of odours are the 'prayers of saints' brought by 'four and twenty elders' (Rev. v. 8). By a vial should be understood friendship with God or perfect spiritual love of Him, in which prayer is made active by spirit and truth.

78. If you suppose that you have no need to weep for your sins during prayer, you must realise how far you are from God, whilst your duty is always to be in Him—and then you will shed warm tears.

79. This is so indeed: having realised your own measure (your poverty and nothingness) you will have your fill of tears, reproaching yourself like Isaiah, that 'being a man, and having unclean lips' and dwelling in the midst of such a people, that is, God's enemies (unclean spirits or thoughts), you dare to stand before the Lord of hosts (Isaiah vi. 5).

80. If you pray truly, you will receive assurances of many things, and angels will come to you as they came to Daniel, and will enlighten you with understanding of causes, the wherefore of all things.

82. Pray in peace and serenity, sing intelligently and in a good state—and you will be like a young eagle soaring high in the sky.

83. Psalmody puts passions to sleep and curbs the impulses of bodily intemperance; and prayer incites the mind to the doing which is its property.

84. Prayer is an activity becoming to the dignity of the mind, or rather, is its real use.

85. Psalmody is the image of diversified wisdom; prayer is the prelude to transubstantial knowledge.

86. Knowledge is an excellent thing; it helps prayer, inciting the power of the mind to the contemplation of Divine knowledge.

87. If you have not yet received the gift of prayer or psalmody, ask persistently, and you will receive.

88. 'And he', the Lord, 'spake a parable unto them to this end, that men ought always to pray, and not to faint' (Luke xviii. 1). So do not grieve nor faint if you have not yet received; for you will receive later. In the parable the Lord says also this: 'Though I fear not God, nor regard man; yet because this widow troubleth

5 *

me, I will avenge her' (Luke xviii. 4, 5). Thus the Lord will also 'avenge his own elect, which cry day and night unto him' (Luke xviii. 7). So be of good cheer and persevere in prayer with diligent patience.

89. Do not wish what concerns you to be as seems (best) to you, but as God wishes; and you will be free from cares and thankful in your prayer.

90. Even if you already appear to be with God, beware the demon of fornication; for it has great fascination and is full of cunning, constantly trying to overcome the transport of your sober mind and to draw it away from God, even when it stands before God with reverence and fear.

91. If you strive after prayer, prepare yourself for diabolical suggestions and bear patiently their onslaughts; for they will attack you like wild beasts and will riddle your body with wounds.

92. Be ready, like an experienced fighter, not to flinch if you should suddenly see some phantom; not to be perturbed if a sword is thrust towards you or a flaming torch into your face; not to be afraid if you see some hideous and artful apparition; but stand firm, professing true faith, and look fearlessly at your enemies.

93. He who endures distress, will be granted joys; and he who bears with unpleasant things, will not be deprived of the pleasant.

94. Beware, lest the sly demons seduce you by some apparition. In such event, remain collected within yourself, turn to prayer and beg God to enlighten you if the apparition comes from him, and if not, that He should quickly drive away the deceitful one. And be bold, for these dogs will not remain if you run to God with warm prayer, but will at once flee far away, invisibly and imperceptibly attacked by God's power.

95. You should also know the following subterfuge of the demons: at times they divide themselves into groups. Some come with a temptation; and when you ask for help others come in the guise of angels and chase away the first, to make you believe that they are true angels, and fall into vainglory, through having been granted such a thing.

96. Try as much as possible to be humble and courageous—and the attack of the demons will not touch your soul nor their

scourge draw nigh to your body, 'for he shall give his angels charge concerning thee, to keep thee in all thy ways' (Ps. xc. 10, 11); and they will invisibly repulse from you every hostile action.

97. If a man, striving to keep his prayer pure, hears the noise, stamping, shouting and cursing of the demons, he will not let his thought drop and will not deliver it to them, but will say to God 'I will not be afraid of evils: for thou art with me' (Ps. xxii. 4), or similar words.

98. During such temptations practise unceasingly a short but intense prayer.

99. If the demons threaten suddenly to appear in the air to stupefy you and ravish your mind, do not fear them and pay no attention at all to their threat. They merely try to frighten you to see whether you attribute some importance to them or hold them in utter contempt.

100. If you stand in prayer before God the Almighty, the Creator and Maintainer, why are you so foolish as to abandon invincible fear of Him and to fear flies and gnats? Do you not hear, then, what the prophet says: 'Thou shalt fear the Lord thy God' (Deut. x. 20).

101. As bread is food for the body and virtue is food for the soul, so spiritual prayer is food for the mind.

102. Pray, not as the pharisee, but as the publican, in the sacred place of prayer, so that you too should be justified of the Lord.

103. Strive not to pray against someone in your prayer, lest you destroy what you are building, by making your prayer an abomination (before God).

104. Let the debtor who owed ten thousand talents teach you that if you do not forgive your debtor you will not be forgiven, for it is said: 'And his lord was wroth, and delivered him to the tormentors' (Matt. xviii. 34).

105. Put aside bodily considerations when you stand in prayer, lest the bite of a flea, a gnat or a fly deprive you of the greatest gain afforded by prayer.

108. You have read, of course, the lives of the Tabennesiot monks in which it is related that when Abba Theodore was preaching before the brethren, two vipers crawled to his feet. In no way perturbed, he arched the soles of his feet and, letting the

vipers crawl under them, continued his sermon to the end; and only then showed the brethren the vipers and told them what had happened.

110. Keep your eye undistracted during prayer and, separating yourself from your body and your soul, live in your mind.

112. While another God-loving monk was practising inner prayer walking in the wilderness, two angels appeared and walked along on either side of him. But he never turned his attention to them for a moment, lest he should lose something better, for he remembered the words of the Apostle, neither 'angels, nor principalities, nor powers . . . shall be able to separate us from the love of God, which is in Christ Jesus our Lord' (Rom. viii. 38, 39).

113. Prayer makes a monk the equal of the angels, for his desire is to 'behold the face of my Father which is in heaven' (Matt. xviii. 10).

114. Never desire nor seek to see any face or image during prayer.

115. Do not wish for a sensory vision of angels, or powers, or Christ, lest you lose your mind by mistaking the wolf for the shepherd and worship the enemies—the demons.

116. The beginning of the beguilement of the mind is vainglory, which moves the mind to try and represent the Deity in some form or image.

117. I shall repeat what I said to beginners: blessed is the mind which keeps perfect silence in prayer.

118. Blessed is the mind which, praying without distraction, acquires ever greater longing for God.

119. Blessed is the mind which, during prayer, is drawn neither to the material nor to possessions.

120. Blessed is the mind which, during prayer, is insensible to all things.

121. Blessed is the monk who regards every man as a god after God.

122. Blessed is the monk who looks on the salvation and progress of all as though they were his own.

123. Blessed is the monk who considers himself as the dregs of all men.

124. A monk is he who, withdrawing from all men, is united with all men.

125. A monk is he who regards himself as existing with all men and sees himself in each man.

126. That man prays who always offers all his first thoughts to God.

127. Avoid all lies and swearing, if you are a monk with a strong desire to pray; otherwise you vainly put on an appearance that is not your own.

128. If you wish to pray in spirit, borrow nothing from the flesh—and you will be free from that cloud which spreads darkness before you during prayer.

129. Entrust your physical needs to God—and it will be clear that you entrust to Him your spiritual needs also.

130. If you are found worthy to be granted God's promises, you will share the Kingdom. Keeping this in mind, should you not endure with joy the present poverty?

131. Do not shun poverty and afflictions—these wings of buoyant prayer.

132. Let virtues of the body be for you a pledge of those of the soul; those of the soul—a pledge of those of the spirit; and those of the spirit—a pledge of transubstantial and essential knowledge.

133. If, praying against some thought, you notice that it is stilled quickly and easily, examine it to see why this came to pass, lest you are caught in a trap and, deluding yourself, become a traitor to yourself.

134. It happens sometimes that the demons suggest some thoughts to you and then urge you to pray against them, to oppose them—and then quickly withdraw to make you fall into delusion, imagining that you have already begun to conquer thoughts and to intimidate the demons.

135. If you pray against some passion or some demon attacking you, remember the words of the psalm, 'I will pursue mine enemies, and overtake them; and I will not turn back until they are consumed. I will dash them to pieces and they shall not be able to stand: they shall fall under my feet' (Ps. xvii. 37, 38). But say it becomingly, arming yourself with humility against your foes.

136. Do not expect to acquire virtue before you have shed

blood in your struggle for it. According to the Apostle we must resist 'unto blood, striving against sin' to be preserved pure (Heb. xii. 4).

137. It happens sometimes that in doing good to one man you suffer harm from another, so that, meeting with injustice, you may say or do something unseemly and thus lose what you have gained. This is precisely the aim of the evil demons. So pay intelligent heed to yourself.

139. At night the evil demons try themselves to confuse a spiritual teacher; but in daytime they do it through people, surrounding him with unpleasant events, slanders and troubles coming from them.

140. Do not refuse to endure these fullers. Let them beat, stamp, stretch and smooth out; through this your garment will be all the brighter.

141. While you are not wholly free from passions and your mind still shows resistance to virtue and truth, you will not find the sweet-smelling incense in your depth (that is, pure and warm prayer).

142. Do you wish to pray? Leave this world and dwell always in heaven, not merely in words, but by angelic doing and Divine understanding.

143. If it is only in adversities that you remember the Judge, how terrible and incorruptible He is, you have not yet learnt to 'serve the Lord with fear, and rejoice in him with trembling' (Ps. i. 11). Know that in the midst of spiritual joys and consolations it is still more necessary to serve Him with fear and devotion.

145. He who remains in sin and continues to anger God, and who shamelessly strives to understand Divine things and to acquire transubstantial prayer, should remember the warning of the Apostle that it is not without danger for him to pray with head uncovered. In the words of the Apostle, such a soul ought 'to have power on her head because of the angels' (1 Cor. xi. 10), having clothed itself in modesty and suitable humility for the sake of those present.

146. Just as long and persistent staring at the sun in its noonday brilliance will bring no good to weak eyes, so imagination about the awesome and transubstantial prayer in spirit and in truth

will bring no good to a passionate and impure mind. On the contrary, the Godhead will rise against it in wrath.

147. If He Who needs nothing and is impartial does not accept the gift of a man who comes to the altar, until he is reconciled with his brother who has something against him (Matt. v. 23), see how one must guard oneself and be circumspect, if one is to bring to the altar of the mind an incense acceptable to God.

149. Attention which seeks prayer will find it. No better thing follows upon attention than prayer, to which we should give all our vigilance.

150. As sight is the best of all senses, so prayer is the most divine of all virtues.

151. Prayer is to be praised not merely for quantity but also for quality. This is shown by the 'two men (who) went up into the temple to pray' (Luke xviii. 10), and also by the words, 'But when ye pray, use not vain repetitions' and so on (Matt. vi. 7).

152. So long as you pay attention only to bodily posture proper for prayer and your mind cares only for the external beauty of the tabernacle, know that you have not yet seen the place of prayer, and its blessed way is still far from you.

153. When, standing at prayer, you are above all other joy, know that you have truly attained prayer.

ST. NILUS OF SINAI

Here are added some texts on prayer from other writings of St. Nilus

154. Prayer and reading are excellent; they stop the aimless wandering of thoughts, shackle the thought which turns on useless things and keep it close by them with profit, occupied without distraction by this excellent doing.

155. Prayer attunes us for converse with God and, through long practice, leads us to friendship with Him; with Him Whose love accepts even worthless men and is not ashamed to enter into friendship with them, so long as the love that lives in them gives them daring.

156. Prayer frees the mind of all thought of the sensory and raises it to God Himself, Who is above all, to converse with Him and daringly ask Him for anything. Thus a man spends his life in purity, as one who, having already experienced communion with God, is thereupon again preparing for this communion.

157. St. Paul teaches us to continue 'instant in prayer' (Rom. xii. 12), grounding ourselves in it by long perseverance (Col. iv. 2, Eph. vi. 18). He also commands us to 'pray everywhere' (1 Tim. ii. 8) so that no idle one can excuse himself because he lives far from the house of prayer. Any place is suitable for prayer. God accepts those who call to Him with a pure heart and righteous deeds, and seeing their disposition, listens to their supplication, even if the place whence they call to Him has nothing special to distinguish it.

158. At times during vigil one should read the psalms quickly, while at other times it is best to intone them. We should vary the method to oppose the wiles of the enemies, who at times incite us to hurry our tongue in quick reading, because the soul is sunk in depression, and at times incite us to stately intoning.

160. Be fond of working with your hands, but still more of the memory of prayer; because the first does not always bring us the fruit of that occupation, while the second does so unceasingly. Do not stop praying until you have paid your due of prayer in full, and do not listen to the thought that it is time to sit down to work. Equally, when you sit at work, do not be too concerned in it, lest you agitate the heart by your haste and make it worthless for prayer.

161. A mind from which the thought of God has been carried away and which has thus become far removed from remembering Him, is also indifferent to sin with the outer senses. For such a mind can guide neither the hearing nor the tongue, since zest to work on itself has gone out of it.

162. Sometimes we try hard to practise pure prayer, and cannot; but it happens also that we do not compel ourselves, yet the soul prays with purity. The first results from our infirmity, the second, from grace from above, which thus calls us to seek purity of soul and teaches us, in each case, not to ascribe it to ourselves if our prayer is pure, but to recognise in this a gift of the Giver. 'We know not what we should pray for as we ought' (Rom. viii. 26). When we try to make our prayer pure and cannot, but are enveloped in darkness, let us moisten our cheeks with tears and implore God to disperse the night of the battle and to let light shine in the soul.

163. Memory of carnal lusts is revolting; for not only does it prevent us from converse with God, but even when the mind seems to be praying, it defiles it with the fantasies of abominable representations. It is good to remain in constant prayer and to exercise the mind in converse with God. But is it so with us? We are frequently diverted from the words of the prayer, we follow thoughts that lead us away, neither denying them nor being saddened by them—which would have shown that our will disagreed with unseemly suggestions. Although our outward aspect is appropriate to prayer, for we kneel and appear to those who see us to be praying, in our thought we imagine something pleasant, graciously talk with friends, angrily abuse enemies, feast with guests, build houses for our relatives, plant trees, travel, trade, are forced against our will into priesthood, organise with great

circumspection the affairs of the churches placed in our care, and go over most of it in our thoughts, consenting to any thought that comes along, in whatever way passion chooses to dispose our heart.

164. Prayer demands that the mind should be pure of all thought and should admit nothing not belonging to prayer, even if it were good in itself. As if inspired by God the mind should withdraw from all things and hold its converse with Him alone.

165. He who divides his time between physical work and prayer subdues his body by labour and moderates its disorderly demands; and since his soul, working together with the body, at last longs for a rest, it disposes it to prayer, as to something easier, and brings it to the work of prayer with fresh strength and zeal. For the soul finds comfort in a change of occupation and in passing from one thing to another, whereas it gets bored when occupied for long with the same thing. It becomes weary of monotony, but welcomes variety of occupations. It seems to it that, by abandoning one occupation, it is freed of all hardship, and so it comes to another with fresh strength, as though it were only now starting work.

166. He who does not like working, feeds passions by idleness and gives his desires freedom to fly to kindred objects. This is specially evident in prayer, for then the attention of the mind is wholly absorbed in what occupies the heart, and thought merely turns over and over the suggestions offered by the stirrings of some passion, instead of conversing with God and asking Him for what profits it. Knowing this, St. Paul vigorously attacks idleness and by his Apostolic authority commands all to work (2 Thess. iii. 6–12). Work is an anchor for thought and gives it a safe direction. Let storms and gusts of wind come from all sides, threatening shipwreck—thought stands firm, kept steadfast by work as by an anchor; even if somewhat agitated by rising suggestions, it is not led into danger, for the bonds that hold it fast are stronger than the driving winds.

167. Those who refuse to work with their hands under the pretext that one should pray without ceasing, in reality do not pray either. By the very fact that they think, through idleness, to give the soul freedom from cares, they entangle it in a labyrinth

of thoughts with no way out and so make it incapable of prayer. A body labouring at some piece of work keeps the thought close by, since the task of thought, like that of the eyes, is to watch over what is being done and to help the body act faultlessly; but a body at rest gives thought freedom to wander, for during rest passions are apt to be set in motion and every lustful memory entices the thought away and captures it like a slave.

168. There is a higher prayer—that of the perfect—which is a certain ravishing of the mind, its complete separation from all sensory things, when with unutterable sighings of the spirit it approaches God, Who sees the heart open like a written book, wherein its will is expressed in wordless images. Thus Paul was ravished to the third heaven, not knowing 'whether in the body' or 'whether out of the body' (2 Cor. xii. 2).

169. Below the first, there is a second kind of prayer, when words are uttered, while the heart is touched, and the mind follows them, and knows to Whom the supplication is addressed.

170. But prayer interrupted by thoughts (the lowest form), and linked with bodily cares, is far from the structure of mind fitting for prayer. In such prayer man does not hear himself, but darts hither and thither in thought, not remembering what words he utters. But if the man who prays is such, will God's ear pay heed to what, in his inattention, he does not himself hear? With those who said, 'Attend to my petition; give ear to my prayer' (Ps. xvi. 1) and 'O Lord, hearken to my voice; let thine ears be attentive to the voice of my supplication' (Ps. cxxix. 2), the mind was wholly and carefully collected and not scattered and spread about over such things as is usual with the negligent, whose thoughts are uncontrolled.

ST. ABBA DOROTHEUS

ST. ABBA DOROTHEUS
Short Biographical Note

Abba Dorotheus lived at the end of the sixth and the beginning of the seventh centuries. He spent his early youth in a diligent study of secular sciences. At the end of his education he lived for a time at his birthplace, not far from the monastery of Abba Serid, perhaps in Ascalon or in Gaza. He was quite well off. Very soon he entered into communication with the great startzi Barsanuphius and John, whose teachings decided him to renounce everything and to take monastic vows in the monastery of Abba Serid, where they had their retreat. Under their direction he completed his monastic education, mainly guided by staretz John. At the same time he performed obediences imposed upon him by the Abbot, who at first placed in his care the hospice and later the infirmary. During this latter obedience he had under his guidance St. Dositheus. After the deaths of Abba Serid and staretz John, when the teacher of them all, the great Barsanuphius, shut himself up completely in his cell, the blessed Dorotheus left the monastery of Abba Serid and became abbot of another monastery. It is probably to that period that belong the homilies he delivered to his disciples. These homilies, twenty-one in all, and a few epistles are all that is left to us from the writings of this father, the light of whose teaching was spread not only among monasteries but among all Christians. The date of his death is not known.

ST. ABBA DOROTHEUS
Directions on Spiritual Training

1. In His loving-kindness God has given us purifying commandments so that, if we wish, we can by their observance be cleansed not only of sins but also of passions themselves. For passions are one thing and sins another. Passions are: anger, vanity, love of pleasures, hatred, evil lust and the like. Sins are the actual operations of passions, when a man puts them into practice, that is, performs with the body the actions to which his passions urge him. For it is possible to have passions and yet not to act from them.

2. The (old) law had as its purpose to teach us not to do what we did not want done to us; consequently it forbade only the actual doing of evil. Now however (in the New Testament) we are required to banish the passion itself, which urges us to do evil —hatred itself, love of pleasures, love of fame and other passions.

3. Listen to what the Lord says: 'Learn of me; for I am meek and lowly in heart: and ye shall find rest unto your souls' (Matt. xi. 29). He shows here the root and cause of all ills and their cure, the cause of all good, namely, that self-exaltation has brought us down and that pardon cannot be obtained except through its opposite, humility. What has brought all our afflictions upon us? Was it not pride? Man was created for every kind of enjoyment and was in the Garden of Eden. But one thing he was forbidden to do, yet he did it. You see the pride? You see the disobedience (the daughter of pride)? Thereupon God said: man does not know how to delight in joy alone. If he does not experience afflictions he will go still further and will perish completely. If he does not learn what are sorrow and labour he will not know what are joy and peace; and so God banished him from the Garden of Eden. Here he was surrendered to his own self-love and his own

will, that they might break his bones and thereby teach him to follow not himself but God's commandments, and that the very sufferings of disobedience should teach him the blessings of obedience, as the Prophet says: 'Thine apostasy shall correct thee' (Jer. ii. 19). So now God's mercy calls: 'Come unto me, all ye that labour and are heavy laden, and I will give you rest' (Matt. xi. 28). He says, as it were: you have laboured and suffered enough and have experienced the evil results of disobedience, come now and be converted: restore yourselves to life by humility, in place of the arrogance by which you put yourselves to death. 'Learn of me; for I am meek and lowly of heart: and ye shall find rest unto your souls' (Matt. xi. 29).

5. Some God-loving men, having cut off the actions of passions after their holy baptism, desired to vanquish passions themselves and become passionless. Such were St. Antony, St. Pachomius and other holy fathers. They conceived the good intention to cleanse themselves 'from all filthiness of the flesh and spirit' (2 Cor. vii. 1). But realising that this is hard to achieve while living in the world, they devised for themselves a special form of life, a special form of activity, that is, a solitary life withdrawn from the world; and they began to flee the world and to live in the wilderness, practised fasting and vigil, slept on bare earth, and endured various other privations, having completely renounced their kith and kin, their goods and possessions.

6. Thus they not only kept the commandments, but also brought gifts to God. Commandments are given to all Christians and it is the duty of every Christian to obey them. It is the same as the tribute that in the world is due to the king. But as in the world there are great and distinguished people, who not only pay tribute to the king but also bring gifts to him for which they are granted special honours, rewards and rank, so too the fathers not only paid tribute to God by obeying the commandments, but also brought Him gifts, such as virginity and poverty, which are not commandments but acts of their own will. For it is said of the first: 'He that is able to receive it, let him receive it' (Matt. xix. 12), and of the second: 'If thou wilt be perfect, go and sell that thou hast, and give to the poor' (Matt. xix. 21).

7. They crucified the world unto themselves, and thereupon

strove to crucify themselves unto the world, imitating the Apostle who says, 'The world is crucified unto me, and I unto the world' (Gal. vi. 14). For when a man renounces the world and becomes a monk, leaves his parents, possessions and all worldly affairs and cares, he crucifies the world unto himself. But when, being made free from external things, he fights also against the very enjoyment or the very desire of things, when he struggles against his own wishes, and mortifies the passions themselves, he crucifies himself unto the world and can boldly say with the Apostle, 'The world is crucified unto me, and I unto the world.'

8. Our fathers, having crucified the world unto themselves, have also crucified themselves unto the world by their efforts. But though, by renouncing the world and retiring into a monastery, we have seemingly crucified the world unto ourselves, we do not want to crucify ourselves unto the world, since we still love its pleasures, are still attached to it, are moved by its glory, have kept in ourselves a fondness for foods, clothes and other vanities. Yet we should not do so, since just as we have renounced the world and its things, so too should we renounce our very attachment to those things.

9. We have left the world, so let us leave also our attachment to it. For attachments tie us again to the world and unite us with it, even if they concern insignificant, ordinary and worthless things. If we wish to be completely transformed and freed from attachments, let us learn to cut off our own desires, even in the least important things. For nothing brings more profit to men than renouncing their own will, since in truth a man gains a greater benefit from this than from any other virtue. Indeed, the cutting off of one's own will and desires can be practised at every moment. Suppose a man is walking; his thought says to him, 'Look at this and at that,' but he cuts off his desire and does not follow it. He meets some people talking; his thought says to him: 'Have a few words with them,' but he cuts off his desire and says nothing. He comes to the kitchen; his thought says: 'Let us go and see what the cook is preparing,' but he cuts off his desire and does not go, and so on and so on. By cutting off his desires in this way he acquires a habit of cutting them off and, beginning with small things, ends by easily and calmly cutting them off in

big things as well. Thus, finally he begins to have no will of his
own at all and remains unperturbed, whatever may happen. Thus
by cutting off their own will men acquire non-attachment and
from non-attachment, with God's help, they rise to complete
passionlessness.

10. A certain staretz said: 'Above all we need humility.'
Why did he say this? Why did he not say that above all we need
self-mastery, since the Apostle says, 'Every man that striveth for
the mastery is temperate in all things' (1 Cor. ix. 25). Or why
did he not say that above all we need the fear of God, since the
Scriptures say, 'The fear of the Lord is the beginning of wisdom'
(Prov. i. 7). Or why did he not say that above all we need mercy
or faith, since it is said, 'By mercy and truth iniquity is purged'
(A.V. Prov. xvi. 6) and, 'Without faith it is impossible to please'
God (Heb. xi. 6). Why then, laying aside all these which are so
needful, does the staretz stress only humility? He shows us by this
that neither fear of God, nor mercy, nor faith nor self-mastery,
nor any other virtue can be achieved without humility. Moreover,
humility destroys all the arrows of the enemy. All the saints
followed the way of humility and laboured at it. 'Look upon
mine affliction and my trouble; and forgive all my sins' (Ps. xxiv.
18), and again 'I was brought low, and he delivered me' (Ps.
cxiv. 6).

11. The same staretz said, 'Humility is neither angered nor
angers anyone. Humility attracts God's grace to the soul; and
God's grace, when it comes, delivers the soul from these two
grievous passions. For what can be more grievous than to be
angry with one's neighbour or to anger him? But what am I saying, that humility delivers from only two passions? It delivers the
soul from every passion and every temptation.'

12. When St. Antony saw all the nets of the devil spread out,
he sighed and asked God, 'Who can escape them?' God answered
him, 'Humility escapes them' and, what is still more wonderful,
added, 'They will not even touch it.' Do you see the power of this
virtue? Indeed there is nothing stronger than humility, for nothing
can conquer it. If some affliction befalls a humble man, he immediately blames himself for deserving it and will not reproach
or blame another. Thus he endures everything that may befall

untroubled, without grief, with perfect calm; and so he is angered by no one and angers none.

13. There are two kinds of humility, as there are two kinds of pride. *The first kind of pride* is when a man reproaches his brother, condemns and reviles him as someone of no account, regarding himself as his superior. If such a man does not speedily come to his senses and try to mend his ways, he comes, little by little, to the *second kind of pride*, which puffs itself up in the face of God Himself and ascribes to itself its achievements and virtues, as though the man has done it all himself, with his own intelligence and knowledge, and not with the help of God. From this can be seen what constitutes the two kinds of humility. *The first* humility consists in considering that one's brother has better judgment and is in all things superior to oneself—or in considering oneself below all men. *The second* humility consists in ascribing one's achievements to God. This is the perfect humility of the saints.

15. No one can describe in words what humility is and how it is born in the soul, unless he learns this from experience. From words alone no one can know it. One day Abba Zossima was speaking of humility, when a sophist who was present asked him: 'Do you not know that you have virtues? After all, you see that you are obeying the commandments: how then in that case do you regard yourself as a sinner?' The staretz could not find how to answer him but said simply, 'I do not know what to say to you, but I consider myself a sinner.' And when the sophist went on bothering him with the question 'How?', the staretz continued to repeat the same thing: 'I know not how, but I truly regard myself such. Do not confuse me.' Or again, when Abba Agathon was nearing death the brethren asked him, 'Are you not afraid, father?' He answered, 'As far as I could I have made myself keep the commandments, but I am a man, and how can I know whether what I have done is pleasing to God. For God's judgment is one thing and man's another.'

16. A staretz once said about what brings a man to humility, 'The ways to humility are bodily labours done intelligently, considering oneself below all others, and ceaseless prayer to God.' Bodily labours bring the soul to humility, because the soul suffers with the body and shares in all that happens to it; as bodily

labours humble the body, the soul is humbled with it. Considering oneself lower than all is a distinctive feature of humility, and if a man practises it and becomes accustomed to it, this by itself implants humility and uproots what we have called the first pride. For how can a man puff himself up before anyone, or blame or belittle anyone if he regards himself as lower than all? In the same way the practice of unceasing prayer obviously goes against the second kind of pride. For it is clear that a man inclines himself towards humility if, knowing that he can achieve no virtue without God's help, he never ceases to pray, asking God to show him mercy. Thus a man who prays without ceasing, if he achieves something, knows why he achieved it, and can take no pride in it; for he cannot attribute it to his own powers, but attributes all his achievements to God, always renders thanks to Him and constantly calls upon Him, trembling lest he be deprived of help. Thus he prays with humility and is made humble by prayer. The more he progresses in virtue the greater becomes his humility, and as his humility grows he receives help and again progresses in humility.

17. In creating man God implanted in him something Divine—a certain thought, like a spark, having both light and warmth, a thought which illumines the mind and shows what is good and and what bad. This is called conscience and it is a natural law. By following this law—conscience—the patriarchs and all the saints pleased God, even before the law was written. But when, through the fall, men covered up and trampled down conscience, there arose the need of written law, of the holy Prophets, of the coming of our Lord Jesus Christ Himself, to uncover and raise it up, to rekindle this buried spark by the keeping of His holy commandments.

18. So now it is in our power either to bury it again or to let it shine in us and illumine us, if we obey. When our conscience tells us to do something and we disregard it, and when it tells us again but we continue to trample on it and not act on it, we bury it. Then it can no longer speak to us clearly for the weight which presses upon it, but like a lamp shining behind a curtain it begins to show us things more and more dimly. Just as no one can recognise their face in water muddied with slime, so we, after

transgression, fail to apprehend the voice of conscience, so that it seems to us not to exist in us at all.

19. Conscience is called the adversary, because it always opposes our evil will; it reminds us of what we ought to do but do not, and condemns us if we do something we ought not. That was why the Lord called it adversary and commanded us: 'Agree with thine adversary quickly, whiles thou art in the way with him' (Matt. v. 25), that is, while you are in this world, as Basil the Great says.

20. So let us guard our conscience, while we are in this world; let us not allow it to accuse us in something, nor disregard it in anything however small. For you must realise that from disregarding this small and insignificant thing we pass to neglect of big things. If someone begins to say 'What does it matter if I eat this scrap? What of it if I look at this or that?', then from this 'What matters this, what matters that?' he will fall into a bad habit and will begin to neglect big and important things and trample down his conscience. Thus becoming hardened in evil, he will be in danger of falling into complete insensitivity.

21. Conscience should be guarded towards God, towards one's neighbour and towards things. In relation to God, he guards his conscience who does not neglect God's commandments and who, even in things not seen by men and that no one demands of us, guards his conscience towards God in secret. Guarding conscience towards our neighbour demands that we should never do anything which, to our knowledge, would offend or tempt him, whether by word or deed, look or expression. Guarding conscience towards things means not to misuse a thing, nor let it be spoiled nor throw it away needlessly. In all these respects conscience should be kept pure and unblemished, lest one should fall into the calamity against which the Lord warns us (Matt. v. 26).

22. St. John says, 'Perfect love casteth out fear' (1 John iv. 18). How is it then that the holy Prophet David says, 'Fear the Lord, all ye his saints' (Ps. xxxiii. 9)? This shows that there are two kinds of fear: the first, initial, the second perfect; one belongs to beginners, the other to perfect saints, who have attained to the measure of perfect love. He who obeys God's will through fear of torment is still a beginner; and he who fulfils the will of

God through love for God in order to please Him, is brought by this love into perfect fear; and through this fear, when once he has tasted the delight of being with God, he is afraid to fall away, is afraid to be deprived of it. It is this perfect fear, born of love, which casts out the initial fear.

23. No one can attain to perfect fear unless he first acquires the initial fear. The wise Sirach says, 'To fear the Lord is the beginning of wisdom . . . The fear of the Lord is a crown of wisdom' (Ecclesiasticus i. 14, 18). By the beginning is meant the initial fear, on which follows the perfect fear of the saints. The initial fear belongs to the state of our soul. It protects the soul from every fall, for it is said, 'By the fear of the Lord everyone departs from evil' (Prov. xv. 27). But a man who departs from evil from fear of punishment, like a slave in fear of his master, gradually comes to doing good voluntarily—at first like a hireling in the hope of some reward for his good action. If he continues thus constantly to avoid evil from fear, like a slave, and to do good in the hope of reward like a hireling, then, abiding by God's grace in the good and thus correspondingly uniting with God, he finally acquires a taste for the good, comes to a certain sense of what is truly good, and no longer wishes to be parted from it. Then he attains to the dignity of son and loves good for its own sake; and although he fears, he does so because he loves. This is great and perfect fear.

24. This sequence is expressed by the Prophet David in the following words: 'Turn away from evil, and do good; seek peace, and pursue it' (Ps. xxxiii. 14). 'Turn away from evil,' that is, avoid all evil in general, turn away from every action which leads to sin. But having said this he did not stop there, but added 'and do good.' For sometimes a man does no evil, but neither does he any good: for example, he harms no one but also does not show mercy; or he does not hate but neither does he love. Having said this David continued, 'seek peace, and pursue it.' He did not merely say 'seek', but pursue it with diligence to acquire it. Follow carefully these words in your mind and note the subtlety shown by the Saint. When it is granted to a man to turn away from evil and thereupon, with God's help, diligently to do good, he becomes at once a prey to attacks from the enemy. And so he

labours, strives, sorrows, now fearing to return to evil like a slave, now hoping for a reward for good like a hireling. In suffering attacks from the enemy, struggling with him and resisting him from these motives, though the man does what is good, he does it with great effort and grief. But when he receives God's help and acquires a certain habit of good, then he finds rest, then he tastes peace, then he experiences what grievous warfare means and what mean the joy and gladness of peace. Then he begins to seek peace, to strive after it assiduously in order to attain it, to possess it wholly and to establish it in himself. He who has reached this stage tastes at last the blessedness of the peacemakers (Matt. v. 9). And henceforth who can impel his soul to do good for the sake of anything but the enjoyment of that good itself? Then such a man knows also perfect fear.

25. The fathers said that man acquires the fear of God if he keeps death and torments in his memory, if each evening he questions himself as to how he spent the day, and each morning how he passed the night, if he is not presumptuous and, finally, if he remains in close communion with a man who fears God. For they relate that once a certain brother asked a staretz, 'What should I do, father, in order to fear God?' The staretz answered, 'Go, live with a man who fears God; and by the very fact that he fears God, he will teach you too to fear Him.' We repel the fear of God from ourselves by doing everything contrary to what has been said—we have neither memory of death nor memory of torments, we have no attention on ourselves and do not question ourselves about how we spend our time, but live heedlessly and commune with men who have no fear of God, and we are presumptuous. This last is the worst of all—it is utter ruin—for nothing drives the fear of God away from the soul more than presumptuousness. Abba Agathon, when asked about it, once said, 'Presumptuousness is like a strong scorching wind, from which all flee when it begins to blow, and which kills all the fruit on trees.' May God save us from this all-destructive passion—presumptuousness.

26. Presumptuousness may have many forms; one may be presumptuous by word, gesture, or look. It may lead a man to chatter, to worldly talk, to doing something ridiculous, provoking

others to unseemly mirth. It is presumptuous, too, if a man touches another without need, points at someone who is laughing, pushes him, snatches something out of his hands, shamelessly stares at him; all this is the work of presumptuousness, all this comes of having no fear of God in the soul and so little by little a man becomes utterly careless. Therefore God, when He gave the commandments of the law, said, 'Ye shall cause the children of Israel to beware of their uncleannesses' (Lev. xv. 31), for without reverence and modesty man cannot honour even God Himself, nor can he keep a single commandment. Hence nothing is more harmful than presumptuousness; it is the mother of all passions, since it banishes reverence, drives the fear of God away from the soul, and gives birth to carelessness.

28. Over whatever you have to do, even if it be very urgent and demands great care, I would not have you argue or be agitated. For rest assured, everything you do, be it great or small, is but one eighth of the problem, whereas to keep one's state undisturbed even if thereby one should fail to accomplish the task, is the other seven eighths. So if you are busy at some task and wish to do it perfectly, try to accomplish it—which, as I said, would be one eighth of the problem, and at the same time to preserve your state unharmed—which constitutes seven eighths. If, however, in order to accomplish your task you would inevitably be carried away and harm yourself or another by arguing with him, you should not lose seven for the sake of preserving one eighth.

29. The wise Solomon says in the Proverbs, 'They that have no guidance fall like leaves: but in much counsel there is safety' (Prov. xi. 14). So you see what the Holy Scriptures teach us? They enjoin us not to rely on ourselves, not to regard ourselves as knowing all, not to believe that we can control ourselves, for we need help, are in need of those who would counsel us according to God. No men are more unfortunate or nearer perdition than those who have no teachers on the way of God. For what does it mean that where no guidance is, the people fall like leaves? A leaf is at first green, flourishing, beautiful; then it gradually withers, falls and is finally trampled underfoot. So is it with a man who has no guide; at first he is always zealous in fasting, vigil, silence, obedience and other virtues; then his zeal little by little cools

down and, having no one to instruct, support and fire him with zeal, he insensibly withers, falls and finally becomes a slave of the enemies, who do with him what they will.

30. Of those who reveal their thoughts and actions and who do everything with counsel the Wise One says, 'in much counsel there is safety' (Prov. xi. 14). He does not say 'in the counsels of many' that is, in seeking counsel from everyone, but in seeking counsel in all things—naturally from one we trust; and not in such a way as to tell one thing and conceal another, but to reveal everything and seek counsel in all things. For such a man, safety is assured 'in much counsel'.

31. When we do not reveal our thoughts and intentions and do not seek the counsel of the experienced, we hold on to our own will and follow our own justifications. Then, apparently doing something good, we spread nets for ourselves, and so without realising it we perish. For how can we understand the will of God or completely surrender ourselves to it, when we trust ourselves and cling to our own will? Therefore Abba Pimen said that 'our will is a brass wall between man and God.'

32. The devil trips up as he likes the man who trusts his own mind and keeps to his own will. But he has no access to a man who does everything with counsel. That is why he hates questions and the guidance in response, hates the very voice, the very sound of such words. Is it not clear why? Because he knows that his evil wiles will at once be exposed when people begin to ask questions and talk of useful things. And there is nothing he fears more than being exposed, for then he can no longer be wily as he wills. When a man asks and hears the advice of someone experienced, 'do this, but do not do that' or, 'now is not the time for that' or sometimes 'now is the time', the devil cannot find how to harm or bring him down, since he always seeks counsel and protects himself on all sides. So the saying 'in much counsel there is safety' is fulfilled for him.

33. The enemy likes those who rely on their own understanding, for they help him and set traps for themselves. I know of no other way for a monk to fall than when he trusts his own heart. Some say a man falls because of this or that, but I know of no

other fall except when a man follows his own lead. If you see a man fallen, know that he followed his own lead. Nothing is more dangerous, nothing more pernicious than this.

34. I am always repeating to you that from insignificant self-indulgences we come to important sins. What is more grievous than the sin of condemning one's neighbour? What else is so hateful and alienating to God? And yet man comes to this great evil through something seemingly unimportant—from allowing himself a small censure of his neighbour. For when this is allowed the mind begins to leave its own sins without attention and notice the sins of its neighbour. And this leads to gossip, reproaches, speaking evil and, finally, pernicious condemnation. Yet nothing angers God more, nothing so despoils a man (of grace) and leads so surely to perdition as fault-finding, speaking evil and condemning one's neighbour.

35. It is one thing to speak evil, and another to condemn or disparage. To speak evil means to say of a man: he lied, or committed adultery, or was angry or did some other wrong. So saying, a man speaks evil of his brother, that is, speaks passionately of his transgression. But to condemn means saying: so and so is a liar, an adulterer, a bad-tempered man. Such a man condemns the very disposition of another's soul, passes judgment on his whole life, in saying that he is such and such, and condemning him as such. And this is a grievous sin.

36. The pharisee, when praying and thanking God for his virtues, did not lie but spoke the truth and was not condemned for this; for we must thank God when it is given us to do something good, since He has helped and assisted us in this. It was not for this he was condemned, nor for saying 'I thank thee, that I am not as other men.' But when he turned to the publican and said, 'or even as this publican' he incurred condemnation. For he condemned the person as such, the very disposition of his soul, his entire life. This is why the publican was 'justified rather than the other' (Luke xviii. 11, 14).

37. God alone has the right to justify or condemn, for He knows the disposition of soul of every man, his strength, his tendencies and gifts, his physical constitution and his capacities; so, in accordance with all this He justifies or condemns each man

justly. For who can know all this rightly except Him, Who has created all and Who knows all.

38. At times we not only condemn but bring our neighbour into contempt. For it is one thing to condemn, and another to bring into contempt. To bring into contempt means when a man not only condemns but also despises another, scorns him and turns away from him as from an abomination. This is worse than condemnation and much more pernicious.

39. Those who want to be saved pay no attention to the failings of their neighbours, but always look for their own and so make progress. Such was the man who, seeing that his brother had sinned, sighed and said, 'Woe unto me! As he has sinned today, so shall I sin tomorrow.' Do you see the wise disposition of his soul, and how he at once found the means of avoiding condemnation of his brother? For in saying 'so shall I sin tomorrow' he prompted himself to fear that he too might soon commit a sin and to pay heed to this—and so he escaped condemning his neighbour. Moreover, not content with this, he prostrated himself at his feet saying, 'This one will repent his sin, while I shall not repent as I ought. I shall not attain to repentance, shall not have the strength to repent.' Do you see the enlightenment of a divine soul?

40. It happens sometimes that the poison of condemnation, overflowing from our soul, seeks to pour into others. And so, meeting another brother who is at peace with all, we hasten to relate to him that this and that has happened, and thus harm him by introducing into his heart the sin of condemnation. We are not afraid of him who said, 'Woe to him that gives his neighbour to drink the thick lees of wine, and intoxicates him' (Hab. ii. 15), but we do the work of the devil and pay no heed. For who is it, if not the devil, whose work is to bring confusion and harm? And so we prove ourselves to be the devil's helpers, to our own and our neighbour's ruin. Why so? Because there is no love in us. 'For charity shall cover the multitude of sins' (1 Pet. iv. 8).

42. Imagine a circle with its centre and radii or rays going out from this centre. The further these radii are from the centre the more widely are they dispersed and separated from one another; and conversely, the closer they come to the centre, the closer

they are to one another. Suppose now that this circle is the world, the very centre of the circle, God, and the lines (radii) going from the centre to the circumference or from the circumference to the centre are the paths of men's lives. Then here we see the same. In so far as the saints move inwards within the circle towards its centre, wishing to come near to God, then, in the degree of their penetration, they come closer both to God and to one another; moreover, inasmuch as they come nearer to God, they come nearer to one another, and inasmuch as they come nearer to one another, they come nearer to God. It is the same with drawing away. When they draw away from God and turn towards external things, it is clear that in the degree that they recede from the central point and draw away from God, they withdraw from one another, and as they withdraw from one another, so they draw away from God. Such is also the property of love; inasmuch as we are outside and do not love God, so each is far from his neighbour. But if we love God, inasmuch as we come near to Him by love of Him, so we become united by love with our neighbours, and inasmuch as we are united with our neighbours, so we become united with God.

43. Why does it happen that at times a man, hearing insulting words, pays no attention to them, but bears them untroubled as though he had not heard them, while at other times he is troubled at once if he hears them? What is the reason for this? People are not troubled for the following reasons. *Firstly*, after prayer or some good exercise a man may be in a right inner state and so is indulgent with his brother and not troubled by his words; it may happen, *also*, that a man feels much affection for someone, and so bears all that comes from him without distress. And *again* it may happen that a man despises him, who wants to insult him, and so disregards his slights. People are troubled from the opposite reasons: because they are not in a good inner state, or because they dislike the man who has insulted them, or for other reasons. But the chief cause of being troubled is that we do not blame ourselves.

44. Abba Pimen said, 'Wherever the man who blames himself may go, whatever harm, dishonour or other tribulation may happen to him, he regards himself in advance as deserving every

unpleasantness and so he is never troubled. Is there anything more free from distress than such a state? . . .'

45. Someone may say, 'If a brother offends me and, having examined myself, I find that I had given him no cause, how can I blame myself?—Indeed, if a man examines himself with fear of God, he will find that he had given every cause, either by word, deed or look. However, even if it proves that this time he had given no cause, he had certainly offended him at some other time in this or some other way, or perhaps had offended another brother and has to suffer for that or, as is often the case, for some other sin. Therefore I say that if a man examines himself with fear of God, and strictly questions his conscience, he cannot fail to find himself guilty and so will blame himself.

46. It may happen that a man sitting in solitude and silence is at peace. But there comes another brother, who in talking says something unpleasant. The man is at once disturbed and says afterwards: 'If he had not come to disturb me, I would not have sinned.' What a ridiculous argument! Did he who spoke to him introduce the passion into him? He only called to the surface the passion that was already there; so now instead of bitterness against his brother, the man should repent of his own passion and blame himself. Such a man is like a rotten loaf of bread, which looks all right outside, but inside is mouldy, so that if anyone breaks it its rottenness appears. Or he is like a clean vessel filled inside with filth and stench, so that whoever opens it will at once release this stench. In the same way this man was living, as it seemed to him, at peace, unaware of the passion inside him. Then the brother said one word to him and revealed the rot concealed within him. So if he wants to be granted mercy he must repent, blaming himself. Only thus will he achieve purity and make progress. As to the brother, he should indeed thank him for having been so useful.

47. The longer a soul sins, the weaker it becomes; for sin weakens and exhausts him who is addicted to it; and so all that befalls him weighs him down. But if a man makes progress in good, the more he progresses the lighter becomes what was heavy before.

48. In every circumstance we must look upwards. Whether

someone does good to us or we suffer harm from anyone, we must look upwards and thank God for all that befalls us, always reproaching ourselves and regarding all the good that happens to us as the work of God's merciful providence, and all the bad as the result of our own sins.

51. Our fathers said that it does not belong to monks to be angry or offend anyone, and again: 'he who has conquered irritability has conquered the demons, but he who is overcome by this passion is a total stranger to monkhood,' and so on. What then must we say of ourselves when we not only succumb to irritation and anger, but also continue resentful? What else can we do but deplore this mean and inhuman state? However, let us pay attention to ourselves, brethren, and let us strive with God's help to free ourselves from the bitterness of this pernicious passion.

52. Troubles frequently arise and unpleasantnesses occur among the brethren, but as a rule they hasten to settle these differences and are pacified. However, it may sometimes happen that, having bowed and made peace, a monk continues to nurse a feeling of hurt against his brother and to cling to thoughts against him. This is resentment; and much care is needed not to become hardened in it and perish. A man who has at once made peace with another, after being irritated with him, has cured his anger, but has done nothing against resentment, and so he continues to be sore with his brother. For resentment is one thing, anger another, irritation another and being disturbed yet another. So that you may understand it more clearly, I will give you an example. To kindle a fire one takes first a small piece of charcoal: this is the word of the brother who offended you. If you can bear it, you extinguish the charcoal. But if you think, 'Why did he say that? If that's the case, then I too shall say this and that to him. If he did not wish to offend me, he would not have said it. So I shall certainly offend him in return.' There you are, putting on some kindling wood, or something else that one puts on to start a fire, and you've produced smoke, which is disturbance. Disturbance is the movement and stirring up of thoughts, which arouse and irritate the heart. And irritation is a vengeful uprising against the man who offended you, which gives rise to presumptuousness. St. Mark said, 'Malice, fed by thoughts, irritates the heart; but

prayer kills it.' Had you borne with that small word of your brother's, you would have extinguished the little piece of charcoal before it had produced disturbance. Yet, if you wish, you can easily extinguish even disturbance, while it is still fresh, by silence, prayer, even by a mere bow from the heart. But if you continue to fume, that is, to irritate and excite the heart by thoughts, 'Why did he . . . so shall I too . . .', this will inflame your heart and give birth to the inflammation of irritation. If you so wish, you can extinguish even irritation before it leads to anger. But if you continue to disturb and irritate yourself, you will be like a man who adds fuel to the fire and so produces flames, which is anger. And anger, if it lingers, turns to resentment, from which a man will not be freed until he sheds his blood (sweat and labour over himself).

53. Thus you have heard about the meaning of initial disturbance, the meaning of irritation, anger and resentment. So do you see how from one word men come to this evil? For if you had blamed yourself from the first, had endured with patience the word of your brother, and had not wished to revenge yourself on him by answering his one word with two, or five and so return evil for evil, you would have been free of all these ills. Therefore I say to you: always cut off passions while they are still young, before they take root and gain strength in you, and begin to oppress you—for then you will have to suffer much from them. It is one thing to pluck a small blade of grass, and another to uproot a large tree.

54. One can return evil for evil not only by deed, but also by word or expression. One man may think that he does not return evil for evil in deed, but in fact returns it by word, or expression, gesture, or look. For all this too can offend one's brother and this too is returning evil for evil. Another may not try to take revenge by deed, word, expression or gesture, but in his heart he harbours resentment against his brother and is bitter against him. Another may have no bitterness against his brother, but if he hears someone reviling, criticising or belittling that brother, he rejoices and so returns evil for evil in his heart. Yet another nourishes no malice in his heart, does not rejoice at hearing of the humiliation of the one who had offended him, and even grieves if he suffers

insult, yet does not rejoice at his success—for instance, is vexed if the other is praised or favoured. This too is an aspect of resentment, though the least serious of them all.

55. It happens sometimes that if someone offends a man, they bow to one another and are reconciled; then he lives at peace with his offender and has no evil thoughts against him in his heart. But some time later the other again happens to say something hurtful and he begins to remember the past offence and be disturbed not only by the second, but also by the first. Such a man is like one who had a wound which he covered with plaster. Although the wound is now healed, the place is still tender; so if someone throws a stone at it, it is hurt more readily than the rest of the body and immediately begins to bleed. . . . This means that the wound is covered over, but is not yet healed completely—there is still a trace of resentment, owing to which the wound is easily reopened if a man receives even a slight knock.

56. We should try to clean up completely the inner infection as well, so that the tender place is well healed with no disfigurement, and it should be impossible to tell that there had been a wound there. How is this attained? By praying wholeheartedly for the offender and saying, 'Lord, help my brother and me for the sake of his prayers.' By praying thus for his brother he shows compassion and love, and asking for help for the sake of his prayers, he humbles himself. And where there are compassion, love and humility, how can irritation or rancour or any other passion have a place? Abba Zossima also said, 'If the devil were to set into motion all the wiles of his malice with all his demons, all his cunning devices will be cast down and destroyed by humility, according to Christ's commandment.' And another staretz said, 'He who prays for his enemy will have no resentment.'

57. Fulfil the advice of the startzi by deeds and you will get a right understanding of what they say. If you fail to do so, you will never learn the work of spiritual striving from words alone. What man, wishing to learn an art, masters it from bare words? No, at first he works and spoils it, works and destroys his work; and so, little by little, by patience and labour, he learns the art with the help of God, Who watches his labour and his intention. But we wish to learn the art of arts merely from words, without work. Is

it possible?! So let us pay heed to ourselves, and work with all diligence while there is still time.

58. One must pay the greatest attention not to be robbed by lies, for a liar does not unite with God. Lies are alien to God. The Scriptures say that a lie is of the devil and that 'he is a liar, and the father of it' (John viii. 44). Thus the devil is called the father of lies, but the truth is God, for He Himself says, 'I am the way, the truth, and the life' (John xiv. 6). You see from Whom we estrange ourselves by lies and with whom we unite! Therefore, if we truly wish to be saved we must love truth with all our strength and all our zeal, and must guard ourselves from all lies, lest they separate us from truth and life.

59. There are three different kinds of lies: one man lies by thought, another by words, yet another by his very life. A man lies by thought if he takes for truth his own suppositions, that is, empty suspicions regarding his neighbour—for instance, when he sees two men talking and conjectures, 'They are speaking about me' and so on. Such a man lies by thought, for all he says is not truth but merely his own opinion, and this leads to evil talk, gossip, enmity and condemnation.—A man lies by word when, for instance, he is too lazy to get up for vigil, and does not say, 'Forgive me, I was too lazy to get up', but says 'I had a fever, I was ill,' and invents dozens of lying words, to avoid making one bow and humbling himself. In the same way if he wants something, he does not say frankly, 'I want this' but twists and turns his words, indicating either poverty or illness, and lies until he gets his desire. People end by not believing such a man even when he speaks the truth.—A man lies by his life if, being an adulterer he pretends to be abstemious, or being grasping feigns to be merciful, or being arrogant assumes a humble appearance.

60. Let us take care of ourselves. Who shall give us back this time if we waste it? The time will come indeed when we shall seek these days and shall not find them. Abba Arsenius used to repeat to himself, 'Arsenius, for what have you left the world?'

61. If we were willing to make even small efforts, we would not suffer either much distress or difficulty. For if a man urges himself to make efforts, then, as he continues them, he gradually makes progress and later practises virtues with tranquillity; for

God, seeing him urge himself, sends him help. So let us urge ourselves, for, although we have not reached perfection, if we make
efforts, through efforts we shall receive help, and with this help
shall acquire all kinds of virtues. Therefore one of the fathers said,
'Give blood and receive spirit,' that is, strive and you will become practised in virtue.

62. As a man who wishes to learn carpentry does not practise
another handicraft, so also those who wish to learn spiritual doing
must be concerned with nothing else, but must strive night and
day to learn, if they are to win it. Yet there should be measure in
all things. Some staretz said, 'Walk the royal road and count the
furlongs.' For virtues lie in the middle between excess and deficiency. Therefore the Scriptures say, 'Ye shall not turn aside to
the right hand or to the left' (Deut. v. 32; xvii. 11) but shall
follow the royal road.

63. In itself evil is nothing, for it is not some kind of creature
and has no substance. But the soul, deviating from virtue, becomes passionate and gives birth to sin, and thereupon suffers, for
it can find no natural rest in it. Is it natural for a tree to have
worms inside? But if some rot starts in it, this rot breeds worms
and the worms eat the wood. So too the soul itself produces evil,
and again itself suffers from evil. Gregory the Theologian said,
'Fire is born of matter; and it devours matter as evil devours the
wicked.'

64. We see the same thing in physical illness. If a man leads a
disorderly life and takes no care of his health, there results either
an excess or deficiency of something in his body, which makes
him ill. But previously there was no illness, and it never existed
of itself; and after the body is cured, it again has no existence at
all. In the same way evil is an illness of a soul that is deprived of
the health belonging to it by nature—and that health is virtue.

81. One should uproot not only passions, but also their causes.
Then one should well fertilise one's disposition by repentance and
mourning, and only then begin to sow good seed, that is, good
deeds. For as with a field, if after clearing and manuring it good
seed is not sown, weeds come up and, finding the soil soft and
friable from being cleared, take deep root in it. So it is with man;
if, having repented of his former deeds and mended his ways, he

does not strive to acquire virtues, then is fulfilled in him the saying of the Gospel about the evil spirit returning again to the house, now swept and garnished, and taking with himself seven other spirits—and the last state of that man is worse than the first (Matt. xii. 43–45).

82. Every man who wishes to be saved must not only refrain from doing evil, but do good, as it is said 'Turn away from evil, and do good' (Ps. xxxiii. 14). For instance, if someone has been given to anger, he must not only not be angry, but must acquire meekness; if he was proud, he must not only not be proud, but must become humble; for each passion has its opposite virtue: pride—humility, cupidity—loving-kindness, fornication—chastity, faintness of heart—patience, anger—meekness, hatred—love.

87. We should not be disturbed even when passion troubles us. Why be surprised, passionate man, and why be disturbed when passion stirs you? You yourself have fashioned it and consent to keep it in yourself—and yet are you disturbed? You have accepted its tokens and you say: why does it trouble me? It is better for you to endure, strive and pray God to help you; for it is impossible for a man who obeyed passions, not to have painful attacks of them. Their vessels, as Abba Sisoy said, are within you; give them back their token and they will leave you. Since we have loved them and brought them into action, it is impossible for us not to be enticed by passionate thoughts, which urge us, even against our will, to obey passions, because we have voluntarily surrendered ourselves into their hands.

88. A man attacked by passionate thoughts before he has begun to act from passion, is still within his city; he is free and has God to help him. So as soon as he humbles himself before God and fights a little, God's help comes to free him from the onslaught of passion. But if he does not fight and, pandering to himself, surrenders to carnal pleasure, God's help withdraws from him and passion entices him to passionate action, after which he will serve this passion whether he wants to or not.

91. The fear of God urges the soul to keep commandments and by means of commandments the house of the soul is built. So let us fear God and build houses for ourselves, to find shelter in

winter, in times of rain, lightning and thunder, for a man without a house suffers great hardships in winter.

92. How to build the house of the soul can be learnt from the building of an ordinary house. He who builds a house puts up walls on all four sides at once, and is not concerned with only one, for then his labour and expenses would be wasted. So it is with a man, who wants to build the house of the soul: he must not take care of only one side of his building, but must build it evenly and harmoniously. This is what Abba John meant when he said, 'I would like a man to acquire every day a little of each virtue' and not to do as some others, who hold on to one virtue and remain in it, practising it alone and taking no care of the others.

93. The house of the soul is built evenly and harmoniously as follows. At first one must lay the foundation which is faith, for 'without faith it is impossible to please' God (Heb. xi. 6). Then on this foundation one should build the house symmetrically, namely: there comes an occasion for obedience, one must put down a stone of obedience; a brother happens to offend you, you must lay a stone of forbearance; an occasion for self-mastery offers, one must lay a stone of self-mastery. So one must lay down a stone from every virtue, for which an occasion presents itself, and in this way erect the building on all sides, placing into it now a stone of compassion, now a stone of cutting off one's will, now a stone of meekness, and so on. With all that, we must take care of patience and courage; for they are the corner-stones which bind together the building and join one wall to another, not letting them lean outwards and come away from one another. Without patience and courage no one can perform a single virtue. It is said therefore 'In your patience possess ye your souls' (Luke xxi. 19).

94. A man building a house puts lime on every stone; for if he places stone upon stone without lime, the stones will fall out and the house will collapse. Lime (in building the soul) is humility, since it is taken out of the earth and is under everyone's feet. And any virtue practised without humility is no virtue. This is said also by the fathers, 'As a ship cannot be built without nails, so a man cannot be saved without humility.' The ordinary house has a roof. The roof of the soul's house is love, which is the perfection of

virtues, just as the roof of a house is the completion of the house. Round the roof is a parapet so that, as the law says (Deut. xxii. 8) children should not fall from it. The parapets of the house of the soul are sobriety, attention and prayer; and the children are the thoughts, which dwell in the soul, protected by sobriety and prayer.

95. But one thing more is required in this building, namely, the builder must be skilled. For if he is not skilled he can make a wall crooked and the house would some day collapse. A man is skilled if he performs virtues intelligently. For it may happen that a man labours at virtues but, because he works without intelligence, he may himself ruin his work or constantly interfere with it; and thus he does not bring the building to completion but only goes on building and destroying.

96. Here is one example out of many. If a man fasts either through vanity, or thinking that he is achieving something specially virtuous, he fasts foolishly and later begins to criticise his brother, considering himself something great. Thus not only does it prove that whilst he put down one stone he took away two, but he is in danger of bringing down the whole wall through his condemnation of his brother. A man who fasts wisely does not think that he does something specially good and does not wish to be praised for his fast. He thinks that through abstinence he will win chastity and thereby will come to humility, as the fathers say, 'The way to humility is bodily labours, performed intelligently' and so on. Such a man proves himself a skilful builder, able to build his house solidly.

97. Do not be deluded by thoughts that virtue exceeds your powers and is impossible for you; but, inspired by faith, boldly make a beginning, show before God your good will and diligence —and you will see the help He will send you to practise virtue. Imagine two ladders, one leading up to heaven, the other down to hell, while you stand on earth between the two. Do not think or say, 'How can I fly upwards from earth and suddenly find myself as high as heaven, that is at the top of the ladder?' All you have to care about is to refrain from going down by doing evil. As to going up, strive to climb little by little by doing the good that offers. Each action will be a step upwards. Climbing thus with God's

help from one rung to another, you will finally reach the top of the ladder.

98. If we seek, we shall find, if we ask, we shall receive. For the Gospels say, 'Ask, and it shall be given you; seek, and ye shall find; knock, and it shall be opened unto you' (Matt. vii. 7). It is said, *ask,* in order that we should call God to our help in prayer; and *to seek* means that, having learnt how virtue comes and what brings it, we should accordingly make our own efforts to acquire it. To *knock* means to practise the commandments; for everyone who knocks does so with his hands, and hands mean activity. Thus we must not only ask, but seek and act, striving, according to the Apostle, to be 'throughly furnished unto all good works' (2 Cor. ix. 8; 2 Tim. iii. 17), that is in full readiness to fulfil God's will wisely, as He wishes and as it pleases Him.

99. The Apostle commanded us to 'prove what is that good, and acceptable, and perfect, will of God' (Rom. xii. 2), in order thereupon to act in accordance with it. What is this good will of God? To love one another, to be compassionate, to be merciful and so on; this is the *good will of God.* And what is the *acceptable will of God*? Not everyone who does something good does it in a manner acceptable to God. It may happen, for example, that someone finds an orphan, poor and good-looking; her beauty pleases him and so he takes her in and brings her up, because she is poor but also because of her beauty. This is the will of God which is *good* but not *acceptable.* It is *acceptable* when he does an act of mercy not from some human impulse, but for the sake of God Who has commanded this, for the sake of the good itself, from compassion alone—and this is acceptable to God. Finally, the *perfect* will of God is when someone does an act of mercy not grudgingly, not indolently, not contemptuously, but with his whole strength and his whole will, bestowing mercy as though he were himself receiving it, and being bountiful as though he himself were receiving the bounty; then the perfect will of God is fulfilled. This is how man fulfils the good, and acceptable and perfect will of God.

100. There are two kinds of gluttony. One is when man seeks food that pleases him and does not always want to eat much, but to eat what pleases his palate. Another is when a man is overcome

by a tendency to eat much; he does not wish for good food and does not care about its taste, but wants to eat and eat, not minding what the food may be, but only caring to fill his belly. The first kind is called frenzy of the palate, and the second frenzy of the stomach. If a man wishes to fast to cleanse himself of sins, he must avoid both these forms of gluttony; for they satisfy not the needs of the body but passion, and if a man is addicted to them it is regarded as sin.

101. However, in fasting one must not only obey this rule about food, but refrain from every other sin in order that, while the stomach is fasting, the tongue also may fast, refraining from slander, lies, idle talk, disparaging one's brethren, anger and every other sin committed by the tongue. One should also fast with the eyes, that is, not look at vain things, not give freedom to the eyes, not look shamelessly and without fear at anyone. The hands and feet should also be kept from any evil action.

103. When you meet others you should, above all, avoid suspiciousness, which leads to evil condemnation. I have many examples which confirm the truth that each man judges others according to his own character. I will give an example. Suppose someone happens to be standing somewhere at night, and three people walk by. On seeing him, one of them thinks, he's waiting for someone to go and commit adultery; another, he must be a thief; the third, he has arranged with someone from nearby to go and pray together, and he is waiting for him. Thus three people saw the same man in the same place, yet they did not form the same opinion of him; each reached a separate conclusion, each obviously conforming to the state of his own soul. As bodies which are unhealthy and bilious transform every food they receive into bad juices, even when the food is wholesome, so an ill-constituted soul receives harm from everything, even if the things it meets with are good. And a man whose soul is well constituted is like one whose body is healthy, so that even if he eats something harmful it becomes transformed in him into good juices. So we too, if the constitution and state of our soul are good, can gain profit from everything, even if the thing is not useful.

106. If you wish that thoughts, holy in faith, should in time of need have a calming action in arresting wrong movements,

thoughts and feelings, study them always, frequently going over them in your mind—and I have faith in God that you will find peace. Also intersperse your prayer with study. Try to make progress in this, so that at a moment of bodily or spiritual affliction you may be able to suffer it without grief, without oppression and with patience.

109. Know that if a man is attacked by some thought or is grieved by it and does not acknowledge it, he only strengthens it against himself, that is, gives the thought more strength to attack and torment him. But if he acknowledges it and begins to struggle and resist the thought and do what is opposed to it, the passion will weaken and will have no power to attack him and bring him sorrow. And later, little by little, striving and receiving help from God, he will overcome the passion itself.

111. When the soul is unfeeling, it is useful frequently to read the Holy Scriptures and the heart-stirring words of the holy fathers, to remember the terrible judgment of God, the departure of the soul from the body and its having to meet the fearsome dark powers, with which it did evil in the course of this short and calamitous life.

ST. ISAAC OF SYRIA (NINEVEH)

ST. ISAAC OF SYRIA (NINEVEH)
Short Biographical Note

St. Isaac was born in Nineveh. Nothing is known of his parents. In the full flower of his youth he, together with his brother, withdrew from the world and all that is of the world, and entered the monastery of St. Matthew. There he took his vows, and began his monastic life.

When he had reached perfection in the spiritual discipline of this monastery and a sufficient measure of attainment in virtues, he was wounded with a desire for silence. So he retired far away from the cenobite monastery and settled in a lonely cell, where he led a completely solitary life, having communion with no one and concentrating his attention only in himself and on God. His brother, who became abbot of this monastery, implored and entreated him to leave his solitude and return to the monastery; but he was so attached to his wilderness that he refused to leave it, even for a short time.

But where his brother's entreaties failed, Divine revelation succeeded. Having refused to listen to his brother, St. Isaac obeyed the Father from above, Who called him to administer the Church of Nineveh. Therefore he left his wilderness and was ordained as bishop of the great city of Nineveh. For the candle was not to be hidden under a bushel in the wilderness, but was to be put on the candlestick of pastorship, to spread far and wide the light of its radiant virtue. But this lasted only a short time: scarcely had this light appeared than it vanished again. The new bishop left his see, for the following reason.

Two men came to see him in his episcopal residence—a creditor and his debtor. The former demanded an immediate payment of the debt, while the latter, acknowledging the debt, begged for a short time of grace. But the creditor said to this: 'If he does not repay his debt at once, I shall immediately take him to court.' St. Isaac remarked: 'If according to the Gospel commandment you should by no means ask back your goods that another has taken away, how much more should you show magnanimity to a man who promises soon to repay his debt.' But the cruel man replied: 'Leave the Gospel commandment out of this for the present.' And he refused to listen to any more.

Then the bishop of God said to himself: 'If they do not obey the Gospel commandments of the Lord, what is there that remains for me to do here?' He saw, moreover, how much the silence and serenity, to which he was used in the wilderness, were disturbed by the unavoidable business of administration; and so he decided to leave his see and return to his beloved skete in the wilderness.

He remained there till death. It is needless to describe his feats in struggling with the flesh and the demons, his great attainments in virtue, demanded alike by active and by contemplative life, or the degree of spiritual perfection and the grace he was granted even in this life; all this can easily be seen from his writings.

St. Isaac wrote much and all he wrote was written from experience. Everything he put down in writing was first experienced by him in active practice, and those whom he guided he taught by his own activity. In the wilderness too he continued to be a spring of pure and life-giving water that never dried, abundantly quenching the thirst of his brethren's souls.

The writings of St. Isaac have reached us in the Syriac and Arabic tongues; about half of them have been translated into Greek, and from Greek into Russian, among other writings of the holy fathers—in all 91 texts.

St. Isaac left earth to dwell in heaven towards the end of the sixth century.

ST. ISAAC OF SYRIA (NINEVEH)

Directions on Spiritual Training

(Short excerpts)[31]

1. Fear of God is the beginning of virtue; it is the offspring of faith and is sown in the heart, when the mind is withdrawn from worldly distractions in order to collect its wandering thoughts into meditation about the future restoration.

2. In order to lay the foundation of virtue, it is best for man to keep removed from worldly affairs and to abide in the law, which illumines the holy paths of righteousness, as the Holy Spirit has shown through the Singer of Psalms (Ps. xxii. 3; cxviii. 35).

3. The beginning of the path of life is always to be instructing one's mind in the Words of God and to spend one's life in poverty. Filling oneself with the one helps to gain perfection in the other. If you fill yourself with study of the Words of God, this helps towards progress in poverty; and progress in non-acquisitiveness gives you leisure to make progress in study of the Words of God. So the two combine to help the speedy building of the whole edifice of virtues.

4. No one can approach God without withdrawing from the world. By withdrawal I do not mean change of physical dwelling place, but withdrawal from worldly affairs. The virtue of withdrawal from the world consists in not occupying your mind with the world.

5. When grace increases in a man, then fear of death on the path of the righteousness he desires (or in the face of obstacles on this path) becomes of no account for him. Then he finds in his soul many reasons why, for fear of God, he should be ready to

31 The subheading is taken from the Dobrotolubiye. (Translators' note.)

suffer afflictions as being something necessary. Then all things unpleasant to the body, and apt to cause it suffering, are as nothing
in a man's eyes, compared with his hopes in the future. But when
grace grows less in a man, all that happens in him and with him
is the reverse; then, owing to investigation (which can be based
only on the tangible), knowledge becomes for him more important than faith, trust in God is not present in all he does, and
Divine Providence in relation to man is understood differently.
Such a man is for ever subject to fears, through the wiles of those
who lurk to shoot privily at him with their arrows (Ps. x. 3).

6. A doubting heart makes the soul timid; whereas faith can
make the will firm, even if the body's members are cut off. In the
measure that love of the flesh has the upper hand in you, you cannot be daring and fearless amid the many battles waged around the
object of your love.

7. Not he is chaste in whom shameful thoughts stop in time of
struggle, work and endeavour, but he who by the trueness of his
heart makes chaste the vision of his mind, not letting it stretch
out towards unseemly thoughts. And while the honesty of his
conscience testifies, in what his eyes see, that he is true (to the
law of purity), pudency hangs like a veil in the secret place of
thoughts, and his innocence, like a chaste virgin, is kept inviolate
for Christ by faith.

8. To drive away the wrong tendencies previously acquired by
the soul, nothing is more helpful than immersing oneself in love
of studying the Divine Scriptures, and understanding the depths of
the thoughts they contain. When thoughts become immersed in
the delight of fathoming the hidden wisdom of the words, a man
leaves the world behind and forgets all that is therein, in proportion to the enlightenment he draws from the words. But even
when the mind floats only on the surface of the waters of the
Divine Scriptures and cannot penetrate to the very depths of the
thoughts contained therein, even then the very fact that he is
occupied with zeal to understand the Scriptures is enough firmly
to pinion his thoughts in ideas of the miraculous alone, and to
prevent them from seeking after the material and the carnal.

9. In everything you meet with in the Scriptures, strive to find
the purpose of the word, to penetrate into the depth of the

thought of the saints and to understand it more exactly. Those whose life is guided by Divine grace towards enlightenment, always feel as though some inner ray of light travels over the written lines and allows the mind to discern from the bare words what is said with great thought for the instruction of the soul.

10. If a man reads lines of great meaning without going deeply into them, his heart remains poor (it gets no food); and the holy force which, through wondrous understanding of the soul, gives most sweet food to the heart, grows dim in him.

11. Each thing is usually attracted to its like. So the soul, being endowed with the spirit, ardently attracts to itself the content of a saying, as soon as it hears words which contain hidden spiritual force. Not every man is moved to wonder by what is said spiritually and possesses great spiritual force concealed in it. Words which speak of virtue require a heart not occupied with the earth; and in a man whose mind is burdened with temporal cares, virtue does not awake thought to love it and seek to possess it.

12. Renunciation of matter by one's being precedes union with God, although, through the dispensation of grace, the latter is in some found to precede the former. The order normal for dispensation differs from the order general among men. But you should preserve the general order. If grace comes first in you, that is its own affair; if it does not come first, you too must climb to the summit of the spiritual tower by the way of all men.

13. The insatiability of the soul in acquiring virtue turns to its use a part of the visible (sensory) desires of the body with which it is joined. Each thing is made good by measure. Without measure even things deemed excellent become harmful.

14. Do you wish to commune with God in your mind?— Strive to be merciful. To the spiritual love which imprints the invisible image (of God in oneself), there is no other path than that a man should first of all begin to be merciful in the measure that our heavenly Father is merciful, as the Lord said (Luke vi. 36).

15. A word not made good by action is like an artist who makes pictures of water on walls, yet cannot quench his thirst with it. When a man speaks of virtue from his own experience, it is the

same as giving to another money earned by his own labours. And if a man sows teaching into the ears of his listeners from what he himself has gained, he opens his lips with confidence, saying to his spiritual children as the aged Jacob said to the chaste Joseph: 'I give to thee Sicima, a select portion above thy brethren, which I took out of the hand of the Amorites with my sword and bow' (Gen. xlviii. 22).

16. Someone said with perfect truth that fear of death afflicts a man, whose conscience condemns him; but a man who bears good testimony in himself desires death as much as he desires life.

17. If something has become deeply united with your soul, you should not only regard it as your possession in this life, but believe that it will accompany you into the life to come. If it is something good, rejoice and give thanks to God in your mind; if it is something bad, grieve and sigh, and strive to free yourself from it while you are still in the body.

18. Always keep in your mind the grievous afflictions of those stricken with sorrow and tribulations, that you may render due thanks for the small and insignificant adversities, which may happen to you, and be able to bear them with joy.

19. In times of cooling and laziness, imagine in your heart those past times when you were full of zeal and solicitude in all things, even the smallest; remember your past efforts and the energy with which you opposed those who wished to obstruct your progress. These recollections will reawaken your soul from its deep sleep, will invest it anew with the fire of zeal, will raise it, as it were, from the dead and will make it engage in an ardent struggle against the devil and sin, thus returning to its former rank.

20. The activity of cross-bearing is of two kinds: one consists in enduring bodily afflictions (bodily privations, inevitable in struggling with passions), and is called activity proper; the other consists in subtle doing of the mind, meditation on God, abiding in prayer, and so on, and is called contemplation. The first purifies the passionate part of the soul, the other brings light to its mental part. Every man who, before perfecting his training in the first activity, passes to the second, being attracted to its delights, not to speak of his own laziness, becomes overtaken by wrath for not having first mortified his 'members which are upon the

earth' (Col. iii. 5), that is, for not having overcome the impotence of thoughts by patient exercise in the activity of bearing the cross, and for presuming to let his mind dream of the cross's glory. This is the meaning of the saying of the saints of old that, if a man's mind conceives an intention to climb on to the cross, before his senses are cured of their sickness and have achieved a state of serenity, he is overtaken by the wrath of God. A man whose mind is defiled by shameful passions, who is quick to fill it with fantasies, has an interdiction set on his lips, because, without first purifying his mind by suffering, without conquering carnal lusts, he puts his trust on what his ear has heard and what is written in ink, and has forged ahead on a path shrouded in darkness, when his eyes are blind.

21. Imagine virtue as the body, contemplation as the soul, and the two together as forming one perfect man, whose two parts—the senses and the mind—are made one by the spirit. Just as it is impossible for a soul to manifest its being before the forming of the body, with its members, has been completed; so too is it impossible for a soul to reach contemplation without active work in virtue.

22. When you hear that it is necessary to withdraw from the world, to leave the world, to purify yourself from all that belongs to the world, you must first learn and understand the term world, not in its everyday meaning, but in its purely inward significance. When you understand what it means and the different things that this term includes, you will be able to learn about your soul—how far removed it is from the world and what is mixed with it that is of the world. 'World' is a collective name, embracing what are called passions. When we want to speak of passions collectively, we call them 'the world'; when we want to distinguish between them according to their different names, we call them passions.

23. When you have learned what the world means, then, by discerning all that is implied in this term, you will also learn what ties you to the world and in what you are freed from it. I will say, more briefly, that the world is carnal life and minding of the flesh. Therefore a man is seen to be free of the world inasmuch as he has wrenched himself free of this.

24. Fear for the body is sometimes so strong in men as to make them incapable of any deeds worthy of honour or praise. But when fear for the soul is added to fear for the body, bodily fear melts in it like wax in the flame.

25. By nature the soul is passionless. Passions are something added to it, through the fault of the soul itself. If formerly the nature of the soul was luminous and pure through absorbing Divine light, and if it likewise becomes such when it regains its former rank, this of itself proves that the soul abandons its nature when it is moved by passions, as the children of the Church assert.

26. The natural state of the soul is knowledge of Divine creatures, both sensory and incorporeal. Its supernatural state is the movement (or action and state) of contemplation of the tran-substantial Deity. The state contrary to its nature is the movement or disposition and life of the soul such as is found in passionate men, who serve passions. Thus it is clear that passions of the soul do not belong to the soul by nature.

27. If you wish to know the innermost in man and you have not yet reached the state when you perceive it by the spirit, you may learn it by each man's words, his mode of life and his disposition. A man who is pure in soul and without sin in his mode of life, always speaks the words of the Spirit with chastity; and he judges both the Divine, and what is in himself, in accordance with the measure of his understanding. But if a man's heart is filled with passions, these passions move also his tongue. Even if he speaks of spiritual matters, he does so under the influence of passion. A wise man notices such an one at the first meeting, and a pure man smells his stench.

28. The practices of a monk are the following: freedom from things of the flesh, labour of the body in prayers and constant memory of God in the heart.

29. Prayer is one thing, and contemplation in prayer is another, although prayer and contemplation mutually engender one another. Prayer is sowing, contemplation the reaping of the harvest, when the reaper is filled with wonder at the ineffable sight of the beautiful ears of corn, which have sprung up before him from the little naked seeds that he sowed.

30. The Saviour began the work of our salvation with fasting.

In the same way all those, who follow in the footsteps of the Saviour, build on this foundation the beginning of their endeavour, since fasting is a weapon established by God. Who will escape blame if he neglects this? If the Lawgiver Himself fasts, how can any of those, who have to obey the law, be exempt from fasting? This is why the human race knew no victory before fasting, and the devil was never defeated by our nature as it is: but this weapon has indeed deprived the devil of strength from the outset. Our Lord was the Leader and the first example of this victory, in order to place the first crown of victory on the head of our nature. As soon as the devil sees some one possessed of this weapon, fear straightway falls on this adversary and tormentor of ours, who remembers and thinks of his defeat by the Saviour in the wilderness; his strength is at once destroyed and the sight of the weapon, given us by our Supreme Leader, burns him up. A man armed with the weapon of fasting is alway afire with zeal. He who remains therein, keeps his mind steadfast and ready to meet and repel all violent passions.

31. Works and deeds gain passionlessness for the soul, mortify the 'members which are upon the earth' (Col. iii. 5) and give quietness from thoughts, when we acquire silence, and when the turmoil produced by impressions from the outer senses ceases in the soul. Otherwise success in this is not possible. For, if a tree is watered every day, can its root ever wither? Does water ever get less in a vessel if more is added daily? But when a man gains silence, his soul readily discerns passions, and the inner man, roused to spiritual work, overcomes them and, from day to day, lifts the soul nearer to purity.

32. How can one say that a man has attained purity?—When he sees all men as being good, and when none appears to him to be unclean and defiled—then he is indeed pure in heart.

33. What should a worker do when he keeps silence in his cell? —What need has a zealous man, sober in soul, to ask how to behave when he is alone with himself? What occupation can a monk have in his cell except to mourn? And what other occupation can be better? His very seclusion and solitude, by their likeness to life in a tomb, far from human joys, teach a monk that his work is—to mourn. And all the saints have left this life in

mourning. So let us beg the Lord to give us mourning. For, if we are granted this blessing, the best of gifts, more excellent than others, then with its help we shall attain purity. And once we have attained it, it will not be taken from us right to the end of our present life.

34. Blessed are the pure in heart, for there is no time when they do not rejoice in the sweetness of tears—in which too they see the Lord at all times. While tears are still wet in their eyes, they are granted a sight of His revelations at the height of their prayer; and no prayer of theirs is without tears. This is the meaning of the Lord's saying: 'Blessed are they that mourn: for they shall be comforted' (Matt. v. 4). For if, with the help of tears, a monk has succeeded in crossing the realm of passions and entering the plain of purity of soul, he meets with the comfort which God grants for their purity to those that mourn. To mourn and shed tears is a gift of the passionless. If the tears of a man, who for a time weeps and mourns, can not only lead him to passionlessness, but even completely free and cleanse his mind of all memory of passions, what can be said of those who day and night exercise themselves in this doing with knowledge?

35. One of the saints said that a body that feared trials, lest it be led to extremity and lose its life, becomes a friend of sin. Therefore the Holy Spirit constrains it to die. For He knows that if it does not die, it will not conquer sin. If a man wishes the Lord to dwell in him, he forces his body to serve the Lord, to work in the commandments of the Spirit, written by the Apostle, and to preserve his soul from the works of the flesh, described by the Apostle (Gal. v. 19). When the body is united with sin, it reposes in works of the flesh, and the Spirit of God does not repose in its fruits. For when the body is being exhausted by fasting and humility, the soul is strengthened by prayer.

36. When the body is greatly burdened by the sufferings of silence, endures privations and want, and comes near to losing its life, it is natural for it to implore you and say: 'Give me a little freedom to live decently; I now walk righteously, for I have been tried by all kinds of bitter sufferings.' But as soon as you take pity on it and give it some small rest from sufferings it begins little by little to cajole you (and its cajolings are very powerful) by whis-

pering: 'We can live as we should even close to the world, by following the same rules which guide us now, since we have been well tried. Put me to the test, and if I am not as you wish, we can always go back. The wilderness will not run away.' Do not trust it, however hard it implores you and whatever promises it makes. It will not do as it says. If you grant its request it will cast you into great downfalls, and you will not be able to rise up from them again.

37. When trials make you despondent and you weary of them, say to yourself: 'Again, you long for impure and shameful life.' And if the body says to you: 'It is a great sin to kill oneself,' answer it: 'I am killing myself because I cannot lead an unclean life. I will die here lest I see the real death of my soul—death in God's eyes. It is better for me to die here for the sake of purity than to lead a bad life in the world. I have willingly chosen this death for my sins. I am killing myself of my own accord, for I have offended the Lord. No longer shall I anger Him. What can I find in a life remote from God? I shall endure these afflictions lest I be deprived of heavenly hope. What is my life in this world to God, if I live it wrongly and anger God?'

38. It is harmful for a monk to see the world and worldly things. What a change occurs in the mind of a man who has for a long time been silent, alone with himself, and who suddenly finds himself once more in the vortex of the world and sees and hears things to which he is not accustomed! Let us not be seduced by those who assert that we suffer no harm from hearing or seeing anything, that we are the same in our thoughts whether we are in solitude or in the world, that our modesty is not troubled either in the cell or outside it, and suffers no change for the worse, and that we feel no stirrings of passions even when we meet people and things. Such things can be asserted only by men so strong in spirit that even if they suffer wounds, they do not feel them. But we have not yet attained to such health, we still bear in ourselves festering wounds, which will swarm with worms if left open and untended even for a single day, instead of being covered with a plaster and bound tight with bandages.

39. Once a soul has surrendered to God with faith and has often experienced His help, it no longer cares for itself, but is

enveloped in wonder and silence; it is impossible for it to return again to its own means of knowledge and apply them, lest it be deprived of Divine Providence, which secretly and unceasingly looks after the soul, cares for it and constantly watches over it. If the soul is thus deprived, it is because it has proved itself to be living in self-reliant fantasies, as though, on the strength of its own knowledge, it were able sufficiently to provide for itself.

40. Those in whom the light of faith is burning are no longer so shameless as to return in their prayers to their former petitions: 'Give us this,' or 'Take away that,' and they have no care for themselves. For at each moment, by the spiritual eyes of faith, they see the Fatherly Providence which gives them the protection of that true Father, Whose infinite love surpasses all fatherly love and Who, more than all, can and has the power to help us in a measure greater than anything we may ask, think or conceive.

41. He who has been given to taste the sweetness of faith, and who thereupon again returns to knowledge on the level of the soul, is like a man who has found a priceless pearl and has bartered it for a copper obol; or again like a man who has abandoned the freedom of being his own master and returned to a beggarly state of fear and slavery.

42. There are three modes by which knowledge ascends and descends. These modes are: body, soul, spirit. Knowledge is the gift of God to the nature of rational beings and was bestowed on them at their very creation. In its nature it is as simple and indivisible as sunlight, but corresponding to its application it undergoes changes and divisions. Listen to the order of this application.

43. *The first degree of knowledge.* When knowledge follows desires of the flesh, it embraces the following modes: wealth, vainglory, adornment, bodily comfort, care for book-learning, such as is suitable in the administration of this world and producing new things through inventions, arts and sciences, and all the other things which crown the body in this visible world. Because of these distinctive features knowledge becomes opposed to faith. It is called naked knowledge, for it excludes all concern for God, owing to the preponderance of the body, introduces into the mind an irrational impotence and limits all its concern to this world alone.

This is how this knowledge conceives itself: as if it were a mental power, which secretly governs man, a kind of divine management, which watches over man and takes perfect care of him. Therefore this knowledge does not ascribe the control of the world to God's Providence; on the contrary, all that is good in man, all that saves him from harm, all that naturally protects him from difficulties and the many adversities which accompany our nature, both secretly and openly, all this appears to this knowledge to be the result of its own care and its own methods.

Such is the opinion this blasphemous knowledge has of itself. It imagines that all things happen through its own providence; and in this it is in agreement with those who assert that nothing rules this world. All the same it cannot exist without constant cares and without fears for the body, and is, therefore, a prey to faint-heartedness, sorrow, despair and fears: fears that come from demons, fears that come from men, rumours about robbers, rumours about murders, worries brought by sickness, by want and lack of the necessities of life, fear of death, fear of sufferings and wild beasts, and of other similar things—all of which make this knowledge like a turbulent sea, on which sailors spend day and night, with no respite from attacks and buffetings by waves from every side.

Since this knowledge is incapable of placing all care of itself on God, through faith and trust in Him, it is constantly occupied in evolving and inventing various contrivances concerned with itself. But when these contrivances happen to fail in some case, it does not see in this the mysterious hand of Providence, and begins to quarrel with people, who resist or oppose it. In this respect, there is implanted in this knowledge the tree of the knowledge of good and evil, the tree which uproots love. Its qualities are pride and arrogance. It is puffed up, while yet it walks in darkness, it values what it has by earthly standards, and does not know that there is something better than itself.

44. *The second degree of knowledge.* When a man renounces the first degree, he becomes occupied with thoughts and desires of the soul; then, in the light of the nature of his soul, he practises the following excellent deeds: fasting, prayer, alms, reading of the Divine Scriptures, virtuous life, struggle with passions and so on.

For all the good deeds, all the excellent features seen in the soul and the wonderful means used for serving in the house of Christ in this second degree of knowledge are the work of the Holy Spirit, Who lends power to its action. At the same time this knowledge also shows to the heart the ways which lead us to faith, and collects in it what is useful for the journey into true life.

But even here knowledge is still material and multiple. It contains only the way which leads and speeds us towards faith. There is yet a higher degree of knowledge. Should a man achieve success in his work, with Christ's help it will be possible for him to be raised to that third degree, if he has laid the foundation of his activity on silent withdrawal from people, reading the Scriptures, prayer and other good works, by which are achieved all that relates to the second knowledge. It is by this knowledge that all that is most beautiful is performed; indeed it is called the knowledge of actions, because by sensory actions, through the senses of the body, it does its work on the external level.

45. *The third degree of knowledge* is the degree of perfection. Hear now how a man becomes finer, acquires that which is of the spirit, and in his life comes to resemble the invisible powers, which perform their service not through sensory actions but through vigilance of mind. When knowledge soars above earthly things and the cares of earthly activities, when it begins to experience thoughts belonging to what is within and hidden from the eyes, when it surges upwards and follows faith in its solicitude for the life to come, in its desire for what was promised us, and in searching deeply into the mysteries that are hidden; then faith itself absorbs this knowledge, is transformed and begets it anew, so that this knowledge becomes all spirit.

Then it can soar on wings to the realms of the incorporeal and touch the depths of the intangible sea, representing to the mind the wondrous workings of the Divine rule in the natures of incorporeal and sensory creatures; (it can) search out the spiritual mysteries, accessible to a fine and simple mind. Then the inner senses awake for spiritual doing, according to the order which will prevail in the immortal and incorruptible life; for then it has, as it were, undergone a spiritual resurrection even in this world, as a true token of the general resurrection.

46. These are the three modes of knowledge. From the time a man begins to distinguish good from evil, and until he leaves this world, the knowledge of his soul remains within these three degrees. The fullness of all wrong and impiety, and the fullness of righteousness, and the probing of all the depths of the mysteries of the spirit, all these are produced by one single knowledge in these three degrees; in it is contained every movement of the mind, whether it ascends or descends, in good, in evil, or in something between the two. These three degrees are called by the fathers: natural, contranatural and supranatural knowledge. They are the three directions along which the memory of a rational soul travels up and down, either when, as has been said, a man acts rightly from his own nature, or when by memory he is ravished on high, above his nature, in supranatural contemplation of God, or when he goes out to herd swine, having squandered the riches of good judgment, slaving with a multitude of demons.

47. The first degree of knowledge renders the soul cold towards efforts to walk according to God. The second warms the soul, hastening its progress towards that which is on the level of faith. The third is rest from activity, enjoying the mysteries of the future life, in a single striving of mind. But since our being is as yet unable entirely to transcend its state of lifelessness and the burden of the flesh, so, while a man lives in the body, he remains in a constant state of changing from one to another. Now, like a miserable beggar, his soul begins its service in the second, the middle degree of virtue; now, like those who have received the spirit of sonship in the mystery of liberation, he rejoices in the quality of spiritual grace which corresponds to its Giver; then again he returns to his humble works performed with the help of the body. For there is no perfect freedom in this imperfect life.

48. In the second degree, the work of knowledge consists in long-drawn exercise and labour. Work in the third degree is the doing of faith, performed not through actions, but through spiritual representations in the mind, in an activity which is purely of the soul, since it transcends the senses. By faith we mean not faith in relation to the distinctions of the Divine Hypostases we worship, or the miracle of dispensation through Incarnation in

man's nature, although this faith is also very lofty; we mean that
faith, which is kindled in the soul from the light of grace and
which fortifies the heart by testimony of the mind, giving it the
certainty of hope which is free from all doubt. This faith manifests
itself not through increased hearing of the ears, but through
spiritual eyes, which see the mysteries hidden in the soul, that invisible Divine treasure, which is hidden from the sight of sons of
the flesh and is revealed by the Spirit to those who receive their
food from Christ's table and learn His laws. As the Lord said: if ye
keep my commandments, I will send you a Comforter, 'even the
Spirit of truth; whom the world cannot receive . . . he shall
teach you all things' (John xiv. 17, 26).

49. *Yet another distinction between different kinds of knowledge.*

Knowledge which is concerned with the visible, or which
receives through the senses what comes from the visible, is called
natural. Knowledge which is concerned with the power of the
immaterial and the nature of incorporeal entities within a man is
called spiritual, because perceptions are received by the spirit and
not by the senses. Because of these two origins (perceptions of the
visible and of the spiritual) each kind of knowledge alike comes
to the soul from without. But the knowledge bestowed by Divine
power is called supranatural; it is more unfathomable and is
higher than knowledge. Contemplation of this knowledge comes
to the soul not from matter, which is outside it, as is the case of
the first two kinds of knowledge; it manifests and reveals itself in
the innermost depths of the soul itself, immaterially, suddenly,
spontaneously and unexpectedly, since, according to the words of
Christ 'the kingdom of God is within you' (Luke xvii. 21). It
does not feed hope with any image in advance, nor can its coming
be observed: but within the image imprinted in the hidden mind,
it reveals itself by itself, without thought. The first kind of knowledge results from constant and diligent work of learning; the
second results from right living and rational faith; the third is
given only to the faith, which sets aside knowledge and puts an
end to actions.

50. Do not doubt the power of our prayers in established services, if it happens that prayers or hourly reading are not followed
by strong stimulation and constant contrition.

51. Accept without fail words spoken from experience, even if the speaker is not learned in books. For though royal treasures may be the greatest of all on earth, yet they do not despise adding an obol taken from a beggar; and rivers are swollen by small streams to become mighty in their flow.

52. Memory of good things and memory of bad things show us, like a pointing finger, either the shamefulness of our thoughts, or the height of our life, and each, according to its nature, strengthens in us thoughts and movements belonging either to the right or to the left. Our traffic with them is in the secrecy of our mind; but this mental traffic depicts our life and in it we can see ourselves.

53. There is a love like a small lamp, fed by oil, which goes out when the oil is ended; or like a rain-fed stream which goes dry, when rain no longer feeds it. But there is a love, like a spring gushing from the earth, never to be exhausted. The first is human love; the second—is Divine, and has God as its source.

54. Do you wish to enjoy the words of your services and to understand the meaning of the words of the Spirit that you utter? Then disregard completely the quantity of verses, take no account of your skill in giving rhythm to the lines, abandon the customary loud chanting, but let your mind sink deep into study of the words of the Spirit, till your soul is roused to heights of understanding and thereby is moved to glorify God or to salutary mourning. There is no peace for the mind in slavish work (in merely reading the set prayers); and disturbance of mind deprives it of the taste of the meaning and of understanding and disperses thoughts. Disturbance may truthfully be called the devil's chariot, for it is Satan's practice to drive the mind like a charioteer, and, carrying with him a load of passions, to enter the luckless soul and plunge it into confusion.

55. Do not oppose the thoughts, which the enemy sows in you, but rather cut off all converse with them by prayer to God. We have not always strength enough so to oppose hostile thoughts as to stop them; on the contrary, in such attempts they frequently inflict us with a wound that is long in healing. Despite all your wisdom and all your good intentions, the enemies will succeed in dealing you a blow. But even if you conquer them, the filth of

such thoughts will pollute your mind and their stench will long cling in your nostrils. But if you use the first method, you will be free of all this and of fear; for there is no help but God.

56. When, while keeping silence in your cell, you turn to work with your hands, do not use this, that the fathers advise, as a cloak for your love of money. To avoid despondency, take up some small task which does not disturb the mind, but do not forget that prayer ranks higher than all else.

57. Be assured that your Protector is always with you—and that, in company with all other creatures, you too are under the one Master, Who by a single lifting of His hand gives order and movement to all things. So stand firm and be of good cheer. Neither demons, nor dangerous beasts, nor vicious men can wreak their will on you and destroy you, unless the Ruler permits it and sets it a definite measure. So say to your soul: 'I have a Protector Who guards me, and no creature can rise against me without command from on high. If it be the will of my Master that the evil ones should gain mastery over the creature, I accept it without grief, since I do not wish the will of my Lord to remain unfulfilled.' In this way, amid trials and temptations, you will be filled with joy, as one who knows and realises in practice that the hand of the Master rules over him and directs him. Thus fortify your heart by trust in the Lord.

58. Not only does the guarding of the tongue speed the mind towards God, but it also gives great hidden strength for performing external actions with the help of the body, and enlightens a man in the secret doing, as the fathers said; for guarding of the lips makes the conscience rise towards God, if only a man keeps silence with understanding.

59. Every thought desiring good is followed by *zeal*, fervent as burning coals. It is wont to protect such thought and shield it from all opposition, obstacles and barriers. Without this virtue no good is produced. Someone, clothed in Christ, called this zeal a watch dog of God's law.

There are two means of arousing, strengthening and inflaming this power of zeal for guarding the house (the soul)—just as there are two means by which it is exhausted, put to sleep and made indolent.

Its awakening and inflaming are brought about, if some *fear* enters a man's mind, that he may lose the blessing he has acquired or aims to acquire, and which may be stolen or destroyed. When this fear is aroused, zeal burns day and night like a red-hot furnace, and like a Cherubim, ever watchful all around, diligently guards his blessing against all hostile attacks from within and without.

The other method of inflaming this zeal is when a longing for virtue gains strength in the soul. The greater this longing in the soul, the greater, in proportion, the zeal for virtue.

The first cause of its cooling is when the very desire for good grows less or dies down in the soul; and the second is when some foolhardy or self-assured thought enters the soul and takes root in it; and the man begins to hope, think and harbour the opinion that he need fear no harm from any power. So he lays down his weapon of zeal, and the house is left unguarded; the dog goes to sleep and for long abandons his watch.

The cause of both one and another alike is the entry into the soul of even the least thought of pride, and its establishment there; or if a man gives himself more to care for transient things; or if he falls a frequent prey to the lures of communications with the world. Or else the cause of it is the stomach, this mistress of all evil. Every time a man engaged in spiritual endeavour enters into communication with the world, his soul immediately loses force. The same happens if he meets with a number of people, for they are bound to pull down his soul by vanity. The mind of a man engaged in spiritual endeavour, who enters into communication with the world, is like a navigator, who is calmly sailing the sea, but suddenly finds himself amidst submerged rocks, and suffers shipwreck.

60. To prefer the will for good is the affair of him who desires it; to accomplish what the will for good has chosen is the affair of God. For this a man has need of God's help. So let us see to it that, if a desire for good arises in us, it is followed by frequent prayers, whereby we entreat God not only to send us His help, but also to show us whether this desire conforms to His will or not. For not every good desire which enters the heart comes from God, but only that desire which is useful.

61. Sometimes a man desires something good, but God does

not help him. This happens because at times a similar desire comes from the devil and is harmful instead of useful; or because what we wish is beyond our powers, since we have not yet achieved a conformable life; or because it is alien to the form of endeavour we have accepted; or because the time has not yet come, when it can be fulfilled or begin to be fulfilled; or because we have neither knowledge nor physical strength sufficient for it; or because the present circumstances are not propitious. Yet the devil uses all his wiles to offer this activity in a favourable light, (so as) to incite us to it and thus disturb our peace of soul or cause harm to the body. So we must carefully examine even our good desires. It is best to act in all things with advice.

62. Virtue is the mother of mourning; mourning gives birth to humility; to humility is given grace. So that the reward that follows is neither to virtue nor to labour for virtue's sake, but to the humility born of them. If humility be lost, the other two are useless.

63. The Lord demands not only that we should follow His commandments, but above all, that we should mend our soul, for which purpose He laid down the commandments. The body acts alike in all actions, whether they belong to the right or to the left; but the mind shows itself to be either right or sinful, according to its disposition.

64. A gift free from trials is a disaster to the receiver. If you do something good before God, and He makes you a gift, pray Him to teach you humility, as much as is good for you, or to appoint a guardian over the gift, or to take it away from you, lest it prove the cause of your ruin. For keeping riches is not useful for every man.

65. Virtues are connected with suffering. He who flees suffering is sure to be parted from virtue. If you desire virtue, give yourself up to every kind of suffering. For suffering engenders humility. Until we have attained true knowledge, we advance towards humility by means of trials. He who rests on his virtue without suffering has the door of pride open before him.

66. When a man is filled with pride, his guardian angel, who is near him and who urges him to care for righteousness, withdraws from him. And when a man has offended this angel and the angel

withdraws from him, a stranger (the spirit of darkness) draws near, and from then onwards the man ceases to care about righteousness.

67. God often permits virtuous men to be tried by something; He permits temptations to rise up against them on all sides, strikes them in their body like Job, casts them into poverty, lets them be shunned by mankind, strikes them in their acquisitions; only their souls are not visited by harm. And, indeed, it is impossible that when we walk in the way of righteousness tribulation should not be met with, and that the body should not be exhausted by pain and labour, and yet remain steadfast, if only we desire to live in virtue. If a man proceeds on his way according to God and meets with something of this kind, it is not right for him to deviate from his way; but he must accept what comes with joy and without questioning, and render thanks to God for sending him this blessing and for being beset by trials for His sake; for God thus lets him share in the sufferings of the prophets, apostles and other saints, who endured tribulations for the sake of this way. Whether these trials come from men, demons or the flesh, let it be a cause for thanksgiving. For God cannot show His favour to a man, who desires to dwell with Him, except by sending him trials for the sake of truth; just as no man can become worthy of this greatness—that is, to be beset by trials and to rejoice—without the grace of Christ.

This achievement is so great that St. Paul plainly calls it a gift, when a man is given to suffer for the sake of his hope in God, as he says to the Philippians: 'For unto you it is given in the behalf of Christ, not only to believe on him, but also to suffer for his sake' (Phil. i. 29). St. Peter also writes in his Epistle: 'But and if ye suffer for righteousness' sake, happy are ye' (1 Peter iii. 14), for you are given to share in the passion of Christ.

It is not fitting that when you live spaciously you rejoice, but in afflictions are cast down and consider them foreign to the way of God. For from ages and generations His way is carved out by the cross and by death. Whence have you got this idea (of treading the way of God in comfort)? Learn from this that you are not on the way of God, but drifting aside from it, that you do not wish to follow in the footsteps of the saints, or that you intend to create a special way for yourself (to be) followed without suffering. The way of God is a daily cross. No one has ascended to heaven through easy life. We know where the easy way leads.

68. Truly righteous men always think themselves unworthy of God; and the very fact that they are truly righteous can be known from their considering themselves despicable and unworthy of God's care. They profess this both openly and in secret, taught so to do by the Holy Spirit, in order to endure labour and straitness while they are in this life. God has prepared for them a time of rest in the life to come. Therefore those who have the Lord dwelling in them do not wish to rest or be freed of suffering, although at times they are secretly granted comfort in spiritual things.

69. Such is the will of the Spirit, that those beloved by Him should live in labours. It is not the Spirit of God that dwells in those who are at rest. The sons of God are distinguished from all others by the fact that they live amid afflictions, whereas the world takes pride in luxury and repose. God does not wish those whom He loves to rest while they are in the flesh; He desires them to live, while in the world, in sorrow, hardships, labours, scarcity, nakedness, want, degradation, insults, with body hard driven and with mourning thoughts, to justify the saying: 'In the world ye shall have tribulation' (John xvi. 33). The Lord knows that those who lead a life of ease cannot abide in love of Him; so he denies them ease and its enjoyment.

70. Through love for God, such as the saints show by suffering for the sake of His name, their heart acquires the *daring* to look at God, their face uncovered, and to ask of Him with hope. Great is the power of daring prayer. Therefore, God lets His saints be tried by every kind of affliction, and lets them too have experience of His help in practice and of how greatly He takes care of them. Through trials and temptations they gain wisdom, and through experience acquire knowledge of all things to protect them from mockery by demons. If God exercised them only in that which is good, they would lack training in the other part and would be blind in battles.

71. If a man is not first tried by experience of evil, he has no taste in the good; so, when he meets with good in evil, he lacks

knowledge to make use of it, as his own property. How pleasing is knowledge derived in actual deed from experience and practice, and what power it gives to a man who has acquired it in himself through long practice; these things are learnt by those who have experienced the help of such knowledge, have seen alike the impotence of their nature and the assistance of Divine power, and are convinced. For they learn this only when, by first withholding the power of His help, God brings them to realise the impotence of their own nature, the difficulties of temptations, the cunning of the enemy, to realise what it is they are fighting, what their own nature is, how well they were protected by Divine power, how much they have advanced on the way, how high the power of God has lifted them, and how helpless they are in struggling against any passion, when this power of God is withdrawn from them. Through all this they acquire humility, draw nearer to God, begin to expect His help and to abide in prayer. Where could they have found all this, if they had not had experience of much evil through falling into this evil with God's sanction? As the Apostle says: 'And lest I should be exalted above measure through the abundance of the revelations, there was given to me a thorn in the flesh, the messenger of Satan' (2 Cor. xii. 7). But by frequent experience of Divine help in temptations, a man acquires firm faith, which makes him unafraid and gives him a good heart in trials.

72. Trial is useful to all men. Those who work are tried, that they may add to their riches; the weak are tried, that they may thereby guard themselves from harm; those sunk in sleep—to prepare them for awakening; those far away—to draw them nearer to God; those who are God's own—that they may rejoice with daring. Every son who is not trained receives without profit the riches from his Father's house. God, therefore, tempts first and oppresses, and then makes manifest His gift.

73. While a man is negligent, he fears the hour of death; when he approaches God, he fears to meet judgment; but when the whole of him is in what lies ahead, both fears become swallowed up by love. Why is this so? Because while a man remains in the knowledge and life of the flesh, death terrifies him. But when his knowledge is spiritual and he leads a righteous life, his mind is at all hours occupied with memory of future judgment; for then

he is rightly placed according to his nature, moves on the level of the soul, is concerned with his proper knowledge and life and is in a state fitting for approach to God. But when he has reached this knowledge of truth, after knowledge of Divine mysteries has been aroused in him and hope of the future has become affirmed, then love swallows both that carnal man who, like an animal, fears to be killed, and the man of reason, who fears Divine judgment. When he becomes a son, he receives the adornments of love, instead of being taught by the rod of fear, and says: 'But I and my house will serve the Lord' (Josh. xxiv. 15).

74. Blessed is he whose thought is always of God, and who ever remains with Him alone in converse with his knowledge. Joy in the Lord is stronger than this life; and whoever has acquired it, not only has no heed for sufferings, but even no regard for his own life. Love is sweeter than life, and understanding according to God, from which love is born, is still sweeter, more so than honey and the honeycomb. To love it is no hurt to suffer painful death for the beloved. Love is bred of knowledge; and knowledge of a healthy soul; health of the soul is a force, which comes from prolonged endurance.

75. Eternal life is repose in God; he who has gained repose in God regards worldly repose as superfluous.

Whether a man has received wisdom from the Spirit, he will know from wisdom itself, which, in his hidden depths and in his senses, teaches him the ways of humility.

Whether a man has attained humility, he will know if he regards it as odious for himself to serve the world by contact with it, or by word; and if the glory of this world is an abomination in his eyes.

76. Passions (in action) result from impacts, produced by the things of this world, which entice us away under pretext of the necessity to satisfy the needs of life; and these impacts will not cease so long as this world stands. But a man endowed with Divine grace, a man who has felt and experienced something higher, does not allow these impacts to enter his heart; for, in their place, another and a better desire has taken possession of him. So neither the impacts themselves nor anything derived from them, approach the heart of such a man; but they remain outside,

inactive, not because passionate impacts have ceased to exist, but because the heart which receives them is now dead to them and lives by something else; not because a man has found rest through practising good judgment and works, but because his mind is no longer troubled by anything and his consciousness is replete in the enjoyment of something else.

77. If we keep the rule of sobriety and practise good judgment with knowledge, the struggle with passionate impacts will in no way come near our mind. But entrance to the heart is denied them not as a result of struggle, but because of the repletion of consciousness and knowledge filling the soul, and because of the desire for the wonderful contemplations to be discovered in the soul.

So long as a man lives, he has need of sobriety, circumspection and alertness, to guard his treasure. But if he leaves his proper post, he becomes weak and is robbed.

One must work not only until one sees the fruits, but until one's very end. For even ripe fruit is often destroyed by hail.

78. If we train ourselves in right discrimination (in the heart), we shall feel ashamed of passions as soon as we meet them. But let us be ashamed of the approach of passions, because of their own guilt also.

79. When you desire to do something for love of God, put death as the limit of your desire. In this way you will rise in actual deed to the level of martyrdom in struggling with every passion, suffering no harm from whatever you may meet within this limit, if you endure to the end and do not weaken. The thought of a feeble reason enfeebles also the power of patience, but a steadfast mind gives strength, such as nature does not possess, even to him who follows its thought.

80. Life in this world is like writing letters on tablets: whenever a man wishes to do so, he can add to them or subtract from them, or make changes in the letters. But the future life is like writings on clean rolls sealed by the royal seal, where no adding or subtracting is allowed. Therefore, while we are still in the midst of change, let us pay attention to ourselves; and while we have power over the record of our life, which we write with our own hands, let us strive to add to it with right living and erase

from it the defects of former life. For while we are in this world, God does not affix His seal either to what is good or what is evil, up to the very moment of our exit from this life.

81. Prayer needs constant exercise to enable the mind to gain wisdom by its prolonged practice. Prayer is preceded by seclusion (solitude, withdrawal of thoughts from everything alien to it). Seclusion is necessary for prayer, and prayer for acquiring love of God; because the result of prayer is to discover reasons for loving God.

82. We must realise that all converse addressed to God and practised in secret, all the concern of a right mind for God, all meditation on spiritual things is established by prayer and goes by the name of prayer and, under this name, is brought together into one—whether you mean various readings, or the voice of your lips glorifying God, or concern and sorrowing for the sake of the Lord, or the making of bows with the body, or psalmody, or all other things which constitute the order of genuine prayer, giving birth to love of God. For love comes from prayer, and prayer from remaining in seclusion. We have need of seclusion, that we may have the possibility the more readily to converse with God.

83. Beware of self-esteem when changes for the better take place in you. Be careful to reveal to the Lord, in your prayer, your weakness and ignorance as regards this subtle self-esteem, lest you are forsaken and succumb to some shameful temptation; for to pride succeeds whoring, and to self-esteem, seduction.

84. If you pile up on one side of the scales all the rest of spiritual efforts and practices, and on the other—silence, you will find that the latter outweighs them all. Many are the counsels that men have; but if a man embraces silence, superfluous for him will be the work of keeping to them and superfluous will prove his former practices; he will prove to have surpassed these activities; for he has neared perfection.

85. Ever let mercy outweigh all else in you. Let our compassion be a mirror where we may see in ourselves that likeness and that true image which belong to the Divine nature and Divine essence. A heart hard and unmerciful will never be pure. A merciful man is the physician of his own soul; for he disperses the darkness of passions as by a strong wind blowing from within

himself. According to the living word of the Gospels this is the blessed loan made to us by God.

86. When you approach your bed, say to it: 'This very night, perchance, you will be my tomb, O bed; for I know not whether tonight, in place of a transient sleep, the eternal sleep of the future will be mine.' And so, while you still have legs, follow the path of doing, before you are tied by bonds that can never be severed. While you still have hands, crucify yourself in prayer before death comes. While you still have eyes, fill them with tears, before they are covered by dust. As a rose wilts at a breath of the wind, so at a little puff on even one of the elements of which you are composed you will die. Establish, O man, in your heart the thought that instant departure confronts you, and constantly say to yourself: 'There, already, at the door is the messenger come for me. Why am I idle? My removal is for ever; there will be no return.'

87. He who loves conversing with Christ, loves to be solitary. But he who loves to be among many is a friend of this world. If you love repentance, love silence. For outside of silence repentance does not reach perfection. If you love silence—the mother of repentance—take pleasure in the insignificant physical discomforts, reproaches, injuries such as will beset you through your silence. Adherence to silence means a constant expectation of death. He who enters upon silence without this thought cannot endure what is unavoidably connected with this way of life.

88. Let us love silence till the world is made to die in our hearts. Let us always remember death, and in this thought draw near to God in our heart—and the pleasures of this world will have our scorn.

89. One man who practised silence said: 'I practise silence, that the verses of my readings and prayers should fill me with delight. And when the pleasure of understanding them silences my tongue, then, as in a dream, I enter a state when my senses and thoughts are concentrated. Then, when with prolonging of this silence the turmoil of memories is stilled in my heart, ceaseless waves of joy are sent me by inner thoughts, beyond expectation suddenly arising to delight my heart.'

90. Another one said: 'Silence cuts off pretexts and causes for

new thoughts, while within one's walls it withers and wilts memories of things which used to concern us. When the old matters wither in the thought, the mind, in setting them aright, returns to its proper dignity.'

91. Yet another one says: 'Choose for yourself a doing which delights—constant vigil by night, when all the fathers used to put off the old Adam and were granted renewal of the mind. During these hours the soul feels immortal life and this feeling divests it of the garments of darkness; and the soul receives into itself the Holy Spirit.'

92. And: 'It is impossible to subjugate these (external) senses to the authority of the soul without silence and withdrawal from men; for since the rational soul is essentially linked and conjoined with these senses, it is involuntarily carried away by them and by its own thoughts suggested by them, unless a man keeps sobriety in secret prayer.'

93. Just as the ear of chastity grows from the seed of the sweat of fasts, so satiety yields the burning of lust, and excess yields impurity. If the stomach is meek and hungry, shameful thoughts cannot enter the soul.

94. O chastity, how greatly is your beauty enhanced by lying on bare earth, by hunger that banishes sleep, by sufferings of the body which, through abstinence from food, seems to have a deep moat between ribs and belly! All food we take in and all pandering to the flesh produce in us shameful images and unseemly fantasies; once born, they incite us to incline secretly towards shameful actions. But an empty stomach makes of our ideas a desert land, silent and undisturbed by any turbulent thought.

95. *Some necessary directions for those who practise silence.*

If during the various offices you keep your mind from wandering, as far as is possible, and a verse suddenly breaks off on your tongue, laying on your soul the bonds of speechlessness, and this happens independently of your free will and comes after a prolonged period of silence, then know that you are making progress in your silence, and that meekness has begun to deepen in you. For bare silence is truly worthy of censure.

If you notice in your soul that with each arising thought, each memory and contemplation which occurs in your silence, your eyes become filled with tears, and tears run freely down your cheeks, then know that the barrier before you has begun to break down, to the confusion of the enemies.

If you find that at times your thought plunges deep into yourself, without your premeditation and outside of the usual order, and if it remains in this state for about an hour, or for some time, and if later you notice that peace reigns in your thoughts, and this experience is always repeated, then know that the cloud has begun to cover your tabernacle of witness (Ex. xl. 34).

If, when you have undertaken this work, you do not find peace from the passions which trouble you, do not be surprised. The bosom of the world remains long in darkness after the rays of the sun have left it; the smell of medicaments and the perfume of incense hang long in the air before they disperse and disappear. How much more so is it with passions: they are like dogs, accustomed to lick the blood in a butcher's shop; when they are not given their usual meal, they stand and bark, until the strength of their former habit is destroyed.

When you are moving forward, you will discover in your soul the following clear evidence: you will be strengthened in all things by hope and enriched by prayer; when you meet people and feel the weakness of human nature, your mind will never lack what will serve usefully in every case (each such case will protect you from pride); shortcomings of your neighbour will cease to be worthy of attention in your eyes; you will long to leave this body with the same intensity of desire with which you long to be in the life to come; you will regard every painful occurrence that may befall you, secretly or openly, as something just and deserved, and will give thanks to God.

96. Passions are brought into motion either by images, or by sensations devoid of images and by memory, which at first is unaccompanied by passionate movements or thoughts, but which later produces excitation.

97. Constant vigil with reading, followed by frequent bowings, will not fail to give peace of heart to the diligent. Those who have gained this peace, have gained it precisely by this means. Those who wish to gain it anew must practise silence together with the foregoing practices. But above all their thought must become

attached to nothing except their own soul; they must practise inner doing and as regards activities must choose precisely those which particularly evoke that specific feeling that strengthens our good state.

98. Every rational being suffers changes without number, and every man is different from hour to hour. A man of discrimination can verify this by putting himself to the test. If he practises sobriety and observes himself with his mind, he will easily see how his thought changes, what this change is, how his peaceful disposition is suddenly disrupted and what is the cause.

St. Macarius wrote of this in his direction to the brethren, admonishing them not to be cast into despair when a change for the worse occurs. For even those who have reached the level of purity constantly descend from a better to a worse state, just as the air at times grows cooler, although they continue to be diligent and allow no self-indulgence. Even when they observe the right discipline, these downfalls occur with them, against their own will.

The blessed Mark asserts the same, saying: 'Changes occur in everyone, as they do in the air.' In *everyone*, that is, not only in the worst and lowest, but also in the perfect. Just as in nature cold is followed by heat, and hail by fine weather, so it is in our work: now there is warfare, now grace comes to our aid; sometimes the soul is tossed about and cruel waves rise against it—then again there is a change, for grace descends and fills a man's heart with joy and God's peace, with chaste and serene thoughts.

99. Thus, when you are storm-beaten, do not despair; and when peace dwells in you, do not get exalted. On the contrary, it is better to examine in yourself the unseemly images and impure thoughts which took root in your mind during the storm, when your thoughts were in turmoil and disorder. Reflect how quickly you inclined towards passions and conversed with them in the darkness of your mind; and realise that all this was sent to make us humble by Divine Providence, which cares for each one of us and provides what is useful for every man.

100. Humility even without efforts gains forgiveness for many trespasses; but without humility even efforts are vain and may lead to much harm. What salt is for any food, humility is for

every virtue. To acquire it, a man must always think of himself
with contrition, self-belittlement and painful self-judgment. But
if we acquire it, it will make us sons of God.

101. The Lord directed us to seek support for our weakness in
prayer, saying: awake, 'watch and pray, that ye enter not into
temptation' (Matt. xxvi. 41). Pray, do not be idle, at all times
'Continue in prayer, and watch in the same' (Col. iv. 2). 'Ask,
and it shall be given you; seek, and ye shall find; knock, and it
shall be opened unto you: For every one that asketh receiveth;
and he that seeketh findeth; and to him that knocketh it shall be
opened' (Matt. vii. 7, 8). But most of all He confirmed His words
and urged us to greater diligence by the parable of a man, who
came to his friend at midnight and asked him for three loaves.
The Lord said: 'I say unto you, Though he will not rise and give
him, because he is his friend, yet because of his importunity he
will rise and give him as many as he needeth' (Luke xi. 8). So
pray, and be not negligent. What a wonderful incitement to
daring!

102. The Lord knows that until we are dead He will not deprive us of the possibility of going astray, that this change is very
close to us, namely, the passage from virtue to vice, and that man
and his nature may absorb what runs counter to them. Therefore
He has commanded us to be diligent and to practise ceaseless
prayer. He commanded us to pray not only for self-protection
against a manifest change, but also because what we are always
meeting is subtle and incomprehensible, and cannot be embraced
by the knowledge of our mind in the states in which we often
involuntarily find ourselves. For, although thoughts may be quite
steadfast and cleave to good, God's Providence frequently leaves
us in the realm of temptations, and casts us therein, as the blessed
Paul says: 'There was given to me a thorn in the flesh' (2 Cor.
xii. 7–9).

103. This world is a contest and a field for contest. This time
is the time of struggle. And there is no law laid down in the time
of struggle and the time of contest; that is, the King lays no limit
on His warriors until the contest is over; then every man will be
brought to the doors of the King of kings and there tried as to
whether he has gained victory in the contest, or has turned his

back. There is only one law there—to watch and to resist. So let us not be negligent in prayer, let us not be lazy in asking help of the Lord, since without Him we can do nothing pleasing to Him. Let us hold firm to the thought that while we are in this world, and remain in the flesh, even though we be exalted to the vault of heaven, we cannot exist without work and labours, or be without care.

104. Perfection in the field of contest consists in repentance, purity and self-perfecting. (A man who has repented begins to struggle with passions—and struggles with them until his heart is purified: purification of the heart is the end of the struggle and the door to the realm of perfection.)

105. Someone was asked: 'What is repentance?' He answered: 'Renouncing what was before and deploring it'; also: 'A humble and contrite heart.'

106. Again he was asked: 'How can a man acquire humility?' He said: 'By constant remembrance of one's trespasses and of the nearness of death, by poor clothes, by always preferring the last place and by gladly undertaking the lowest and most degrading tasks on every occasion: by not being disobedient, by keeping silence, by not liking to go to meetings, by wishing to remain unknown and not elected for any post, by never keeping a single thing entirely at his own disposal, by hating conversations with a number of people, and by not liking gains, and above all by being in his mind above blaming and accusing any man, and above envy —by not being a man who lays his hand on others but who suffers the hands of others being laid on him, and does his own work in solitude and carries no cares in the world except himself. To be more brief: the life of a stranger in this world, poverty and solitude—these are the things which give birth to humility and purify the heart.'

107. The sign of having reached perfection is this: if a man were to be condemned ten times a day to be burned alive for loving his neighbours, and yet not be content with this, as was shown by Moses (Ex. xxxii. 32), Paul (Rom. ix. 3) and other apostles. God surrendered His own Son to death on the cross, through love for His creatures. If He had something more precious to give, He would have given it to us, to make our race His own.

Imitating Him, all the saints, in pursuit of perfection, strive to emulate God by the perfection of their love for their neighbour.

108. No one can ascend to the level of this love unless a secret feeling of hope is born in him. Those who love this world cannot acquire love for men. When a man acquires this love, then he is clothed both in this love and in God Himself. And he who has acquired God must not only refuse to gain anything else in addition, but must divest himself even of his own body. But if a man is clothed in love for this world and this life, he will not be clothed in God until he abandons it all. For God Himself has testified to this, saying: 'If any man come to me and hate not . . . his own life' renouncing all things, 'he cannot be my disciple' (Luke xiv. 26). It is needful not only to renounce, but to hate it.

109. Why is hope so sweet, and why does it make all efforts easy?—Because at such a moment a natural desire (for good being) awakes in the soul of the saints, while hope gives them to drink of it abundantly from its cup, and quenches their thirst. Hence they no longer feel the hardships of labour, but become insensitive to efforts and griefs, and throughout their whole progress think that they walk on air, and do not tread the path with human feet; for they see not the hardships of the way, no mountains or rivers bar their path, and the rough places become plain (Isaiah xl. 4). Their attention is on the Father's bosom, and at every moment hope itself directs their vision, as with a pointing finger, towards the distant goal, invisible, yet seen by the hidden eyes of faith, while desire for this distant goal sets aflame all parts of their souls like a fire. Thither alone is every thought directed, and thither they all hasten to attain. Hope so inflames them, as with fire, that they can give themselves no rest, but press forward with joy, ceaselessly and impetuously.

110. Passionlessness means not only not feeling passions, but also not accepting them within. Owing to the many and various virtues, both evident and hidden, acquired by the saints, passions are withered in them and so cannot easily arise against the soul, and their mind has no need to be on constant watch for them; for it is at all times filled with thoughts, which are consciously evoked in their reason by meditations and conversations on the most excellent qualities. As soon as passions begin to stir, the mind is

suddenly ravished away from them by some understanding which has penetrated it; and, according to the blessed Mark, passions remain in them, as it were, idle.

111. If, by the grace of God, a mind is occupied with performing virtuous deeds and has approached knowledge, it is little affected by what constitutes the bad and foolish part of the soul. For knowledge ravishes it on high and estranges it from all that is in the world. Owing to the purity of the saints, the subtlety, acuteness and quickness of their mind, and also owing to their work and achievement, their mind is purified and becomes illumined, as their flesh becomes drained. Because of their training in silence and its long practice, they speedily and easily attain to inner contemplation and are filled with wonder at what is revealed. They are wont to abound in contemplations, their mind never lacks for subjects of understanding, and they are never left without that which produces in them the fruits of the spirit. Long experience erases from their hearts recollections, which evoke passions there, and the power of the devil grows weaker. For when the soul does not befriend passions by thinking of them, then, since it is constantly occupied with another concern, the power of passions can no longer hold the spiritual senses of the soul in its claws.

112. Just as self-esteem ravishes the soul aloft and gives it freedom to float amid the clouds of its thoughts and to wander all over creation; so humility collects the soul into singleness by silence—and makes it concentrate within itself. As the soul, living in the body, is hidden from sight and communion with people; so a truly humble man not only does not wish to be seen or known by others, but more, his will is to plunge away from himself into himself, to become nothing, as if not existing, not yet come into being. And while such a man is hidden, enclosed within himself and withdrawn from the world, he remains wholly with his Lord.

113. A humble man never stops to look at gatherings, crowds, excitements, noise, merrymaking; he does not pay attention to words, conversations, calls or anything that disperses the senses; he is not wishful to possess many things and be constantly occupied with activities, but wants to be always free, without cares, that he may keep his thoughts from going out of him. For he is sure that

if he becomes involved in many things, he will be unable to keep
his thoughts undisturbed, since numerous activities produce many
cares and a swarm of complicated thoughts; and this opens the
door to passions, banishes calm discrimination and closes the door
to peace. Therefore a humble man protects himself from all the
multiple, and thus ever remains in stillness, quiet, peace, modesty
and reverence.

114. A humble man is never hurried, hasty or perturbed,
never has any hot or flitting thoughts, but at all times remains
calm. Nothing can ever surprise, disturb or dismay him, for he
suffers neither fear nor change in tribulations, neither surprise nor
elation in enjoyment. All his joy and gladness are in what is
pleasing to his Lord.

115. A humble man does not dare even to pray or petition God
about something, and does not know what to ask for; he simply
keeps all his senses silent and waits only for mercy and for whatever the Most Worshipful Majesty may be pleased to send him.
When he bows down with his face to the earth, and the inner·eyes
of his heart are raised to the gates of the Holy of Holies, where He
dwells Whose abode is—darkness, before Whom the Seraphims
close their eyes, he dares only to speak and pray thus: 'May Thy
will be done upon me, O Lord!'

116. Walk before God in simplicity, and not in subtleties of
the mind. Simplicity brings faith; but subtle and intricate speculations bring conceit; and conceit brings withdrawal from God.

117. When you face God in prayer, become in your thought
like a speechless babe. Do not utter before God anything which
comes from knowledge, but approach Him with childlike
thoughts, and so walk before Him as to be granted that fatherly
care, which fathers give their children in their infancy. It is said:
'The Lord preserves the simple' (Ps. cxiv. 6), not only those who
are small in body, but also the wise in the world, who have renounced their knowledge and become babes by their own will, so
as to learn that all-sufficing Wisdom, which is not acquired by
book-learning. Beg of God that He may grant you to come to the
measure of such faith. Pray for it diligently, ask for it fervently,
implore with great zeal, until you receive it. You will be granted
this boon, if first you force yourself with faith to place all your

cares on God, and exchange your own stewardship for God's providence. And when God sees that this is your will, that with all purity of thought you place more trust in Him than in yourself and have forced yourself to put more hope in God than in your soul, then that unknowable power will come to dwell in you and you will clearly and without doubt be conscious that this power is with you; that power in consciousness of which many go through fire and are not afraid, and walk upon waters with thought unharassed by fear of drowning.

118. Does it not seem to you that by some men this spiritual knowledge may be acquired through natural knowledge? Not only is it impossible that this spiritual knowledge should be received by natural knowledge, but it cannot even be experienced in feeling by a man who zealously exercises himself in natural knowledge. If any such wishes to approach this other, spiritual knowledge, he can come no nearer to it until he renounces natural knowledge, with all its subtle twistings and manifold methods, and until he brings himself to the state of mind of a child. On the contrary, the habits and ideas of natural knowledge are a great hindrance for him, until he has succeeded little by little in effacing them. This spiritual knowledge is simple and does not shine in natural thoughts. Until the mind is freed from the multitudes of thoughts and has achieved the single simplicity of purity, it cannot experience spiritual knowledge.

119. Once you have trusted yourself to the Lord, Who is all-sufficient to protect you and look after you, do not return to cares of this kind, but say to your soul: 'In all things He, to Whom I have once entrusted my soul, suffices for me. I do not exist here; He knows this.' Then you will indeed witness God's miracles, you will see how, at all times, God is near to save those who fear Him, and how His Providence encompasses them, though it remains unseen. But, because the Protector, Who is with you, is unseen by physical eyes, you must not doubt, and think He is not there; for He often becomes manifest even to physical eyes, to gladden you.

120. As soon as a man rejects all visible help and human hope, and follows after God with faith and a pure heart, grace straightway follows after him and reveals its power in help of various

kinds. First it reveals its power in visible things relating to the body, and helps man by ministering to it, in order that he should experience most forcefully the power of Divine Providence, which takes care of him. Having experienced help in what is visible, he becomes convinced of help in what is hidden, for here grace makes plain before him the intricacies of difficult thoughts and ideas, and so man easily discovers their meaning, their mutual relationship, their delusiveness, and how they arise from one another—and harm the soul. At the same time grace puts to shame before his eyes all the wiles of the demons and points, as with a finger, to what he would have suffered had he remained ignorant. Then is born in him the thought that he must entreat his Creator by prayer for everything both great and small.

121. When the grace of God strengthens the thought that he should put his trust in God in all this, then, little by little, he begins to enter into temptations. And grace allows temptations corresponding to his stature to be sent him, that he should bear their force. In these temptations help comes to him in an evident manner, to give him good heart, until he gradually learns his lesson, acquires wisdom, and begins to despise his enemies in his trust in God. For a man cannot become wise in spiritual warfare, know his Protector, be aware of his God and become inwardly affirmed in his faith in Him, except in proportion to the strength of the trial he has endured.

122. As soon as grace notices that a shade of doubt has entered a man's thoughts and he has begun to think highly of himself, it immediately lets the temptations, which assail him, multiply and gain strength, until he realises his weakness and again clutches at God in humility.

123. Do not be surprised that when you draw near to virtue, grievous and intense tribulations come to you on all sides: for virtue is not considered virtue, if it does not involve hard work. This is why St. John (Kolobos, or the Prophet) said: 'It is usual for virtue to encounter difficulties; virtue attached to ease is worthy of condemnation.' And the blessed Mark says: 'Every virtue made perfect is called a cross, when it fulfils the command-ment of the Spirit.' The Apostle teaches that: 'All that will live godly' in fear of the Lord and 'in Christ Jesus shall suffer

persecution' (2 Tim. iii. 12). And the Lord says: only 'whosoever will lose his life for my sake shall find it' (Matt. xvi. 25). Therefore to begin with He offers you a cross, so that you should first dedicate yourself to it, and only later send your soul to follow after Him.

124. Nothing is stronger than desperation. It knows no conqueror, whether from the right or the left. When in his thought a man deprives his life of hope, nothing can equal him in daring. No enemy can resist him, and no rumour of affliction can weaken his resolution; for every affliction which may come is lighter than death, whereas he has bent his head to receive death.

125. At all times, the hope of ease has been wont to make men forget what is great, good and virtuous. Both in the past and now, it is this and nothing else, that has deprived men of force, so that not only do they not gain victory, but are even despoiled of their best. In short, if a man neglects the kingdom of heaven, it is only through hope of some small comfort in this life. Who does not know that birds approach the net in the hope of finding rest?

126. When the mind becomes eager for virtue, then too the outer senses allow no hardship to overcome them. When the heart becomes fervent with the spirit, then the body is not vexed by afflictions, nor visited by fear, and shrinks from no terrors; for then the mind is adamant, and firm enough to oppose all temptations. So let us be fervent—and negligence, which engenders laziness, will flee from us. Fervour gives birth to courage and gives the soul victorious power. What power of the demons is strong enough to withstand the natural fervour which the soul hurls against them?

127. Our ancient fathers knew that our mind cannot always stand in one place and keep its vigil, that at times it cannot even detect what it is that harms it. Therefore they embraced poverty as a weapon and withdrew into the wilderness, where are no human occupations causing passions, that they might have no occasions for irritation, desires, resentment. Thus they protected and strengthened themselves against it all, using the wilderness as an impregnable tower.

128. When a man lives in poverty, the thought of leaving this world constantly comes to him, and he takes ceaseless care to

prepare for it; he shuns all ease, the thought of scorning the world is lively in his mind, his heart grows steadfast to meet dangers without fear, he is not afraid of death, since his eyes are turned towards it at all hours; if he meets with afflictions, he accepts them with gladness and joy, knowing that they bring crowns. But if he happens to acquire something transient, at that very same moment love for the body begins to awaken in his soul, and thoughts arise about physical ease and the means to get all that serves it: then steadfastness of heart is taken from him, steadfastness such as he had when in his detachment from possessions he was above the world; then his soul begins to be agitated by thoughts which bring fear for his life, since a firm trust in God has withdrawn from him.

129. *Various sayings*

As a man whose head is under water cannot inhale pure air, so a man, whose thoughts are plunged into the cares of this world, cannot absorb the sensations of that new world.

As poisonous stench upsets the physical organism, so does an unseemly sight the peace of the mind.

As glass cannot remain whole when it hits a stone, so, if a saint spends a long time in converse with a woman, he cannot remain pure and undefiled.

As trees are wrenched from their roots by a strong and constant flow of water, so love for the world is uprooted in the heart by a flow of temptations surging against the body.

As bitter medicines destroy the impurity of bad juices in the body, so grievous afflictions purify the heart from evil passions.

As a man cannot remain unscathed who spares his enemy on the field of battle, so a man engaged in spiritual warfare cannot save his soul if he spares his body.

As a young girl, frightened by some terrifying sight, runs to her parents, clutches their garments and cries for help, so too with the soul; the more it is oppressed and driven by fear of temptations, the more it hastens to cling to God, invoking Him in ceaseless prayer. So long as, one after another, temptations continue to afflict it, it increases its supplications; but as soon as it is granted a respite, it gives itself up to dissipation of thoughts.

As a man who has brought a great gift to the king is rewarded by a gracious look, so, if a man's prayer is accompanied by tears, the great King of ages, God, forgives him the full measure of his sins and rewards him with a benevolent look.

As a man who carries a precious pearl on a road infested with brigands is in constant fear of being attacked and robbed, so a man who carries the pearls of chastity and journeys in the world—this road swarming with enemies—cannot be free from fear of these robbers, until he reaches the sanctuary of the tomb, that is, the land of repose.

As a man, who drinks wine on a day of mourning, becomes intoxicated and forgets to mourn the sadness of his situation, so a man intoxicated with love of God forgets in this world, that is, in this house of weeping, all his hardships and sorrows and, in his intoxication, becomes insensitive to all sinful passions. His heart is strengthened by hope in God, his soul is as light as a feathered bird, his mind constantly soars above the earth, his thoughts hover far above all that is human, and he enjoys immortality with the Most High.

130. Humility is the garment of the Deity. The incarnate Word was clothed in it and, through it, conversed with us in our bodies, covering the radiance of His greatness and His glory by this humility, lest the creature be scorched by the sight of Him. The creature could not have looked at Him, had He not taken on some part of it, and thus conversed with it. Therefore every man who clothes himself in garments of humility becomes clothed in Christ Himself, since Christ desired to be clothed also in His inner man in that likeness, in which He was seen by His creature and in which He lived with it.

131. Humility is a certain mysterious force, which perfected saints receive when they have completed their life. This force is given by the power of grace only to those who are perfect in virtue, for this virtue includes all in itself.

132. Not every man who is modest, silent and meek has attained to the level of humility; nor likewise a man who is humbled by the recollection of his trespasses and is filled with contrition about them, although such a thing is indeed praiseworthy. Such a man does not yet have humility, but strives to approach it—he only desires humility, but does not yet possess it.

A man who has perfect humility has no need to invent reasons for being humble, but shows humility without effort or self-compelling.

133. If anyone should ask how to acquire humility, we would answer: 'It is enough for the disciple that he be as his master, and the servant as his lord' (Matt. x. 25). See how much humility was shown by Him Who has given us this commandment and Who gives us this gift; imitate Him and you will acquire it.

134. We must try in every way to avoid all that excites evil passions in us, but above all to cut off the causes of passions in ourselves and that which brings even the least passion into motion. But if, despite this, passions start moving, we must resist them and fight against them. The best method to achieve both alike is to plunge deep into the inner man and remain there in seclusion, constantly tending the vineyard of one's heart. When our mind remains there in solitude and seclusion, it is grace and not the mind, which wages war against passions.

135. The purpose of the advent of the Saviour, when He gave us His life-giving commandments as purifying remedies in our passionate state, was to cleanse the soul from the damage done by the first transgression and bring it back to its original state. What medicines are for a sick body, that the commandments are for the passionate soul. It is clear that commandments are directed against passions, for curing the delinquent soul.

136. Harm has come to us from transgressing the commandments. It follows, therefore, that health is restored by keeping them. Without keeping commandments, without first of all following this road which leads to purity of soul, we must not even hope or aspire for the soul to be purified. Do not say that God can grant us purification of soul through grace, even without our keeping the commandments. This is for the Lord to judge, and the Church does not direct that we should ask for such a thing. The Jews, at the time of their return from Babylon to Jerusalem, travelled by the natural way; but Ezekiel arrived there by supernatural means and it was by Divine revelation that he was made a witness of the renewal that was to come. So too with purity of soul. Some going by the road that many have trodden, through keeping commandments, in a life of many labours, arrive by sweat

and blood at purity of soul; others are granted it by the gift of grace. The wonderful thing is that it is not permissible to ask in prayer for purity to be granted us by grace, nor to refuse to lead a life of practising the commandments. For when the rich man asked the Lord: 'Master, what shall I do to inherit eternal life?' (Luke x. 25) the Lord said clearly: keep the commandments. When the rich man persisted, wishing to know more, He said: 'If thou wilt be perfect, go and sell that thou hast, and give to the poor, and thou shalt have treasure in heaven: and come and follow me' (Matt. xix. 21). This means: become dead to all that you have, and then live in Me; depart from the old world of passions, then enter the new world of the spirit. For by saying: Take up your cross (Matt. xvi. 24), the Lord taught man to die to all things in the world. And when a man has killed the old man in himself, or his passions, He says to him: 'Follow me.' The old man cannot go the way of Christ.

137. The blessed Basil the Great and the two blessed Gregorys, who were lovers of the wilderness and praised silence, did not embrace silence before exercising themselves in the performance of commandments, but first lived in the world and kept the commandments as they must be kept by those living with others, and then they arrived at purity of soul and were granted spiritual contemplation. Only then did they hasten and go out into the wilderness and a life of silence, to abide thenceforth with their inner man; thus the eyes of their mind were opened and they remained in spiritual contemplation until grace called them to be shepherds of the Church of Christ.

138. The wilderness puts passions to sleep. But not this alone is demanded of man—to put passions to sleep; he must also uproot them, that is, master them when they stubbornly persist against us. And sleeping passions awake as soon as they meet with a cause which moves them to action. So let us desire the wilderness not only because it puts passions to sleep; but let us desire that, being deprived of the sensory and far from all men, we should acquire wisdom there; let us desire the renewal of our inner spiritual man in Christ; let us wish at all hours to watch over ourselves, let our mind be awake, ever ready to protect itself, and let it never be robbed of the memory of its hope.

139. That we might have likeness to our great Father in heaven, our Lord commanded us to be merciful, but monks prefer silence to mercy. How can this be reconciled?

Our Lord commanded us to be merciful, that we might have likeness to our Father in heaven, because the merciful draw near to God. When we, monks, revere silence, we do not exclude mercy but strive, as far as we can, to withdraw from vain cares and turmoil. It is not our aim to go against our duty (towards our neighbours), but we practise silence in order to keep our thoughts on God, which, more than all else, can restore us to our purity and bring us nearer to God. If it should happen that for a certain time the brethren have urgent need of us, we must not neglect this need. So let us constantly urge ourselves to be inwardly merciful to every rational creature. For so we are taught by the Lord, and it is this, and not something empty, that characterises our silence. And it is needful not merely to preserve this inner mercy of ours, but, when circumstances demand, not to neglect to give proof of one's love outwardly as well.

140. The Lifegiver resumed the fullness of the commandments in two which embrace all the rest—love of God, and a like love of God's image. The first satisfies the purpose of spiritual contemplation; the second—of contemplation and activity. For the essence of God is simple, invisible and has essentially no need of anything; and consciousness, when plunged into itself, has essentially no need of bodily activity in relation to God; its activity in this is simple and is manifested in but one part of the mind, corresponding to the simplicity of that worshipful Cause, which is above physical senses. And the second commandment, that is, love of men, owing to the duality of nature demands that what we fulfil invisibly in consciousness, we should likewise wish to fulfil in the flesh.

Since activity always precedes contemplation, it is impossible for any man to rise to the realm of the higher, unless he first fulfils by activity what is lower. No man has the right to say about love of neighbour that he progresses in it in his soul, if he neglects that part of it which is fulfilled by the body, in accordance with his strength and the time and place. For only this can prove that perfect love exists in a man. And if we are faithful and true in this, as far as we can be, our soul is given power to stretch upwards to the great realm of high Divine contemplation in simple and quite incomparable apprehensions. Where there is no possibility to express love of neighbour in physical visible actions, then it is enough before God for love of neighbours to be practised only in the soul.

141. He who wishes to love God above all else must take care of the purity of his soul; and purity of soul is acquired by overcoming and destroying passions. Passions are a door closed in the face of purity. Unless a man opens this closed door, he will not enter into the pure and chaste realm of the heart. And without this the soul cannot have daring in the hour of prayer; for this daring is the fruit of purity and of the labours to acquire it. This is the order in which it is all done: patience, joined with self-compulsion, does battle against passions for the sake of purity; if the soul overcomes passions, it acquires purity; and true purity endows the mind with daring in the hour of prayer.

142. Let us give up praying God for something high; but, above all, let us acquire patience to endure everything that befalls us; and in great humility and contrition for what is in us and for our thoughts, let us beg for remission of our sins and for peace of the soul. One of the fathers wrote: 'If a man does not count himself a sinner, his prayer is not accepted by the Lord.' It is written: 'The kingdom of God cometh not with observation' (Luke xvii. 20). On our side let us make every effort to put in good order the realm of our heart by deeds of repentance and a life pleasing to God; and what is of God will come by itself, if the place in the heart is pure and undefiled. To seek things 'with observation,' that is, high Divine gifts, is not approved by the Church of God; and those who have received them acquired pride and downfall. And this is not a sign that a man loves God, but a disease of the soul. How can we seek high Divine gifts, when Paul boasts of afflictions, and counts it a high gift of God to share in the sufferings of Christ.

143. So long as the soul is sick with passions, its senses have no perception of the spiritual; and the soul does not even know how to desire it, but desires it only from hearsay and writings. The power of the soul is cured of these diseases by the hidden practice

of commandments, with sharing in Christ's passion. Originally, our nature received renewal through the Incarnation of Christ, and became a participant of Christ's passion and death; and then, after renewal, it became sanctified by the shedding of blood, and able to receive new and perfect commandments. Now if these commandments had been given to men before the shedding of blood, before our nature had been renewed and sanctified, then it is possible that even the new commandments, like those of old, would have merely cut off vice in the soul, but would have been unable to destroy the very root of vices in it. But now it is not so; now secret doing and the new and spiritual commandments, which the soul keeps with fear of God, renew and sanctify the soul and secretly restore health to all its members. For it is clear to all which passion is silently cured in the soul by each commandment, and their effectiveness is evident both to the healer and the healed, as it was with the woman who had an issue of blood.

144. The passionate part of the soul can be made whole also by grace, as happened with the blessed apostles. But this is the result of a special Divine choice; as a rule the soul is made sound by means that conform to the law. In other words, if, by practice of commandments and the difficult labours of true living, a man overcomes passions, he thereby gains health of the soul by unexceptional means conforming to the law; he receives milk from outside the materiality of this world, he has cut off his former character and is reborn, as at first, in the spiritual; and when by grace he has received the apprehensions of the inner man, he becomes visible in the realm of the spirit, and through grace receives into himself the new world, that is not multiple.

145. When mind is renewed and heart sanctified, then all the apprehensions, which arise in a man, correspond to the nature of the world he enters. First there arises in him love for the Divine and desire for communion with the angels and for revelation of the mysteries of spiritual knowledge. His mind experiences spiritual knowledge of creatures and in it is lit the light of contemplation of the mysteries of the Holy Trinity and likewise the mysteries of the Divine dispensation for our sakes; and later it enters into complete union and therewith knows hope of the future.

146. If a soul confined in the realm of passions could truly understand the spiritual, it would have no need to question and speculate on the mysteries of the spiritual world. But it is clear that learning and knowledge bring no profit if passions are present, and do not suffice to open the door that is closed in the face of purity. But when passions are removed from the soul, then the mind is illumined, set in a pure place in our being, and has need no longer of questions; since it clearly sees the blessings which can be gained in this place. For, just as the outer senses need not be taught to sense the beings and things with which they come into contact, but each sense naturally perceives what it meets with; so you should form the same picture of spiritual contemplation. For if the mind, in gazing at the hidden mysteries of the spirit, is in its natural state of health, it clearly sees the glory of Christ; it does not question, does not have to learn, but delights in the mysteries of the new world, above freedom of will, according to the warmth of its faith and hope in Christ.

147. If you wish the mysteries of the new world to dwell in your heart, first enrich yourself with physical works, fast, vigil, service, effort, patience, subjugation of thoughts and so forth. Fetter your mind by reading the Scriptures and entering deeply into them, keep the commandments written before your eyes, and by constant prayerful converse and going deeply into yourself in prayer, uproot from your heart every image and every likeness you have received in the past. Accustom your mind always to go deeply into the mysteries of our Saviour's dispensation; cease asking for knowledge and contemplation which, in their own place and at their own time, exceed all description by words, and persist in the practice of commandments and the labours of acquiring purity, and beg the Lord to grant you a wise way of living. The beginning, middle and end of such living is the following: renunciation of all things by union with Christ. If you wish to contemplate mysteries, cultivate the commandments in yourself by actual practice, and not merely by aspiring to know them. Spiritual contemplation acts in us in a realm of purity.

148. The contemplation belonging to the sons of the mystery of faith is conjoined with faith and grazes in the pasture of the

Scriptures. Words, which knowledge cannot grasp, become comprehensible to us with the aid of faith, and we receive the knowledge of them in that contemplation, which follows purification. In respect of the spiritual mysteries, which are above knowledge and which cannot be apprehended by the physical senses or the reasoning power of our mind, God has given us faith, by which we learn only that these mysteries exist. But this faith gives birth to hope (hope, that is, of understanding them). By faith we profess that God is the Lord, the Almighty, Creator and Maker of all things. Thereupon, urged by conscience, we decide that we must keep His commandments and understand that fear keeps the old commandments, but that love keeps the life-giving commandments of Christ, as the Lord says: 'If ye love me, keep my commandments. And I will pray the Father, and he shall give you another Comforter' (John xiv. 15, 16). The coming of the Comforter means the gift of the revelation of spiritual mysteries; therefore in receiving the Spirit, Who entered the Apostles, lies the whole perfection of spiritual knowledge. The Lord promised to pray His Father to give them a Comforter, to abide with them for ever, provided they followed the commandments and purified themselves. Thus you see that, as a reward for keeping the commandments, the mind is granted the grace of mysterious contemplation and the revelations of spiritual knowledge.

149. The keeping of commandments has this power when it is done for love of their Bestower, and not from fear. Therefore the rightful door leading to contemplation is love. In all ascents to revelations of knowledge and to contemplations of the mysteries, it is Divine love that leads in and out those who have acquired it. So first we must acquire love, and thereupon contemplation of the spiritual will be natural for us. Realise the wisdom of the blessed Paul when, putting aside all the gifts bestowed by grace, he asked for the most essential—the one by which all gifts are received and preserved, that is, love (1 Cor. xiii.). Love is the place of revelations; and in this place contemplation is revealed to us by itself. Just as with the progress of natural growth the soul receives more and more knowledge about things existing in the world, and learns new things from day to day; so in spiritual things a man receives spiritual contemplation and Divine perception, and learns

this in proportion to the growth of his mind in wise living. And when it comes to the realm of love, it contemplates the spiritual in its rightful place.

150. So long as a man makes efforts, striving to force the spiritual to come down to him, it resists. And if in his arrogance he dares to lift his eyes to the spiritual and strives to reach it by his understanding out of its proper time, his sight soon becomes dimmed and, instead of reality, he sees images and phantoms. As soon as you realise this by discrimination and reflection, you will cease to aspire to contemplation out of its proper time. If it should seem to you that even now (before you have entered the realm of purity and love), something you see is contemplation, this contemplation is but the shadow of a phantom, and not contemplation. For everything immaterial has a likeness and an illusory image—but there can also be true contemplation. Even in the natural order one sometimes sees what is real, and at other times its opposite—instead of reality the eye sees a shadow, sees water where there is no water, sees buildings suspended in the air, when in fact they stand on the ground. By the example of these material phenomena, judge also of what is immaterial.

151. If the sight of the mind is not cleansed by practice of commandments and by the works of a life of silence, if it does not gain the light of love in its perfection and grow in stature to renewal in Christ, it cannot become a true seer of Divine contemplation. And all likenesses of spiritual things, which the mind may try to conceive for itself, are called illusion, and not reality. The fact that the mind sees one thing instead of another is due to its not being purified. The same thing happened to profane philosophers who regarded as spiritual that about which they had no true teaching from God—and who discoursed on those things with unseemly presumption, divided the one God into many gods, spoke and agreed among themselves in blasphemous thoughts and called this insane fantasy of their thoughts a doctrine of nature.

152. True contemplation of natures, both sensory and supersensory, and of the Holy Trinity Itself, is given in the Revelation of Christ. Christ taught and showed it to men when at the outset, by His Hypostasy, He accomplished the renewal of man's nature,

restored and gave man his original freedom, and Himself paved the way by which we can ascend to Truth through His life-giving commandments. Our nature is capable of seeing true, and not illusory, contemplation only after a man has shed the old passionate man by enduring sufferings, effort and grief, as a new born babe sheds the covering which emerges from the mother's womb. Then the mind, spiritually reborn, becomes capable of receiving the contemplation of its birthplace.

153. This contemplation serves as food for the mind until it becomes able to receive contemplation of a kind higher than the first. For one contemplation passes a man on to another contemplation, until finally the mind is led into the realm of perfect love. Love is the dwellingplace of the spiritual and comes to dwell in a pure soul. When the mind has entered the realm of love, then grace becomes active, and the mind receives spiritual contemplation and sees hidden mysteries.

154. There are two modes, as I have said already, in which the gift of revelations of mental contemplation is given. Sometimes it is given by grace as a reward for ardent faith, and sometimes for practice of commandments and purity. By grace, as in the case of the blessed Apostles, who purified their minds not by practice of commandments but by ardent faith; for they believed in Christ in simplicity, and followed Him without doubts and with their heart aflame. And when Christ had completed His blessed dispensation, He sent them a Comforter, the Spirit, Who purified and perfected their mind, Who by His action put to death the old passionate man in them, and by His action brought to life their new spiritual man. Thus, too, St. Paul was first mysteriously renewed, and afterwards received the contemplation of the revelation of the mysteries. The Scriptures do not record the terms in which Christ spoke with him, but it is recorded what Ananias said to him: 'Brother Saul, the Lord, even Jesus, that appeared unto thee in the way as thou camest, hath sent me, that thou mightest receive thy sight, and be filled with the Holy Ghost' (Acts ix. 17). And when he baptised him, Paul was filled with the Holy Ghost, and experienced the secret mysteries of revelations, just as did the holy Apostles to whom the Lord said: 'I have yet many things to say unto you, but ye cannot bear them now. Howbeit when he,

the Spirit of truth, is come, he will guide you into all truth . . .
and he will shew you things to come' (John xvi. 12, 13).

155. It was precisely when the blessed Paul received the Holy
Ghost and was renewed by Him that he was granted the mysteries
of revelation, began to contemplate by the spirit of revelations
and delighted in this contemplation, heard ineffable words, saw
visions transcending nature, was ravished by contemplations of
heavenly powers and rejoiced in the spiritual. Let no one think,
as the heretics (called Euctites) assert in their madness, that he
achieved these heights by his own desire! The mind is totally incapable of reaching thither. On the contrary, Paul was caught up
by the spirit of revelations, as he himself wrote in his Epistle to
the Corinthians (2 Cor. xii. 2, 4), contrary to the assertions of
these vain people, who likened themselves to the holy Apostles
and took the fantasies of their thoughts for spiritual contemplations.

156. Touching men who are filled with passions, and yet
undertake to investigate the laws of the corporeal and the incorporeal and so are like those who, being themselves sick, lecture
on the rules of preserving health, one of the saints wrote: 'When
the blessed Paul heard about disciples who had neglected the
commandments and had not vanquished passions, yet aspired to
the bliss of contemplating the mysteries, which is possible only
after purification from passions, he said: first put off the old man
of passions and after that hope to put on the new man, renewed
by the knowledge of the mysteries into a likeness of the Creator,
and do not aspire to my bliss or that of the other Apostles, which
was an action of grace, because God hath ''mercy on whom he
will have mercy, and whom he will he hardeneth'' (Rom. ix. 18).
For who will stand up against His countenance or resist His will?
At times God gives freely; at others He demands works and
purification, and only then bestows the gift; and sometimes even
after works and purification He does not give at once, but keeps
the gift to bestow contemplation in its proper place.'

157. We find that He acts thus also with regard to a compara-
tively lesser gift, namely the remission of sins. For, behold,
baptism gives freely and demands nothing except faith; but if a
man repents his sins after baptism, God does not forgive him

freely, but demands works, sufferings, sorrows, contrition, tears, a long time of mourning—and then He forgives. The Lord forgave the thief freely, merely for his confession uttered on the cross, and promised him the kingdom; but in the case of the woman who had sinned he demanded also faith and tears.

158. A soul which loves God, in God and in Him alone finds peace. First release yourself from all your outward attachments, then your heart will be able to unite with God; for union with God is preceded by detachment from matter.

A child is given bread to eat after he has been weaned from milk; and a man who intends to make progress in Divine things wishes first to withdraw from the world, like a child from the arms and breasts of his mother.

Works of the body precede those of the soul, just as clay preceded the soul that was breathed into Adam. He who has not performed works of the body cannot have works of the soul, for the latter are born of the former as an ear of wheat is born of a single seed. And he who has no works of the soul is also deprived of spiritual gifts.

160. He who with understanding flees vainglory, has tasted the life to come in his soul.

He who flees comfort in this life, has already seen the life to come in his mind. But he who is bound by love of possessions is the slave of passions.

Do not think that love of possessions means acquiring only gold and silver; it is acquiring anything to which your will is tied.

Do not praise a man who endures bodily sufferings but gives free rein to his senses, I mean ears, open and uncontrolled lips and roving eyes.

161. Know that to forgive the sins of one's debtors is an act of righteousness. Then you will see your mind filled with serenity and light.

If a merciful man does not rise above personal righteousness, he is not merciful; that is, a truly merciful man not only gives alms from his own possessions, but gladly suffers wrong from others, and has mercy on them.

He who lays down his soul for his brother is merciful, and not he who shows mercy to his brother by alms alone.

He also is merciful who, when his brother smites him on the cheek, is not so shameless as to retaliate and sadden his brother's heart.

162. Love to practise vigil that you may find comfort come near your soul.

Practise reading in silence, that your mind may always be raised to God's wonders.

Love poverty with patience, that you may gather your wandering mind into singleness. Learn to hate spacious life, that you may keep your thoughts untroubled. Refrain from multitude of concerns and take care for your soul alone, to save it from being robbed of inner stillness.

163. Do not shackle your freedom by things which serve pleasure, lest you become a slave of slaves.

Love poor garments to humble the thoughts which are born in you, namely, arrogance of heart. He who likes glitter cannot have free thoughts, for the heart inwardly attunes itself to outward appearances.

164. Humility is followed by self-mastery and restraint in everything.

Through constant self-restraint, humility comes to contemplation and adorns the soul with chastity; whereas vanity, through constant turmoil and confusion of thoughts, gathers impure treasures from everything it meets, and defiles the heart. It looks with unseemly eyes at the nature of things, and fills the mind with shameful images; but humility brings spiritual harmony through contemplation and urges its possessor to glorify God.

165. It is better for you to free yourself from the bonds of sin, than to free slaves from their slavery.

It is better for you to make peace with your soul in singleness of your tripartite nature, that is body, soul and spirit, than by your teaching to bring peace among men at variance.

Gregory says: 'It is good to preach for God's sake, but better to make oneself pure for God.'

It is more useful for you to care about raising what has fallen in your soul through passions, by urging your thoughts towards the Divine, than it is to raise the dead.

166. In all the days of your life, wherever you may go, con-

sider yourself a stranger, to escape the harm engendered by freedom of behaviour.

Let your lips always utter blessings, and you will not be slandered; for slander begets slander, and blessing begets blessing.

In all you do, regard yourself as inadequate to teach—and you will prove wise throughout your life.

Do not pass on to another what you have not yourself experienced, lest you feel shame for yourself, and lest comparison with your life reveals your lie.

167. Beware of reading heretical teachings, for they, more than all else, can arm the spirit of blasphemy against you.

Read often, and insatiably, the books of teachers on Divine Providence, for they lead the mind to discern order in God's actions and creatures, give it strength and by their penetration prepare it to receive illumined thoughts and impel it in purity towards understanding God's creatures.

Read the Gospels, which God gave the whole universe for understanding, that your mind may go deep into the marvels of God.

Let your reading be done in a stillness, which nothing disturbs; be free from all cares for the body and turmoil of life, so that, when the sweetness of understanding comes, you should be aware in your soul of this most sweet taste, surpassing all sensation, and your soul should savour it.

168. Purify your soul, free yourself from cares concerning things outside your nature, shroud your understanding and movements in the cloak of chastity and humility and, through this, you will find what lies inside your nature, since to the humble mysteries are revealed.

169. If you intend to dedicate your soul to the work of prayer, which purifies the mind, and to night vigil, in order to acquire an illumined mind, withdraw from the sight of the world, cease meeting people, do not let friends visit you in your cell, as is customary, even on seemingly good pretexts, except those who think and live as do you and your fellows in retreat. Fear the disturbance of conversations within the soul and, withdrawing from outer conversation, combine mercy with prayer, and your soul will see the light of truth. For in so far as the heart ceases to

be disturbed by external objects, so can the mind move from understanding Divine thoughts and actions up to knowledge and wonder. For it is easy for the soul to change one conversation for another, if we show even a little diligence.

170. To change one conversation for another (an empty for a soul-saving one) occupy yourself with reading the Scriptures and the lives of the saints. And when you stand up to do your rule of prayer, instead of thinking of what you have seen and heard in the world, you will find in yourself thoughts of the Divine Scriptures you have read, and these thoughts will make you forget memories of worldly things; and thus the mind will come to purity. This is the meaning of the written word—that reading helps the soul when it stands up to pray; and also, that by prayer the soul becomes enlightened in reading. And again, instead of extraneous admixture, reading provides food for the different kinds of prayer, and thus enlightens the soul, helping it always to pray without laziness or distraction.

171. For lovers of the flesh and the belly to study spiritual things is just as unseemly as for a whore to discourse on chastity.

A very sickly body cannot stand rich food. In the same way, a mind occupied with worldly things cannot approach study of the Divine.

A fire is not lighted with damp wood; and Divine ardour is not kindled in a heart that loves ease.

As a man, who has not seen the sun with his own eyes, cannot describe its light by hearsay, and does not perceive this light, so is it with a man, whose soul has not tasted the sweetness of spiritual works.

172. If you have something above your daily needs, give it to the poor and thereupon go daringly to offer your prayers, that is, converse with God as a son with his Father.

Nothing can bring the heart nearer to God than alms; and nothing bring such stillness in the soul as willing poverty.

When you give, give generously, your face expressing kindness, and give more than you are asked for.

Do not try to discriminate the worthy from the unworthy, but let all people be equal in your eyes for a good deed. For in this way you can attract even the unworthy towards the good, since the soul is easily led to the fear of God by means of bodily things.

173. Sweep your cell clean of everything superfluous, for this will lead you to abstinence, however unwillingly. Scarcity of all things teaches a man to be abstinent.

He who gains victory in external warfare—I mean the war waged against the soul by the senses—hearing, sight, and so on—need have no fear of inner warfare.

When a man has barred the city gates, that is, the senses, he fights within and does not fear those devising evil outside the city.

Blessed is he who, knowing this, does not exert himself in a multitude of works, but who has translated all his physical activity into the work of prayer.

174. At such time that God brings your heart to be touched, constantly practise bows and prostrations.

Let your heart be in no way troubled if, at such time, the demons try to persuade you that you should be doing something else; and then look, and wonder, at the result in yourself.

Nothing is more important and difficult in spiritual struggle, and nothing excites more envy in the demons, than if a man prostrates himself before the cross of Christ, praying day and night, and is as though his hands were bound behind him.

Do you wish to keep your ardour from cooling and your tears from drying? Occupy yourself in this way; and blessed are you if you practise it day and night, and ask for nothing else.

If you do not strive, you will not find, and if you do not knock at the door with ardour and constantly keep vigil before it, you will not be heard.

175. Until the outer man dies to the whole world, not only to sin, but also to every activity, and equally until the inner man dies to evil thoughts and the natural stirrings of the body weaken, so that sinful sweetness no longer arises in the heart, until then the sweetness of the Divine Spirit will not arise in a man, his members will not acquire purity in this life, Divine thoughts will not enter his soul, and will remain not sensed and not seen. And until in his heart a man has made passive the cares of life, except for the indispensable needs of his nature, and entrusts this care to God, spiritual ecstasy will not spring forth in him.

176. He who, with feeling and conviction, keeps in mind the thought of the equality to which their common end leads all men, has need of no other Teacher to renounce all worldly things.

He who does not voluntarily shun the causes of passions is involuntarily led into sin. And the causes of sin are the following: wine, women, wealth, physical health; not, however, because they are essentially sinful, but because they readily incline nature to sinful passions. Therefore a man should take heed and beware of them.

Poverty is abhorrent to men, but a puffed up soul and a wandering mind are more abhorrent to God. People reverence riches; God honours a humble soul.

177. If you wish to make a right beginning in your doing, first prepare yourself for the temptations which will assail you. For the enemy has the habit of visiting a man with terrible temptations as soon as he sees him starting a righteous life with ardent faith. By this he strives to frighten him and thus cool the ardour of his right intention, so that he no longer burns to please God by his works. Therefore prepare yourself to meet courageously the temptations which are wont to assail virtues, and only then begin to practise them.

179. Sow alms in humility, and you will reap mercy at the time of judgment.

Regain the good you have lost by means of that through which you have lost it. You have lost chastity; God will not accept your alms if you remain in adultery, for He demands from you the sanctity of the body.

Every disease is cured by its corresponding remedies. You are overcome by envy; why do you exert yourself in struggle against sleep?

180. While the offence is still small and unripe, destroy it, before it has time to produce wide branches and has begun to ripen. Do not give yourself up to negligence, while this fault seems small to you; for later you will find in it an inhuman master and will run before it like a slave, a prisoner. A man who fights a passion at its inception quickly masters it.

181. A man who can bear an injury with gladness, even if he holds in his hands the means to repel it, receives comfort from

God for his faith. And a man who humbly suffers accusations made against him, has reached perfection and the holy angels marvel at him. For no other virtue will be as high or as hard to practise.

182. Do not trust yourself, thinking that you are strong, until you have been tried and have found yourself unchangeable.

Do not rely on your own strength, lest you be left to fall out of weakness; then through your fall you will realise how weak you are.

Do not trust your knowledge, lest the enemy gets into communication with you and catches you by his guile.

Never boast of your works when you speak, lest you be put to shame.

In all things a man boasts of, God lets him suffer change, that he may learn humility through degradation.

183. Always raise your eyes to God, for God's Providence and Protection envelops all men, but It is invisible, and reveals Itself only to those who have cleansed themselves of sin, and who constantly think of God and of Him alone. Especially does God's Providence become revealed to them when, for His sake, they enter into temptation. For then they sense God's Providence, as though seeing it with physical eyes, in proportion to the measure and cause of the temptation, which overtakes each one of them, to incite them to courage, as it was with Jacob, Joshua, the three youths, Peter, and other saints, to whom God's Providence appeared in some human form, to hearten them and affirm them in righteousness.

184. Is there need to say anything about men engaged in spiritual endeavour, strangers to the world, and about hermits? They have made the wilderness a city, have transformed it into the home and abode of the angels. For the righteousness of their life, angels have always come to them, and, as warriors of the same King, they have often fought side by side. All their life have they loved the wilderness and, from love of God, had their dwelling in the mountains, caves and precipices of the earth. Since they have abandoned the earthly and conceived a love for the heavenly, thus imitating the angels, the holy angels themselves have deemed it right not to conceal from them their countenance, and have fulfilled their every wish, giving them all possible help.

185. Once a man has dedicated himself for all time to God, he spends his life in tranquillity of mind.

Without uncovetousness, the soul cannot be free of the turmoil of thoughts; and until it brings the senses into silence it will not experience tranquillity of thought.

Without experiencing temptations, no one can acquire spiritual wisdom.

Without diligent reading, you will not know fineness of thoughts.

Without stillness of thoughts, the mind will not attain to the hidden mysteries.

Without hope in faith, the soul cannot daringly venture into temptations.

Without a clear experience of God's protection, the heart is not capable of hope in God.

If the soul does not taste of the sufferings of Christ with understanding, it cannot have communion with Christ.

187. Our nature has become such that it acquires passions with ease; many are the temptations in this world, evil is not far from you; it springs forth within you and lies under your feet. Temptations are as close to men, as the two eyelids to one another. God has wisely arranged this for your profit, that you should constantly knock at His door, that the fear of afflictions should sow memory of Him in your mind, that you should approach Him in prayer and your heart be illumined by constant remembrance of Him. God has not created you impervious to afflictions, lest you too, desiring to be a god, should share the inheritance of him who was first an angel of light, but later through exalting himself became Satan. Neither has He created you inflexible and immovable, lest you become akin to the nature of inanimate creatures.

188. Ceaselessly purify yourself before God, and keep memory of Him in your heart, lest by remaining long without this memory you prove to have no daring when you approach Him. For daring before God comes of frequent converse with Him and much prayer.

Men communicate with one another by means of the body; but man communes with God by remembering Him in his soul, directing his attention to God in prayer and giving himself wholly up to God.

By long preserving the memory of God, the soul from time to time is brought to a state of ecstasy and wonder.

'Let the heart of them that seek the Lord rejoice. Seek ye the Lord' ye condemned men, 'and be strengthened; seek his face continually' (Ps. civ. 3, 4)—be sanctified by the holiness of His countenance and be cleansed of your sins.

189. When temptation assails an unrighteous man, he has no trust whereby he may call upon God and expect salvation from Him, since in easy times he retreated from the will of God.

Before affliction overtakes you, pray to God, and in the time of sorrow you will find Him—and He will hear you.

Noah's ark was made ready in time of peace; and the wood for it took a hundred years to fashion. In the time of wrath the unrighteous perished, but it became a protection to the righteous.

190. Those in whom the world is dead suffer injuries with joy; but those in whom the world is alive cannot bear injuries: moved by vanity, they are angry, and from this foolish movement are cast into turmoil or encompassed with sorrow.

He who wishes to progress in the virtue of bearing injuries with patience and magnanimity must withdraw from his relatives and become an exile; for one cannot make progress in this virtue in one's birthplace.

Only the great and the strong can bear such sufferings in the midst of their relatives—and those alone can do this, in whom the world is dead, since they no longer hope for any consolation in this life.

193. Bodily labours without purity of mind are like a barren womb and withered breasts, for they cannot approach the knowledge of God. Such people tire the body but neglect to uproot passions in the mind, and so they reap nothing.

As a man who sows among thorns can reap nothing, so a man who harms himself by spitefulness and covetousness can succeed in nothing, but groans on his bed, unable to sleep for the worries about his affairs which oppress him.

194. If the soul is illumined by memory of God and unceasing

day and night vigil, the Lord sends there (within) for its protection a cloud, which envelops it by day and a flame to illumine it by night; thus light shines in its darkness.

195. As a cloud hides the light of the moon, so the vapours of a full stomach banish Divine Wisdom from the soul.

The flame of a fire is to dry wood what a full stomach is to the body. As one inflammable matter, added to another, strengthens the flames, so diversity of foods strengthens the stirrings of lust in the body.

Knowledge of God does not dwell in a pleasure-loving body; and a man who loves his body will not gain Divine grace.

As the fruit of the womb comes to life amidst the pains of childbirth, and brings joy to the mother, so with the oppression of the gullet there is born in the soul the fruit of the knowledge of Divine mysteries.

As the father takes care of his children, so Christ takes care of a body enduring harships for His sake—and is always near its lips.

196. He is a stranger, whose mind stands outside all things of life.

He is a monk, who stays outside the world and is ever praying to God, so that he may gain future blessings.

A monk's wealth is the comfort he finds in mourning, and the joy of faith, which shines in the secret places of his mind.

He is chaste who, besides preserving his body undefiled by carnal intercourse, is ashamed even of the least reminder of it.

If you love chastity, banish shameful thoughts by exercising yourself in reading and prolonged prayer; then you will have a weapon against the natural impulses to such thoughts: but without this it is impossible to have purity of soul.

197. If you are truly merciful, do not grieve inwardly when something that belongs to you is unjustly taken from you, and do not tell others of your loss.

Let the loss you suffer from your offender be swamped in your mercy, as the tang of wine is swamped by a large amount of water.

Show the fullness of your mercy by the good with which you repay those who have offended you, as did the blessed Elisha with his enemies, who intended to capture him (4 Kings vi. 13–23).

198. A man, who is truly humble, is not indignant when he is

wrongly accused, and says nothing to justify himself against false accusation, but accepts slander as truth; he does not attempt to persuade people that he is calumniated, but begs forgiveness. Some people have voluntarily attracted accusations they did not merit; others have endured being called adulterers, being far from adultery, and testified by their tears that they bear the fruit of sin they had not committed, and have wept asking their offenders forgiveness for the iniquity they had not done, their soul all the while being utterly pure and chaste. Others, to avoid being praised for the excellent rules of their life, practised in secret, have pretended to be half-wits, while in truth they were permeated with Divine salt and unshaken in their stillness, so that, at the height of their perfection, they had holy angels to proclaim their merits.

199. When the Saviour spoke of the many mansions of His Father, He meant the different degrees of mind that are given dwellings in that realm, that is, the diversities and distinctions of spiritual gifts to be enjoyed according to the stature of mind. For he called the mansions many, not because they are in different places, but because the difference lies in the degree of gifts. Just as each man enjoys the physical sun according to the clarity and receptive power of his sight, and as one lamp gives differing degrees of illumination in a house, although the light is not divided into many lights; so in the life to come all the righteous are indivisibly put to dwell in one realm, but each of them is illumined by the one spiritual Sun, according to his own measure, and attracts to himself joy and gladness according to his quality, as it were from one and the same air, from one place, the throne of vision and image. And no one sees the measure of his neighbour, whether he be above or below him, lest the sight of the greater grace of his neighbour and his own lack should cause him sadness and grief. There each, according to his own gift of grace, has inward joy in his own measure. But, outside them all, there is one vision and realm; and apart from the two degrees, namely one realm on high and one below, there is between them the multiplicity of varying gifts.[32]

200. When the devil wishes to defile the mind by a lustful

[32] The last sentence is obscure in the Russian. (Translators' note.)

241

memory, he first tries men's patience by love of vanity, and the inception of this thought has no appearance of passion. He usually acts thus in the case of men who guard their mind and in whom he cannot readily introduce an unseemly thought. When he snatches a man from his fortress and the man starts to converse with the first thought and move away from his fortress, the devil confronts him with something reminiscent of fornication and turns his mind towards unseemly subjects. At first the mind is troubled by these sudden suggestions, but later makes its peace with them, and still later passes from thought to action. But if the mind recoils and forestalls the first suggestion of thoughts, then, with God's help, it can speedily overcome the passion.

201. It is better to repel passions by the memory of virtues, rather than by resisting them; for when passions leave their realm and arise for battle, they imprint on the mind their own images and likenesses. Such a struggle gains great power over the mind, grievously agitating the thoughts and casting them into confusion. But if a man acts by the first rule we have mentioned, when passions are repulsed they leave no trace in the mind.

202. Until a man has received the Comforter, he has need of the Divine Scriptures to imprint the memory of good in his thought, to keep his striving for good constantly renewed by continual reading, and to preserve his soul from the subtleties of sinful ways; for he has not yet acquired the power of the Spirit, which repels errors and captures soul-saving memories. When the power of the Spirit has penetrated the power of the soul acting in a man, then, in place of the law of the Scriptures, the commandments of the Spirit take root in the heart and a man is secretly taught by the Spirit and needs no help from sensory matter. For, so long as it is from matter that the heart has its teaching, error and forgetfulness straightway follow the lesson; but when teaching comes from the Spirit, its memory is kept inviolate.

203. Like an unfledged bird is that mind which, while repenting, is but newly freed from the bonds of passions and, during prayer, strives to rise above the earth but cannot, so crawls on the face of the earth, having no strength to fly. Yet with the help of reading, effort, fear and care for many virtues, it collects its thoughts together, for it is incapable of knowing anything except

that. And for a short time this keeps the mind undefiled; but later come memories, which trouble and defile the heart; for the man has not yet experienced that calm air of freedom where the mind enters only after a long while through forgetting all earthly things. For he has acquired only physical wings, that is virtues performed outwardly, but has not yet seen contemplative virtues and has no experience of them. But they are the wings of the mind, on which a man is brought near to heaven, quitting the earth.

204. So long as a man serves the Lord through something sensory, images of that sensory object become imprinted in his thoughts, and he pictures to himself the Divine in material images. But when he receives perception of that which is inner, then, according to the measure of this perception, his mind begins to rise, from time to time, above the images of things.

205. When your soul is nearing the way out of darkness, then this will be for you a sign: your heart is aflame, burns like fire day and night; and so the whole world seems to you like dust and dung; you even have no desire of food, for the sweetness of new flaming thoughts, constantly arising in your soul. Suddenly fountains of tears open up in you, flowing freely like an inexhaustible stream and mingling with all your activities, with your reading, your prayer or meditation, your eating or drinking or aught else. When you see this in your soul, be of good cheer, for you have crossed the sea. Then be diligent in your work, stand watchfully on guard, that grace may increase in you from day to day. But until you see this, you have not yet accomplished your journey nor reached the mountain of God. If, after receiving the blessing of tears, they cease and your ardour cools, though there is no other change, that is, no physical weakening to cause this, woe unto you! What have you destroyed by falling into vainglory, or negligence, or laziness?! But what comes after tears, we shall describe later.

206. If you have no works, do not speak of virtues.

Sufferings for God and for His sake are more precious to God than any prayer or offering; and the smell of their sweat is better than any incense.

Regard all virtue performed without bodily labour as premature, stillborn fruit of the womb.

The offerings of the righteous are the tears of their eyes, and a sacrifice pleasing to God is their sighings during vigil.

The righteous, burdened by the weight of their body, will call to the Lord and will send their supplications to God in their infirmity; and at the cry of their voice the Holy Hierarchies will come to their aid, to strengthen and comfort them with hope; for the holy angels, being close to holy men, have a share in their sufferings and sorrows.

207. Wine warms the body, and the Word of God the mind.

Men inflamed by ardour are ravished into meditation on the object of their hope and prepare their mind for the life to come.

Men drunk with wine see no obstacles before them; and men intoxicated with hope know no suffering nor anything worldly.

Blessed are those who, from love of God, have girded their loins with unquestioning simplicity for this sea of suffering, and who do not turn back.

Those who embark upon this rough journey with hope, do not turn back and do not stop to investigate. But, having crossed the sea and looking back on the stormy passage, they give thanks to God for delivering them from the narrows, rapids and roughness of the way, of which they knew nothing.

When hope embarks on this passage, it crosses the sea with its first ardour, having no care at all for the body nor deliberating in itself as to whether or no its labour begun will in any wise succeed.

When you wish to undertake work for God, first make a testament, like one who is no longer to live in this world, one who is prepared for death and has despaired of his present life, one who has reached the limit of his span.

Start all good work with courage, and do not undertake such labours with a divided soul; nor let your heart waver in its trust in God, lest your labours be profitless and your work a burden.

208. The doings of those who live according to God are the following:

One man may pass the whole day in beating his head against the ground, and do this instead of performing the services, that is, the hours.

Another may accompany his long and constant prostrations with a number of prayers.

Yet another replaces the Divine services by copious tears and is content with that.

Another tries to penetrate the meaning of what he reads and connects this with a definite rule.

Another so mortifies his soul with hunger that he cannot perform Divine services.

Another makes his service unceasing by a constant and warm study of psalms.

Another spends his time in reading which warms his heart.

Another surrenders himself to captivity, pondering over the Divine meaning of the Holy Scriptures.

Another, moved to wonder at the marvels which strike him in the verses, is restrained from his customary reading and possessed by silence.

Another, having tasted all this and had enough, has turned back and become inactive.

Another, having tasted just a little, is filled with vainglory and falls into error.

Another has been prevented from keeping to his rule by some grievous illness and weakness; yet another, by the predominance of some habit, or some desire, or ambition, or vanity, or covetousness, or passionate attachment to material gains.

Another has stumbled, but has risen again and has not turned back until he has received the pearl of great price.

209. The beginning of everything is a right intention before God (decision to please God).

After withdrawal from the affairs of the world, this is followed by: hunger, reading, all-night sober vigil according to each man's strength, and many bows[33] which it is useful to practise during the hours of the day and often at night.

Let the smallest measure for you be thirty bows—thereupon bow to the holy cross and end thus.

[33] The Russian поклонъ has no English equivalent: it includes bows and prostrations. (Translators' note.)

But there are people who increase this number of bows, according to their strength. Others choose to spend three hours solely in prayer, with mind held sober, lying prostrate on the ground with thoughts free from wandering. (In other words, some pray often but not for long at a time; others pray but once, but remain long in prayer.)

210. Our adversary, the devil, has the old-established habit of cunningly diversifying his attacks against those who have entered upon spiritual endeavour. He changes the method of attack by using different weapons against them and by adjusting himself to the person's intention.

The first method of enemy attack.

Those whose will is indolent and whose thoughts are weak are attacked strongly from the very beginning by powerful temptations. The devil does this to overpower them with fear from the very first endeavour, to make the way look difficult and hard to them and to make them say: 'If the beginning of the way is so grievous and hard, can anyone endure to the end the many struggles which face him?'

The devil does not wage war against them for long, but soon turns them to flight. This happens because they entered upon work for the Lord with doubt and coldness. And God commands that we should undertake this work with readiness to die for the sake of pleasing Him, and He promises to crown the faithful labourer with the honour of martyrdom.

Because they did not decide from the first to give themselves up to death, they prove weak to that extent. So they show themselves unstable in every struggle, since they love themselves and wish, above all, to spare their body. And so the enemy drives them like a tempest, seeing in them no strength of soul such as he is wont to meet in the saints.

In proportion to a man's will to strive towards God, God too helps and assists him, and shows His care of him. And the devil cannot approach a man or lead him into temptations unless a man is negligent, or God allows it.

211. *The second method of attack.*

In the case of men whom the devil sees to be full of courage, men who disregard death and undertake their work with great zeal, the devil does not at once go out to meet them, and does not engage them in battle at their first impetus, knowing that zealous warriors are not easy to overcome.

Therefore, while he sees them to be such, he does not dare to touch them, until he has noticed their zeal cooling and sees that they have laid down the weapons they had fashioned in their thoughts, and cast them off by changing the Divine words and memories which had helped and assisted them.

As soon as they begin to turn away from their first thoughts, and start inventing on their own what serves to overcome those thoughts through the seductions of speculations which spring from themselves, and when of themselves they begin to dig for their souls a moat of perdition through the wandering thoughts which are born of laziness, and bring coldness to mind and heart—then the devil assaults them without mercy.

The devil refrains from attacking them until then, because a certain power encompasses those who strive towards God with ardent zeal, trust Him and believe in Him. For this reason God repels from them the violence of the devil's malice, and it does not come near them. The enemy is restrained by the sight of the Protector, Who is always shielding them. For so long as a man does not throw away from himself the causes of help—prayers and the labours of humility—the Protector and Helper never leaves him.

212. You, who set out in the footsteps of God, remember then, throughout your life of endeavour, the first beginning and first zeal you had when entering the path, and the ardent thoughts with which you first left your house and entered the fighting ranks. Examine yourself each day, that there should be no cooling of your soul's ardour in relation to any of the weapons that you carry, nor in the zeal which was aflame in you at the start of your endeavour. Constantly raise your voice in the warrior's camp, encouraging and urging to valour the sons of right, and show to the enemy that you are keeping watch. At the same time, invoke God with good hope, weep at His goodness, shed tears and labour until He sends you a Helper. And then you will never be conquered.

213. *The third method of enemy attack.*

When the enemy sees the power, such as a man acquires from

God in reward for his zeal and his calling to Him with faith, he tries to find some other means to make the angel who is helping him withdraw; namely, he strives to evoke in him proud thoughts, to make him think that his whole strength depends on his own powers and that it is by his own strength that he keeps himself safe from his adversary and murderer. If a man believes these thoughts suggested by the enemy, God's help withdraws from him and he falls into the enemy's hands. But if a man does not give way to these suggestions, but holds fast to the memory of His Helper and never ceases to raise the eye of his heart to heaven, the enemy devises new means of attack against him.

214. *The fourth method of enemy attack* consists in the enemy beginning to oppress a man through the needs of nature (especially the need of a wife and the need to have wherewith to exist).

(Concerning the first need.) Although he cannot force a man to commit anything in actual deed, since the man is fenced off by silence, and his dwelling place is far from the opportunities and causes of sin, yet he endeavours to make a man's mind see it in imagination and tries to provoke in him false fantasies in the mask of truth. Moreover, to make him desire what he imagines, he stimulates him and forces his mind to dwell on shameful thoughts, consent to them and become guilty of them. For the enemy knows that in a man engaged in spiritual endeavour, the issue of victory or defeat lies in his thought and is decided in a moment—let but thought merely move from its place, and descend to earth from its heights, let but for one moment man's will show its consent, which has happened to many through a dream image of a woman's beauty. And if they have gone one or two stages towards the world, the enemy has frequently managed actually to bring women to them. By this or similar means the enemy has sometimes gained victory over the careless and those weak of heart. But others have proved stronger than these temptations and, with the help of Divine grace, have overcome the enemy with his fantasies.

(Concerning the second need.) Often, too, the enemy has made them see in their imagination gold, precious things and other treasures and at times even actually showed them in the hope of stopping a man in his progress and, through such imaginings, catching him in one of his nets. Such things are allowed in order to test men and see whether, when deprived of these things in their seclusion, and living amid scarcity and want, they do in fact love God, and whether, when they meet such things, they try to despise them for love of God and, being seduced by them, do not let themselves be overcome, but regard them as nothing compared with love of God. True doers stand firm and, having passed through the test, become purified like gold in a furnace; but the weak and negligent are often overcome even by a small want, and they turn back, renouncing their endeavour.

215. As soon as a man realises his weakness and genuinely feels it, he at once rouses his soul from indolence and becomes cautious. But no one can feel his weakness unless even a small temptation, either of body or soul, is allowed to assail him—and he is granted deliverance from it. For then he sees clearly the futility of his own efforts and measures, he sees that the circumspection, abstinence and guarding of his soul, through which he hoped to find security, brought him no profit and that deliverance came independently of it all. Hence he is shown that by himself he is nothing and is saved by God's help alone.

A man, who has learnt the need of God's help, prays much. And the more he multiplies his prayer, the greater becomes the humility of his heart. For no man who prays and asks can be otherwise than humble: 'A broken and humbled heart God will not despise' (Ps. l. 17).

As soon as a man becomes humble, mercy is not slow to envelop him. Then the heart is aware of God's help, and acquires a certain power of assurance (in God) which arises in it. And when a man is aware that God's help is actually assisting him, his heart becomes filled with faith in very truth.

From this he understands that prayer is the refuge of those who seek help, the source of salvation, the treasure-house of hope, the harbour from storms, the support of the weak, protection in temptations, the shield of deliverance in battle, an arrow directed against the enemies—and it is revealed to him that the whole multitude of spiritual blessings becomes accessible to him through prayer. From then on he begins to delight in the prayer of faith; he no longer prays with labour and weariness, but with heartfelt joy and wonder, constantly making movements of thanksgiving and innumerable genuflexions.

216. Through great desire for God's help, a man draws near to God, remaining in prayer. But in as far as he approaches God in his intention, so God approaches him with His gifts, and for his great humility does not withdraw His grace from him.

Sometimes, however, the bountiful God keeps back from him the gifts of grace, to spur him to approach God and so that, because of his need, a man should ceaselessly stand before God, Who is ready to spill forth what will help him.

Some petitions God is quick to grant, namely those without which no one can be saved; while He is slow in granting others. In some circumstances He repels and disperses the scorching power of the enemy, while in others He lets a man fall into temptations, that this trial may cause him to approach God—that he may gain experience from temptations, and, having the proof of his weakness before his eyes, be confirmed more and more in humility.

If a righteous man has not realised his impotence, his actions are, as it were, on the edge of a razor—and he is not far from downfall and from the pernicious lion of pride. A man who does not know his weakness lacks humility; and a man who lacks humility has not yet reached perfection; a man who has not reached perfection always remains in fear, for his city is not upheld on iron pillars and thresholds of brass, that is, humility. Without humility the task of man (his pursuit) cannot be completed and his charter of freedom does not yet bear the seal of the Spirit. Until then he remains a slave and his work is not free from fear.

217. Therefore for His saints the Lord leaves such causes as provoke humility and contrition of heart in intense prayer, so that those who love Him should come near Him through humility. He frequently frightens them by the passions of their nature and the insinuations of shameful and unclean thoughts, and often too by the reproaches, insults and blows of men, and sometimes by bodily diseases and ills, at other times by poverty and the lack of essential means, or by the torment of great fear, by abandonment, manifest attacks of the devil and various terrifying happenings.

And all this in order that they should have causes for humility and should not fall into the sleep of negligence.

218. When it happens that your soul is inwardly filled with darkness and that, just as the rays of the sun are at times shut off from the earth by clouds, so the soul is deprived for a time of spiritual comfort, and when the light of grace becomes dimmed within because a cloud of passions covers the soul, and because the joy-creating force is weakened in you, so that your mind is shrouded in unaccustomed darkness; then let not your thought be troubled, but be patient; read the books of the teachers, force yourself to pray—and wait for help. It will be quick in coming, it will be there before you know. For as the face of the earth is delivered by the rays of the sun from the darkness of the clouds enshrouding it, so prayer can destroy and disperse the clouds of passions in the soul and illumine the mind by the light of comfort and joy.

219. So long as you have not reached the realm of tears, that which is hidden within you still serves the world—that is, you still lead a worldly life and do the work of God only with your outer man, while the inner man is barren; for his fruit begins with tears.

When you reach the realm of tears, then know that your mind has left the prison of this world, has put its foot on the path of a new age and has begun to smell the scent of new and wondrous air. Tears begin to flow because the birth of the spiritual child is near. Grace, the common mother of all, wishes mysteriously to bring forth a Divine image into the light of the life to come.

But these tears are of a different order from those which come from time to time to those practising silence (sometimes during contemplation, sometimes while reading, or at the time of prayer). I am not speaking of this order of *tears*, but of such as flow *unceasing day and night*.

The eyes of a man who has reached this degree become like a spring of water *for up to two years and more*, after which he comes to the *stilling* of thoughts.

After the stilling of thoughts, as far as nature permits it in part, there comes *that rest* of which St. Paul speaks (Heb. iv. 3).

In this peaceful tranquillity the mind begins to *contemplate mysteries*.

Then the Holy Spirit begins to reveal to him heavenly things— *and God comes to dwell in him* and resurrects in him the fruit of the Spirit.

But hear further: when you enter the realm of stillness of thoughts, the profusion of tears is taken from you—and tears come to you in moderation and at the proper time.

220. There are three stages through which man makes progress: the stage of beginners, the intermediate stage, and the stage of the perfect.

When a man is in the *first stage*, although his manner of thinking is inclined towards the good, yet his mind still moves in passions.

The second stage is a state between the passionate and the passionless, and thoughts from the right and the left alike arise in the man, and he does not cease to shed both light and darkness.

Moreover, if he stops for a short time the frequent reading of the Divine Scriptures and the representation of Divine ideas in his mind, accompanied with circumspection in external things, which gives birth to inner watchfulness, then he is swept into passions.

If he continues to feed his ardour for spiritual things in the said manner—by seeking, by striving, by feeding good thoughts with reading the Scriptures and thus keeping them from leaning to the left, by guarding his soul with love and cleaving to God in patient and untiring prayer, then God will finally open His door to him, especially for his humility; for mysteries are revealed to the humble (and this is the *third stage*).

221. Hope in God is preceded by labour for God and by the sweat of this labour.

If you believe in God, you do well. But faith demands works, and hope in God becomes manifest in suffering for virtue.

Do you believe that God takes care of His creatures and is omnipotent? Then let your faith be accompanied by suitable works—and God will hear you. Do not try to hold the wind in your fist, that is faith without works.

It often happens that a man unwittingly travels a road where there is a wild beast, or murderers, or something of the kind; but the universal Providence of God saves him from harm, either by delaying his progress until the wild beast has gone off, or by making him turn aside through meeting someone.

At times an evil snake lies on the path and is invisible; but, unwilling to abandon a man to this trial, God suddenly makes the snake hiss, move away and crawl in front of the wayfarer, who on seeing it takes care and is saved.

It often happens that a house, or a wall, or a stone, is about to fall while someone is sitting below, and God, in His loving-kindness, commands an angel to keep it from falling, until those sitting below move or are called away; and as soon as they leave He allows what was falling to fall.

All these and the like are acts of the general and all-pervading Divine Providence; but a righteous man has over him a special providence which never leaves him.

The rest of men are ordained by God to use reason in managing their affairs and, with God's Providence, to use also their own knowledge. But a righteous man has replaced knowledge by faith, which makes him fear nothing and be 'confident as a lion' (Prov. xxviii. 1).

And since his constant care is towards God, God also says of him: 'I am with him in affliction; and I will deliver him, and glorify him. I will satisfy him with length of days, and shew him my salvation' (Ps. xc. 15, 16).

A man indolent and lazy in his work cannot have this hope. But if a man is with God in all things, if he approaches Him by means of righteous works and the eyes of his heart never sleep but are raised to His grace, he can speak of himself in the words of the divine David, saying: 'Mine eyes have failed by my waiting on my God' (Ps. lxviii. 3).

222. When we seek to flee from the world, nothing separates us from it, kills the passions in us and enlivens us for spiritual life so much as mourning and an understanding contrition of heart. On the other hand, nothing so strengthens our fellowship with the world and removes us from the treasures of Wisdom and knowledge of Divine mysteries as frivolity and wandering thoughts, with licence of behaviour. This is the work of the dissolute demon.

So with love I implore you to beware of the malice of the enemy, lest through your foolish talk the ardour of love for Christ, Who tasted gall on the cross for your sake, should grow cool in your soul and lest, in place of this sweet work and daring before God, the devil fill your soul with many fantasies when you are awake, and, in your sleep, seduce it with unseemly dreams, whose evil stench is abhorrent to the angels.

Force yourself to imitate the humility of Christ, to kindle the more quickly the fire He has put in you, a fire destroying all those movements of the world, which kill the new man and defile the house of the Holy and Almighty God. For I dare to say with St. Paul that we are 'the temple of God' (1 Cor. iii. 16). So, since God Himself is pure, let us purify His temple to make Him wish to dwell therein. And since God is holy, let us make holy His temple; let us adorn it with all kinds of good and honourable deeds, scent it with the perfume of repose in God's will, and with pure prayer of the heart. Then the cloud of His glory will envelop the soul and the light of His greatness will shine forth in the heart.

223. A man who is full of cares cannot practise silence; for his numerous occupations disrupt his silence and quiet, even against his will.

A monk should put himself before the face of God, and always be raising his eyes to Him, if he truly wants to guard his mind, repel the alien movements stealing in, and in the stillness of thoughts discern what comes in and goes out.

While you are not free from cares you can expect no light in your soul, nor silence and stillness while your senses are un-bridled. Without unceasing prayer it is impossible to come near to God. After the work of prayer, a new care laid upon the mind leads to dispersal of thoughts.

Tears, beating one's breast during prayer and ardent zeal to prolong prayer evoke in the heart the warm sweetness of tears and it rises towards God in rapture, calling: 'My soul has thirsted for the living God: when shall I come and appear before God?' (Ps. xli. 2). He alone, who has drunk of this wine and has then been deprived of it, knows in what pitiable state he was left, and what was taken from him because of his weakening.

224. How harmful it is for those who lead a life of silence to

meet men and converse with them! As a sudden hailstorm bruises and destroys the fruit on trees, so meetings with people, however brief, bruise the fresh-opened flowers of virtues, which so richly adorn the stem of the soul, planted by the brooks of waters of repentance (Ps. i. 3).

As a strong hoar-frost withers the green seedlings which come out of the earth, so meetings with people wither the root of the mind, which has begun to produce the green shoots of virtues.

As a noble and honoured man, when drunk, forgets his nobility and is open to ridicule for the alien thoughts which spring from wine, so chastity of the soul is disturbed by the sight of men and converse with them; a man forgets his caution, the intention of his will is effaced from his mind and the basis for a praiseworthy way of life is destroyed.

225. Do not consider that among all the practices of a monk there is anything more important than night vigil. If a monk is free from the distraction of physical occupations and of cares for transitory things, the mind, by its help, is quick to soar on high as on wings and to rise to delighting in God. If a monk keeps vigil of the mind with good judgment, he will appear, as it were, incorporeal. It is impossible that those who spend their whole life in this occupation should be left by God with no reward for their sobriety, watchfulness of heart and careful directing of their thoughts towards Him. A soul which labours at keeping vigil will have the eyes of Cherubim, to keep them constantly raised on high and to contemplate heavenly visions.

226. A man who has chosen this divine work must take every care to protect himself during the day from the turmoil of crowds and the cares of occupations; otherwise he will endure the labour of refraining from sleep, but will gain no fruit from it; for in this case it will be impossible for his mind to practise psalmody and prayer as it should. But when, in place of cares, a man's occupation during the day is reading the Divine Scriptures, which strengthen the mind and which particularly refresh prayer and help vigilance, so closely connected with prayer, then, in this reading he finds a guide to lead him on the right path, finds that in which lies the seed of all that feeds contemplation in prayer, and

which keeps the thoughts from wandering and constantly sows in the soul remembrance of God.

227. Ceaseless silence, accompanied by reading, moderation in food, and vigil soon rouse thought to wonder, unless there is some cause disturbing to silence. The thoughts which with no intention or effort spontaneously arise in those who keep silence make both eyes shed copious tears that run down their cheeks, and are like fonts of baptism.

228. Until a man begins to hate the causes of sin, sincerely and from the heart, he cannot be free from the feeling of enjoyment produced by an act of sin. This is the most grievous fight of all (that is, with enjoyment of sin), which resists a man even at the cost of blood. Thereby man's freedom in the singleness (exclusiveness) of his love for virtue is put to the test.

In this struggle lies the force of sin, by which the enemy is wont to disturb the souls of the chaste, compelling them to experience what they had never in any way accepted in themselves. And this is the time of invisible endeavour, which can be very hard if the attacks, strengthened by an acquired habit, gain great power over those who have been accustomed to surrender to defeat by consenting to their own thoughts.

229. Beware of idleness, for it conceals a sure death; and without it one cannot fall into the hands of those who strive to capture us. On the day of judgment God will judge us not about psalmody, not for neglect of prayer, but for the fact that their omission opens the door to demons. When, finding there is room for them, they enter and close the doors of our eyes, they torment us and do with us that which subjects us to condemnation and grievous punishment from God.

The practice of this rule (psalmody and prayer) in the cell is established by the wise from the spirit of revelation, for the protection of our life; but the unwise consider its omission as of no consequence. Since they take no account of the ensuing harm, the beginning and middle of their way is ignorant licence, the mother of passions.

230. We cannot prevent causes for passions from being in us, and so we are tempted even against our will. We do not wish to sin, but we often accept with pleasure the causes which lead to

sins; then these causes become instrumental in making sins active. He who loves what causes passions involuntarily becomes a slave to passions.

He who hates his sins will cease to sin; and he who confesses them will receive absolution. It is impossible for a man to get free from the habit of sin if he does not first acquire a hatred of sin; and it is impossible to receive absolution before a confession of sins.

231. While a man bears within himself the poison of intoxication with his sins, everything he does seems fitting to him. And when nature leaves its rightful place, it is no matter whether intoxication be with wine or with lusts, for one and another alike drive it from its proper state—each will produce an identical inflammation in the body; the means may be different, the result is the same.

232. If you remain alone in your cell and have not yet acquired the power of true contemplation, always occupy yourself with reading troparions and the appointed prayers, with memory of death and hope of the future.

All this collects the mind into singleness, and keeps it from whirling, until true contemplation comes; for the strength of the spirit is greater than that of passions.

In hope of the future, occupy yourself with remembering God, try to grasp thoroughly the meaning of the troparions and beware of all external things, which excite desires in you; at the same time be watchful even in the small things you do in your cell.

Examine your thoughts, and pray to be given eyes in everything you do; this will open a source of joy in you; and then you will find such sorrows as are sweeter than honey.

233. No one can conquer passions, save only by visible and concrete virtues; and no one can overcome the wanderings of thoughts, save only by the study of spiritual knowledge.

Our mind is volatile; if it is not tied by some meditation, it never stops wandering. And it cannot be kept from wandering without gaining perfection in the aforesaid virtues; for unless a man overcomes the enemies he cannot be at peace.

Passions impede the hidden virtues of the soul; and unless they are first deposed by visible virtues, inner virtues cannot be seen behind them.

234. Love for God is by nature hot, and when it grips a man beyond measure, it throws the soul into ecstasy. A man who feels this love exhibits a remarkable change: his face becomes fiery and joyful, and his body is warmed; fear and shame leave him; a terrible death he counts as joy; the contemplation of his mind allows no kind of interruption in his thought of the celestial; he is aware of no impulse excited by objects, for, even if he does something, he is quite insensible of it—so ravished is his mind in contemplation, and his thought is always as it were conversing with someone.

This spiritual rapture intoxicated the Apostles and martyrs of old. Some travelled the world over, working and suffering persecutions, while others never lost heart in the most terrible tortures, but endured them with courage. Yet others wandered in deserts, mountains and caves, and amidst disorder were the most well-ordered; they were thought to be out of their minds, but were the wisest of the wise.

235. A life of spiritual endeavour is the mother of sanctity; from it is born the first experience of perception of the mysteries of Christ—which is called the first stage of spiritual knowledge.

A defiled soul does not enter the pure kingdom, and does not unite with the spirits of the saints.

Make smooth the quality of your chastity by tears, fasting and solitary silence.

A small suffering endured for God is better than a great deed performed without suffering. That which is done without labour is the righteousness of worldly men, who bestow charity with the outer man, but gain nothing within themselves. But you must strive within yourself and suffer with Christ, to be worthy to partake of the glory of Christ. The mind will not be glorified with Jesus, if the body does not suffer for Christ.

236. There are two means of mounting the cross: one is crucifixion of the body, the other, ascent into contemplation. The first is the outcome of freedom from passions, and the second the effect of active works of the spirit.

The mind does not submit if the body is not submissive to it.

The kingship of the mind is the crucifixion of the body; and the mind does not submit to God, unless freedom has submitted to reason. He who submits to God is near to having all things submissive to him.

237. The foundation of all good things, the return of the soul from the enemy's prison, the way leading to light and life—all this is contained in the following two methods: collecting oneself into one, and always fasting, that is, setting oneself the rule of wise and judicious abstinence in food, of remaining constantly in one place, and of ceaseless occupation with thought of God.

This makes the senses obedient, the mind sober, tames the fierce passions arising in the body, produces luminous movements of thought, care in the practice of virtues, tears and the memory of death, and pure chastity, freed of all fantasy tempting to thought; in short, hence come the freedom of the true man, spiritual joy and resurrection with Christ in the Kingdom.

If a man neglects these two methods, he must know that not only will he harm himself in all that was spoken of earlier, but will undermine the very foundation of all virtues and will come to the two contrary vices, namely, bodily wandering and dishonourable gluttony. These are the beginnings of things opposed to the aforesaid—and they prepare in the soul a place for all passions.

238. The enemy, knowing the times of our natural needs, which incite nature to seek their satisfaction, knowing that a roving eye and indulgence of the belly incite the mind to whirl around, tries at precisely these times to make us increase our daily needs, and to sow in us images of evil thoughts, so that in the intensity of struggle passions may gain ascendancy over nature and force a man to sink into sin. Since the enemy observes such times, it behoves us to be wise, particularly at those same times and not allow ourselves heedlessly to obey the will of the suggested thoughts, not to cede victory to hunger, and above all not to leave the place of our silence nor go where this can easily happen to us, lest thereby we provide excuses for leaving the wilderness altogether.

239. The enemy stands with us day and night before our eyes, he watches, waits and spies for some door to our senses to open and let him in. And if we let ourselves be negligent in some

one thing, this cunning and shameless cur shoots his arrows at us.

At times, nature of its own accord begins to like ease, laxity, laughter, wandering thoughts, laziness—and becomes a source of passions and rebellious turmoil; and sometimes the enemy instils all this into the soul.

Beware of indulging yourself in small things, lest you end by being lax in big things and come to grievous downfalls. Even a small carelessness, as someone said, often leads to great dangers. Always to be sober, even in small and insignificant things—this is wisdom.

240. Do not be disheartened in the work which is to give you life, and do not shirk dying for it; for faintness of heart is a sign of despondency, and negligence is the mother of both alike.

A timid man shows that he is a prey to two diseases: love of life and lack of faith.

Love of life is a sign of little faith. But a man who scorns it testifies by this that he believes in God with his whole soul, and awaits the future.

Vigour of heart and scorn of dangers come from one of two causes: either from great faith in God or from hardness of heart. Hardness of heart leads to pride, but faith leads to humility of heart.

241. A man cannot acquire hope in God, unless he first fulfils His will as much as he is able. For hope in God and courage of heart are born of the testimony of conscience, and only through truthful testimony of our mind can we have trust in God.

Testimony of the mind consists in the fact that conscience in no way accuses a man of negligence in anything he ought to do within his powers. 'If our heart condemn us not, then have we confidence toward God' (1 John iii. 21). So confidence comes from progress in virtues and a good conscience.

242. A man preserves constant silence and does not speak for the following three reasons: either for human glory, or from ardent zeal in virtue, or because he has some Divine converse within him and his mind is drawn towards it.

Virtue is not the display of many and various actions done with the body, but is the heart itself wise in hope; for a right aim attaches it to God.

The mind can work righteousness without actions of the body; but a body without wisdom of heart can gain no profit for all it may do.

At the same time, if a man of God finds a chance of right action, he does not refrain from showing his love for God by the labour of his doing.

243. In your struggle with the stirrings of carnal lust count withdrawal from the sight of women as a stout weapon; because the enemy cannot produce in us what nature has the power to do. Do not think that nature forgets what God has naturally sown into it for begetting children and for testing those who persist in this spiritual effort. But withdrawal from the objects of desire destroys the lust in our members, makes us forget it and annihilates it.

Objects, when unseen, produce but a slight, barely perceptible movement; but when they are seen they evoke passions by their proximity, feed them as oil feeds the flame of a lamp—and a passion already dead and withered, is kindled anew.

A natural movement, not combined with something external, cannot disturb purity of will and infringe our chastity, since God has not given nature the power to overcome man's righteous desire to strive towards Him.

But if we deliberately allow ourselves, at times, to be attracted by something sensory, and give ourselves either to eating and drinking beyond measure, or to the proximity of women, to looking at them and talking of them, which quickly kindles and spreads in the body the fire of lust, then we replace the naturally gentle movement in the body by one that is violent and unbridled, for these are added to nature by the impulses of our will.

All that God has created, He created beautifully and harmoniously. And as long as this degree of harmony with what we are by nature is preserved in us, natural movements cannot force us to stray from the path. Then only harmonious movements arise in our body, which merely inform us of the existence in us of a natural passion, but produce no excitement or turmoil so strong as to interfere with chastity.

244. At times too movement in the members is allowed by

God because of our conceit. Of these attacks we know that after a long time of keeping attention in ourselves and of regular work, even when we think we have made some progress, we are made to suffer them that we may learn humility.

Other attacks come from our indolence or excessive indulgence to the flesh, when we try to avoid all things that are painful and difficult in the course of our life, particularly constant seclusion in our cell and physical hardships. Straitness, difficulty and painfulness of living shackle and destroy voluptuousness; while licence, plenty and comfort of the body loosen, feed and increase it.

God and His angels rejoice when we suffer hardships, and the devil with his helpers—when we are at ease. Sufferings and straitness broaden and assist our practice of commandments, while ease makes room for passions and thus restrains and stops the practice of commandments.

When the body is kept within bounds, thoughts cannot indulge in dangerous flights. If a man bears labours and sufferings with gladness, he can easily bridle his thoughts, for his labours make them inactive.

When, remembering his past sins, a man chastens himself, God looks upon him with benevolence. God rejoices that, for having strayed from the path, he has laid a penance on himself—for this is a sign of repentance. The more he constrains his soul, the more God's benevolence towards him grows.

But every joy, whose cause is not in virtue, immediately provokes lustful movements.

245. Virtues follow one another in succession, that the path of virtue may be less hard and grievous, that a man may succeed in them progressively and in this find relief, and that thus even the difficulties themselves, endured for the sake of virtue, may become dear to him as something good.

Thus, no one can become really free from covetousness unless he is prepared to endure trials gladly.

And no one can endure trials unless he is convinced that the sufferings, in which he is prepared to share, may lead to something worth more than bodily comfort.

A man who deprives himself of material things, but has not cut off the activity of his senses—I mean sight and hearing—prepares greater sufferings for himself and will have to endure greater distress and greater tribulation. For if mental images of things, without the things themselves, produce painful feelings in a man, what are we to say if the things themselves are near and around us? In that case, the sensations produced by these things make a man suffer exactly what he suffered in the past through action itself; for the memory of his habit of them does not leave his thought.

How excellent in this respect is solitude! Then only thoughts remain to act as tempters; but even in the taming of thoughts it is a great and powerful help.

246. Do not seek advice from a man who does not lead a life similar to yours, even if he be very wise. Confide your thoughts to a man who, though he lacks learning, has studied the work in practice, rather than to a learned philosopher, who reasons on the basis of his speculations, with no practical knowledge.

To acquire experience means not merely to approach things and glance at them, gaining no knowledge of them, but through long dealing with them to discern clearly by experience their usefulness and harm.

Often a thing looks harmful from outside, but inside is full of profit; and conversely a thing frequently seems to be useful, while inside it is filled with harm.

Therefore follow the advice of a man, who has himself experienced all, and knows how to judge patiently what needs discrimination in your case, and can point out what is truly useful for you.

247. When in your journeying you find unfailing peace— beware; for you are far from the straight road, laboriously trodden by the feet of the saints.

While you are still on your way to the city of the kingdom, let this be for you a sign that you are drawing near to the city of God: that you meet powerful trials; and the nearer you draw and the more you progress, the more trials multiply and assail you.

Therefore, as soon as in the course of your journey you feel in your soul the greatest and strongest temptations, know that at that time your soul has in fact mysteriously entered a new and higher stage, and that in the state where it is now placed grace has been increased for it; for God leads the soul into suffering trials in exact proportion to the grace He bestows.

If the soul is weak and has not strength enough for great trials, and therefore asks to be spared them, and God listens, then know for certain that inasmuch as the soul lacks strength for great trials, it is inadequate too for great gifts; and in so far as great trials are forbidden to come near it, great gifts are forbidden also. For God does not grant a great gift without a great trial. In His wisdom, which is beyond the understanding of His creatures, God determines gifts in proportion to trials.

248. Trials which come when a man enters upon righteous life and when his life *grows in righteousness,* differ from trials which are allowed to come *to teach a proud heart.*

Trials to the soul, which come from the rod of the spirit and serve *progress* and growth, trials through which the soul is taught, tested and brought to spiritual endeavour are the following: laziness, heaviness in the body, infirmity of the members, despondency, confusion of thoughts, apprehensiveness caused by bodily exhaustion, temporary desertion of hope, darkening of thoughts, lack of human help, scarcity of the bodily necessities of life, and other similar things.

These trials bring to the soul a feeling of loneliness and defencelessness, darkening of heart and humility. Yet the Divine Providence proportions these trials to the strength and needs of those who suffer them. In them are blended both comfort and defeat, light and darkness, struggle and help, in short, straitness and spaciousness. And this is a sign that, with God's help, a man is making progress.

249. Trials which God allows to attack men *who puff themselves up* in the face of God's goodness and who offend Him by their *pride,* are the following: withdrawal of the force of wisdom which men possess, constant presence of a lustful thought which gives them no peace, and which is allowed in them to curb their conceit; quick temper; desire to have everything their own way, to argue, to reprimand others; a heart that despises everyone; a mind gone completely astray; blasphemy against the name of God; absurd and laughable suspicions that they are scorned by people, deprived of the honour due to them, that demons mock them and

put them to shame, both openly and secretly by every kind of means; and, finally, the desire to be in touch with the world and circulate in it, to talk endlessly and chatter senselessly, to be always in search of news and even of false prophecies, to promise much that is beyond their strength. These are spiritual trials.

To physical trials belong: painful, complicated attacks, prolonged and difficult to cure, constant meetings with bad and godless people, falling into the hands of wrongdoers, sudden stumblings and dangerous falls, events ruinous to them and their relatives.

All these that we have set forth belong to trials of pride. They start in a man when he begins to appear wise in his own eyes. And he goes through all these calamities to the extent that he becomes possessed by such proud thoughts; pride enters you to the extent that you have such thoughts.

250. There is yet another kind of trial—by faintness of heart through lack of patience. Every hardship and every affliction, if not accompanied by patience, produces an increased torment; for patience repels afflictions, while faintness of heart is the mother of torment. Patience is the mother of comfort, and is a certain strength born from largeness of heart. It is hard for a man to find such strength in afflictions without a gift from God, received through unfailing prayer and the shedding of tears.

When it is God's pleasure to subject a man to great tribulation, He lets him become a victim to faintness of heart. This gives birth to the force of despondency, which overwhelms him and oppresses his soul; and this is a taste of gehenna, because it produces a thousand temptations: confusion, irritation, protesting and bewailing one's lot, wrong thoughts, wandering from one place to another, and so on.

The cause of all this is your negligence. It is you yourself who have not troubled to find a remedy for it. The remedy for it all is only one—humility of heart. Without this no one can destroy the obstacle of these evils. In proportion to his humility a man is given patience in afflictions; in proportion to his patience the burden of afflictions is made lighter and he receives comfort; in proportion to the comfort he receives, the love for God increases in him, and in proportion to this love, his joy in the Holy Spirit grows. God does not remove trials from His servants, but gives them patience in trials as a reward for their faith and for surrender to His will.

251. Bodily life in accordance with God consists of bodily work—physical efforts to purify the body from passions in virtuous activity.

Mental life is the work of the heart, steadfastly carried on, diligently keeping in mind the judgment; likewise it is unceasing prayer of the heart, thinking of God's Providence and care, both general and in particular, which is manifest in the whole world, and protecting oneself from hidden passions, lest something passionate be encountered in the hidden and spiritual realm.

252. As grace added to grace, men after baptism are given repentance; for repentance is a second regeneration granted by God.

Repentance is the door of mercy; by this door we enter into God's mercy, and there is no entry into mercy but this.

Repentance is the second grace and is born of faith and fear; fear is the paternal rod ruling us until we attain the spiritual paradise of blessings; after that it leaves us.

Paradise is the love of God, wherein is delight in all blessings. The tree of life is the love of God from which Adam fell away. From that day joy no longer met with him; but he worked and laboured in a land of thorns.

Men deprived of the love of God, if they walk in righteousness, eat that bread of the sweat of their labours, which the first created one was ordained to eat after his fall.

The fruit of living in love is life from God, and one who lives in love smells the air of resurrection, while still in this world. Love is the kingdom. The Lord gave His Apostles the mysterious promise that they would eat of it in His kingdom. For it is said: 'That ye may eat and drink at my table in my kingdom' (Luke xxii. 30) and what can this mean, if not love? This is the 'wine' that maketh 'glad the heart of man' (Ps. ciii. 15). Blessed is he who drinks that wine!

253. As it is impossible to cross the wide sea without a ship or a boat, so no one can reach love without fear.

We can cross the fetid sea, which lies between us and the inner paradise, only in the boat of repentance, manned by the oarsmen of fear. But if the oarsmen of fear do not control the ship of repentance, by which we cross the sea of this world to God, then we sink in this fetid sea.

Repentance is the ship, and fear is its helmsman, while love is the Divine harbour. Fear leads us aboard the ship of repentance, takes us across the fetid sea of life and guides us to the Divine harbour which is love.

To this harbour come all those who labour and are heavy laden —by repentance. And when we reach love, then have we reached God, and our journey is accomplished, and we have come to the island of that yonder world where dwell the Father, the Son, and the Holy Ghost.

254. There is knowledge which comes in advance of faith, and there is knowledge which is born of faith. The knowledge which precedes faith is natural knowledge, and knowledge born of faith is spiritual knowledge.

Natural knowledge discriminates between good and evil and is called natural discernment, by which we distinguish good from evil naturally, without being taught.

God has implanted this discernment in a rational nature, but teaching increases and amplifies it.

There is no man who does not have it. It is the force of natural knowledge in the rational soul, which (force) is brought constantly to act in it (in the soul).

The honour bestowed upon rational nature is discernment, which discriminates between good and evil; the Prophet rightly likens those who have lost it to senseless cattle (Ps. xlviii. 12).

255. Natural knowledge which precedes faith is the way to faith and to God. Being implanted in our nature by God, it itself convinces us that we must believe in God, Who brought all things into being.

This faith produces fear in us; and fear impels us to repent and to act. Thus (that is, for what he does) man is given spiritual knowledge, or perception of the mysteries, which gives birth to the faith of true contemplation.

It is not simply of bare faith that spiritual knowledge is born; but faith gives birth to the fear of God, and when we begin to act from fear of God, the action of this fear gives birth to spiritual knowledge, as St. John Chrysostom says: 'When a man has acquired will conformable to the fear of God and a right way of thinking, then he quickly receives revelation of what is hidden.' Revelation of the hidden is what he calls spiritual knowledge.

256. But indeed it is not the fear of God that gives birth to this spiritual knowledge, for this knowledge is granted as a gift for the works of the fear of God. The works of the fear of God are repentance; and repentance, having completed its full course, brings a man to the place where he is given spiritual knowledge.

Spiritual knowledge is perception of the hidden. When a man perceives this that is invisible, then in his perception a new faith is born, not opposed to the first faith, but confirming it. It is called contemplative faith. Until then it was hearing, now it is vision; and vision is more sure than hearing.

257. All this is born of that natural knowledge, which distinguishes good from evil. It is the good seed of virtue.

From this natural knowledge in man there come constant stabs of conscience—continual memory of death and a certain tormenting care which lasts till his very end—and further, grief and mourning, fear of God and natural shame—contrition about former sins and proper diligence—remembrance of the way common to all, and concern to be rightly provided for it—tearful imploring of God to be granted a righteous entrance into the gate, through which every living being has to pass—scorn of the world and an intense struggle for virtue.

All this is acquired through natural knowledge—and with this let each man compare his work.

If it proves that a man has acquired all this, it means that he is following the natural way; but when he surpasses this and enters into love, he rises above nature. Then for him all struggle, fear, labour and weariness are ended.

These are the effects of natural knowledge. And we find them in ourselves, if we do not obscure this knowledge by our pleasure-loving will. At this stage we shall remain until we come to love, which frees us of it all.

On the basis of all we have said, let every man examine and test himself, to see where he is walking, whether in what is against nature, according to nature or above nature.

258. A good thought falls into the heart only by God's grace; and an evil thought comes near a man only to tempt and to test.

A man who has reached knowledge of the measure of his weakness has reached perfect humility.

A heart aroused to constant thanksgiving attracts Divine gifts. The Lord suffers all human weaknesses, but abhors a man who is always complaining, and does not leave him without a lesson.

Grace is preceded by humility; chastisement is preceded by a high opinion of oneself.

A proud man is allowed to fall into irreverence—a man boasting of active virtue is allowed to fall into wantonness—a man who glories in his wisdom is allowed to fall into the dark nets of ignorance.

259. A man who, while remembering God, respects every man, by a hidden movement of God's hand himself receives help from every man.

A man who protects the injured has God as his Helper; a man who stretches his hand to aid his neighbour has God's arm to support him.

A man who accuses his brother of fault has God for his own Accuser.

A man who corrects his brother in his private chamber, cures himself of his own fault; but he who accuses a man before others increases the pain of his own sores.

A friend who exposes another in secret, is a wise physician; but he who tries to cure another before the eyes of many, is a reviler.

260. God admonishes with love—He does not wreak vengeance (may this never be!); He seeks only to make whole His image, but does not harbour anger.

A man who does good for the sake of a reward is apt to change quickly.

However perfect a man may become in this life in his striving after God, he must always remain behind Him; but in the future life God shows him His countenance—though not what He is.

However much the righteous enter into contemplation of God

in this life, they see only an image as in a mirror; but there, truth itself appears to them.

261. Fire flaring up in dry wood is hard to put out; if Divine warmth enters a heart, which has renounced the world, its flame does not die—and it is more impetuous than fire.

When the power of wine enters the members, the mind forgets to be strict in anything; when memory of God takes possession of the pastures of the soul it wipes memory of all the visible from the heart.

Perception of the future life while in this world is like a small island in the sea; and he who approaches it is no longer troubled by the waves of the appearances of this life.

While a monk sees that he still needs time to work, parting with his body grieves him; but when he feels in his soul that he has redeemed time and has obtained his pledge, he longs for the future life.

While the merchant is at sea, he has fear in his members, lest the waves rise against him and engulf his hope of doing business. While the monk is in the world his life is beset by fear, lest a tempest awake in him and destroy the work at which he has laboured from youth to old age.

262. When a sailor is at sea he looks at the stars, and by them directs his course until he reaches harbour. But a monk looks at prayer, for it sets him right and directs his course to that harbour towards which his life is leading in hourly prayer.

A swimmer plunges into water stripped of his garments, to find a pearl; a monk, stripped of everything, goes through his life to discover in himself the pearl—Jesus Christ; and when he finds Him, he seeks no longer for aught existing beside Him.

263. It is harmful for a virgin to frequent gatherings and be among crowds, and for the mind of a monk to converse with many.

A bird, wherever it may be, hastens back to its nest, to hatch there its young; and a discriminating monk hastens to his place, to create in himself the fruit of life.

Clouds obscure the sun, and much talk darkens the soul which has begun to be illumined by prayerful contemplation.

They say of the bird called the siren, that every man who hears the sweet sound of its voice is so charmed that, following it in the wilderness, he forgets his very life in the sweetness of its song, falls down and dies. The same happens with the soul. When heavenly sweetness enters it, the sweet sound of God's words is imprinted by feeling on the mind and the whole soul surges up in its wake, forgetting its life in the flesh; the body loses its desires, and the soul rises out of this life to God.

264. Unless a tree first sheds its old leaves, it cannot grow new branches; so a monk, unless he casts off from his heart memories of his former actions, cannot bear new fruit and grow new branches in Jesus Christ.

They say that in a shell, where a pearl is born, lightning produces a kind of spark, which attracts a certain matter from the air, whereas until then it remains merely flesh; and until a monk's heart receives heavenly matter through understanding, its doing remains ordinary and its shells hold no fruit of comfort.

265. Do not approach the words of the mysteries, contained in the Divine Scriptures, without prayer and asking God's help, but say: 'Grant me, O Lord, to be open to receive the power contained in them.' Regard prayer as the key to the true meaning of what is said in the Divine Scriptures.

When you wish to approach God with your heart, first prove your love for Him by bodily labours. It is in them that lies the beginning of living. And the Lord placed them at the foundation of perfection.

Count idleness as the beginning of darkness of soul; and meetings for conversations as darkness upon darkness. If even useful talk, when it has no measure, produces darkness, how much more so does vain talk. A soul becomes worthless from excess of lengthy conversations.

266. Good measure and a certain rule in life enlighten the mind and protect it from confusion.

Confusion of mind, coming from lack of order (want of established rules) produces darkness of soul, and darkness produces new confusion.

Peace (of soul) results from good order, and of peace is born light; light and peace make the air of the mind clear and luminous.

267. A greedy soul is deprived of wisdom, and a merciful soul will be taught wisdom by the Spirit.

The key to Divine gifts is given to the heart by love of neighbour, and, in proportion to the heart's freedom from the bonds of the flesh, the door of knowledge begins to open before it.

How beautiful and praiseworthy is love of neighbour, if only its cares do not distract us from love of God!

268. How pleasant to talk with our spiritual brethren, if only we can at the same time keep our converse with God!

It is good to seek conversations with our spiritual brethren if a right measure is preserved, that is, so long as it does not cause us to lose our hidden life and doing, and our unceasing converse with God.

This latter is disturbed at the very outset of the former, for the mind is not adequate for carrying on two conversations.

Immoderate conversation is harmful even with spiritual brethren; as regards people of the world, it is harmful even to look at them from a distance; even without seeing them, the mere sound of their voice disturbs the peace of the heart.

269. Since the soul, in its nature, is better than the flesh, the soul's body is better than the physical body.

But just as the creation of the body originally preceded the breathing of life into it, so works of the body precede work of the soul.

Even if practices are not very lofty but are unvaryingly persisted with, they are a great force. A feeble drip, that goes on dripping, pierces hard stone.

When the time draws near for your spiritual man to be resurrected in you, joy is kindled in your soul, and your thoughts are held captive within you by that sweetness, which is in your heart. But while the world is attempting to rise in you again, wandering of thoughts increases.

By the world I mean the passions which are born of wandering of the mind.

When they are bred and reach maturity, they become sins and bring a man to death.

Just as children are not born without a mother, so passions are not born without wandering of thoughts, and sin is not committed without converse with passions.

270. If patience grows in our souls, it is a sign that we have secretly received the blessing of consolation.

When the soul is intoxicated with the joy of its hope and with Divine gladness, the body feels no afflictions, even if it is infirm. Then it has strength to bear redoubled hardships without losing force.

Thus it is when the soul enters into that spiritual joy.

If you guard your tongue, God grants you the blessing of piercing of the heart, that you may see in it your soul and thereby enter into spiritual joy.

Inasmuch as a man has wrought for God, his heart is given daring in his prayer; and inasmuch as a man has many distractions, he is deprived of God's help.

271. *The first thought* which, in God's loving-kindness, enters a man and guides his soul to life *is the thought of the end of this human state*, which enters *the heart*. This thought is naturally followed by scorn of the world; and this is the start of every good movement which leads a man to life. And it is this that the Divine power, which accompanies a man, lays as a foundation when it wishes to manifest life in him. And if a man does not kill this thought in himself by worldly cares and vain talk, but rears it in silence, dwells on it in contemplation, and makes it his concern, it will lead him to deep contemplation, such as no one can describe in words. Satan abhors this thought, and attacks it with all his forces to destroy it in a man, and if it were possible he would give a man the kingdom of the whole world, could he but distract him and wipe this thought from his mind. For the sly one knows that if this thought remains in a man, his mind is no longer on this earth of illusion and no wiles can come near him.

272. *The next* stage, which follows this, is when a man, progressing in the good life and approaching the experience and practice of contemplation, is granted from above the *grace to taste the sweetness of spiritual knowledge*.

The beginning of this stage is the following: first a man is convinced of God's Providence for men, he is illumined with love for the Creator and is filled with wonder alike at the wise ordering of sentient beings and at God's great care for them.

This is the beginning of Divine sweetness in him and the kindling of his love for God, which flames in the heart and burns up the passions of soul and body.

This love, accompanied by great zeal and good conscience, begins to flare up suddenly—and a man is intoxicated, as with wine, and his heart made captive to God.

Thereupon this force begins to gain strength and firmness in him, in proportion to his effort to lead a good life, to guard himself, to spend his time in reading and prayer.

273. Let us not be perturbed if we are in darkness. I mean that special darkness in which the soul languishes at times and is, as it were, among the waves; and whether a man reads the Scriptures, or practises his rule, in whatever he does darkness follows upon darkness.

He leaves his work, and very often is even unable to go near it. That hour is full of despair and fear; hope in God and the comfort of faith in Him are completely lost by the soul, and the whole of it is filled with doubt and fear.

But God does not abandon the soul to such a state for long, and soon makes a way to escape (1 Cor. x. 13).

But I will tell you, and give you this advice: if you have no strength to master yourself and to prostrate yourself in prayer, then wrap your head in your cloak and sleep, until this hour of darkness is over, but do not leave your cell.

People subjected to this temptation are mostly those who wish to lead a life of the mind, and who, on their way, seek the comfort of faith. Therefore at this hour what torments and wearies them most is the wavering of their mind. This wavering is often followed by impious thoughts, and a man is sometimes seized by doubt of the resurrection, and other things of which it is better not to speak.

Those occupied by physical work are entirely free of these temptations. They are assailed by another kind of despondency, familiar to every one, which in its mode of action differs from these and similar temptations.

Blessed is a man who endures it without going out of his door.

However, this struggle is not ended in an hour; and grace does not return suddenly to dwell in the soul, but gradually. One thing alternates with another: at times temptation comes, at others, comfort.

274. A man whose zeal is not controlled by reason never achieves peace of mind; and a stranger to peace is a stranger to joy. If peace of mind is called perfect health, and unreasonable zeal is opposed to peace, this means that a man full of wrong zeal is a prey to a grievous disease.

A heart filled with concern about the impotence and weakness of his outward physical work takes the place of all this physical work. Physical work without concern of the mind is like a body without a soul.

A man who grieves in his heart, but gives freedom to his senses, is like a man who suffers physically but whose mouth is open to every kind of harmful food; or a man with an only son, whom he gradually kills with his own hands.

275. Deeds without mercy are before God like a man killing a son in the presence of his father.

Compared with God's providence and God's mercy the trespasses of all flesh are as a handful of sand thrown into the sea. And as a strongly flowing spring is not obstructed by a handful of dust, so the mercy of the Creator is not stemmed by the vices of the creatures.

To bear a grudge and pray, means to sow seed on the sea and expect a harvest.

As a flame of fire cannot but mount upwards, so must the prayers of the charitable ascend to heaven.

As water flows downhill, so does the force of irritation, when it finds a way into our heart.

276. Humility may come from fear of God, from love for God, and from joy.

A man humble from fear of God is always accompanied by modesty in all his members, a right ordering of the senses and a contrite heart.

A company of the humble is beloved by God, like the company of the Seraphim.

A chaste body is more precious before God than a pure offering.

These two virtues—humility and chastity—prepare in the soul a pledge of betrothal for the Holy Trinity.

277. Watch your stomach, but not as you watch your sight; for a struggle in the home is undoubtedly easier than one outside.

Do not believe, brother, that inner thoughts can be stopped unless the body is brought into a good and orderly state.

Fear habits more than enemies. He who feeds a habit in himself is like a man who gives food to fire.

Once a habit demands something and its request is not fulfilled, the next time you will find it weaker. But once you fulfil its will, the next time you will find it fall on you with much greater force.

278. He who is fond of mocking and of showing off before people should be no friend of yours; otherwise he will teach you the habit of giving way to weakness.

If anyone begins to criticise his brother in your presence, keep your head downcast. As soon as you do this, you will show yourself circumspect before God and before him.

If you give something to one in need, let cheerfulness on your face precede the gift, and speak to him words of comfort. If you do this, your friendly look will be dearer to his mind even than a gift that is more than he needs.

Let all your actions be preceded by bodily chastity and a pure conscience, for without them every act is vain before God.

279. If you are persecuted, do not persecute; if you are crucified, do not crucify; if you are offended, do not offend; if you are slandered, do not slander.

To seek justice against a man is not fitting in Christian life; there is no hint of it in Christ's teaching.

Rejoice with those who rejoice, and weep with those who weep; for this is a sign of purity.

Suffer with the infirm; shed tears with the sinners; rejoice with the penitent.

Be friends with all men, but in your thought remain alone.

280. Denounce no one, revile no one, even men of the most wicked lives. Spread your cloak over one who is falling and cover him.

Know that the reason why we must not go out of the door of our cell is that we should not know the wicked deeds of men;

then in the ignorance of our mind we shall see all men as good and saintly.

If you cannot labour with your body, at least make efforts in your mind.

If you cannot fast for two days, fast at least till evening; if you cannot fast till evening, be careful not to overeat.

If you are not a peacemaker, at least do not be addicted to strife.

If you cannot close the mouth of a man who is judging his brother, at least refrain from joining him in this.

281. Know that if fire goes forth from you and scorches others, God will demand from your hand the souls which your fire has scorched. And if you yourself do not send forth fire, but are in agreement with one who does, and enjoy it, during judgment you will be counted among his accomplices.

Whatever ways men tread in the world, they find no peace until they come to hope in God.

The heart finds no respite from labours and stumblings, until hope enters it and brings it peace and joy. Lips we worship said of hope: 'Come unto me, all ye that labour and are heavy laden, and I will give you rest' (Matt. xi. 28).

The light of the mind gives birth to faith; faith gives birth to the comfort of hope; hope makes strong the heart.

282. The Son of God suffered on the cross; therefore we, sinners, boldly rely on repentance.

Sufferings of the mind suffice to replace all labour of the body.

St. Gregory says: 'He is a temple of grace who is united with God, and is always concerned with thought of His judgment.'

The blessed Basil says: 'Unceasing prayer produces a clear thought of God in the soul, and the setting up in ourselves of memory of God is the coming of God to dwell in us.' Thus we become the temple of God. A contrite heart serves to prepare us for our rest in God.

283. What we gather during our negligence shames us during our prayer.

Sobriety helps a man more than works; and licence (letting thoughts go) harms him more than (bodily) inactivity.

Inactivity produces domestic strife, which disturbs a man, but he has power to stop it. For as soon as he gives up inactivity and goes back to the place of his work, these attacks fall away and withdraw. But what comes from licence is not the same as what comes from inactivity. So long as during his inactivity a man stays within the realm of his freedom, he can turn back and, by establishing his rule, regain order in himself; for he is still within the realm of his freedom. But by giving himself licence (for thoughts with enjoyment) he goes outside the realm of his freedom. If a man had not completely given up watching over himself, he would not be forcibly and involuntarily constrained to submit to what brings him no peace.

284. O man, do not give licence to any of your senses, lest you lose the possibility of regaining your freedom. Inactivity is harmful only to the young, but licence harms also the old and the perfect. Those whom inactivity leads to evil thoughts can again return to watching over themselves and re-establish themselves in their lofty life. But those who, founding their hope on their works, have neglected to watch over themselves, are made captive and led from lofty to dissolute life.

285. Not only when we make a slip in something should we grieve, but particularly when we become set in that same thing; for even the perfect frequently slip, but to become set therein is complete darkness.

The grief we feel when we slip is accepted by grace as a pure doing.

If, trusting in repentance, a man deliberately slips a second time, he is dishonest with God; death comes to him unexpectedly and he does not reach the time when he hoped to fulfil the works of virtue.

286. Every man who gives free rein to the senses, gives free rein to the heart, for the work of the heart fetters the outer senses.

If a man practises this work with good judgment, it shows clearly in three ways: he is not tied by material profits, he dislikes indulging his belly and he never allows himself to be irritated. Where these three defects exist, there is no true order within, even if outwardly all appears irreproachable.

A reasonable disdain of things of the flesh produces non-attachment, scorn of ease and of the admiration of men.

If a man accepts readily and joyfully a loss for the sake of God, he is inwardly pure.

A man who does not look with gratification on someone who has done him honour, and is not indignant if he is insulted, has in this life become dead to the world.

287. Do not feel hatred for a sinner, for we shall all be taken to account. If you have to oppose him for the sake of God, weep for him.

And why should you hate him? Hate his sin, and pray for him, and so imitate Christ, Who was not wroth with sinners, but prayed for them.

Be a preacher of God's goodness, for God rules over you, unworthy one; for although your debt to Him is so great, yet He is not seen exacting payment from you and gives you great rewards for the small efforts you make.

288. Fear God out of love for Him, and not for the awesome name that He is given.

Love Him as you should love Him, and not for what He will give you in the future, but for what we have received in the present, and for this world alone, which He has created for us.

Who persuaded Him in the beginning to bring us into being?

Who intercedes for us before Him, when we do not remember Him?

When we were not, who brought this body of ours to life?

Whence comes the thought of knowledge to enter the clay?

What immeasurable goodness it is that leads again our sinful nature to regeneration!

Come, ye men of understanding, and be filled with wonder! Whose mind is sufficiently wise and amazed to wonder worthily at the mercy of our Creator?

289. In the degree that a man despises this world and shows zeal in fearing God, God's Providence comes near him—and he is secretly aware of the help of Providence and pure thoughts are given him to understand it.

If a man willingly deprives himself of worldly blessings, God's mercy accompanies him and His loving-kindness supports him to the degree that he deprives himself of them.

The souls of those who are not strong enough to win true life by a voluntary renunciation of all things God leads to virtue by involuntary sufferings, as we see in the beggar Lazarus.

God is near the grieving heart of a man who calls to Him in his affliction. Even if the Lord sometimes subjects a man's body to privations and other afflictions, to the soul of the sufferer He shows great loving-kindness, according to the severity of his suffering in his afflictions.

290. If the desire for love of Christ does not so conquer everything in you that joy in Christ strips you of passions in every affliction, then know that the world in you is more alive than is Christ.

When illness, want, exhaustion of the body, fear of harming the body perturb your thought enough to tear you away from the joy of hope and your constant care to please the Lord, then know that the flesh lives in you, and not Christ.

To speak simply, whatever attachment is master in you over the rest, it is that that lives in you.

If you suffer no lack in anything you need, your body is healthy and no adversities threaten you, and if you say that, with all this, you can advance towards Christ in purity, then know that your mind is sick and you are deprived of the taste of Divine glory.

291. That you may not say that there has been no man whose mind could rise completely above his infirmity, when his body was being destroyed by trials and afflictions, no man whose love for Christ could conquer the sufferings of his mind, I shall call to your memory the martyrs. See how their patience, supported by the force of their love of Christ, overcame great sufferings and physical pain.

And not they alone showed such fortitude; there have been philosophers, pagans, who did not know the true God, but who showed a wonderful strength of courage. One of them laid down a rule for himself to keep silence—and did not break this rule even when threatened with death. Others completely mastered natural lust; yet others easily endured calumnies; some calmly suffered grievous diseases; and others showed patience in afflictions and great tribulations.

If they endured it all for the sake of an empty glory and hope, must not we the more greatly endure, we monks, called to communion with God?

ST. MAXIMUS THE CONFESSOR

ST. MAXIMUS THE CONFESSOR

Short Biographical Note

St. Maximus was of noble birth, a native of Constantinople. After completing the full education required at that time, in theology, philosophy and so forth, he was taken by the Emperor Heraclius into his court and carried out the duties of first secretary, with praiseworthy success.

When the monothelitic heresy arose, in the birth of which even the Emperor and the Patriarch were guilty, and discords began both in the palace and the city, as well as in other parts of the empire, St. Maximus considered it as the proper occasion to satisfy his ever-present desire to leave the world and enter some monastery. Resigning from his duties, he entered the Chrysopolis monastery (A.D. 641) and began, with all zeal, to practise asceticism in accordance with strict statutes of the fathers, showing to all and in every respect an example worthy of imitation. So, when a new abbot had to be chosen for the monastery, he was unanimously elected for this office; he carried out its duties fittingly, indulging neither himself nor others.

Meanwhile the monothelitic heresy grew and spread, supported by the court and the Patriarch; and discord grew with it. Hating discords, St. Maximus left the monastery and went to Rome. On his way, he stayed for a time in Carthage in Africa where, in the Council convoked there, he denounced the unsoundness of monothelism, represented in the person of the Patriarch of Constantinople, Pyrrhus, who happened to be there as a private individual. Then he sailed to Rome, where he soon took part again in a Council against the monothelites, a Council convoked by the Pope St. Martin on the occasion of the Emperor's command to accept and sign a 'typikon', or creed, he had composed,

283

in which he had included the monothelitic heresy. This Council condemned and anathematised monothelism, the typikon of the Emperor and all those who accepted this heretical doctrine. Thereupon this decision of the Council was promulgated everywhere, both in the East and West.

The enraged Emperor gave orders for the Pope St. Martin and St. Maximus to be seized and brought to Constantinople. When they arrived there St. Martin, after incredible tortures, was sent to be imprisoned in the Chersonese where he died (A.D. 655). As regards St. Maximus, they began assiduously to try to win him over, first in the Emperor's palace, then in a place of confinement in Constantinople; after this in Visia, a small town in Thrace, where the holy martyr was imprisoned for the first time; then, when he was again brought back to Constantinople, attempts were made in a more solemn and threatening manner, in the monastery of St. Theodore, where he was lodged. The enquiry was conducted by senators, but bishops also were sometimes present. The purpose was to persuade St. Maximus to agree to their doctrine, or at least to sign the typikon, or, if not, to keep silent. They did not succeed. The truth of Orthodoxy proved victorious on the lips of St. Maximus every time and not only reduced his adversaries to silence but forced them to bow down to it. They tried to shake the courage of the defender of truth by promises, threats and advice as to how to circumvent the truth without it being noticed by others, and finally, at the last session, by flogging. Nothing was of any avail and St. Maximus was banished to a second place of imprisonment, being taken through Selimbria to Pervera, on the western shores of the sea of Marmora.

But the enemies of truth could not rest, and St. Maximus was once more recalled to Constantinople for final admonitions, which were conducted with great persistence but without success, in three stages: in the imperial palace, in prison, then again in the palace where the final verdict was pronounced: to keep the martyr alive but to submit him to torture more grievous than death. For that purpose he was delivered into the hands of the city eparch.

Finally, after inhuman tortures and abuses the saint was

banished to a distant land, Mingrelia, and there cast into the prison of Schemara, where he suffered every kind of want for three years, and finally departed to the Lord. Before his death, St. Maximus was comforted by a certain prophetic vision. This was in A.D. 662. The memory of St. Maximus is celebrated on January 21st.

ST. MAXIMUS THE CONFESSOR
Four Centuries on Love
Foreword to Elpidios

In addition to my discourse on ascetic life I am sending to your honour, Father Elpidios, a writing on love, in four Centuries corresponding to the number of Gospels. It may not match your expectations, but it is the best our powers can do. Still, I would like your Holiness to know that even this is not the fruit of my own mind. But having read the writings of the holy fathers and gathered from them what is relevant to my subject, I have condensed much into little in the form of sayings and texts, for greater ease of memory and reflection. I am forwarding this to your Reverence, begging you to read it with a good disposition, seeking only what is useful and paying no attention to clumsiness of style; but pray for my unworthiness, for I lack all spiritual fruit. I also beg you not to take my writing as a burden, for I am fulfilling the commandment of obedience. I say this because nowadays there are many of us, who burden the conscience by instructive words, yet those who teach by deeds or learn through deeds are few.

Pray pay careful attention to each text, for it seems to me that not all is easily clear to everyone. Many people will find that much of it will need careful enquiry, although at the first glance it may seem to be simple. Maybe things which will thus become revealed will prove useful. But of course, by the grace of God, the same result may be achieved if someone reads it not with an inquisitive spirit but with fear of God and love. But if a man should read this or some other book not for spiritual profit but in order to find passages with which to reproach the writer, that he may vaingloriously show himself to be the more knowledgeable, to such a man nothing useful will ever be revealed in anything.

First Century on Love[34]

1. Love is that good disposition of the soul in which it prefers nothing that exists to knowledge of God. But no man can come to such a state of love if he be attached to anything earthly.

2. Love is born from passionlessness; passionlessness—from hope in God; hope—from patience and magnanimity; these two —from self-mastery in all things; self-mastery—from fear of God; fear—from faith in the Lord.

3. He who believes in God fears the torments of hell. He who fears torment restrains himself from passions. He who restrains himself from passions bears tribulations with patience. He who bears tribulations acquires hope in God. Hope in God frees the mind of all earthly attachment. A mind thus freed acquires love of God.

4. He who loves God prefers knowledge of God to all things created by Him, and ever strives for it with desire.

5. If all that exists exists by God and for God, and God is better than anything which came into being through Him, then a man who abandons God and occupies himself with lower things thereby shows that he prefers above God what has come into being through Him.

6. A man whose mind cleaves to God with love holds as nought all visible things, even his own body, as though it were not his.

7. If the soul is better than the body, and if God, Who created the world, is incomparably better than His creation, then a man who prefers the body to the soul and the world to God, Who created it, is in no way different from those who worship idols.

8. He who has torn his mind away from love of God and from staying in His presence, and lets it attach him to anything sensory,

34 The Greek 'Ἀγάπη. (Translators' note.)

prefers the body to the soul and prefers what came into being through God to its Creator.

9. If the life of the mind is enlightenment by knowledge and this light is born from love of God, then is it well said that there is nothing higher than love of God.

10. When, urged by love, the mind soars to God, it has no sensation either of itself or of anything existing. Illumined by the limitless Divine light, it is insensible to all the created, just as is the physical eye to stars in the light of the sun.

11. All virtues assist the mind in its love of God, but pure prayer above all. Borne on its wings towards God, the mind is outside all that exists.

12. When, through love, the mind is ravished by knowledge of God and, standing outside all that exists, is conscious of God's infinity, then in its ecstasy it becomes aware of its own nothingness, and in all sincerity repeats the words of Isaiah, 'Woe is me! for I am pricked to the heart; for being a man, and having unclean lips, I dwell in the midst of a people having unclean lips; and I have seen with mine eyes the King, the Lord of hosts' (Isaiah vi. 5).

13. He who loves God cannot but love every man as himself, although the passions of those who are not yet purified find no favour with him. Therefore, when he sees them converted and reformed, he rejoices with great and ineffable joy.

14. A passionate soul is unclean, filled with thoughts of hatred and lust.

15. He who sees in his heart a trace of hatred towards another for some fault of his, is a complete stranger to love of God. For love of God can in no way tolerate hatred of man.

16. 'If ye love me, keep my commandments,' says the Lord (John xiv. 15). 'This is my commandment, That ye love one another' (John xv. 12). Thus he who does not love his neighbour, does not keep the commandment; and he who does not keep the commandment, cannot love the Lord.

17. Blessed is the man who can love all men equally.

18. Blessed is the man who is attached to nothing subject to corruption and time.

19. Blessed is the mind which, passing by all creatures, constantly rejoices in God's Beauty.

20. He who extends care for the body as far as lusts, and who feels rancour against his neighbour for something transitory, serves the creature rather than the Creator.

21. He who protects his body from lustful pleasures and from diseases has it as his ally in serving better things.

22. He who flees all worldly lusts places himself above all worldly tribulations.

23. He who loves God must of necessity love his neighbour too. And such a man cannot hoard possessions, but so manages them as to please God, giving to each man what he needs.

24. He who bestows alms, imitating God, does not distinguish good from bad, righteous from wicked in their bodily needs. He gives alike to all, according to their need; though he prefers a virtuous to a sinful man for the good disposition of his will.

25. Although God, good and passionless in His nature, loves all men equally as His creatures, He exalts a virtuous man as one akin to Him in disposition, and in His goodness shows mercy to a wicked one, and, punishing him in this life, converts him. So, too, a right-thinking and passionless man loves all men equally—the virtuous for his nature and for the good disposition of his will, and the wicked both for his nature and from compassion, showing him mercy, since he has no sense and walks in darkness.

26. Love is made manifest not merely through giving away one's possessions, but even more so by teaching the word of God and by bodily service.

27. A man who has sincerely renounced worldly things and without hypocrisy serves his neighbour from love, frees himself the more readily of all passions and comes to share in Divine love and Divine knowledge.

28. He who has attained to love of God in himself hath, like the divine Jeremiah, 'not been weary of following' the Lord (Jer. xvii. 16), but endures valiantly every labour, insult and abuse, never thinking evil of anyone.

29. When someone insults you or humiliates you in any way, beware of angry thoughts, lest because of this insult they tear you away from love and remove you to the realm of hatred.

30. When reproaches and dishonour weigh heavy on you,

know that they have been of great use to you, for through humiliation Providence has cast out vanity from you.

31. As memory of fire does not warm the body, so faith without love does not produce the light of knowledge in the soul.

32. As the light of the sun draws a healthy eye to itself, so knowledge of God naturally lifts a pure mind to itself through love.

33. A mind is pure if it has come forth from ignorance and is illumined by Divine light.

34. A soul is pure if it is free from passions and is constantly gladdened by love of God.

35. Passion is worthy of condemnation as being unnatural movement of the soul.

36. Passionlessness is a peaceful state of the soul in which it is not readily moved to evil.

37. He who by his diligence has gained the fruits of love does not fall away from it, even if a thousand evils assail him. You will find proof of this in Christ's disciple, Stephen and others like him. Christ Himself also prayed to the Father for His murderers, and asked Him to forgive them, for they knew not what they did (Luke xxiii. 34).

38. If the qualities of love are to suffer long and be kind (1 Cor. xiii. 4), it is clear that a man who is angry and bears malice is a stranger to love. But a stranger to love is a stranger to God, for 'God is love' (1 John iv. 8).

39. Do not say that you are the temple of the Lord, says the divine Jeremiah (Jer. vii. 4). Neither should you say, only faith in our Lord Jesus Christ can save me. For this is impossible unless you acquire love for Him, a love testified by deeds. As regards faith that is bare, 'the devils also believe, and tremble' (James ii. 19).

40. The works of love are—diligently to do good to one's neighbour, to be magnanimous, patient and to use things with good judgment.

41. He who loves God grieves no one and is grieved by no one for the sake of transitory things; he causes grief and is grieved only by the soul-saving grief, by which the blessed Paul was grieved and grieved the Corinthians (2 Cor. ii. 4).

42. He who loves God leads the life of an angel on earth, fasting and keeping vigils, singing psalms and praying, and always thinking good of every man.

43. Whatever a man desires he strives to attain; but since God is infinitely better and more desirable than any desirable things and blessings, how great must be the zeal we show to reach Him, Who is good and desirable in His nature.

44. Do not corrupt your flesh with shameful deeds; do not pollute your soul with evil thoughts: and the peace of God will descend upon you, bringing with it love.

45. Weaken your flesh by hunger and vigil, and practise without laziness psalmody and prayer—and the consecration of chastity will descend upon you, bringing with it love.

46. He who has been granted knowledge of God and has been illumined by it through love, is never puffed up by the spirit of vainglory; but a man who has not attained to it, is easily swayed by the latter. However, if he looks up to God in whatever he does, doing all things for His sake, with God's help he will easily escape this disease.

47. He who has not yet attained to knowledge of God inspired by love, thinks highly of what he does according to God. But a man who has received it repeats in his heart the words of our forefather Abraham, when God appeared to him, 'I am earth and ashes' (Gen. xviii. 27).

48. He who fears the Lord has humility as his constant companion and, by its reminders, ascends to love and gratitude to God. Recalling his former life according to the spirit of the world, his various sins, the temptations befalling him since his youth and how the Lord freed him from them all and led him from a life of passions to life in God, in addition to fear he receives also love; and ceaselessly with deep humility he gives thanks to God, the Benefactor and Ruler of our life.

49. Do not pollute your mind by retaining in yourself thoughts of anger and lust, lest, falling away from pure prayer, you sink into the spirit of despondency.

50. The mind loses its daring impetus towards God, when it converses with evil and impure thoughts.

51. When a foolish man, swayed by passions, becomes troubled

by anger, he takes senseless flight from his brethren; but when he is inflamed by lust, on repenting he runs to them all the more, to talk with them. But a sensible man behaves differently in both cases. In the case of anger he cuts off the causes of indignation and frees himself from vexation against the brethren; in the case of lust he abstains from irrational impulses and idle talk.

52. In time of temptations do not leave your monastery, but endure agitation of thoughts with courage, especially those which bring sorrow and despondency; for being thus tried by afflictions providentially, you will acquire a firm hope in God. But if you leave your monastery, you will prove yourself to be inept, cowardly and inconstant.

53. If you wish not to fall away from love of God, do not let your brother go to sleep vexed against you, nor go to sleep yourself vexed against him, but 'go . . . first be reconciled to thy brother, and then come' (Matt. v. 24) with a clear conscience and offer to Christ your gift of love in diligent prayer.

54. If, in the words of the divine Apostle, a man has all the gifts of the Spirit and has no love, it profits him nothing; how great, then, must be our diligence to acquire it (1 Cor. xiii. 3).

55. If 'love worketh no ill to his neighbour' (Rom. xiii. 10), does not a man who envies his brother, or resents his good repute, who besmirches his name with malicious talk or slanders him through his own ill nature, make himself a stranger to love and worthy of eternal damnation?

56. If love is 'the fulfilling of the law' (Rom. xiii. 10), does not a man transgress the law and deserve eternal torment if he bears malice against his brother, plots against him, curses him and rejoices in his downfall?

57. If 'he that speaketh evil of his brother, and judgeth his brother, speaketh evil of the law, and judgeth the law' (James iv. 11) and if the law of Christ is love (John xiii. 34), will not the slanderer fall away from the love of Christ and will he not become himself the cause of his own eternal torment?

58. Do not lend your ear to the tongue of the slanderer, nor your tongue to the ear of him who likes malicious talk, speaking or listening with enjoyment to words against one's neighbour,

lest you fall away from love of God and find yourself exiled from eternal life.

59. Accept no censure of your father, neither encourage his reviler, lest the Lord be angered by your actions and forbid you the land of the living.

60. Close the mouth of him who pours slander into your ears, lest you commit with him a double sin, by yourself acquiring the habit of this pernicious passion, and by failing to prevent him from reviling his neighbour.

61. 'But I say unto you,' says the Lord, 'Love your enemies, bless them that curse you, do good to them that hate you' (Matt. v. 44). Why has He commanded this? To free you of hatred, vexation, anger, rancour and to grant you the greatest attainment, perfect love, which no man can have who does not love all men equally, like God, Who loves all men equally, and 'will have all men to be saved, and to come unto the knowledge of the truth' (I Tim. ii. 4).

62. 'But I say unto you, That ye resist not evil: but whosoever shall smite thee on thy right cheek, turn to him the other also. And if any man will sue thee at the law, and take away thy coat, let him have thy cloke also. And whosoever shall compel thee to go a mile, go with him twain' (Matt. v. 39–41). Why? To preserve you from anger, agitation and vexation, to teach him by your gentleness, and to put you both under the yoke of love, for the Lord is good.

63. We preserve passionate images of anything towards which we have at any time felt passionate. Therefore whoever overcomes passionate images by this very fact disdains also the objects of his imagination. For it is much harder to wrestle with memories of things than with the things themselves, just as it is easier to sin in thought than in actual deed.

64. Some passions belong to the body, others to the soul. The causes of bodily passions are in the body, and the causes of passions of the soul are in external objects. But love and self-mastery cut off one and another alike: love—those of the soul, self-mastery—those of the body.

65. Some passions belong to the excitable power of the soul, others to the desiring power. Both are provoked by the senses,

but they are provoked when the soul is outside the bounds of love and self-mastery.

66. It is harder to overcome passions of the excitable power of the soul than those of the desiring power. For this reason the Lord has given us a stronger remedy against them—the commandment of love.

67. All other passions affect only one part of the soul—either the excitable, or the desiring, or else the thinking, as for instance, forgetfulness and ignorance. But despondency, embracing all the powers of the soul, straightway, at a single breath, brings almost all the passions into motion and therefore presses more heavily than all other passions. Good, therefore, are the words of the Lord that give the remedy against it, 'In your patience possess ye your souls' (Luke xxi. 19).

68. Never wound any of the brethren, especially when he is guiltless, lest he cannot bear the pain and goes away; for then you will never escape the reproaches of your conscience, which will always cause you grief during prayer and drive your mind away from boldly soaring to God.

69. Suffer no one to tempt you with suspicion against any man. For those who let themselves be exposed in one way or another to temptations by incidents, whether voluntary or involuntary, do not know 'the way of peace' (Rom. iii. 17) which, through love, leads its lovers to knowledge of God.

70. He has as yet no perfect love, whose disposition towards men depends on what they are like, loving one and hating another for this or that, or sometimes loving and sometimes hating one and the same man for the same reasons.

71. Perfect love does not divide human nature, which is one, according to men's different characters; but looking always on this nature, it loves all men equally; it loves the good as friends and the wicked as enemies, doing good to them, being long-suffering, enduring things caused by them, never returning evil for evil, but even suffering for them if occasion demands, in order, if possible, to make friends even of them. But if this proves impossible, it still retains its good disposition towards them, always showing the fruits of love equally to all men. Thus our Lord God Jesus Christ, showing His love for us, suffered for the whole of

mankind and gave equally to all the hope of resurrection, although each one makes himself worthy either of glory or of the torment of hell.

72. He who does not count equally as nothing honour and dishonour, riches and poverty, pleasures and afflictions, has not yet attained perfect love. Perfect love counts as nothing not only these things, but even temporal life and death.

73. Listen to the words of those who attained perfect love: 'Who shall separate us from the love of Christ? shall tribulation, or distress, or persecution, or famine, or nakedness, or peril, or sword? As it is written, For thy sake we are killed all the day long; we are accounted as sheep for the slaughter. Nay, in all these things we are more than conquerors through him that loved us. For I am persuaded, that neither death, nor life, nor angels, nor principalities, nor powers, nor things present, nor things to come, nor height, nor depth, nor any other creature, shall be able to separate us from the love of God, which is in Christ Jesus our Lord' (Rom. viii. 35–39).

74. Hear again what they say about love of neighbour: 'I say the truth in Christ, I lie not, my conscience also bearing me witness in the Holy Ghost, that I have great heaviness and continual sorrow in my heart. For I could wish that myself were accursed from Christ for my brethren, my kinsmen according to the flesh: who are Israelites' and so forth (Rom. ix. 1–4). Thus also spoke Moses and other saints.

75. He who does not disdain ambition and lusts, as well as love of money, which is born of them and which nurtures them, cannot cut off the causes of angry irritation; and he who does not cut them off cannot attain perfect love.

76. Humility and suffering (bodily privations) free a man from all sin; for the one cuts off passions of the soul and the other— passions of the body. The blessed David acted thus, as is clear from his prayer to God, 'Look upon mine affliction and my trouble; and forgive all my sins' (Ps. xxiv. 18).

77. Through the commandments the Lord makes passionless those who obey them; and through the Divine teaching He gives them the light of knowledge.

78. All teaching speaks either of God or visible and invisible

creatures, or of the providence and judgment manifested in them.

79. Loving-kindness cures the excitable part of the soul; fasting withers lust; prayer purifies the mind and prepares it for contemplation of what is. For the Lord gave us commandments corresponding to the powers of the soul.

80. 'Learn of me;' says the Lord, 'for I am meek and lowly in heart' (Matt. xi. 29). Meekness gives protection from the stirring of the excitable part, and humility frees the mind from arrogance and vainglory.

81. The fear of God is twofold. One is born of the threat of punishment, which gives rise successively to self-mastery, patience, hope in God and passionlessness, from which comes love. The other is connected with love itself and produces reverence in the soul, lest the daring of love lead to disrespect of God.

82. Perfect love casts out the first fear from the soul which has acquired it and which no longer fears torment; and the second, as I have said, remains always connected with the soul. The following words of the Scriptures apply to the first, 'By the fear of the Lord every one departs from evil' (Prov. xv. 27), and 'The fear of the Lord is the beginning of wisdom' (Prov. i. 7). To the second apply the words, 'The fear of the Lord is pure, enduring for ever and ever' (Ps. xviii. 9), and, 'There is no want to them that fear him' (Ps. xxxiii. 9).

83. 'Mortify therefore your members which are upon the earth; fornication, uncleanness, inordinate affection, evil concupiscences and covetousness,' and so forth (Col. iii. 5). By earth the Apostle here designates the minding of the flesh; by fornication—sin committed by deed; by uncleanness—consent to it; by inordinate affection—passionate thought; by evil concupiscence —simple acceptance of a concupiscent thought; by covetousness —the material of which passion is born and nurtured. All these, as aspects of the minding of the flesh, the divine Apostle enjoins us to mortify.

84. Memory at first brings into the mind a simple thought; and if this lingers there, it arrives at stirring up passion. If you do not eliminate the passion, it bends the mind to consent to it; when this comes to pass, man is led to sin by action. Therefore the wise

Apostle, writing to Christians converted from paganism, first ordains them to cease committing sin by action, and then, proceeding inversely, to arrive at its cause. The cause which engenders and nurtures passions is, as was said above, covetousness which, in my opinion, means here surfeit, the mother and nourisher of fornication. For covetousness is evil in relation not only to possessions but also to food, just as restraint is good in relation not only to food but also to possessions.

85. As a bird tied by the leg, when it starts to rise upwards is pulled back to earth by the string, so the mind which has not yet attained passionlessness, although rising to the knowledge of heavenly things, is pulled back to earth by the passions.

86. When the mind is wholly freed from passions, it advances unchecked towards the contemplation of what is, directing its progress towards knowledge of the Holy Trinity.

87. When the mind is pure, then the apprehensions it receives of things incite it to their spiritual contemplation. When it becomes impure through laziness, the representations it forms of other things are simple; but when it perceives something to do with man, it transforms it into shameful and evil thoughts.

88. If no worldly thought ever impinges upon your mind during prayer, know that you are not outside the realm of passionlessness.

89. When the soul begins to feel itself in good health, then its dreams also become pure and serene.

90. As the physical eye is attracted by the beauty of visible things, so is a pure mind by knowledge of the invisible. By invisible I mean incorporeal.

91. It is a great work not to be attached to things, but a much greater to be without passion towards their images; for the war that evil spirits wage against us through thoughts is much harder than the war arising from the things themselves.

92. He who has made progress in virtues and has become enriched by knowledge, already sees things as they are in their nature, and always says and does everything in accordance with sound understanding, never deviating from it. For we are virtuous or sinful according to whether we use things sensibly or stupidly.

93. The sign of perfect passionlessness is when, both in the

waking state and in sleep, representations of things are always simple when they enter the heart.

94. By fulfilling the commandments the mind becomes stripped of passions; by spiritual contemplation of the visible it is stripped of passionate representations of things; by knowledge of the invisible it withdraws from contemplation of visible things; finally, by knowledge of the Holy Trinity it abandons even the knowledge of things invisible.

95. As the sun, when rising and giving light to the world, shows both itself and the objects it illumines so the Sun of truth, shining in a pure mind, reveals both Himself and the understanding of all that is and is to be through Him.

96. We know God not in His own essence, but through the magnificence of His creation and through His providence for creatures. We see in them, as in a mirror, His boundless goodness, wisdom and power.

97. A mind that is pure remains either in simple thoughts about human things, or in natural contemplation of the visible, or in contemplation of the invisible, or in the light of the Holy Trinity.

98. When it contemplates visible things, the mind investigates their natural properties, or what these properties signify, or else seeks their cause.

99. When it exercises itself in the contemplation of things invisible, it seeks to know their natural properties, the cause of their existence, what follows from this, and God's providence and judgment concerning them.

100. When the mind is in God, at first its ardent love seeks to understand His essence; but it finds comfort not in the knowledge of what is in Him, for this is impossible and unattainable for all created beings alike, but in the knowledge of what invests Him, such as eternity, infinity, indescribability, goodness, wisdom and the power which creates all, maintains all and judges all. Only one thing in Him can be understood by all men—that He is limitless; and the very realisation of His incomprehensibility is a knowledge which transcends the mind, as said men wise in theology—Gregory and Dionysius.

Second Century on Love

1. A sincere lover of God prays wholly without distraction, just as he who prays without distraction loves God sincerely. But that man cannot pray without distraction whose mind is nailed to something earthly. Thus he whose mind is attached to something earthly does not love God.

2. A mind which lingers long on some object of sense is certain to have a passion for it, such as desire, or regret, or anger, or rancour. And so long as it does not regard this thing as of no importance whatever, it cannot become free of the passion.

3. Passions, taking hold of the mind, attach it to material objects; and, separating it from God, force it to be occupied with them. On the other hand, love of God, when it takes possession of the mind, severs its bonds, persuading it to value neither objects of sense nor even temporal life itself.

4. The task of the commandments is to make representations of things simple; but the task of reading and contemplation is to make the mind devoid of matter and form. And the result of this is prayer without distraction.

5. To free the mind completely from passions so that it may be able to pray without distraction, the active method is not sufficient, unless it is accompanied by various spiritual contemplations. The former frees the mind of intemperance and hatred; the latter deliver it from forgetfulness and ignorance, and in this wise it receives the possibility of praying as it ought.

6. The highest state of pure prayer has two forms. One belongs to men of active life, the other to men of contemplative life. One is engendered in the soul by fear of God and good hope; the other by love of God and extreme purity. The sign of the first order is when a man collects his mind, freeing it of all worldly thoughts, and prays without distraction and disturbance, as if God Himself were present before him, as indeed He is. The sign of the second

is when, in the very act of rising in prayer, the mind is ravished by the Divine boundless light and loses all sensation of itself or of any other creature, and is aware of Him alone, Who, through love, has produced in him this illumination. In this state, moved to understand words about God, he receives pure and luminous knowledge of Him.

7. What a man loves, that he desires to grasp with all his strength; and all that obstructs him in this he pushes aside, lest he lose it. Thus a lover of God applies himself to pure prayer and casts out every passion which hinders this end.

8. He who rejects the mother of passions, self-love, will with God's help readily cast out all other passions, such as anger, sadness, rancour and the rest. But he who is possessed by the first suffers the sting of the others, even against his will. And self-love is passionate love of the body.

9. Men love one another, either commendably or reprehensibly, for the following five reasons: either for the sake of God, as a virtuous man loves all men and is loved even by those who are not virtuous; or from nature, as parents love their children and are loved by them; or from vanity, as a man praised loves his praiser; or for the sake of gain, as a rich man is loved for what is received from him; or from love of lust, as a man who serves his stomach and what is below it loves the giver of feasts. The first of these is commendable, the second is intermediate, the others are passionate.

10. If you hate some, neither love nor hate others and love some moderately but others very intensely, then learn from this unequalness that you are still far from perfect love, which enjoins equal love for all men.

11. 'Turn aside from evil, and do good' (Ps. xxxvi. 27), that is, fight with enemies to weaken the passions and then keep watch, lest they increase anew. Again fight to acquire virtues, and then again keep watch to preserve them. This would be 'to cultivate and keep' (Gen. ii. 15).

12. With God's permission our tempters either inflame the desiring power of the soul, or agitate the excitable, or obscure the thinking power, or else heap sufferings on the body, or rob us of bodily needs.

13. The demons either tempt us themselves or incite against us people who have no fear of God. They tempt us themselves when we go into seclusion from men, as the Lord was tempted in the wilderness. They tempt through people when we have dealings with them, again as they tempted the Lord through the pharisees. But if we keep our eyes fixed on our example, that is, the Lord, we shall repulse them alike in each case.

14. When the mind begins to progress in love of God, the spirit of blasphemy begins to tempt it and to suggest thoughts, which no man can invent, but which can be devised only by their father, the devil. He does this from the envy he feels towards the lover of God, so that he should be cast into despair by such thoughts and no longer dare to soar to God in his habitual prayer. However, the evil one gains no advantage from this for his end; on the contrary he makes us more steadfast. For by being attacked and fighting back we become more experienced and sincere in our love of God. 'Let their sword enter into their own heart, and their bows be broken' (Ps. xxxvi. 15).

15. When it turns towards the visible the mind naturally apprehends things through the medium of the senses. Neither the mind, nor the natural apprehension of things, nor the things, nor the senses are evil, for they are all created by God. What then is evil in this? Obviously it is passion, which attaches itself to the natural apprehension of things. And passion need have no place in the natural apprehension of things, if the mind is awake.

16. Passion is an unnatural movement of the soul, due either to senseless love or irrational hatred of something sensory or because of something sensory: from a senseless love of food, or women, or possessions, or transitory glory, or of something else sensory, or by reason of such; from senseless hatred when, as was said above, people hate irrationally some of the above-mentioned things or someone because of them.

17. Or again, evil is an erroneous judgment about things apprehended, accompanied by their wrong use. Thus right judgment concerning intercourse sees its purpose in childbearing. But a man who sees in it nothing but lustful pleasure, errs in his judgment, taking the bad as good. Such a man commits abuse. One

should reason similarly about the understanding and use of other things.

18. When the demons separate your mind from chastity and surround it with lustful thoughts, call to the Almighty with tears, saying, 'Mine enemies have compassed about my soul. . . . Thou art . . . my joy, to deliver me from them that have compassed me' (Ps. xvi. 9; xxxi. 7), and you will be delivered.

19. Grievous is the demon of fornication and he presses heavily upon those who struggle with this passion, especially if one neglects to practise moderation in food, and in meetings and conversations with women. At first he imperceptibly captures the mind by impulses to lustful pleasure, and thereupon enters through the door of memory into the man who practises silence, sets his body aflame and presents various shameful images to his mind, provoking him to consent to sin. If you do not wish this to continue in you, practise fasting, labour, vigil and blessed silence, with diligent prayer.

20. Those who never cease to pursue our soul, strive by means of passionate thoughts to cast it into sin either by thought or deed. But when they meet a mind which refuses to accept them, they are 'ashamed and confounded'; and when they find the mind occupied with spiritual contemplation, they are 'turned back and grievously put to shame speedily' (Ps. xxxiv. 4; vi. 10).

21. He performs the office of a *deacon*, who anoints the mind for holy endeavours and drives out passionate thoughts; he performs the office of a *priest*, who enlightens the mind by knowledge of what is and destroys false knowledge; he performs the office of a *bishop*, who completes the mind's perfection by the sacred unction of knowledge of the worshipful Holy Trinity.

22. The demons grow feeble when our passions diminish through keeping the commandments; they perish when the soul becomes passionless; for then they vanish from it completely, no longer finding there what supported them and served them as weapons in their fight against it. This is the meaning of the words, 'they shall be feeble, and perish at thy presence' (Ps. ix. 3).

23. Some men refrain from passions through fear of men, others through vanity, others through self-mastery; but yet others are delivered from passions by God's providence.

24. All the words of the Lord comprise the following four subjects: commandments, teachings, threats and promises, and for their sake we endure every hardship such as fasting, vigil, sleeping on bare earth, privations and labours in work of obedience, insults, dishonour, torture, death and the like. 'By the words of thy lips,' says the Prophet, 'I have guarded 35 hard ways' (Ps. xvi. 4).

25. The reward of self-mastery is passionlessness; of faith, knowledge. Passionlessness gives birth to discernment, and knowledge, to love of God.

26. By leading an active life, such as it should, the mind progresses in sound judgment; and by leading rightly a life of contemplation it progresses in knowledge. The first leads to the power to discriminate between virtue and vice; the second introduces a man into the knowledge of the properties of corporeal and incorporeal beings. But the mind is granted the gift of theology only when it has fiown through all this on wings of love and has reached its dwelling in God. Then the spirit contemplates the attributes of God, as far as this is possible for the human mind.

27. If you wish to be a theologian, do not seek to find what God is in Himself, for this can be discovered not only by no human mind, but by no mind which is below God. But examine as far as possible the attributes investing Him, such as: eternal presence, boundlessness, indescribability, goodness, wisdom and His power as Creator, Provider and Judge of all. For he is already a great theologian among men who uncovers, however little, these attributes of God.

28. Strong is the man who has combined knowledge with action, for by the latter he withers lust and tames excitation, and by the former gives wings to his mind and goes forth to live with God.

29. When the Lord says, 'I and my Father are one,' He means their oneness of essence; and when He says, 'the Father is in me, and I in him' He shows the inseparability of the Hypostases. So the Tritheists, who separate the Son from the Father, fall into an abyss on either side. For if they admit that the Son is co-eternal

35 The English version of the Septuagint inserts 'myself from' in italics. (Translators' note.)

with the Father, yet separate Him from the Father, they are forced to say that He is not born of the Father and thus fall into a heresy which recognises three gods and three principles; or, if they admit that the Son is born of the Father, yet separate Him from the Father, they are forced to admit that He is not co-eternal with the Father, and to subject to time the Lord of time. According to the teaching of the great Gregory we should preserve the unity of God and profess three Hypostases, each with His distinctive property. For, according to his teaching, the Trinity is divided but indivisibly; and is combined but dividedly. A wonderful union and division! But where is the wonder if the Father and the Son were combined and divided as man and man are combined and divided, and nothing more?

30. He who is perfect in love and has reached the summit of passionlessness knows no difference between his own people and strangers or between believer and infidel, between bond and free, or even male and female. Being above the tyranny of passions and seeing one human nature, he looks equally on all men and is equally disposed towards them all. There is in him 'neither Jew nor Greek, there is neither bond nor free, there is neither male nor female,' but all in all is Christ (Gal. iii. 28).

31. From the passions lying in our souls the demons borrow the means to incite in us passionate thoughts. Then by these they overcome the mind and force it to descend to consent to sin. Having conquered the mind in this they lead it to sin by thought; and, this done, they lead it like a captive to sin by deed. Finally, having thus devastated the soul through thoughts, they withdraw together with them. There remains in the mind only the idol (mental image) of sin of which the Lord says, 'When ye therefore shall see the abomination of desolation . . . stand in the holy place' (Matt. xxiv. 15). 'Whoso readeth, let him understand' that the holy place and the temple of God is the human mind, where the demons, having devasted the soul by passionate thoughts, have erected the idol of sin. As to the fact that the words of the Lord have come to pass historically as well, I think that no one who has read Josephus Flavius will have the slightest doubt. Some say, besides, that it will be the same in the days of Antichrist.

32. Three principles move us to good: the seeds (of good which are) in our nature, the holy Powers, and our will for good. Seeds we have from nature—when, for example, we treat others as we wish to be treated by them, or when we see a man in want and in trouble and naturally show compassion to him. Holy Powers—when feeling an impulse to some good deed, we find (in ourselves) blessed assistance, and are successful. Finally, will for good—when we distinguish good from evil and choose the good.

33. In the same way, three principles incite us to evil: passions, demons and will for evil. Passions—when we desire something unreasonably, such as food at the wrong time or without need, or a woman with no intention of procreation, and unlawfully; also when we feel anger or bitterness against someone wrongly, for example, against a man who has reviled us or has caused us harm. Demons—when during our inattention they choose a suitable time and suddenly assail us and with great force provoke the aforementioned passions or others like them. Finally, will for evil—when, knowing the good, we choose the bad.

34. The reward for efforts in virtue is passionlessness and knowledge. For they lead us to the Kingdom of Heaven, just as passions and ignorance lead us to eternal torment. Therefore a man who seeks them for the sake of human glory and not because they are good, hears the words of the Scriptures, 'Ye ask, and receive not, because ye ask amiss' (James iv. 3).

35. Many human actions are good in themselves, but for some reason become bad. For example, fast and vigil, prayer and psalmody, alms and hospitality are good actions in themselves; but when done from vanity they are no longer good.

36. In all our actions God looks at the intention, whether we do them for Him or from some other motive.

37. When you hear the words of the Scriptures, 'Who will render to every man according to his deeds' (Rom. ii. 6), remember that God renders good not for an action done without right intention, even though it may seem good, but precisely for what is done with right intention. For God's judgment looks not only on what is done, but also on the intentions with which it is done.

38. The demon of pride exercises his wiles in two ways: he either persuades a monk to ascribe his right actions to himself, and not to God, the Giver of all blessings and Helper in all right activities, or, when the monk does not consent to this, urges him to despise the less perfect brethren. The man does not realise that, in influencing him thus, the demon incites him to deny God's help. For by despising those who have proved unable to be as correct as himself, he makes a display of himself, as a man who has done specially well by his own efforts. And this, as the Lord said, is impossible, 'for without me ye can do nothing' (John xv. 5). For our weakness is such that even if we desire good, we cannot achieve it without the Giver of all blessings.

39. He who has realised the weakness of human nature has received by experience the knowledge of God's power of help. When with this help such a man has accomplished certain things and striven to accomplish others, he never despises anyone. For he knows that, just as it helped him and freed him from many passions and evils, so it has the power to help all men, if God so wishes, and especially those who make efforts for His sake. Although for certain reasons God does not at once free all men from passions, as a good and compassionate Physician, He heals in His own time any who runs to Him.

40. When passions are inactive pride enters, either if the causes of passions are concealed, or if the demons feign to retreat.

41. Almost every sin is committed for the pleasure of self-gratification, and is therefore effaced by suffering and grief—voluntary or involuntary—resulting from repentance or from some affliction deliberately sent to us by Divine Providence. 'For if we would judge ourselves, we should not be judged. But when we are judged, we are chastened of the Lord, that we should not be condemned with the world' (1 Cor. xi. 31, 32).

42. If some unexpected trial comes upon you, do not blame him through whom it came, but seek the reason for its coming; and you will be corrected. For, whether through this person or another, you had to drink the bitter cup of the judgments of God.

43. The more wicked your disposition, the less you must reject suffering, that you may be humbled by it and thus throw out pride.

44. Some temptations bring men pleasures, others grief, yet others physical suffering. For the Physician of souls, according to His own judgment, applies the remedy, which corresponds to the cause of passions lurking in the soul.

45. Temptations are sent to some to efface previously committed sins, to others to arrest sins being committed at the moment, and again to others to prevent sins yet to come. In addition there are temptations sent to test a man, as in the case of Job.

46. A man of good sense, realising how beneficial are the judgments of God, thankfully endures the tribulations they bring him, holding none guilty but his own sins. But a foolish man, when he sins and is punished, regards as the culprit of his ills either God or men, not discerning the wisdom of Divine Providence.

47. Some remedies arrest the movement of passions and do not allow them to grow; and others weaken them and make them wither. Thus fasting, labour and vigil prevent the growth of lust; and solitude, contemplation, prayer and love of God weaken it and lead to its disappearance. Likewise in relation to excitability: magnanimity, not bearing malice, and meekness arrest it and prevent its growth; and love, almsgiving, kindness and compassion diminish it.

48. If a man's mind is constantly bent towards God, his desire too increases in its longing for God, and the whole of his excitable power is transformed into love of God. For the mind, becoming wholly luminous through its long participation in Divine illumination, and having subdued and mastered its desiring part, effects a transformation, as has been said, into continual longing and unfailing love for God—translating it entirely from the earthly to the Divine.

49. Not to envy, not to be angry, not to bear malice against one who offends does not yet mean to have love for him; for even without love a man can refrain from returning evil for evil, according to the commandment. But it is not so easy to return good for evil without forcing oneself, for spontaneously to do good to those who hate you belongs to perfect spiritual love alone.

50. Not to love another does not mean to hate him, just as not

to hate does not mean to love. But a man can be neutral in relation
to another, that is, neither hate nor love. For as a rule a loving
disposition is produced in the soul by the five causes mentioned
in the ninth text of this second century:—one praiseworthy,
another intermediate and three blameworthy.

51. When you notice that your mind is pleasurably occupied
with material things and lingers gladly on thoughts of them, then
know that you love them more than you love God. For 'where
your treasure is, there will your heart be also' (Matt. vi. 21) says
the Lord.

52. A mind that cleaves to God and dwells in Him by prayer
and love is wise, good, strong, compassionate, merciful, magnanimous; in brief, it bears within itself almost all the Divine
attributes. But a mind that falls away from God and forms friendship with material things, surrendering to lustful pleasures, becomes animal or bestial and fights with men for such things.

53. The Scriptures mean by the world, objects of the senses,
and those who occupy their minds with them are men of the
world. To shame them, the Scriptures say: 'Love not the world,
neither the things that are in the world. If any man love the world,
the love of the Father is not in him. For all that is in the world, the
lust of the flesh, and the lust of the eyes, and the pride of life, is
not of the Father, but is of the world' (1 John ii. 15, 16).

54. A monk is he who has withdrawn his mind from sensory
objects and who ceaselessly cleaves to God by self-mastery, love,
psalmody and prayer.

55. A herdsman in the spiritual sense is the name for a man of
action, for in spiritual life right moral actions have the significance
of the herding of working cattle. Therefore Joseph tells his
brethren to say 'We thy servants are herdsmen' (Gen. xlvi. 34).
But the shepherd is a man of contemplation, for by sheep are
meant thoughts grazing on the mountains of contemplation,
guarded by the mind. Therefore 'every shepherd is an abomination to the Egyptians', that is to the enemy powers (Gen. xlvi. 34).

56. When the body is urged by the senses to its pleasures and
lusts, a depraved mind joins it in its tendencies and fantasies. But
a virtuous mind refrains and draws back from passionate fantasies
and tendencies, striving all the harder to improve its movements.

57. Some virtues are of the body, others of the soul. Those of the body are—fasting, vigil, sleeping on bare earth, service, handicraft so as not to be a burden to others or to be able to give alms, and so on. Virtues of the soul are—love, magnanimity, meekness, self-mastery, prayer and so on. Thus if because of some need or because of our physical state, such as illness, or for some such reason we are unable to practise the above mentioned physical virtues, the Lord, who knows the reason for this, indulgently forgives us. But if we do not practise virtues of the soul, we shall have no excuse, for they are not subject to such obstacles.

58. Love of God disposes a man to scorn all transitory pleasures and all physical sufferings and afflictions. Let all the saints bear witness of this to you, for they have suffered much for Christ.

59. Beware of the mother of evil—self-love, which is an irrational love for the body. For it is from this that are born, with seeming justification, the three first and fundamental passionate and irresistible thoughts, namely—those of gluttony, cupidity and vainglory, using as pretext the natural bodily needs, and thereupon giving birth to the whole tribe of passions. This is why it is so necessary, as has been said, to beware of self-love and to fight it with great watchfulness. For its destruction means the destruction of all its offspring.

60. The passion of self-love suggests to the monk that he should spare his body and be indulgent to it in food under the pretext of wise management of the body and preserving its health, in order that, gradually leaning more and more towards it, he should fall into the abyss of lustful pleasures. In the case of a layman, self-love suggests that, as he is a layman, he should 'make . . . provision for the flesh, to fulfil the lusts thereof' (Rom. xiii. 14).

61. The highest state of prayer, it is said, is when the mind while praying leaves the flesh and the world and is completely devoid of matter and form. He who keeps this state inviolate truly prays without ceasing.

62. As the body at death is separated completely from all the things of this life, so the mind, dying under the action of perfect prayer, is wrenched away from all worldly representations. And if it does not die this death, it cannot be and live with God.

63. Let no one deceive you, humble monk, by the thought that you can be saved while serving lustful pleasures and vainglory.

64. As the body commits sin by deeds and has the bodily virtues to guide it and make it chaste, so the mind commits sin by passionate thoughts, and to guide it has the virtues of the soul, that make it chaste by looking at things purely and without passionate attachment.

65. As days are followed by nights and summers by winters, so vainglory and lustful pleasures are followed by sorrows and grievous sufferings, either in this or the future life.

66. It is impossible for the sinner to escape the future judgment without voluntary painful labours in this life, or without sufferings from involuntary afflictions.

67. It is said that God allows the demons to attack us for five reasons. The first is that, through being attacked and fighting back, we should learn to distinguish virtue from sin. The second is that, having acquired virtue by struggle and labour, we should keep it firm and unalterable. The third, that progressing in virtue we should not think highly of ourselves but should learn humility. The fourth, that having experienced in practice the wickedness of sin we should hate it with perfect hatred. Finally, the fifth and the most important is that having been freed from passions we should not forget our weakness and the strength of Him, Who has helped us.

68. As the mind of a hungry man dreams of bread and the mind of a thirsty man of water; so the mind of a glutton visualises various kinds of food; of a voluptuary—women's faces; of a vain man—human homage; of a money-loving man—profits; of a spiteful man—revenge against his offender; of an envious man—ill-fortune visiting the man he envies. The same happens with other passions, for a mind assailed by passions forms passionate images, whether the body is asleep or awake.

69. When lust grows, the mind dreams in sleep of things which bring pleasure, and when excitability grows it sees things that bring fear. Passions are strengthened by unclean spirits who, helped by our negligence, stimulate them. And passions are diminished by holy angels, who urge us to practise virtues.

70. Frequent stimulation of the desiring power of the soul produces therein an irresistible habit of lustful pleasures, and frequent arousing of the excitable power makes the mind timid and deprives it of courage. The first is cured by long practice of fasting, vigil and prayer; the second by kindness, compassion, love and mercifulness.

71. Evil spirits wage war against us either by means of things, or passionate representations of things; by things—against those who move and have their being among them, and by representations—against those who are withdrawn from things.

72. Just as it is easier to sin in thought than in deed, so equally is struggle against representations harder than struggle against things.

73. Things are outside the mind, but their representations are inside it. So it is in the mind's power to use them rightly or wrongly. For a wrong use of representations is followed by a wrong use of things.

74. The mind receives passionate representations in three ways: through the senses, through the state of the body and through memory. Through the senses, when such things as arouse our passions, producing an impression on the senses, evoke passionate thoughts in the mind. Through the state of the body, when, as a result of intemperance in food, or from the action of the demons, or from some illness, the state of the body changes and incites a man to passionate thoughts or to revolt against Providence. Through memory, when memory revives representations of things, for which we have passionate feelings, and thus engenders passionate thoughts in the mind.

75. Some of the things given us by God for our use are in the soul, others in the body, yet others around our body. In the soul are its powers; in the body—the senses and other members; around the body—food, possessions, money and so forth. A right or wrong use of these things, and the resulting effects, shows us as being either virtuous or sinful.

76. Some of the above-mentioned effects occur in what is ir the soul, others in what is in the body, yet others in what is around the body. In the soul—knowledge and ignorance, remembering and forgetting, love and hate, fear and daring, joy and

sorrow, and so on. In the body—enjoyment and weariness, sharp and dull senses, health and ill-health, life and death, and so forth. In what lies around the body—fecundity and barrenness, wealth and poverty, honour and dishonour, and so forth. Of these some are deemed good by men, others bad, whereas in reality none of them are bad, but can be either good or bad according to the use made of them.

77. In itself knowledge is good, just as is health. But to many people the opposite has proved more useful. Since for the wicked knowledge leads to no good, although, as has been said, it is good in itself. Neither does health lead to anything good in them, nor wealth nor joy, for they put them to no good use for themselves. For such men the opposite is more useful, and therefore this (that is, the opposite) is not bad in a true sense, although it appears bad.

78. Do not make wrong use of thoughts, lest of necessity you make wrong use of things as well, for if you do not first sin in thought you will never sin in deed.

79. 'The image of the earthy' (Adam) means the principal vices: foolishness, cowardice, intemperance, injustice. 'The image of the heavenly' is the principal virtues, such as good judgment, courage, chastity, justice. But 'as we have borne the image of the earthy, we shall also bear the image of the heavenly' (1 Cor. xv. 49).

80. If you wish to find the way leading unto life, seek it in that Way, Who said, 'I am the way, the truth, and the life'; 'I am the door' (John xiv. 6; x. 9); and there you will find it. But seek diligently, for 'few there be that find it' (Matt. vii. 14), lest you are left behind by the few, and find yourself among the many.

81. A soul is turned away from sin by the following five impulses: fear of men, fear of judgment, hope of future reward, love of God or finally pangs of conscience.

82. Some say that there would be no evil in creatures were it not for a certain extraneous power, which entices us to evil. But this power is nothing more than our own neglect of the natural activity of the mind. Thus those who take care of this activity always do good and never do evil. Therefore, if you too desire this, throw off negligence and with it you will throw off evil,

which is a wrong use of thoughts accompanied by a wrong use of things.

83. According to nature, our rational part should obey the word of God and control our irrational part. Let this order be followed in all things—and there will be no evil in creatures, nor will there be anything driving them to evil.

84. Some thoughts are simple, others complex. Simple thoughts are passionless, complex thoughts—passionate, as being compounded of passion and representation. Moreover we can see that many simple thoughts follow in the tracks of the complex, when they begin to move towards sin in thought. Take gold, for example. A passionate thought about gold may arise in a man's memory and he may mentally wish to steal it; behold, he has already committed sin in his mind. Memory of gold was followed by memory of a purse, a chest, a store-room, and so forth. In this case the memory of gold was complex, since it was connected with passion, and the memories of the purse, the chest and so on were simple, for the mind felt no passion towards them. It is the same with any other thought: a vainglorious thought, a thought about a woman, and others. For not all thoughts which follow upon the passionate thought are themselves passionate, as was shown in this example. From this we may recognise which thoughts are passionate and which are not.

85. Some say that during our sleep the demons come to touch the shameful parts of our body and thus excite the passion of fornication; thereupon, through memory, the excited passion brings to the mind an image of a woman. Others think that the demons themselves appear to the mind in the guise of a woman, and then, touching the shameful parts of the body, excite desire for women, which results in corresponding fantasies. Yet others think that the prevailing passion of the approaching demon provokes a corresponding passion in the man and that in this way the soul is incited to thoughts and introduces images through memory. And so it is with other passionate fantasies: some say it happens in one way, others in another way. But whatever be the method, the demons are powerless to provoke a passion, whether the body is asleep or awake, if love and self-mastery are present in the soul.

86. Some commandments of the law should be observed both physically and spiritually; others only spiritually. For instance, 'Thou shalt not commit adultery,' 'thou shalt do no murder,' 'thou shalt not steal' and others of this kind, should be observed both physically and spiritually—and spiritually in a three-fold manner. Yet the commandments of circumcision, of keeping the sabbath, of slaughtering a lamb, of eating unleavened bread with bitter herbs and similar things—only spiritually.

87. There are three principal moral states among monks: the first, when he commits no sin in action; the second, when he does not allow passionate thoughts to linger in the soul; the third, when he looks in thought without passion on images of women and of those who have offended him.

88. He is uncovetous, who has renounced all possessions and has nothing on earth except his body, and who, having lost all attachment to his body, has entrusted to God and to pious men all care of himself.

89. Some men acquire possessions without passion, and so do not grieve at their loss, as did those who 'took joyfully the spoiling of' their 'goods' (Heb. x. 34). Others acquire them with passion and so grieve at the idea of losing them, as did the rich man mentioned in the Gospels, who 'went away sorrowful' (Matt. xix. 22); and if they lose them in actual fact are mortally afflicted. Thus the loss of possessions reveals whether the man owned them with passion or without passion.

90. The demons fall on men, who have reached great heights in prayer, by introducing into their minds simple thoughts of sensory things and thus distracting them from prayer. They attack those, who study to acquire knowledge, by making passionate thoughts linger in them for a long time; and those who practise active life, by enticing them to commit sin in deed. The accursed ones use all kinds of means with all men to separate them from God.

91. Those whom Divine Providence exercises in piety in this life are tried by the following three temptations: either by pleasant gifts, such as health, beauty, many children, riches, fame and other similar things; or by grievous events, such as loss of children, of possessions, of fame; or else by sufferings of the body, such as, illnesses, tortures and so forth. To the first the

Lord says, 'Whosoever he be of you that forsaketh not all that he hath, he cannot be my disciple' (Luke xiv. 33). And to the second and third, 'In your patience possess ye your souls' (Luke xxi. 19).

92. It is said that the following four causes change the state of the body and thereby produce in the mind either passionate or passionless thoughts: angels, demons, air and food. Angels, it is said, change it by word; demons by touch; air by its variations, food by the quality of what is eaten and drunk, and its excess or scantiness. In addition, changes are produced by memory, hearing and sight after the soul has experienced the effect of joyful or sorrowful circumstances. Having experienced their effect, the soul produces a change in the bodily state, and the changed bodily state, as has been said, gives the mind corresponding thoughts.

93. Death, rightly speaking, is being separated from God; and the sting of death is sin, which Adam received in himself, and so was at once banished from the tree of life, from the garden of Eden and from God, which was necessarily followed by bodily death. But life, in the true meaning of the word, is He Who said, 'I am . . . the life' (John xiv. 6); He Who, being dead, restored the dead to life.

94. When one writes something, one does so either for one-self, in order to remember it, or for the use of others, or for both reasons, or to bring harm to some, or for the sake of appearances, or through necessity.

95. 'Green grass' (Ps. xxii. 2)[36] is active virtue; and 'the water of rest'—knowledge of the created.

[36] The Septuagint version of Ps. xxii is as follows:

1. The Lord tends me as a shepherd, and I shall want nothing.

2. In a place of green grass, there he has made me dwell: he has nourished me by the water of rest.

3. He has restored my soul: he has guided me into the paths of righteousness, for his name's sake.

4. Yea, even if I should walk in the midst of the shadow of death, I will not be afraid of evils: for thou art with me; thy rod and thy staff, these have comforted me.

5. Thou hast prepared a table before me in presence of them that afflict me: thou hast thoroughly anointed my head with oil; and thy cup cheers me like the best wine.

6. Thy mercy also shall follow me all the days of my life: and my dwelling shall be in the house of the Lord for a very long time.

(Translators' note.)

96. 'The shadow of death' is human life. He who is with God and with whom God is, can say daringly, 'Yea, even if I should walk in the midst of the shadow of death, I will not be afraid of evils: for thou art with me' (Ps. xxii. 4).

97. A pure mind sees things rightly; speech, trained by practice, puts what is seen, as it were, before the eyes of others; and an open ear receives it. But he who lacks these three blames the speaker.

98. He is with God who knows the Holy Trinity, Its creation and Its providence, and who keeps free from passions the part of his soul susceptible to passion.

99. It is said that 'the rod' is God's judgment, and 'the staff' is Providence. He who has acquired knowledge of this can say, 'Thy rod and thy staff, these have comforted me' (Ps. xxii. 4).

100. When the mind has been stripped of passions and is illumined by the contemplation of what is, it can be in God and pray as it ought.

Third Century on Love

1. A rational use of representations and objects brings chastity, love and knowledge; and an irrational use—lack of self-mastery, hatred and ignorance.

2. 'Thou hast prepared a table before me' and so forth. 'Table' means here active virtue; for it is prepared by Jesus Christ against those who oppress us. 'Oil,' which anoints the mind, means contemplation of creatures; the 'cup' of God is the knowledge of God; His 'mercy' is His Word, Who is God: for by His incarnation He follows us all the days of our life until He overtakes all those who are to be saved, as He did with Paul. 'The house' means the kingdom in which all the saints will come to dwell; 'very long time' means eternal life. (Ps. xxii. 5, 6.)

3. Sins happen to us from wrong use of the powers of the soul, that is, the desiring, the excitable and the thinking powers. Wrong use of the thinking power results in ignorance and foolishness, and wrong use of the excitable and desiring powers—hatred and lack of restraint. Right use of them means knowledge, good judgment, love and chastity. And if this be so, then nothing of what was created and received existence from God is evil.

4. It is not food that is evil but gluttony; not childbearing but fornication; not money but cupidity; not glory but vainglory. If this be so there is no evil in anything that is, except wrong use, which results from our mind neglecting to cultivate our nature (the powers of the soul, and their right direction).

5. According to the blessed Dionysius, the evil in demons is: irrational excitability, mindless desires and headlong fantasy. But irrationality, mindlessness and precipitancy in rational beings mean loss of reason, of mind and of circumspection. But loss is a sequel to possession. Hence there was a time when they had reason, mind and reverent circumspection. If this be so, then

demons too are not essentially evil, but have become evil through wrong use of their natural powers.

6. Some passions give birth to intemperance, others to hatred, yet others to both intemperance and hatred.

7. Eating too much and too well causes inchastity; cupidity and vainglory cause hatred of one's neighbour; their mother, self-love, is the cause of both.

8. Self-love is passionate and irrational love of the body. The qualities opposed to it are love and self-mastery. It is clear that he who has self-love has all the passions.

9. 'No man ever yet hated his own flesh' (Eph. v. 29) says the Apostle; yet he keeps under his body and brings it into subjection (1 Cor. ix. 27), giving it nothing except 'food and raiment' (1 Tim. vi. 8), and even those only because they are indispensable for life. Thus they love it without passion and feed and clothe it as a servant of Divine things merely to replenish its needs.

10. If one loves someone, one strives to please him in all possible ways. Thus if a man loves God he will certainly strive to do what pleases Him. And a man who loves the flesh does what gives satisfaction to the flesh.

11. Pleasing to God are love, chastity, contemplation and prayer; and pleasing to the flesh are gluttony, lack of restraint and all that increases them. This is why 'they that are in the flesh cannot please God' (Rom. viii. 8); but 'they that are Christ's have crucified the flesh with the affections and lusts' (Gal. v. 24).

12. When the mind inclines towards God, it has the body as its servant and gives it no more than is needful for its life; but when it inclines towards the flesh, it becomes a servant of its passions and makes always 'provision for the flesh, to fulfil the lusts thereof' (Rom. xiii. 14).

13. If you wish to be free of thoughts, cure yourself of passions; then you will easily banish thoughts from the mind. Thus, in relation to the passion of fornication, fast, practise vigil, work and withdraw from men; in relation to anger and sadness, count as nothing honour and dishonour and other earthly things; in relation to rancour, pray for those who have offended you—and you will be delivered.

14. Do not take your measure from the weakest among men but, rather, broaden yourself into the measure of the commandment of love. If you take men as your measure, you will fall into the abyss of arrogance; but broadening yourself into the measure of love, you will reach the height of humility.

15. If you are indeed keeping the commandment of loving your neighbour, why do you implant in yourself the bitterness of annoyance against him? Is it not clear that above love you prefer the transitory, and in protecting it you wage war against your brother?

16. It is not so much for the sake of necessity that gold is desirable to men, as because it enables many to satisfy their lust for pleasures.

17. There are three causes for love of riches: lust for pleasures, vainglory and lack of faith; and lack of faith is stronger than the other two.

18. A man addicted to pleasures loves money in order to enjoy himself with its help; the vainglorious man, to gain fame; and the man without faith to hide and keep it for fear of hunger, or old age, or illness, or banishment, putting more trust in riches than in God, the Creator and Provider for every creature, down to the last and smallest living being.

19. Four kinds of men amass riches: the three mentioned above, and the fourth—a good householder. It is clear that only the last one amasses riches rightly, that his hand should never fail to give whatever each may need.

20. All passionate thoughts either stimulate the desiring part of the soul, or provoke the excitable part, or obscure the thinking part; from which it results that the mind becomes blind for spiritual contemplation and the soaring of prayer. Therefore a monk, especially if he practises silence, must watch his thoughts vigilantly, and recognise and cut off their causes. He should recognise them in the following manner: the desiring part of the soul is stimulated by passionate memories of women, and the cause of these lies in lack of restraint in food and drink and frequent, imprudent dealings with women. They are cut off by hunger, thirst, vigil and solitude. The excitable part of the soul is provoked by passionate memories of people who have offended

one, and the cause of these lies in love of pleasures, vainglory and love of things, for a passionate man grieves if he loses them or cannot obtain them. He cuts them off by scorning such things, as of no value, through love of God.

21. God knows Himself and knows His creatures, and the holy Powers know God and know God's creatures. But the holy Powers know God and His creatures not as He Himself and His creatures are known by God.

22. God knows Himself from His own blessed essence, and He knows His creatures from His wisdom, by which and in which He created all things. But the holy Powers know God, Who is above all participation, by participation (in His knowledge), and they know His creatures by apprehending that in them which is to be contemplated by the mind.

23. Creatures are external to mind; but their contemplation the mind receives within itself. It is not so, however, in God the eternal, the infinite and indescribable, Who has given from Himself, to all that is, being, well-being and ever-being.

24. In God, the Holy One, that is to say, in God's goodness and wisdom, the rational and intelligent nature participates by its very being, by its capacity for well-being, and by the gift from grace of ever-being. Through this grace it knows God. As to His creatures, it knows them, as has been said, by apprehending the all-ordering wisdom, which it contemplates in them, and which, being subtle, takes shape immaterially in the mind.

25. When God brought into existence the rational intelligent nature, in His infinite goodness He endowed creatures possessing it with four divine qualities to maintain, protect and preserve them:—being, ever-being, goodness and wisdom. He gave the first two to the nature and the latter two to the moral faculty. To the nature—being and ever-being, to the moral faculty—goodness and wisdom, in order that through participation the creature should become what He Himself is by nature. This is why it is said that man is created in God's image and likeness, as one who is, created in the image of Him Who is; as one who ever is, in the image of Him Who ever is, although not without beginning, yet without end. As being good, he is created in the likeness of Him Who is good, as being wise in the likeness of Him Who is wise, becoming

through grace what God is by nature. Every rational creature is in God's image; but in His likeness are only the good and the wise.

26. All rational and intelligent nature is divided into two orders; angelic nature and human nature. All angelic nature is again divided into two principal moral fellowships and communions—the holy and the damned, that is, the holy Powers and the ungodly demons. And the whole human race is divided only into two fellowships—the righteous and the unrighteous.

27. God, Who is Being itself, Goodness itself, Wisdom itself, or rather, Who is above all these, is wholly without opposites. But since creatures have being only through participation and grace (the rational and intelligent possessing in addition the capacity for goodness and wisdom), they contain the opposites, namely, the opposite of being—non-being; the opposite of capacity for goodness and wisdom—malice and ignorance. Their ever-being or non-being lies in the power of their Creator, but their participation or non-participation in God's goodness and wisdom lies within the will of rational creatures.

28. Supposing that the being of creatures has been with God from eternity and that they have received from Him merely their qualities, the Greeks say that their being too has no opposite and that opposites are to be found only in their qualities. But we affirm that it is only God's Being that has no opposites, since It is eternal, and boundless and gives eternal life to all other being. But the being of creatures has non-being as its opposite, and their ever-being or non-being is in the power of Him Who properly Is. But since He neither repents of His gifts nor changes them, as the creature is, so it will always be, being maintained by His almighty power, although, as has been said, it contains non-being as its opposite. For it has been brought into being from non-being and its being or non-being is in God's will.

29. As evil is privation of good and ignorance is privation of knowledge, so non-existence (non-being) is privation of existence (being)—not privation of What properly Is, for this has no opposite, but privation of being which exists through participation in What properly Is. Privation of the first two depends on the will of the creature; privation of the last depends on the will of

the Creator, Who, in His goodness, always wishes creatures to be, and always to be receivers of His gifts.

30. All creatures are either rational and intelligent, admitting of opposites, that is, virtue and vice, knowledge and ignorance; or they are heterogeneous bodies composed of opposites, such as earth, air, fire and water. The former are totally incorporeal and immaterial, although some of them are joined to bodies; the latter consist entirely of matter and form.

31. In their nature all bodies are motionless but are moved by the soul. Some souls have reason, others lack reason, yet others lack sensibility.

32. Of the powers of the soul, one is for nourishment and growth, another for representations and impulses, and yet another for reasoning and thinking. Plants have only the first; dumb animals have the second in addition to the first; and men have the third together with the first two. The first two powers are perishable, the third is regarded as imperishable and immortal.

33. The holy Powers, communicating enlightenment to one another, transmit also to human nature the virtue and the knowledge that are in them. Virtue—that is, goodness in imitation of God, whereby they do good to themselves, to each other and to the creatures below them, thus rendering them godlike. Knowledge—such as a higher knowledge of God, for 'Thou, O Lord, art most high for ever' (Ps. xci. 8); or a deeper knowledge of corporeal beings; or a more exact knowledge of incorporeal beings; or a more clear knowledge of Providence, or a more precise knowledge of Judgment.

34. Impurity of mind consists, first, in erroneous knowledge; second, in ignorance of something general—I refer to the human mind, for it does not belong to an angel to be ignorant even of anything particular; third, in passionate thoughts; fourth, in consent to sin.

35. Impurity of soul consists in this, that it does not act in accordance with nature; for of this are born passionate thoughts in the mind. The soul acts in accordance with nature when its passionate powers, that is, the excitable and the desiring, remain passionless under the impulse of things, or of thoughts about them.

36. Impurity of body is sin committed by deed.

37. He loves silence, who is unattached to worldly things. He loves all men, who loves nothing human. He has knowledge of God and of the Divine, who is drawn into evil by no one either on account of their misdeeds, or by thoughts about them bred of suspicion.

38. It is a great thing not to have a passionate attachment to things, but a still greater to be passionless in face of their representations in the mind.

39. Love and self-mastery keep the mind passionless both towards things and towards their representations.

40. The mind of a lover of God arms itself not against things and their representations, but against the passions connected with these representations. In other words, it rises not against a woman, nor against a man who has offended it, nor against their images, but against the passions connected with these images.

41. The whole struggle of a monk against the demons consists in separating passions from representations; for otherwise it is impossible for him to look at things without passion.

42. An object is one thing, a representation another, passion yet another. An object is, for example, a man, a woman, gold and so forth; a representation—a simple memory of some such object; passion—either an irrational love or an undiscerning hatred of one of these things. It is against such passion that the monk wages war.

43. Passionate representation is thought compounded of passion and representation. If we separate passion from representation, there remains pure thought. We separate the two, if we wish, by means of spiritual love and self-mastery.

44. Virtues free the mind from passions; spiritual contemplations free the mind from simple representations; pure prayer presents it to God Himself.

45. Virtues exist for the sake of knowledge of creatures, knowledge for the sake of him who knows, he who knows for the sake of Him who is known unknowably and Who knows beyond knowledge.

46. Since God suffices unto Himself, He brought creatures from non-being into being, not because He had need of something

but in order that they should rejoice, sharing in His bliss in accordance with their capacity; and that He should take joy in His works, seeing them rejoicing and ever insatiably satiating themselves from the Insatiable Source.

47. The world has many poor in spirit, but not in the proper sense; many who mourn, but either about loss of property or loss of children; many who are meek, but towards impure passions; many who hunger and thirst, but only to usurp wrongly what is not theirs and to collect unfair profits; many merciful, but to the body and things of the body; many pure in heart, but out of vanity; many peacemakers, but they subjugate the soul to the flesh; many who are persecuted, but for their own wrongdoings; many who are reviled, but for shameful sins. Only those are blessed who act and suffer for Christ and according to Christ. Why? 'For their's is the kingdom of heaven,' and 'they shall see God' (Matt. v. 3, 8), and so on. They are not blessed because they act thus and endure, for those mentioned above do likewise; but because they act and endure for the sake of Christ and in accordance with Christ.

48. In everything we do, as has often been said already, God looks at the aim, whether it is for Him or for some other purpose that we act. So, when we wish to do something good, let us have as our aim not to please men but to please God, so as to have our eyes always fixed on Him, doing everything for Him, lest we bear the labour but lose the reward.

49. When you pray, banish from your mind both simple representations of human things and contemplations of everything created, lest being occupied by imaginings of the lesser you fall away from Him, Who is incomparably better than all that is.

50. If we truly love God, by this very love we shall banish passions. And to love Him means to prefer Him to the world, and the soul to the flesh, with scorn for all worldly things, and with constant dedication of oneself to Him, by self-mastery, love, prayer, psalmody and so forth.

51. If for a long time, being mindful of God, we diligently concern ourselves with the passionate part of our soul, we shall no longer be led astray from the right path by the impact of thoughts; but understanding their causes more clearly and cutting

these off, we begin to show more forethought, so that the words of
the Prophet are realised in us: 'Mine eye has seen mine enemies,
and mine ear shall hear the wicked that rise up against me'
(Ps. xci. 11).

52. When you see that your mind acts rightly and justly amidst
worldly thoughts, know that your body too remains pure and free
of sin. But if you see your mind occupied by sinful thoughts and
do not stop it, then know that your body too will not fail to
succumb to them.

53. As things are the world for the body, so representations
are the world for the mind. And as the body commits adultery
with the body of a woman, so the mind commits adultery with
representations of women by the image of its own body; for man
sees in imagination the image of his body in intercourse with the
image of a woman. In the same way he revenges himself through a
mental image of his body on a mental image of the man who has
offended him. It is the same with other sins; for what the body
does in actual deed in the world of things, the mind does mentally
in the world of mental images.

54. Should we not be filled with horror, tremble and be quite
beside ourselves when we hear that God 'the Father judgeth no
man, but hath committed all judgment unto the Son,' (John v.
22)? And the Son cries, 'Judge not, that ye be not judged'(Matt.
vii. 1), 'Judge not, and ye shall not be judged' (Luke vi. 37); and
the Apostle says, 'Judge nothing before the time, until the Lord
come' (1 Cor. iv. 5) and, 'Wherein thou judgest another, thou
condemnest thyself' (Rom. ii. 1). Yet, in spite of this men neglect
mourning their own sins and, taking judgment out of the hands of
the Son, themselves judge and condemn one another, as if
they were without sin. The heavens are filled with horror
and the earth trembles, but they, insensitive as they are, feel no
shame!

55. He who is inquisitive about others' sins, or who judges his
brother on suspicion, has not yet laid the basis of repentance and
has not taken the trouble to learn his own sins which are indeed
heavier than a great weight of lead. He does not know why a man
is slow of heart, nor wherefore he loves vanity and seeks falsehood
(Ps. iv. 2) and so, like one demented and wandering in darkness,

he turns away from his own sins and his fancy finds sins in others, whether real or imaginary, on mere suspicion.

56. Self-love, as has often been said, is the cause of all passionate thoughts, for it gives birth to the three principal concerns of the desiring part of the soul—gluttony, cupidity and vanity. Thereupon gluttony gives birth to thoughts of fornication; cupidity to greed of gain; vanity to pride. All the rest follow from each of these three, such as thoughts that are angry, sad, malicious, despondent, envious, slanderous and others. These passions bind the mind by means of material things and drag it down to earth, pressing down on it like a heavy stone, when in its nature it is lighter and finer than fire.

57. The beginning of all passions is self-love, and the end is pride. Self-love is irrational love of the body. Who cuts it off, cuts off too all the passions coming from it.

58. As parents by the flesh are attached to those who are born of them, so the mind is naturally attached to its thoughts. And as in the eyes of passionately fond parents their own children appear to be the most beautiful and well-behaved, when in fact they are the most worthy of complete ridicule, so to a foolish mind its own thoughts seem to be the most reasonable, even if they are the most absurd. But a wise man does not so regard his thoughts; even when he has proof that they are true and good, he mistrusts his judgment all the more and makes other wise men judges of his thoughts and judgments, lest he should run, or had run, in vain (Gal. ii. 2)—and he accepts confirmation from them.

59. When you overcome one of the most vile passions, such as gluttony, or fornication, or anger, or greed of gain, you become assailed immediately by a vainglorious thought; and when you overcome it, a thought of pride takes its place.

60. While all the vile passions possess the soul, they banish from it the thought of vanity; but being overcome, they open to it the door of the soul.

61. Vanity gives birth to pride, whether it be banished or remains. When banished it produces a high opinion of oneself, when it remains—arrogance.

62. Vanity is eliminated by acting secretly, and pride by ascribing to God all that is well done.

63. He who has been granted knowledge of God and has truly tasted its sweetness scorns all pleasures born of the desiring power.

64. He who is ruled by earthly desires wants either good food, or the satisfaction of movements below the belly, or human glory, or riches, or something else following from these. And if the mind finds nothing better than these things, to which to transfer its desire, it will never to the end of its life be resolute enough to abandon them. But what is infinitely better than them is knowledge of God and of things Divine.

65. Those who scorn pleasures do so from fear, or from hope, or on the strength of realising their nothingness; or from love of God.

66. A knowledge of Divine things, which lacks devotion to them, does not persuade the mind entirely to scorn the material, but it resembles a simple thought about some sensory object. This is why one can find many people, who possess much knowledge and yet wallow in carnal passions like sows in the mire (2 Peter ii. 22). For having achieved a degree of purification at the time when they strove after good, and having received a certain measure of knowledge concerning it, they have later fallen into laziness and so become like Saul who, having been granted the throne, began to lead a life unworthy of a king and so was overthrown with terrible wrath.

67. Just as a simple thought of human things makes the mind neglect what is God's, so a simple knowledge of the Divine does not persuade it entirely to scorn things that are human. For here truth still remains in shadows and conjectures, and therefore has need of the blessed devotion. of holy love to tie the mind to spiritual contemplations and to persuade it to prefer the non-material to the material, the mental and the Divine to the sensory.

68. Not everyone who has cast out passions and has made his thoughts simple has by this fact alone turned them towards the Divine. He may be devoted neither to things human nor things Divine; but this happens to men whose life is merely active, who have not yet been granted knowledge and who refrain from passions either from fear of torment or from hope of the Kingdom of Heaven.

69. 'For we walk by faith, not by sight' (2 Cor. v. 7), and our knowledge is like seeing through a glass, darkly. Hence we need to exercise ourselves long in this knowledge, so that, through long instruction and much application to it we may become firmly practised in uninterrupted contemplations.

70. If, having for a time cast out the causes of passions, we practise spiritual contemplations, yet do not always spend our time at it and do not make it our sole occupation, we easily turn back to carnal passions; and we have gained no other fruit than simple knowledge coupled with self-esteem, the end of which is a gradual dimming of the knowledge itself and a final reverting of the mind to material objects.

71. A blameworthy passion of love occupies the mind with material objects; but a praiseworthy passion of love makes it cleave to the Divine. For, as a rule, on whatever objects the mind lingers with attention, to these it inclines fondly; and where it inclines fondly, there it brings desire and love, whether they be Divine objects, immaterial, akin to itself, or things of the flesh and passions.

72. God created both the invisible and the visible worlds; likewise He created both the soul and the body. If the visible world is so beautiful, what must the invisible world be like! And if the latter is so much better than the former, how much higher than both is God their Creator? Now, if the Creator of all good things is better than all creation, why has the mind abandoned the best of all to occupy itself with the worst, that is, carnal passions? Is it not clearly because it has become accustomed to it, since it has been mixing with the worst from birth and has never yet experienced that which is best of all? Therefore, if by long abstinence from sensory pleasures and by instruction in Divine things we little by little alienate it from this habit, in the course of its progress it will lean more and more towards the Divine, will realise its own dignity and, finally, will transfer all its devotion to God.

73. He who speaks of his brother's sin without passion does so for two reasons—either to correct him or for the benefit of another. But if he speaks of it without this purpose either to the man himself or to another, he speaks either to blame or to slander

his brother. Such a man will not escape being abandoned by God, but will inevitably fall into this or another sin and, being exposed and condemned by others, will be shamed.

74. One should not apply the same judgment to sins which appear alike in action, but should judge them differently (according to the cause of sin). For it is one thing to sin from habit, another to sin spontaneously from an irresistible impulse. In the latter case a man had no thought of it before committing the sin, neither is he drawn to it after committing it; on the contrary he grieves and is greatly tormented by the occurrence. It is quite different with a man who sins from habit; for even before sinning he had not ceased to sin in his mind, and after committing it he still remains with the same disposition.

75. He who practises virtues from vanity also seeks knowledge from vanity. Such a man no longer does or says anything for edification, but in all things seeks praise from those who see his actions or hear his words. This passion is exposed when, if some of those people happen to criticise his actions or his words, he is greatly vexed, not because he had failed to edify them (for he never had this aim), but because he is humiliated and degraded by them.

76. The passion of cupidity becomes revealed if a man always accepts with joy and gives with sorrow. Such a man cannot be a truly good householder. (See par. 19.)

77. A man endures his sufferings for the following reasons: from love of God, in the hope of reward, from fear of torment, from fear of men, from a natural power to endure, for the sake of the pleasure to come, for some mercenary gain, from vanity, or through necessity.

78. It is one thing to be freed from thoughts and another to be freed from passions. Men are often freed from thoughts when the objects of their passion are not before their eyes. Yet the passions meanwhile lie concealed in the soul and manifest themselves when the objects appear. Therefore one must observe the mind when objects are present and learn towards which of them it has a passion.

79. He is a true friend who, when his brother is tempted, endures with him, without anxiety or consternation, his sorrows privations, afflictions and tribulations as though they were his own.

11*   329

80. Do not disdain your conscience, which always gives you the best counsel; for it offers you advice from God and the angels, frees you from hidden defilements of the heart and, when you leave the world, gives you daring towards God.

81. If you wish to be wise as well as modest, and not be a slave to the passion of self-esteem, always seek what is hidden from your reason. Then, finding how much and how varied is what is unknown to you, you will marvel at your ignorance and will humble your pretensions. And, having realised your nothingness, you will learn many great and marvellous things. But illusion about your knowledge prevents you from learning.

82. He is sincere in wanting to be saved who is not averse to healing remedies; and these remedies are sorrows and tribulations brought by various adversities. He who resists adversities knows neither what commerce takes place here on earth, nor with what profit he will go hence.

83. Vanity and cupidity mutually engender one another. For some become rich through vanity and others, having become rich, are puffed up with vanity. But it is in the world that it is thus. A monk is filled with vanity when he has no possessions, and if he has money, he hides it, ashamed at having something unbefitting to his calling.

84. A monk's vanity expresses itself in his being vain of his virtue and its consequences; his pride is expressed in pride of achievement, in belittling others and ascribing success to himself instead of to God. For a man of the world, the object of vanity and pride is beauty, wealth, power and sagacity or worldly good sense.

85. What is success for a man of the world is failure for a monk, and what is success for a monk is failure for a man of the world. For a man of the world success lies in riches, fame, power, pleasures, physical well-being, many children and other similar things; a monk involved in these perishes. Success for a monk lies in poverty, obscurity, lack of power, abstinence, mortification, privations and so on; but involuntary subjection to such things is a great calamity for a man who loves the world, for he is then often in danger of hanging himself, as many have done.

86. Food is created for two reasons—nourishment and remedy. Therefore those who use it for some other purpose than

that for which it is given us by God, are condemned as pleasure-loving. In all things wrong use is sin.

87. Humility is born of pure prayer, with tears and contrition. For prayer that is always calling for God's help does not let us rely insanely on our own strength and wisdom, nor exalt ourselves before others, which are two terrible maladies of the passion of pride.

88. It is one thing to fight a simple thought, lest it arouse passion, and another to fight a passionate thought, lest we consent to sin. Both these forms of struggle prevent thoughts from lingering in us.

89. Rancour is inseparable from discontent. So when it is with bitterness that the mind sees in itself, as in a mirror, the face of the brother who has offended it, it is evident that it has rancour. 'The ways of those that remember injuries lead to death' (Prov. xii. 28), for 'he that remembers injuries is a transgressor' (Prov. xxi. 24).

90. If you feel rancour against someone, pray for him; and by prayer separating distress from the memory of the wrong he has done you, you will arrest the movement of passion; and by a feeling of friendliness and affection you will completely banish this passion from the soul. If another man bears malice against you, be kind and humble towards him, live in peace with him and you will free him from the passion.

91. It is hard to cure a man from the sufferings of envy, for he regards as a personal misfortune what he envies in you. Perhaps the only way to calm him is to conceal this thing from him. However, if the thing is useful to many and yet causes grief to the one, which side is one to take? One should take the side of what is useful to many. All the same, as far as possible, do not neglect the one, nor be too taken with the treacherousness of the passion, for you are aiding not the passion but the man who suffers from it. Be humble and regard him as superior to yourself, giving him preference at all times, in all places and in any affairs. As to your own envy, you can stop it if you rejoice at the joy of him, whom you envy and grieve with him when he grieves, fulfilling the precept of the Apostle 'Rejoice with them that do rejoice, and weep with them that weep' (Rom. xii. 15).

92. Our mind is placed between two entities, each suggesting what belongs to it: one virtue, the other vice; that is, between an angel and a demon. But the mind has the power and strength to follow or oppose which it wills.

93. The holy Powers direct us to good, and the natural seeds of good and our own will to good help us; as to suggestions from the demons, they are strengthened by passions and the will to evil.

94. A pure mind is at times taught by God Himself Who visits it; at other times it is the holy Powers that suggest to it the good, or again at others it is the nature of the things it contemplates.

95. A mind that has been granted knowledge should keep its thoughts of things free from passion, its contemplations free from error, its state of prayer serene. Yet it cannot always preserve this state for, instigated by the demons, movements of the flesh force their way in and obscure it as if by smoke.

96. Not all that which saddens us makes us angry; for occasions for sadness are more frequent than occasions for anger. For instance, something is broken, something is lost, someone is dead. In such cases we feel only sad, but in others we feel both sad and angry, if we are not lovers of wisdom.

97. When the mind receives representations of things, it is apt to take on new forms in accordance with each. And when the mind contemplates things spiritually it undergoes varying changes, corresponding to each contemplation. But when it is in God it remains entirely without image or form. For, contemplating the unchanging, it too becomes unchanging and wholly luminous.

98. A soul is perfect whose desiring power is wholly directed towards God.

99. A mind is perfect when, through true faith, it has inconceivably gained knowledge of the Inconceivable, has surveyed all His creation in general and has received from God an all-embracing knowledge of His providence and judgment in His creatures, as far as this is accessible for man.

100. Time is divided into three parts. Faith extends over all three, hope over one, and love over two. Faith and hope have limits, but love, uniting with what is beyond the endless, and ever increasing, remains through endless ages. Therefore 'the greatest of these is charity' (1 Cor. xiii. 13).

Fourth Century on Love

1. When the mind reflects on the absolute infinity of God, on this unfathomable and greatly desirable deep, it is first filled with wonder; and then it is struck with amazement how God has brought into being from nothing all that is. But as there is no end of His greatness, so too is His wisdom unsearchable. (Ps. cxliv. 3.)

2. For how will he not be filled with wonder, who contemplates this unapproachable and awe-inspiring cause of goodness? How will he not be transported to ecstasy who ponders on how and whence came the nature endowed with mind and word, and the four elements of which bodies are made, when there was no substance preceding their birth? What is this power which, passing to action, brought them to being? But the children of the Greeks do not accept this, being ignorant of His all-powerful goodness and His wisdom and intelligence, which surpass all comprehension and give life to all things.

3. God, Creator through eternity, in His infinite goodness creates when He wills by His consubstantial Word and Spirit. Do not ask, How is it that, although He is always Good, He only now manifested Himself as Creator? For I tell you that the inscrutable wisdom of the Infinite Being escapes human comprehension.

4. The Creator has manifested and brought into action at the moment He wished the knowledge of everything that is, knowledge pre-existing in Him from eternity. For no one can question whether the Almighty God can accomplish anything when He so wishes.

5. As to the reason why God has created one thing or another —seek to discover it, for this can be known. But how, and why not so long ago—do not investigate, for this is beyond your reason. For some Divine things are comprehensible, others are not comprehensible for man. Speculation, if not bridled, may

cast one down a precipice, as said one of the saints (Gregory the Theologian).

6. Some say that creatures have been coexistent with God through eternity; but this is impossible. For how can creatures, in every sense finite, be coexistent through eternity with the One, Who is in every sense Infinite? And how can they be creatures if they are coeternal with the Maker? But this is what the Greeks say, who introduce a God, Who is the Maker not of existence, but merely of qualities. We, on the other hand, recognise that God is omnipotent and say that He is the Maker not only of qualities, but also of beings possessing these qualities. If this be so, then the creatures are not coexistent with God in eternity.

7. The Deity and what is Divine is in a certain sense cognisable and in another sense incognisable. Cognisable by the contemplation of His attributes; incognisable in what He is in Himself.

8. In the simple and infinite nature of the Holy Trinity do not seek some tendency or capacity, lest you make it complex like the creatures—which is absurd and incompatible with God.

9. The infinite, omnipotent Nature, the Maker of all, alone is simple, unique, without qualities, peaceful, tranquil, without movement. But every creature is composed of essence and accidents and always has need of Divine Providence, for it is not free from change.

10. Every nature endowed with mind and senses, when brought into being, received from God the capacity to take in impressions from things: rational nature received the capacity to think, sensory nature—to sense.

11. God only communicates; the creature both receives and communicates; it receives being and well-being, and communicates only well-being; the corporeal nature in one way and the incorporeal in another.

12. The incorporeal nature communicates well-being by speech, by action and by being contemplated, and the corporeal only by being contemplated.

13. The ever-being and non-being of the rational and intelligent nature lies in the will of Him who has made all things and 'they were very good' (Gen. i. 31); but to be good or bad as they choose depends on the will of creatures.

14. Evil is to be seen, not in the nature of creatures, but in their wrong and irrational movements.

15. A soul moves rationally when its desiring power has acquired self-mastery, the excitable strives after love, turning away from hatred, and the mental abides in God, by prayer and spiritual contemplation.

16. He has not yet attained perfect love and profound knowledge of Divine Providence who, in time of trial, when affliction befalls him, does not have magnanimity, but cuts himself off from love for his spiritual brethren.

17. The aim of Divine Providence is to reunite by means of right faith and spiritual love those who were cut asunder and scattered by evil. It was in order to 'gather together in one the children of God that were scattered abroad' (John xi. 52) that the Saviour suffered. So he who refuses to bear the burden of arduous circumstances, endure sorrows, suffer pain walks outside the love of God and the aim of Providence.

18. If 'charity suffereth long, and is kind' (1 Cor. xiii. 4), does not he who is fainthearted in sorrowful happenings, who bears malice against those offending him or who cuts himself off from love for them, fail to conform to the aim of Divine Providence?

19. Pay heed to yourself lest it be in you and not in your brother that lurks the evil that cuts you off from him; and hasten to make your peace with him, lest you forsake the commandment of love.

20. Do not neglect the commandment of love; for through it you will be a son of God, but transgressing it you will become a son of gehenna.

21. Love between friends is destroyed if you envy or are the object of envy; if you cause or suffer loss; if you revile or suffer revilement; and finally if you feed and keep suspicious thoughts against your brother. Have you never done or suffered something of this sort, because of which you abandon love for your friend?

22. Suppose a trial has come to you through your brother and distress has led you to hatred, do not be conquered by hatred but conquer it by love. This is how you can conquer it: pray God sincerely about him, accept his excuses, or cure yourself by

excusing him, regard yourself as the cause of the trial and resolve to endure until the cloud has passed by.

23. He is long-suffering who waits till the end of the trial and receives praise for what he has endured.

24. 'A man slow to wrath abounds in wisdom' (Prov. xiv. 29); for he relates all happenings to the ultimate end and in its expectation bears all afflictions. And 'the end', says the Apostle, is 'everlasting life' (Rom. vi. 22). 'And this is life eternal, that they might know thee the only true God, and Jesus Christ, whom thou hast sent' (John xvii. 3).

25. Do not be hasty in rejecting spiritual love, for no other way to salvation remains for men.

26. If yesterday you regarded a man as a spiritual brother and virtuous, do not deem him today to be vicious and wicked through hatred for him, which was born in you from suggestions of the evil one; but through long-suffering love and thinking of yesterday's good cast out today's hatred from your soul.

27. If yesterday you praised a man as good and extolled him as virtuous, do not revile him today as vicious and wicked, through your love being turned to hatred, excusing your wicked hatred for him by blaming him; but continue the same praises, even though bitterness still possesses you—and you will speedily come back to salutary love.

28. Do not let the bitterness, which still endures in you against your brother, make you change your customary praise of him in conversations with other brethren by imperceptibly introducing censure into your words; but speak of him in conversation with wholehearted praise and pray for him sincerely, as if for yourself—and you will soon be delivered from pernicious hatred.

29. Do not say, 'I do not hate my brother', when you are averse to remembering him, but listen to the words of Moses, 'Thou shalt not hate thy brother in thine heart: thou shalt in any wise rebuke thy neighbour, so thou shalt not bear sin on his account' (Lev. xix. 17).

30. If, through some temptation, your brother persistently speaks evil of you, do not be removed from the state of love and

do not allow the same evil spirit to trouble your thought. You will not be removed from it if, while being reviled and calumnied, you will bless him and wish him well. This is the way of loving wisdom in accordance with Christ, and he who follows this way will dwell with Him.

31. Do not regard as well-meaning those who repeat to you words which engender in you vexation or enmity against a brother, even if they appear to speak the truth; but turn away from such, as from deadly snakes, to put a stop to their malicious talk, and to save your own soul from bitterness.

32. Do not wound your brother with insinuations, lest you receive the same in return and thus banish the loving disposition from both, but with loving boldness 'go and tell him his fault' (Matt. xviii. 15) to banish the causes of bitterness and free him and yourself from vexation and agitation.

33. Examine your conscience with the greatest care to see whether it is your own fault that your brother does not make peace with you, and do not reject its accusations by false reasonings, for conscience knows what is hidden in you and will accuse you at the moment of your leaving this world, and will be a stumbling-block during prayer.

34. When you are at peace with your brother, do not remember what was said by him in a moment of vexation, whether it was something said to your face, or to another in your absence and later repeated to you, lest, accepting thoughts of rancour, you return again to pernicious hatred of your brother.

35. A rational soul which nurses hatred for a man cannot be at peace in relation to God, Who has given us the following commandment, 'But if ye forgive not men their trespasses, neither will your Father forgive your trespasses' (Matt. vi. 15). Even if your brother does not want to make peace, preserve yourself from animosity by praying for him sincerely and speaking ill of him to no one.

36. The inexpressible peace of the holy angels rests on these two dispositions: love of God and love for one another; and the same is true of the peace of all the saints of all times. So excellent are the words of the Saviour, 'On these two commandments hang all the law and the prophets' (Matt. xxii. 40).

37. Do not indulge yourself, and you will not hate your brother. Do not love yourself, and you will love God.

38. If you wish to live with spiritual brethren, at their door renounce all personal wishes, for otherwise you can be at peace neither with God nor with those who live with you.

39. He who has acquired perfect love and has organised his whole life in accordance with it says, 'by the Holy Ghost' 'that Jesus is the Lord' (1 Cor. xii. 3). And the opposite results in the contrary.

40. Love of God loves always to give wings to the mind to speak of God and Divine things; and love of neighbour disposes it always to think well of him.

41. He who loves empty glory or is attached to something material is apt to be vexed with people about temporal things, or bear malice against them, or have hatred for them, or be a slave to shameful thoughts. All this is foreign to a soul which loves God.

42. When you no longer say or do something shameful in your mind, when you bear no malice against a man who has done you harm or has slandered you, and when your mind during prayer is constantly free of matter and form, know that you have attained the measure of passionlessness and perfect love.

43. It is no small feat to become free of vainglory. Men free themselves from it by the practice of virtues in secret and by frequent prayer; and the sign of freedom is to bear no malice against a man who speaks or has spoken ill of you.

44. If you wish to be righteous, give to each part of you, that is, to the soul and the body, what befits it: to the thinking part of the soul, reading, spiritual contemplations and prayer; to the excitable—spiritual love opposed to hatred; to the desiring—chastity and self-mastery; to the body, food and clothing only inasmuch as they are needful.

45. The mind acts in accordance with its nature when it keeps passions in subjection, contemplates the meaning of all that is and abides with God.

46. As good health and illness are seen in the body of an animal, and light and darkness in the eye, so virtue and vice are found in the soul, knowledge and ignorance in the mind.

47. A Christian gains wisdom in these three ways: by

commandments, by doctrine and by faith. Commandments free the mind from passions, doctrine leads it into knowledge of What Is, and faith—to the contemplation of the Holy Trinity.

48. Some who engage on spiritual work repel only passionate thoughts, others cut off passions themselves. Passionate thoughts are repelled either by psalmody, or prayer, meditation or some other appropriate activity; passions are cut off by scorn of those things towards which a man feels passion.

49. We can be passionate towards a woman, possessions, fame, and so forth. A man can arrive at indifference and disdain of woman if, upon renouncing the world, he compels himself as he ought to drain his body by self-mastery; of possessions, if he persuades his thought to be content with what he has; of fame, if he prefers the practice of virtues in secret, seen by God alone. It is the same with all other passions. He who scorns all these things is freed from all dislike.

50. He who has renounced worldly things, such as wife, possessions, and so forth, has made the outer man a monk, but not yet the inner man. But he who has banished passionate representations has made a monk also of his inner man, that is the mind. It is easy to make the outer man a monk if one so wishes; but it is no small task to make a monk of the inner man.

51. What man in this generation has totally freed himself of passionate representations and has attained pure prayer detached from all things, which is the sign of inner monkhood?

52. Many passions lurk in our souls; they show themselves when their objects appear.

53. A man may not be troubled by passions while their objects are absent, if he has reached a small degree of passionlessness; but as soon as these objects appear, passions at once begin to draw the mind towards them.

54. When the object of passion is absent, do not think you have perfect passionlessness. But when the object appears and you remain unaffected by it or by its memory later, know that you have entered its precincts. Yet do not be neglectful even then, for although long practice of virtue kills passions, if you neglect it they will awaken once more.

55. He who loves Christ is certain to imitate Him as much as

he can. And Christ never ceased doing good to men; was long-suffering in the face of ingratitude and revilement; and when He was scourged and put to death by men, He endured this, imputing evil against no one. These three actions are acts of love for the neighbour, without which a man deceives himself if he asserts that he loves Christ or that he will gain His Kingdom. For the Lord said, 'Not every one that saith unto me, Lord, Lord, shall enter into the kingdom of heaven; but he that doeth the will of my Father' (Matt. vii. 21). And again, 'He that hath my commandments, and keepeth them, he it is that loveth me' (John xiv. 21), and so forth.

56. The whole purpose of the Saviour's commandments is to free the mind of intemperance and hatred and lead it into love for Him and the neighbour, which gives birth to the light of holy and active knowledge.

57. If you have been granted by God a certain knowledge, do not neglect love and self-mastery; for, by purifying the passionate part of the soul, they make plain for you the way to knowledge.

58. The way to knowledge is passionlessness and humility, 'without which no man shall see the Lord' (Heb. xii. 14).

59. Since 'knowledge puffeth up, but charity edifieth' (1 Cor. viii. 1) join love to knowledge and you will be free of arrogance, will be a spiritual householder, edifying yourself and all who come near you.

60. Love edifies because it envies not and is not bitter against those who envy, nor does it make public boast of what in it is enviable. It does not consider itself as having already attained perfection (Phil. iii. 12), and if it does not know something, is not ashamed to admit its ignorance. In this way it protects the mind from being puffed up and encourages it always to make progress in knowledge.

61. Knowledge is usually followed by conceit and envy, especially in the beginning. Conceit manifests itself only within, and envy both within and without: within (my envy) towards those who possess knowledge, without (envy towards me) on the part of those who are ignorant. Love prevents these three defects: conceit, because it 'is not puffed up'; inner envy, because 'it envieth not'; outer envy, because it 'suffereth long, and is kind'

(1 Cor. xiii. 4). Thus he who has knowledge should acquire also love, that it may keep the mind from harm in all things.

62. He who has been granted the gift of knowledge and yet nurses bitterness, rancour or hatred towards another is like one who pricks his eyes with thorns and thistles. Thus knowledge of necessity has need of love.

63. Do not be wholly concerned with the body, but setting it a task within its powers, turn your whole mind inwards. 'For bodily exercise profiteth little: but godliness is profitable unto all things' (1 Tim. iv. 8) and so on.

64. He who remains within and takes constant care of the inner is chaste, long-suffering, kind, humble; and not only this, but also he is active in contemplation, theology and prayer. This is what the Apostle means by saying, 'Walk in the Spirit' and so forth (Gal. v. 16).

65. He who does not know how to walk in the Spirit takes no care about passionate representations, but turns all his care to the flesh and either he is indulgent to his belly, dissolute, irritable, ill-tempered, resentful, thus darkening his mind, or he undertakes excessive hardships and thus stifles his thought.

66. The Scriptures do not deprive us of anything given by God for our use, but curb immoderation and correct lack of judgment. In other words they do not forbid eating, bearing children or having money and spending it rightly, but they do forbid gluttony, adultery and so on. They do not even forbid us to think of these things—for they are made to be thought about—but they forbid thinking passionately of them.

67. Some things we do for God are done in obedience to commandments, others are done not from commandments, but, as it were, as a voluntary offering. It is in obedience to commandments that we love God and our neighbour, love our enemies, do not commit adultery, do not kill and so on, for failure to obey these leads to condemnation. It is not in obedience to commandments that we preserve virginity and lead a celibate life, renounce all possessions, live in solitude and so on. Such actions have the significance of offerings, whereby, if through weakness we should fail to fulfil some commandment, we may incline our good Master to have mercy.

68. He who has chosen celibacy or virginity must have his loins girded about and his light burning (Luke xii. 35): the loins girded about by self-mastery, and the light burning by prayer, meditation and spiritual love.

69. Some brethren think that they cannot have the gifts of the Holy Spirit, for, through negligence in practising the commandments, they do not know that he who has true faith in Christ possesses within him the epitome of all the gifts of God. But since, through our inaction, we are far from that active love of Him, which would show us the Divine treasures concealed within us, we justly regard ourselves as excluded from God's gifts.

70. If, according to the words of the Divine Apostle, Christ dwells in our hearts by faith (Eph. iii. 17) and in Him 'are hid all the treasures of wisdom and knowledge' (Col. ii. 3), then in our hearts are to be found all the treasures of wisdom and knowledge. And they are revealed to the heart according to the measure of purification of each man by the commandments.

71. This is the 'treasure hid in a field' (Matt. xiii. 44) of your heart, which you have not yet found because of your inaction. For if you had found it, you would have sold all that you had and bought that field. But you have abandoned that field and work nearby, where there is nothing but thorns and thistles.

72. Therefore the Saviour says, 'Blessed are the pure in heart: for they shall see God' (Matt. v. 8). They will see Him and the treasures that are in Him, when they purify themselves by love and self-mastery; the more they are purified, the more will they see.

73. Therefore He says also, 'Sell that ye have, and give alms' (Luke xii. 33), 'and, behold, all things are clean unto you' (Luke xi. 41), since you are no longer concerned with things relating to the body, but strive to cleanse of hatred and intemperance your mind, which the Lord calls 'heart' (Matt. xv. 19). For all those things defiling the mind prevent it from seeing Christ, Who lives in it by the grace of holy baptism.

74. The Scriptures call virtues ways; and the greatest of all virtues is love. Therefore the Apostle says, 'And yet shew I unto you a more excellent way' (1 Cor. xii. 31)—one that makes us

scorn all material things and prefer nothing temporal to the eternal.

75. Love for God opposes lust, for it urges the mind to refrain from sensory pleasures; love for neighbour opposes anger, for it makes it scorn riches and fame. They are the two pence the Lord gave to the host at the inn (Luke x. 35) for him to take care of you. But do not prove ungrateful, associating yourself with thieves, lest you be again wounded and left not half alive but dead.

76. Cleanse your mind of anger, rancour and shameful thoughts; and then you will be able to recognise Christ coming to dwell in you.

77. Who has illumined you with faith in the consubstantial, worshipful and Holy Trinity? Who gave you knowledge of the dispensation by the Incarnation of one of the Persons of the Holy Trinity? Who taught you about the incorporeal beings, the origin and the end of the visible world, or the resurrection of the dead and eternal life, or about the glory of the Kingdom of Heaven and the terrible Judgment? Is it not the grace of Christ, which lives in you and is the pledge of the Holy Spirit? What is greater than this grace? Or what is better than this wisdom and knowledge? What is higher than these promises? If, even after this, we remain idle and negligent and do not cleanse ourselves of passions, which blind our mind and prevent us from seeing these truths more clearly than the sun itself, we should blame ourselves and not deny the presence of grace in us.

78. God, having promised you eternal blessings and given the pledge of the Spirit in your heart, commanded you to take care of your life, that your inner man, freed from passions, should even in the present life begin to taste these blessings.

79. If you are granted high Divine contemplations, strive all the more after love and self-mastery, that you may keep your passionate part untroubled and have a never ceasing light in your soul.

80. Restrain the excitable power of your soul by love; mortify the desiring power by self-mastery; give wings to the thinking power by prayer, and the light of your mind will never be dimmed.

81. The causes which destroy love are the following: dishonour, loss suffered, calumny either against faith or mode of life, beatings, blows, wounds and the like, whether this happens to oneself or to one's relatives or friends. He who abandons love for any of such reasons has not yet understood the aim of Christ's commandments.

82. Strive as much as you can to love every man. If you cannot do so yet, at least do not hate anyone. But you will not be able to do even this, unless you scorn all things earthly.

83. If someone has abused you, do not hate him, hate the abuse and the demon who instigated him to it. If you hate the man who abused you, you hate a man and so transgress a commandment. Thus what he has done in word, you do in deed. And if you keep the commandment, show towards him works of love and help him if you can to turn him away from evil.

84. Christ does not wish you to feel hatred or malice, anger or bitterness against anyone, in whatever manner or for anything temporal. The four Gospels preach this to all men.

85. Many of us talk, yet few act. But no one must distort the word of God to indulge his negligence; it is better to confess one's weakness, not concealing God's truth, lest, together with transgressing commandments, we become guilty in misinterpreting the word of God.

86. Love and self-mastery free the soul from passions; reading and meditation free the mind from ignorance; and standing in prayer puts man before God Himself.

87. When the demons see that we despise the things of this world, not wishing to hate men for their sake and fall away from love, they instigate slanders against us, so that we should not bear the bitterness and should hate the slanderers.

88. No suffering is harder for the soul to bear than that of slander, whether against faith or conduct. And no one can remain indifferent to it unless, like Susannah, he keeps his eyes on God, Who alone has the power to free men from afflictions, as He freed her, to show men the truth convincingly, as He showed it of her, and to comfort the soul with hope.

89. Inasmuch as you pray for your slanderer, so will God

convincingly reveal the truth about you to those who have given way to temptation.

90. God alone is essentially good, and only a man who imitates God is good in the disposition of his soul; for his chief aim is to unite the wicked with Him, Who is essentially good and thus make them good. To this end, being reviled he blesses; being persecuted, he suffers it; being defamed, he brings comfort; being slain, he prays for his slayers (1 Cor. iv. 12, 13). He does all, lest he fall away from his chief aim—love.

91. The Lord's commandments teach us to make right use of indifferent things. A right use of indifferent things renders the state of the soul pure; a pure state of soul gives birth to sound judgment; sound judgment gives birth to passionlessness, which engenders perfect love.

92. He still lacks passionlessness who, when temptation comes, cannot disregard the fault of his friend, whether real or only apparent. For passions concealed in the soul of such a man, becoming excited, blind the mind and prevent it from seeing the rays of truth and distinguishing the good from the bad. Should we not assume that neither has such a man as yet attained to perfect love, for 'perfect love casteth out fear' of judgment (1 John iv. 18).

93. 'Nothing doth countervail a faithful friend' (Ecclesiasticus vi. 15); he regards as his own the misfortunes of his friend and shoulders both them and him, suffering even unto death.

94. Friends are many, but in good times. In time of trial, it is hard to find even one.

95. One should love every man wholeheartedly, but one should put one's hope in God alone and serve only Him with all one's might. For while He protects us, our friends too show us favours and no enemies have power to harm us. But when He withdraws from us, all our friends also turn away from us and all enemies have power over us.

96. There are four principal ways in which God withdraws from us: one is providential withdrawal, as in the case of the Lord Himself, in order by seeming withdrawal to save those who are thus deserted; another—a testing withdrawal, as with Job and Joseph, to reveal one as a pillar of strength and the other as a

pillar of chastity; yet another is withdrawal for the purpose of spiritual education, as with Apostle Peter, in order, through humility, to preserve in him the abundance of grace. And finally there is withdrawal by turning away, as with the Jews, in order through punishment to bring them to repentance. All these kinds of withdrawal are salutary and filled with Divine grace and loving-kindness.

97. Only faithful keepers of commandments and true intimates of God's designs do not abandon their friends when, with God's permission, they are visited by trials. But those who neglect the practice of commandments and are not initiated in the mysteries of God's designs, rejoice with their friend in good times and abandon him when he suffers in time of trial. Sometimes they even take the side of his adversaries.

98. The friends of Christ love all men sincerely, but are not loved by all. Friends of the world neither love all nor are loved by all. Friends of Christ keep the bonds of love to the end; but friends of the world only until some discord arises between them about something worldly.

99. 'A faithful friend is a strong defence' (Ecclesiasticus vi. 14). For in good times he is a good counsellor and a devoted helper, and in adversity—a sincere intercessor and a defender, who shares in suffering.

100. Many have said much about love, yet if you seek it, you will find it only among the disciples of Christ. For they alone had true Love to teach them the love of which it is said, 'And though I have the gift of prophecy, and understand all mysteries, and all knowledge; . . . and have not charity, . . . it profiteth me nothing' (1 Cor. xiii. 2, 3). For he who has love has God Himself, for 'God is love' (1 John iv. 16). To Him be glory for ages of ages. Amen.

2. Contemplative and Active Texts selected from the Seven Centuries of the Greek Philokalia[37]

1. There is one God—without beginning, beyond all comprehension, possessing the power to be in its entirety, completely excluding all thought of *when* and *how* He is, being in His essence inaccessible and unknowable to any creature. (1, 1)

2. All that is is called thinkable, knowable, something for the knowledge of which there exist demonstrable principles. God is called unthinkable, but from the thinkable and the knowable is derived belief that He is. (1, 8)

3. Knowledge of created things has for evidence their specific principles, which can be observed by natural means, and by which these things are naturally defined. But of God, through the principles contained in these things, there can be only belief that He is; belief giving to the righteous a profession and faith in His existence that are stronger than any evidence. Faith is true knowledge based on principles not subject to proof, being the evidence of things which are beyond reason and word. (1, 9)

4. God is the beginning, the middle and the end of all that is: the beginning, as Creator, the middle, as Provider, the end, as the Consummator (περιγραφή), for, as the Scriptures say, 'of him, and through him, and to him, are all things' (Rom. xi. 36). (1, 10)

5. No soul is more worthy of respect than one which by nature possesses reason. God, being good, in creating each soul according to His image, gave it self-movement (freedom). Thereafter each according to its own will either chooses honour or incurs dishonour, voluntarily, by its actions. (1, 11)

37 The translators offer here a selection from the texts chosen by Theophan. The figures at the end of each paragraph refer to the Greek original. (Translators' note.)

6. As it is written, God is the Sun of righteousness (Mal. iv. 2), shedding the rays of His goodness on all alike. But the soul, according to its disposition, is either wax, if it loves God, or mud, if it loves matter. As it is in the nature of mud to be dried up by the sun, and it is natural for wax to be softened by it, so every soul attached to matter and to the world, receiving admonishments from God to make it see reason and rejecting them by its disposition, becomes hardened like mud and, like Pharaoh, casts itself into perdition; but every God-loving soul in such case softens like wax and, receiving the imprints of the images of Divine things, becomes in spirit the dwelling of God. (1, 12)

7. If a man has illumined his mind by Divine understandings, has taught his tongue constantly to worship the Creator by Divine psalmody and has sanctified his senses by looking with purity at all things, then he has added to the natural blessing of being in God's image, the well-being of God's likeness through voluntary good disposition. (1, 13)

8. He preserves his soul undefiled, who compels his mind to think only of God and of His perfections, who uses his speech for rightly interpreting and expounding these perfections, and who has taught his senses to look rightly on the visible world and all that is therein, and to proclaim to the soul the greatness of the intelligence there concealed. (1, 14)

9. Having freed us from bitter slavery to the tyrants—the demons—God, in His loving-kindness, has given us the yoke of veneration for Him—humility, which curbs all the power of the devil, assists those who have taken this yoke in all that is good, and keeps it inviolate. (1, 15)

10. He who believes, fears God; he who fears God is humble; he who is humble becomes meek, acquiring a disposition remote from the unnatural movements of anger and lust; he who is meek keeps the commandments; he who keeps the commandments is purified; he who is purified is illumined; he who is illumined is deemed worthy to recline with the bridegroom—the Word—in the treasure-house of mysteries. (1, 16)

11. As a labourer, exploring a field's suitability for planting with trees, at times unexpectedly finds a treasure, so every

spiritual worker, who is humble and sincere and the disposition of whose soul is level and free from the weeds of earthly passions, when questioned about his success, like the blessed Jacob, 'What is this which thou hast quickly found?' can answer 'That which the Lord thy God presented before me' (Gen. xxvii. 20). For when God grants us wise contemplations of His wisdom, with no effort or expectation on our part, we understand that we have suddenly acquired a spiritual treasure. A skilful and experienced worker is a spiritual labourer, who transplants, like a wild tree, into a spiritual field, what he sees in visible things by means of the senses, and in doing so he finds a treasure—a grace-given vision of Divine wisdom, manifested in created things. (1, 17)

12. He who seeks knowledge for display and fails to gain it, should not envy his brother and be smitten with sorrow. Rather should he go through the labour established as preparation for knowledge—the labour of active virtue. Labouring over this lovingly, first of all with the body, he will prepare his soul for receiving knowledge. (1, 20)

13. Those who strive rightly after knowledge of things, with devout intention, having no thought of display before others, will meet with most luminous contemplations concerning them and will find indications towards a most exact knowledge of themselves. To those the law says: having entered the promised land, you will inherit 'great and beautiful cities which thou didst not build, houses full of all good things which thou didst not fill, wells dug . . . which thou didst not dig, vineyards and oliveyards which thou didst not plant' (Deut. vi. 10, 11). For he who lives not for himself, but for God, is filled with Divine gifts, which are not always manifest because of the threat of an attack of passions. (1, 21)

14. A hypocrite, while he thinks he is not found out, keeps peace and is silent, content with the glory he enjoys from appearing to be righteous; but when he is found out, he pours out venomous words, hoping to cover his own shame by reviling others. The Scriptures liken such a man to a generation of vipers, since he is wicked, and enjoins him to bring forth fruit meet for repentance, that is, to change the hidden disposition of his heart to conform with what he appears to be. (1, 23)

18. A wise man, both in teaching and in learning, wishes to teach and to learn only what is useful. But a man who only appears to be wise, both in asking questions and in answering them, offers only what feeds curiosity. (1, 28)

19. Such gifts of grace as a man has received through God's benevolence he must pass on without jealousy to others, according to the word of the Lord, 'Freely ye have received, freely give' (Matt. x. 8). He who hides the gift in the earth falsely accuses the giver of being hard (Matt. xxv. 24), and rejects virtue for the sake of sparing the flesh. But he who sells the truth to the enemies and is thereupon condemned, cannot bear the disgrace, being vainglorious, and so hangs himself. (1, 29)

20. Those who still fear the battle with passions and dread the attacks of invisible foes, must be silent, that is, in their fight for virtue they must not use the method of arguing but must turn to prayer, casting upon the Lord their care and protection. In Exodus it is said to such, 'The Lord shall fight for you, and ye shall hold your peace' (Ex. xiv. 14). As for those who, after the defeat of their pressing foes, are filled with gratitude and so seek to understand which virtue they should undertake to practise, they should only keep open the ear of their heart and pay heed to what the Lord says, as Israel was commanded, 'Hear, O Israel' (Deut. vi. 4)! As for him who, when his heart is purified, conceives an irresistible desire to know God, to him reverent daring is befitting, and accordingly it is said to him, 'Why criest thou to me?' (Ex. xiv. 15). Thus for him to whom, for his fear, silence is ordained, recourse to God alone is fitting; for him who is ordained to listen it is fitting that he be ready to hear and to fulfil the Divine commandments; and for him who has attained to spiritual understanding it is fitting to cry to God in prayer, without ceasing, both asking to be delivered from evil and giving thanks for blessings received. (1, 30)

21. A soul can never reach knowledge of God, if God Himself does not condescend to it and touch it, raising it to Himself. And the human mind could never soar high enough to receive Divine light, if God Himself did not lift it up, as far as the human mind can be lifted up, and did not enlighten it with Divine illuminations. (1, 31)

22. A man who merely has faith removes the mountain of sin, according to the Gospel (Matt. xvii. 19, 20), by an actively good life, casting out of himself his former attachment to sensory things, inconstant and changeable as they are. But a man who has been able to become a disciple receives from the hands of the Word fragments of loaves of spiritual knowledge, fills thousands with them and thus manifests by deeds the power of the Word to give increase (Matt. xv. 32 et seq.). And he who was able to become an Apostle, heals 'all manner of sickness and all manner of disease' and casts out unclean spirits (Matt. x. 1). He casts out unclean spirits, that is, he banishes the action of passions; he heals sickness, that is, by hope he leads to righteous disposition those who had lost it; he cures all manner of disease, that is, he arouses and strengthens those weakened by laziness, reminding them of the judgment. But he who has received the 'power to tread on serpents and scorpions' (Luke x. 19) destroys the beginning and end of sin. (1, 33)

23. An Apostle and a disciple, of course, also has faith; but a disciple is not always an Apostle, although he always has faith. He who simply has faith is not thereby a disciple or an Apostle. However, through his mode of life and contemplation, it is possible also for this third (the believer) to ascend to the rank and dignity of the second (the disciple), and this second to the rank and dignity of the first (the Apostle). (1, 34)

24. What lies in time and goes according to the temporal order comes to a stop when it reaches completion, for then its natural growth is finished. But what is brought forth by the grace of God according to the order of virtuous living, when it reaches completion proceeds to grow again—for here the end of one serves as the beginning of another. He who by active virtue has put a stop to the corruptible passions in him, by this very fact has begun other Divine transformations 'from glory to glory' (2 Cor. iii. 18), since God, acting in him, never ceases, just as He never began, to enact good. For just as the attribute of light is to shed light, so the attribute of God is to enact good. For this reason according to the law—which corresponds to the state of temporal things, being born and dying—sabbath is kept by rest from actions; but according to the Gospels, which correspond to the state of

spiritual and mental things, it is celebrated by doing active good, although those are indignant at this who do not understand that the sabbath is made for man and not man for the sabbath, and that the Son of Man is Lord also of the sabbath (Mark ii. 27, 28). (1, 35)

25. For the soul to taste spiritual joys, the mere overcoming of passions is not enough, unless it also acquires virtues through keeping commandments. 'Rejoice not', says the Lord, 'that the spirits are subject unto you', that is, the actions of passions; 'but rather rejoice, because your names are written in heaven' (Luke x. 20), that is, because through the grace of sonship, as a reward of virtue, your name is inscribed among the passionless. (1, 77)

26. Until we have completely freed our mind from our nature and from all that is below God, we cannot regard ourselves as having acquired an unchanging habit of virtue. For only when love makes firm this disposition in us can we know the power of God's promise, because the perfect immutability of those who are worthy is established, as we must believe, there where power has been already rooted by mind through love. And a man who has not gone out of himself and of all that could be an object of thought, and has not become grounded in the silence which surpasses all thought (the stilling of all movements of the mind), can in no way be free from change. (1, 81)

27. The great Moses began to worship God only after he had pitched his tabernacle without the camp; that is, after having firmly established his heart and mind outside all visible things. And after he had entered the darkness, that is the place of knowledge without matter or form, he remained there performing the most sacred mysteries (or being ordained in them) (Ex. xxxiii. 7; xx. 21). (1, 84)

29. A man who fulfils the law by his life and conduct refrains merely from passionate deeds, sacrificing to God the actions of irrational passions. This suffices for his salvation owing to his spiritual infancy. (1, 94)

30. A man, guided by the words of the prophets to renounce passionate deeds, adds to this renunciation also rejection of all the sympathy for them or the accord with them, which form themselves in the soul; lest, while showing himself as abstaining

from sin with his worse side, that is the flesh, he should unresistingly sin in secret with his better side, that is the soul. (1, 95)

31. He who has sincerely embraced life according to the Gospels cuts off the beginning and the end of sin in himself, practises every virtue in mind and deed and brings to God the offering of praise and profession, as one liberated from active attacks of passions, free from inner struggle against them, and having but one insatiable joy, which feeds the soul with the hope of future blessings. (1, 96)

32. Sensory perception, or the perception of sensory impressions, belongs to the *man of action*, who labours over attaining the virtues. Non-perception by the senses, or being unmoved by sensory impressions, belongs to the *contemplative*, who concentrates his mind on God, wresting it away from the flesh and the world. Striving to separate the soul from the natural bonds of sympathy for the flesh through *active* effort on the right way, the first often feels weary and his good disposition is weakened. But the second, having removed the thorns of this sympathy by practising and remaining in *contemplation*, can no longer be beguiled or held by anything; for he has become cleansed of the things, by which those seeking to take possession of him were wont to wound and hold him. (1, 99)

33. As the fruit of disobedience is sin, so the fruit of obedience is virtue. And as disobedience is followed by transgression of commandments and breaking of the bond with Him, Who gave the commandments, so obedience is followed by keeping the commandments and closer union with Him Who gave them. For he who has kept a commandment through obedience has done what is right and has preserved unbroken the union of love with the Giver of commandments. And he who, through disobedience, has transgressed a commandment, has committed a sin and has separated himself from the union of love with the Giver of the commandment. (2, 7)

34. If, after breaking the bond through transgression, a man seeks to re-establish this bond, he first withdraws from passions, then from passionate thoughts, then from nature and all that belongs to it (that is, from the material world), then from things of the mind and knowledge of them (that is, from the spiritual

world); finally, having passed through the multiplicity of mani-
festations of Providence (the flux of events), he approaches in
some incomprehensible manner Unity Itself; here alone he sees
his own immutability and rejoices 'with joy unspeakable' (1 Peter
1, 8), having received 'the peace of God, which passeth all
understanding' (Phil. iv. 7), and which ever protects from downfalls him who has been granted it. (2, 8)

35. Fear of gehenna forces those introduced into this path
(beginners) to avoid sin; desire of blessings to be bestowed gives
to those, who make progress, readiness in practising virtues; but
the mystery of love raises the mind above all creation, rendering
it blind to all that is below God. For only to those, who have
become blind to all that is below God, does the Lord give
wisdom, shewing them the most Divine (Ps. cxlv. 8). (2, 9)

37. Let him who dedicates himself to knowledge set the steps
of his soul immoveably before the Lord, as God said to Moses
'thou shalt stand there for me' (Ex. xxxiv. 2). However, if those
who love wisdom read attentively the following, 'There be some
of them that stand here, which shall not taste of death, till they
have seen the kingdom of God come with power' (Mark ix. 1),
they must realise that there is some difference even amongst those
who stand before the Lord. For not to all of those who stand
before Him does the Lord always appear in glory; but to those
who are only being introduced to the way to Him (beginners),
He comes in the guise of a servant, and to those who are strong
enough to follow Him in His ascent of the high mountain of His
Transfiguration, He appears in the aspect of God, as He was before
the creation of the world. Thus is it possible that one and the
same Lord should appear in different aspects to those who approach Him—to some in one, to others in another, the appearance varying in accordance with the faith of each. (2, 13)

38. It is said of a man who leads a life of action that he
temporarily inhabits the flesh as a stranger, whose aim is, by the
practice of virtues, to cut off from his soul all sympathy for the
flesh and to tear himself away from material attractions. And of a
man who leads a life of contemplation, it is said that he is but a
stranger even in virtue itself, as one who as yet sees the truth
as through a glass, darkly. For he has not yet seen, through

experience, as it were face to face, the actual aspect of the blessings hoped for, as they really are. And every saint in relation to future blessings 'walks in a shadow' crying 'I am a sojourner in the land, and a stranger, as all my fathers were' (Ps. xxxviii. 6, 12). (2, 17)

39. It is good to forget all and to seek the Lord as we are commanded (Ps. xliv. 10; civ. 4). For although, because our present life is what it is, when we seek God we cannot reach the limit of His depth, yet perhaps having reached some small fraction of His depth, we shall see the Holy of Holies and the spirit of the spiritual. Figuratively, this is shown by the Bishop when from the Holy place (the first part of the tabernacle), which is holier than the forecourt, he enters the Holy of Holies, which is holier than the holy. (2, 19)

40. If the Son of God the Father, God the Word, became the Son of man and man, that men might become gods and sons of God, let us believe that we shall be there, where Christ Himself is now, as the 'head of the body' (Col. i. 18), having become in His human nature the forerunner for us to the Father. For in the host of gods, that is, those saved, God will stand in the midst, bestowing (according to each man's worth) the honours of heavenly beatitude, but without placing the worthy apart from one another. (2, 25)

41. He who still fulfils the passionate desires of the flesh, lives in the land of the Chaldees as a servant and maker of idols. But when, after sound reflection, he comes to a certain realisation of the mode of life which naturally befits him (and has a feeling for it), then, leaving the land of the Chaldees, he goes to Charrhan in Mesopotamia (Gen. xi. 28–31), that is, to a state adjoining both virtue and sin, not yet pure from the beguilement of the senses. But when he passes beyond the boundaries of this inter-mediate sensory understanding of the good, he enters the good land, that is the state free from all sin and ignorance, which God, Who is not false, shows and promises to give as the reward for virtue to those who love Him. (2, 26)

42. He who strives to acquire wisdom in the spirit of right-eousness, and who has set himself in battle order against the in-visible powers, should pray that both natural discrimination (between good and evil), the light of which is not great, and the

enlightening grace of the Spirit should be with him; the former guides the flesh, as if it were a child, to active virtue, and the second, like a light, leads the mind to prefer above all else wisdom as its spouse (Wisdom of Solomon viii. 2); wisdom whereby strongholds are pulled down 'and every high thing that exalteth itself against the knowledge of God' (2 Cor. x. 4, 5). Joshua shows the same when he asks in prayer, 'Let the sun stand over against Gabaon,' that is, let the light of the knowledge of God on the mountain of mental contemplation never go down in him, 'and the moon over against the valley of Ælon' (Josh. x. 12), that is, may the natural discrimination between good and evil, which lies above the weakness of the flesh, remain steadfast in relation to virtue. (2, 33)

43. Gabaon is higher mind; and *the valley* is flesh, subdued by death. *The sun* is the Word, enlightening the mind, giving it the power of contemplation and freeing it of all ignorance; and *the moon* is the natural law, compelling the flesh lawfully to submit to the spirit and take on the yoke of the commandments. The moon is taken as a symbol of the natural because of its mutability. However, in the saints nature is not mutable, owing to their immutable habit of virtue. (2, 34)

44. It is not outside themselves that those who seek the Lord should seek, but within themselves that they must seek Him with faith, testified by deeds. 'The word is nigh thee', says the Apostle, 'even in thy mouth, and in thy heart: that is, the word of faith' (Rom. x. 8), for seeking the word of faith means seeking Christ Himself. (2,35)

45. Neither, when we reflect on the height of God's infinity, should we despair of His loving-kindness, as if from such height it could not reach us; nor, when we remember the measureless depth of our fall through sin, should we disbelieve in the possibility of the virtue, which is dead in us, rising again. Both are possible for God—descent to illumine our mind with knowledge, as equally restoring virtue in us, lifting us to Himself by means of righteous deeds. 'Say not in thine heart,' says the Apostle, 'Who shall ascend into heaven? (that is, to bring Christ down from above:) Or, Who shall descend into the deep? (that is, to bring up Christ again from the dead.)' (Rom. x. 6, 7). (2, 36)

46. Those who live, like animals, for the sake of the senses alone, misuse God's creations in indulging the passions. They do not listen to the word of wisdom, made plain to all, enjoining them to know and glorify God through His creatures and to understand whence we come, what we are, for what purpose we are created and whither we should strive by means of the visible; they wander in darkness all their life, clutching with both hands nothing but ignorance of God. (2, 41)

47. Those who listen only to the letter of the Holy Scriptures, and who shackle the dignity of their soul by serving the law with their body, think to propitiate God by the sacrifice of dumb animals. They care much for the body and its external purifications, but pay no attention to the beauty of the soul, disfigured by the wounds of passions. Yet it is for the soul's sake that all the variety of visible things has been created and all the law and the word of God have been given. (2, 42)

49. 'The doors were shut . . . for fear of the Jews' (John xx. 19) means that, for fear of the spirits of evil in the land of revelations, those who are firmly established on the heights of Divine contemplations shut their senses like doors and receive God the Word, Who, appearing to them in an unknown way, not according to the order of sensory events, gives them through 'Peace be unto you'—passionlessness, and through breathing on them—participation of the Holy Ghost, bestows on them power over evil spirits and shows the signs of His mysteries (John xx. 19-22). (2, 46)

50. The *land of the Chaldees* is passionate life, where sinful idols are set up and worshipped. *Mesopotamia* is the mode of life inclining now towards one side, now towards its opposite. And the *promised land* is a state (of the spirit) filled with all (spiritual) blessings. Every man who, like the Israel of old, does not take care of this good disposition falls again into slavery to passions and is deprived of the freedom granted to him. (2, 48)

51. It should be noted that none of the saints ever went voluntarily to Babylon; for it would be foolish and unseemly for those who love God to choose the bad in place of the good. If some of them were led there involuntarily, together with the people, we understand by such those men who, not from

themselves, but through special circumstances, for the sake of saving those who need guidance, leave the exalted word of knowledge and pass to teaching about passions. For the same reason, the great Apostle deemed it more necessary to abide in the flesh, that is to continue to give moral teaching to disciples, when his whole desire was to abandon moral teaching and to be with Christ through simple spiritual contemplation, which is above the world (Phil. 1. 23, 24). (2, 49)

54. He who prays for supersubstantial bread does not of course receive the whole of the bread, as it is in itself, but as much as the receiver can receive. The Bread of Life (John vi. 35) gives Himself to all who ask, since He loves men, but not to all equally: to those who have wrought great deeds of righteousness He gives more, and to those who are poor in such deeds, less—to each as much as the degree (or good disposition) of his mind can receive. (2, 56)

55. For the man who lives actively, the Lord is present through virtues; and from a man who does not value virtue, He is absent. And again, for a man of contemplation, He is present through the true knowledge of things; but from a man who in some measure errs in this He is absent. (2, 58)

56. In the beginning of education in righteousness, it usually looks as if righteousness refers only to the body. And in the first approach to right worship of God, our conversation is more according to the letter than the spirit. Later, gradually coming closer to the spirit and refining teachings that are after the flesh by spiritual contemplations, we come to dwell purely in pure Christ, as far as is possible for men; so that we can say with the Apostle, 'though we have known Christ after the flesh, yet now' (in His glory) 'henceforth know we him no more' (2 Cor. v. 16). This is due to a simple (or pure) approach of the mind to the Word, with no veils covering Him, for we have already achieved the ascent from the knowledge of Christ after the flesh to beholding 'his glory, the glory as of the only begotten of the Father' (John i. 14). (2, 61)

57. He who has begun to live his life in Christ, has surpassed both the righteousness that is under the law and natural righteousness; that is the meaning of the Divine Apostle when he says,

'For in Christ Jesus neither circumcision availeth any thing, nor uncircumcision' (Gal. vi. 15), meaning by the word circumcision, righteousness under the law, and by the word uncircumcision, hinting at similar righteousness according to the law of nature. (2, 62)

59. 'I am the door' (John x. 9) said the Lord. For those who have accomplished rightly the path of virtues in the course of a sinless active life are led by Him into the realm of knowledge where, like light, He shows them the shining treasures of wisdom. He is alike the way, and the door, the key, and the kingdom; the way, as the One Who guides; the key, as the One Who opens to the worthy the entrance to Divine treasures; the door, as the One Who gives entry; the kingdom, as the One to be inherited and Who, through participation, is present in all. (2, 69)

60. The Lord is called *light, life, resurrection, truth*. *Light*, as He Who illumines souls and banishes the darkness of ignorance, as He Who enlightens the mind with understanding of things, beyond the grasp of the mind, and Who reveals mysteries accessible only to the pure; *life*, as He Who lends to souls which love Him the movement proper to the realm of Divine things; *resurrection*, as He Who rouses the mind from deadening attachment to material things and cleanses it from all corruption and death; *truth*, as He Who gives those who are worthy a never changing disposition towards good actions. (2, 70)

61. A man glorifies God in himself, not when he pays reverent homage to Him merely by words, but when, for the sake of God and His commandments, he endures with patience sufferings and labours. Such a man is glorified in return by the glory, which is in God, bearing in himself by participation the blessing of passionlessness, as a reward for virtue. For every man, who glorifies God in himself by sufferings endured for virtue in his active life, is himself glorified in God through passionless illumination by Divine rays in the state of contemplation. And the Lord, going to His voluntary passion, says 'Now is the Son of man glorified, and God is glorified in him. If God be glorified in him, God shall also glorify him in himself, and shall straightway glorify him' (John xiii. 31, 32). It is clear from this that sufferings for the sake of virtue are followed by the Divine gifts of grace. (2, 72)

62. So long as the soul is in the process of moving from strength to strength and from glory to glory, that is, progresses from virtue to greater virtue and ascends from knowledge to greater knowledge, it never ceases to be a sojourner, as is said, 'My soul has long been a sojourner' (Ps. cxix. 6). For great is the distance, and many the degrees of knowledge to be passed until it comes to 'the place of thy wondrous tabernacle, even to the house of God, with a voice of exultation and thanksgiving and of the sound of those who keep festival' (Ps. xli. 4), ever adding voice to voices, spiritual voice to spiritual voices, as it makes progress in spiritual contemplations, with joy in what is contemplated—joy and proper thanksgiving. These festivals are celebrated by all who have received the Spirit into their hearts, crying, Abba, Father (Gal. iv. 6). (2, 77)

63. *The place of thy wondrous tabernacle* is a passionless and steadfast disposition towards virtues, thanks to which God the Word comes to adorn the soul with the varied beauties of virtues like a tabernacle. The *house of God* is knowledge compounded of many and varied contemplations, thanks to which God visits the soul to fill it with much wisdom. The *voice of exultation* is the leaping of the soul at the sight of many virtues. *Thanksgiving* is giving thanks for the glorious food or for being filled with wisdom. *Sound* is the constant secret singing of praise which results from the blending of the two, that is, of exultation and thanksgiving. (2, 78)

64. He who has valiantly overcome carnal passions and has gained enough victories over evil spirits, and who has banished their thoughts from the domain of his soul, should pray to be given a clean heart and for the right spirit to be renewed within him, that is, by the grace of God to be cleansed completely of evil thoughts and be filled with thoughts that are Divine. (2, 79)

65. He who has made his heart clean not only learns the meaning and significance of secondary things, which are below God, but, having passed through them all, he sees in some sort even God Himself, which is the uttermost limit of blessings. Visiting such a heart, God deigns to engrave in it with the Spirit His own writings, as on Moses' tablets, inasmuch as it has increased itself in stature through good activity and contemplation, in accordance with the commandment which

ordains mysteriously, 'increase and multiply' (Gen. xxxv. 11). (2, 80)

66. The mind of Christ, which the saints receive according to the words 'We have the mind of Christ' (1 Cor. ii. 16), comes, not by our losing our own mental power, nor as essentially and personally passing into our mind (taking its place), but as illumining, by its quality, the power of our mind and transporting its action into singleness with itself. In my opinion, a man has the mind of Christ, if he thinks of all things in the spirit of Christ and is brought by all things to thought of Him. (2, 83)

67. We are called the body of Christ, according to the words of the Apostle 'Ye are the body of Christ, and members in particular' (1 Cor. xii. 27), not because by losing our own bodies we become His body, nor because He personally passes into us or is particularised into members; but because, like the flesh of Christ, our flesh also is freed from the corruption of sin. For as Christ by nature was without sin as a man, both in flesh and soul, so we too who believe in Him and have put Him on in the Spirit may, by exerting our will, be in Him without sin. (2, 84)

68. So long as a man is still in this life, no matter how perfect he may be in doing and contemplation, according to the conditions of earthly existence, it is only in part that he has knowledge, prophecy, the pledge of the Holy Spirit, but not in all their fulness; for he has still to come at some time to the state of perfection, in which those who are worthy are shown truth face to face, as it is in itself. Then he will not have fulness only in part, but will carry in himself entire fulness by participation. For the Apostle says that then all (that is, those who are saved) will 'come . . . unto the measure of the stature of the fulness of Christ' (Eph. iv. 13); 'In whom are hid all the treasures of wisdom and knowledge' (Col. ii. 3), after the manifestation of which 'that which is in part shall be done away' (1 Cor. xiii. 10). (2, 87)

69. Some enquire, what will be the state of those deemed worthy of perfection in the Kingdom of God? Will there be progress and movement (from better to still better) or will there be only one state, established and unchanging? What will bodies and souls then be like and how can it be thought about? Upon reflection, someone may reply to this that in life in the flesh food

has a double significance—it serves for growth and for the maintenance of those who are fed: namely, until we have come unto the perfect measure of bodily stature we are fed for growth, but when the body stops growing, it is fed not for growth but for maintenance. In the same way, food has a double meaning in relation to the soul. It is fed by virtues and contemplations while it is making progress until, having passed beyond all that is, it comes unto the measure of the stature of the fulness of Christ. When it has reached this, it stops progressing or adding to its growth by ordained methods, and, being directly fed with incorruptible food by means which pass all understanding and which, perhaps for that reason, are above growth, it now receives food only for maintaining the godlike perfection granted to it, and for testifying to the immeasurable joys brought by this food. Receiving through this food the well-being, which now never varies nor deserts it, it becomes a god through participation in Divine grace, since it has itself ceased from all actions engendered by the mind and the senses and, at the same time, has brought to rest the natural actions of the body, which becomes godlike in its company in the measure possible for it. Then God alone shines through body and soul, vanquishing their natural features with overwhelming glory. (2, 88)

72. He who by efforts in practising good has succeeded in mortifying the 'members which are upon the earth' (Col. iii. 5), and through fulfilling the commandments of the Word has conquered the world that is in him, will have no tribulations, since he has already abandoned the world and has begun to dwell in Christ—Christ Who has overcome the passionate world and is the Giver of all peace. For he who has not abandoned attachment to the material is bound to have tribulations, since his feelings change with the changing of what is changeable in nature. But he who has begun to dwell in Christ will on no account feel material changes whatever they may be. Therefore the Lord says, 'These things I have spoken unto you, that in me ye might have peace. In the world ye shall have tribulation: but be of good cheer; I have overcome the world' (John xvi. 33). In other words, in Me, the Word, you shall have peace, being freed from the vicissitudes and turmoil of earthly things and passions, whereas in the world, that

is in attachment to material things, you shall have tribulations, for there all things are constantly changing into one another. Tribulations will come both to the man who practises virtue, owing to the effort connected with it, and to the man who loves the world, owing to material losses and privations. But in one they are salutary, while in the other they are destructive and pernicious. But for both, peace is in the Lord: for the first, because, after the labours of virtuous life, He gives him the peace of passionlessness in the state of contemplation; for the second because, through repentance, He removes from him the customary attachment to corruptible things. (2, 95)

76. One is the Being, Who is good, transubstantial and without beginning, the Unity in Three Hypostases, the Father, the Son and the Holy Spirit, the infinite coexistence of three infinites; concerning Whose being, how He is, what He is and of what nature He is no understanding is possible for created minds. It flees from all understanding by conjectures of the mind, while in no way moving out from its essential inner place of secrecy, and the knowledge of Him surpasses immeasurably all knowledge. (3, 1)

77. There is one God, the Father, of Whom the One Son is begotten and from Whom the One Holy Spirit flows; Unity unconfounded and Trinity undivided; Mind without beginning, Sole Begetter of the One Word, Who is essentially without beginning, and the Source of the One, everlasting Life, that is, the Holy Spirit. (3, 4)

78. There is one God, Unity without beginning and eternal, without parts and undivided; being both Unity and Trinity. (3, 5)

79. God the Christ is born and, by assuming flesh with a rational soul, becomes man—He, Who from non-being has given being to all that is, and to Whom the Virgin gave birth supernaturally, losing no attributes of virginity. For as He became man without changing His nature or losing His power; so also He both makes Her a mother and preserves Her a Virgin who gave Him birth, simultaneously denoting one miracle by another and veiling one by the other. In Himself, in His essence, God is always hidden in mystery; and if at times He emerges from His essential mystery, He does so in such manner that, by its very

manifestation, He makes it even more mysterious. Thus He makes the Virgin a bearing Mother in such a way that the very giving of birth itself makes the bonds of virginity indissoluble. (3, 9)

80. Let us look with faith upon the mystery of the Divine Incarnation and give only praise without inquiry to Him, Who condescended in this way for us. For who, relying on the power of his reason to inquire, can tell how God the Word is conceived? How is His flesh formed without seed? How is He born without corruption? How is she a Mother, who, even after giving birth, remained a Virgin? How does He, Who is above all perfection, increase in stature (Luke ii. 52)? How, being pure, did He receive baptism? How did He give food, who was Himself subject to hunger? How did He give strength, who was Himself subject to weariness? How, Himself subject to suffering, did He bring healing? How, Himself mortal, did He restore others to life? And to mention last what is first, how can God be man and, what is still more mysterious, how can the Word be in hypostasis substantially in the flesh, while in nature remaining hypostatically in the Father? How is it that one and the same is both God in nature and has become by nature man, in no way renouncing either of the two natures—neither the Divine, according to which He is God, nor ours, according to which He became man?—Faith alone can embrace all these mysteries, since it professes the existence of things that are above word or reason (Heb. xi. 1). (3, 13)

85. As physicians, treating the body, do not prescribe the same remedy to all, so also God, in treating sicknesses of the soul, has more than one means of healing; and giving each soul what it needs, He makes it whole. So let us give thanks to Him when we are being healed, even if what happens to us brings suffering; for the end is bliss. (3, 20)

91. The end of all good is love, for all who walk therein it guides, transports and brings near to God, Who is the highest good and the Source of all good; for love is always faithful, it never fails and remains ever unchanged. Faith is the foundation of hope and love, which follow it, since it firmly establishes the truth. Hope is the strength of love and of faith, standing on its either side to the right and to the left, since it shows them, by its very self, how worthy of faith (is the object of faith), how worthy of

love (is the object of love) and teaches how to make a way thither. Love is their fulfilment, for it embraces everything desirable that follows from them, and there gives repose. For, in place of faith in what is and of hope of what will be, it leads a man through itself (and in itself) into possessing it, as being present and into partaking of it as something actual. (3, 26)

92. There are three very great and most pernicious evils which, in brief, give birth to all wickedness: ignorance, self-love and hatred, which are intimately connected and mutually support one another. For ignorance of God engenders self-love, and from self-love comes hatred in relation to what is of the same nature. No one denies that the evil one produces and incites them in us, teaching us to misuse our powers—reason, desire and energy. (3, 31)

93. By reason, in place of ignorance, we should soar to God, seeking Him through knowledge; by desire, cleansing it from the passion of self-love, we should strive wholly to God alone, with all our longing; by energy, freed from hatred, we should use all our powers to find only God and to create in ourselves the blessed Divine love that unites with God and shows God's lover to be God—that love which comes from these two (knowledge of God and desire of God) and for which they exist. (3, 32)

94. When we cast off self-love, as I have said, this origin and mother of all evil, then all that comes from it, with it will fall away. For when it is not there, no kind and no trace of evil can ever keep footing in us. (3, 33)

99. God created us that we should become 'partakers of the divine nature' (2 Peter i. 4) and of His immortality, and that we should be like Him (1 John iii. 2) through deification by grace; to this end, everything is created and exists, and things that as yet are not, are brought into existence and born. (3, 42)

101. Self-love and men's minding of the flesh have separated men from one another and, having distorted the law, have split the single nature (of those endowed with a single nature) into many parts; they have been the origin of that hardness of heart which now possesses everyone and through this quality have set nature itself against itself. Therefore every man who, by sound sense and right thinking, succeeds in destroying this disharmony

of nature, shows mercy to himself before others, for he tempers his heart as it should·be by nature. Moreover, this tempering naturally brings him nearer to God and shows in him what it means to be in God's image, and how beautifully God in the beginning made our nature in His likeness, reflecting clearly His own goodness, equal to Himself in all things, not turbulent, peaceful, unrebellious, closely linked by love with God and with itself—a nature through which we embrace God with desire (that is, as the desired Good), and each other with sympathy (as being of the same nature). (3, 46)

102. In His loving kindness God became man in order to gather human nature to Himself, and to destroy its tendency to evil, by which it is divided against itself and never ceases to rise up against itself, due to the volatile mobility of its disposition towards others. (3, 47)

104. The beguilement and sweetness of sin usually vanish when it has actually been committed. Therefore man, finding by experience that every sinful pleasure is always followed by painful unpleasantness, has conceived the utmost yearning for pleasure and the utmost revulsion from unpleasantness and pain. He seeks the first with all his strength and strives by every possible means to prevent the second, thinking—what is quite impossible—in this way to separate the one from the other—and to delight his evil self-love by pleasure alone, with no distress at all; and he forgets, as is usual in the blinding effect of passion, that sinful pleasure is never free from the bitterness of pain. For the bitterness of sorrow is naturally mixed with sinful pleasure, although those who experience it forget this when passionate pleasure possesses them; for what possesses us always so occupies our attention that it completely hides from our sight what is to follow. Thus running after pleasures through self-love, and for the same reason trying to avoid all bitterness, we engender in ourselves innumerable pernicious passions. (3, 53)

105. But no one experiences such feelings of pleasure and bitterness who has become free of every tendency of the flesh and unites or rather cleaves with his mind to God, the most precious and the highest Good, truly worthy of love. (3, 54)

107. Where reason is not the master, the senses usually hold

sway. As a rule, this power of the senses is mixed with the power of sin which, through pleasure, leads the soul to pity the flesh, its kindred by nature. As a result it undertakes, as if it were natural to do so, a passionate and pleasure-loving care of the flesh and leads a man away from a rightly natural life, urging him to be for himself the instigator of evil, which has no independent existence. (3, 56)

108. Evil for a rational soul is to forget its natural good, thanks to a passionate attitude to the flesh and the world. When mind becomes the master, it abolishes this attitude through its knowledge of the spiritual order of things, rightly interpreting the origin and nature of the world and the flesh, and driving the soul to its kindred domain of the spirit, where the law of sin never enters, since there there is no sense, which could serve sin as a bridge to transmit it to the mind (or to the mental domain of the spirit). For the former relationships of the senses with the soul are already destroyed and all sensory images are passed and left behind, so that, having transcended them, the mind is no longer sensitive to them, being a stranger to them both in nature and disposition. (3, 57)

109. As the mind, keeping passions in its power, makes the senses instruments of virtue, so the passions, holding the mind in their hands, dispose the senses towards sin. It is necessary to look and think soberly how the soul should keep to a suitable mode of action, by using for creating and establishing virtues what was formerly used to commit sins. (3, 58)

110. The Holy Gospels introduce renunciation of life in the flesh and adoption of life in the spirit. I am speaking of those who die daily (1 Cor. xv. 31) as men, that is, die to the human life in the flesh in this world, and live only in the Spirit for God; according to the Apostle, they no longer live their own life but have Christ living in them (Gal. ii. 20). Similarly, those people are also regarded as dead to the flesh who suffer in this world great tribulations, sorrows and oppression and endure with joy persecutions and all kinds of trials. (3, 59)

111. Every passion is composed and born of a conjunction between some sensory object and the senses, accompanied by a deviation of the natural active powers—I mean, excitation, or

desire, or reason—from their proper, natural mode of action. If now, having discerned the purpose of their conjunction with one another, that is, the conjunction between the sensory object, the senses and the natural active power taking part in this, the mind by the use of reason succeeds in recalling each of them to the order natural to it and in seeing each of them separately, that is, the sensory object without relation to the senses, the senses without their link with the sensory object, and the active power involved, desire, say, or some other, without its passionate disposition towards the object or the senses; if, I repeat, the mind succeeds in doing this, without letting the passion itself direct its mental vision, it will grind very small this passionate conjunction, whatever it may be, like the golden calf of old (Ex. xxxii. 20), and scatter it upon the water of knowledge, completely abolishing even the most subtle thought of the passion, through restoring the things which provoke it to the order which is theirs by nature. (3, 60)

113. A firm and trustworthy basis for hope of the deification of human nature is God's Incarnation, which makes of man a god in the same measure as God Himself became man. For it is clear that He who became man without sin can also deify nature, without transforming it into the Deity, raising it to Himself in the measure that He humbled Himself for man's sake. Speaking of this mystery the great Apostle says, 'That in the ages to come he might shew the exceeding riches of his grace in his kindness toward us through Christ Jesus' (Eph. ii. 7). (3, 62)

115. Pleasure and pain, and the desire and fear that ensue, were not originally created together with human nature, otherwise they would belong to the features determining this nature. According to the teaching of the great Gregory of Nyssa they were introduced after our being had lost the inherent perfection of its nature, having been grafted upon the least rational part of our being. And through them, immediately after the transgression of the commandment, our likeness to dumb animals instead of to the blessed image of God manifested itself visibly and clearly, for, with the darkening of the status of rational beings, human nature had rightly to endure punishment from the very thing through which it had acquired features of irrationality. Thus God has

wisely arranged that, through this, man should come to realise the superiority of reason. (3, 65)

116. Even passions are of use in the hands of those who zealously lead good and righteous lives, if we wisely tear them away from the carnal and use them to acquire the heavenly—namely, when we make of desire an impetuous movement of spiritual yearning for Divine blessings; of love of pleasure—a vivifying joy caused by rapture of the mind before Divine gifts; of fear—a prudent care not to be subjected to future torment for sins; of sorrow—repentance directed towards correcting present evil. Briefly, if we use these passions to destroy or prevent existing or expected evil, as well as to acquire and preserve virtue and knowledge, we shall be like wise physicians, who abolish or prevent the harm caused or to be caused to the body by poison, by using the body of the poisonous creature—the viper. (3, 66)

117. The law of the first Testament purifies our nature of all filth by active love of wisdom; but the law of the New Testament, by the hidden guidance of contemplation, leads the mind away from the material towards the immaterial aspect of things akin to it. (3, 67)

118. The Holy Scriptures call the *fearing* (guided by fear) only those who are being introduced (beginners) and are but on the threshold of the Divine court of virtues. Those who have acquired appropriate experience in understanding and in the method of practising virtues are usually called *progressing*. And those who by spiritual understanding have reached the very summit of true knowledge of virtues are called *perfect*. Thus, a man who has renounced the old churning around in passions and, under the action of fear, has turned his whole disposition towards the Divine commandments, lacks none of the blessings fitting for beginners, although he has as yet gained no experience in virtue and has not shared in the wisdom spoken 'among them that are perfect' (1 Cor. ii. 6). In the same way the man who progresses lacks no blessings belonging to his degree, although he has not as yet attained that height of knowledge of Divine things which belongs to the perfect. And the perfect, who have already been mysteriously granted a contemplative knowledge of God and have purified their mind of every material image, also show

themselves to be rooted in the love of God, which bears a full and faultless likeness to the image of God's beauty. (3, 68)

119. Fear is of two kinds: one pure and the other impure. The fear born on account of trespasses through the expectation of torment is impure, for it is caused by awareness of one's guilt; it does not remain for ever, for it disappears when the sin is removed by repentance. But the fear which, apart from this apprehensive anxiety caused by sins, is always present in the soul, is pure and will never disappear; because it is in a certain way appropriate towards God as a tribute from His creatures, showing a natural reverence before His greatness, which is above all kingdom and all power. (3, 69)

120. The Holy Spirit is in all in general, since He encompasses all, provides for all and brings into motion in all the natural seeds (of good). But in those who are under the law, He is the definer, for He points out the transgression of commandments and throws light on the promise predicted about Christ. In all those who live according to Christ He is present, in addition, as the conferrer or producer of sonship. As the giver of wisdom, He exists in none of these simply and unconditionally, but only in those who, having reached understanding, have made themselves worthy of His Divine presence in them by their godlike life. For every man, even if he is a believer, who does not do the will of God has a foolish heart, the harbourer of evil thoughts, and a body guilty of sin, since it is always filled with unclean passionate lusts. (3, 73)

127. The Divine Apostle calls the various actions of the Holy Spirit 'diversities of gifts' bestowed by one and the same Spirit (1 Cor. xii. 4). Such manifestation of the Spirit is granted according to the measure that each man has in him faith and shares in a particular gift; that is to say, every believer, according to his faith and the actual temper of his soul, receives a corresponding action of the Spirit, which gives him disposition and strength sufficient to fulfil one commandment or another. (3, 96)

128. Just as one man is given the word of wisdom, another the word of knowledge, another faith, another some other of the gifts enumerated by the great Apostle (1 Cor. xii. 8-12), so one receives by the Spirit, according to the measure of his faith, the gift of perfect, direct love of God, which is wholly free from the

material; another, by the same Spirit, receives the gift of perfect love of neighbour; another some other gift, also by the same Spirit, as I have said, since each has his own gift acting in him. For every active and strong tendency towards fulfilling a commandment the Apostle calls a gift of the Spirit. (3, 97)

129. Faith is a force which keeps all things well-ordered within, or it is the right order itself which gives a supernatural, direct and perfect union between the faithful and the object of his faith—God. (4, 8)

130. Since man is composed of soul and body he is under the action of two laws, that is, the law of the flesh and the law of the Spirit; the law of the flesh has a sensory action, and the law of the spirit a mental or spiritual action. Moreover, acting in a sensory manner, the law of the flesh habitually links man with matter, whereas the law of the spirit, acting mentally or spiritually, brings about direct union with God. Thus it is quite in order that if a man 'shall not doubt in his heart' (Mark xi. 23), that is, shall not interrupt the direct union with God accomplished by faith, he, being passionless, and above all, having become godlike through his union with God by faith, 'shall say unto this mountain, Remove hence to yonder place; and it shall remove' (Matt. xvii. 20). This saying points like a finger to the fact that the minding and law of the flesh is indeed heavy and hard to move, and for our natural powers is totally immoveable and unshakeable. (4, 9)

131. The power of irrational love of life, or animality, has become so deeply rooted in human nature through the senses, that many regard man as being no more than flesh, which is capable only of enjoying the present life. (4, 10)

132. Saying 'Seek ye first the kingdom of God, and his righteousness' (Matt. vi. 33), that is first of all the knowledge of truth, and then active training in acquiring a righteous disposition, the Lord showed clearly that the faithful should seek solely the knowledge of God and virtue adorning it with deeds. (4, 16)

133. Many are the things which the faithful should seek in order to acquire knowledge of God and virtue, such as: liberation from passions, endurance of temptations, understanding of virtues and of the kinds of activities corresponding to them,

banishment of the soul's predilection for the flesh, alienating the senses from their attachment towards the sensory, completely estranging the mind from all the created and, speaking generally, an innumerable quantity of things required to turn away from sin and ignorance and to acquire knowledge and virtue. Therefore the Lord said, 'And all things, whatsoever ye shall ask in prayer, believing, ye shall receive' (Matt. xxi. 22), indicating by this that the devout should, with faith and understanding, seek and ask for all things generally, which assist in knowledge of God and virtue, and these things alone; for all these things are salutary for our soul and the Lord always gives them to those who ask of Him. (4, 17)

135. There are three powers in the soul—the thinking, the excitable (the energetic) and the desiring. By the thinking power we seek to understand what is good, by the desiring power we desire the good we have understood, by the excitable power we strive and fight for it. Those who love God, striving with these powers towards Divine virtue and knowledge and seeking with one, desiring with another, striving with the third, receive incorruptible food and knowledge of Divine things, which enriches the mind. (4, 25)

136. When God created human nature, together with giving it being by His will, He combined with it the power to perform what is needful. By this power I mean the impulse (tendency) to fulfil virtues which is essentially inherent in our nature, and is consciously manifested in action according to the will of him who possesses it. (4, 27)

137. If a man keeps only to a sensory discrimination between things according to whether they are pleasant or unpleasant, discrimination characteristic of the body, then, transgressing the Divine commandment, he eats of the tree of the knowledge of good and evil. In other words, owing to the irrationality or foolishness of the senses, he is only able rightly to discern one thing—namely, what serves for preserving the body whole, and therefore to accept the pleasant as good and shun the unpleasant as bad. But if he keeps entirely to mental discrimination, which rightly distinguishes the temporal from the eternal, then, having kept the Divine commandment, he eats of the tree of life, that is

of wisdom formed in the mind, which can rightly discern one thing, namely, what serves for the salvation of the soul, and which therefore accepts the glory of eternal blessings as good and rejects corruptible, temporal blessings as evil. (4, 34)

138. For the mind, the good is a passionless disposition towards the spiritual, and evil—a passionate leaning towards the sensory. But for the senses, the good is passionate movement towards the body, instigated by pleasure-loving lust, and evil—the unpleasant state caused by its privation. (4, 35)

140. Together with thoughts about sensory objects, the evil one maliciously introduces also images of their external aspects and forms, and the mere outer aspect of these things evokes passionate desire of them, if our intellectual activity is interrupted in its passage to the mental and spiritual through the medium of the senses. It is here that the enemy succeeds in corrupting the soul, throwing it into passionate agitation. (4, 38)

141. The word of God is light and fire, because it illumines natural thoughts and scorches unnatural ones; and also because it disperses the darkness of sensory life for those who, through fulfilling the commandments, strive after the better life they hope for. As to those who, from love for the flesh, cling in self-will to this dark night of (sensory) life, it punishes them by the fire of judgment and condemnation. (4, 39)

142. By its nature, the power of our mind is capable of knowing corporeal and incorporeal beings. But it receives knowledge of the Holy Trinity only through grace, merely in believing *that* It is, but never attempting to probe *what* It is in essence, as the mind of demons (does).

149. So long as the mind has in itself a living memory of God, it seeks the Lord through beholding (Ps. xxvi. 4, 8), not simply, however, but in the fear of the Lord (2 Chron. xxvi. 5), that is, together with obeying the commandments. For he who seeks the Lord without obeying the commandments does not find Him, since he seeks the Lord not in the fear of the Lord. And 'the Lord prospered him' (ibid.) for the Lord prospers everyone, who does what he ought with understanding, by teaching him various virtues and by revealing to him the true meaning of created things. (4, 62)

150. Without faith, hope and love no evil can be finally eliminated and no good can be perfectly established in us. Faith induces the mind, when attacked, to run to God and urges it to be bold with the conviction that all kinds of spiritual weapons are ready to hand. Hope is for the mind a trustworthy pledge of Divine help, promising the destruction of the enemy powers. And love makes it hard, or rather quite impossible, to tear it away from its kindred union with the Divine, even in time of battle, making the whole strength of its disposition cling to the desire of God. (4, 68)

152. Turning to God in itself shows clearly that Divine hope has been fully absorbed by the heart, since without it no one, anywhere and on any occasion, can be impelled towards God. For the function of hope is to present the future as the present to the eyes of those attacked by the enemy might, and to assure them that God, for Whom and because of Whom the saints must fight, has in no way deserted them and is protecting them. For no one can ever turn to good without some expectation, whether hard or easy to gain. (4, 71)

153. Every mind girded with Divine power has as elders or princes—*the thinking power* in which is born intelligent faith, teaching it always to see God ineffably present and to enjoy the future blessings through hope, as though they were present; *the desiring power,* in which love for God becomes established, making the will cleave to desire of the most pure Deity and keeping the disposition unswervingly directed towards the object of desire; and *the excitable power,* in which Divine peace comes to dwell in strength, directing all the movement of desires towards love of the Deity. Every mind has the assistance of these powers in uprooting evil and in planting and preserving virtues. (4, 73)

155. He who, during an uprising of passions, valiantly locks up the senses, who completely banishes imagination and memories of sensory things, and wholly suppresses the natural impulses of the mind to investigate what lies outside it, will victoriously put to shame, with the help of Divine grace, the evil and tyrannical uprising of passion and the devil, trying to coerce him. (4, 76)

160. Natural desires and pleasures do not make culpable those

who experience them, since they are a necessary consequence of the way we are made. For natural things give us pleasure even apart from our will—whether it be food that we happen to get to satisfy the hunger we were feeling, or drink quenching the thirst from which we were suffering, or sleep which renews our strength weakened by vigil, or anything else we may have to satisfy our natural needs, which is necessary for the well-being of our nature and helpful to those zealous to acquire virtues. All this is fitting also for those who strive to avoid sinful inclinations; yet within reasonable bounds, which do not allow a man to become a slave to blame-worthy and unnatural passions, arising in us of their own accord and having no other origin but the movements of natural requirements and desires, uncontrolled by reason; for though they are inherent in us, it is not for the purpose of accompanying us into immortal and everlasting life. (4, 90)

161. It is the work of the highest goodness not only to have created the divine and incorporeal natures of mental creatures as a reflection of the ineffable Divine glory, making them capable, according to their receptivity, of apprehending all the unthinkable splendour of inaccessible beauty, but also to have imprinted clear traces of its greatness in sensory creatures, which are in many respects inferior to mental beings; for these traces can transport directly to God a human mind, which ponders deeply over them, making it soar above all visible things and leading it, as it were, into the realm of higher bliss. (4, 96)

163. He who combines doing with knowledge, and knowledge with doing is the throne of God and a footstool for His feet: His throne through knowledge and His footstool through doing. And if anyone called heaven such a human mind, purified of every imagining of material things and always occupied, or rather adorned, by detached thoughts of the Divine, in my opinion he would not have gone beyond the limits of truth. (5, 1)

164. The initial impulse to the movement of any passion is usually provided by an object of sense akin to it. For without such an object as would attract the powers of the soul through the medium of one sense or another, the passionate movement would never arise, since passion does not exist without an object of sense. If there were no woman, there would be no fornication; if

there were no meats there would be no gluttony; if there were no gold there would be no cupidity. Thus the origin of every passionate movement of our natural powers is a sensory object, or a demon who by its means incites the soul to sin. (5, 3)

165. Between God and man there stand objects apprehended through the senses and objects contemplated by the mind. Desiring to reach God the human mind must not be enslaved by sensory objects in active life and must in no wise be kept back by mental objects in contemplative life. (5, 5)

167. The wrath of the Lord is a diminution or cessation of Divine gifts, which (cessation) is of benefit to every mind which thinks highly or much of itself, and which boasts of the blessings granted to it by God, as though they were the fruit of its own virtue. (5, 10)

169. He who thinks that he has already reached the summit of virtues will never seek the original source of blessings, for he attributes the power to make progress in good to himself alone, and thus deprives himself of what can make firm and secure his salvation—that is, God. But a man, who is aware of his own natural want of strength in good, will not cease in his urgent striving towards Him, Who can make good what he is lacking. (5, 14)

177. Blessed is he who has truly realised that God accomplishes in us, as in instruments, every action and contemplation, virtue and knowledge, victory and wisdom, goodness and truth, so that we bring absolutely nothing into it from ourselves except a disposition of desiring the good. Possessed of this disposition the great Zorobabel said, addressing his speech to God, 'Blessed art thou, who hast given me wisdom: for to thee I give thanks, O Lord of our fathers. From thee cometh victory, from thee cometh wisdom, and thine is the glory, and I am thy servant' (1 Esdras iv. 60, 59). As a truly grateful servant he referred everything to God, Who had given it all. For, having received it from God, he had wisdom; and in giving thanks, he ascribed to God all the power of the blessings given him, which combined, as is said, victory and wisdom, virtue and knowledge, action and contemplation, goodness and truth. For combining with one another, they send forth rays of the one light and glory which is God's. (5, 28)

178. All the perfections of the saints were clearly gifts of God. Thus none possessed anything, except the blessing bestowed upon him, meted out by God Himself, as the Lord of all, in the measure of the gratitude and good disposition of the receiver, who keeps possession only of what he dedicates to God. (5, 29)

179. Each one of us, according to the measure of our faith, receives a manifest action of the Spirit, so that everyone becomes for himself a bestower of grace. Consequently, no right thinking man will ever envy another, who abounds in gifts of grace, for it rests with him to acquire the disposition, which is a necessary condition for receiving Divine gifts. (5, 34)

180. The cause of the differences in the distribution of Divine gifts is the proportion of faith in each man (Rom. xii. 6). And in accordance with how we believe we also have a zealous readiness to act in the spirit of faith. Thus a doer (in the spirit of faith) by the measure of his activity shows the measure of faith, at the same time receiving grace in the measure that he has believed. And he who does not act thus shows by the measure of his inaction the measure of his unbelief, at the same time being deprived of grace in the measure he has fallen into unbelief. So a man who envies those who act righteously acts wrongly, since it is clearly in his own, and not in others' hands, to increase his faith and works and then to receive grace, which comes in the proportion of faith (and corresponding works). (5, 35)

181. 'And the Spirit of God shall rest upon him,' says Isaiah, 'the spirit of wisdom and understanding, the spirit of counsel and strength, the spirit of knowledge and godliness shall fill him; the spirit of the fear of God' (Isaiah xi. 2, 3). To these gifts there are correspondences:—to *fear*—abstinence from evil deeds; to *strength*—performing good deeds; to *counsel*—discerning what is contrary to duty; to *godliness*—an unerring view of what is meet; to *knowledge*—realising by experience the meaning hidden in the virtues; to *understanding*—a total orientation of the soul towards what is realised; to *wisdom*—a union with God, which passes all understanding, and which, by participation, makes of man a god. (5, 38)

182. The spirit of the *fear of God* is abstinence from evil deeds; the spirit of *strength* is diligent striving and movement towards an

energetic fulfilment of commandments; the *spirit of counsel* is experience in discriminating (between good and evil), in accordance with which we fulfil the commandments with understanding, sifting the worse from the better; the *spirit of godliness* is an unerring view of the forms of the practice of virtues, guided by which we never depart from the sound judgment of the reason; the *spirit of knowledge* is a true understanding of commandments and their principles, upon which the outer forms of virtues are based; the *spirit of understanding* is uniting oneself with the forms and principles of virtues (resolve to fulfil the former and to act in accordance with the latter), or rather the transformation (of oneself in accordance with them), which creates a fusion of natural powers with the forms and principles of virtues; the *spirit of wisdom* is ravishment towards the Cause of the deepest spiritual meanings contained in the commandments and union with It, through which we are mysteriously initiated into the meaning of things which is in God, as far as this is possible for men, and communicate it to other men in speech welling up from the heart as from some fountain. (5, 39)

184. No one, when sinning, can bring as an excuse the weakness of the flesh. For union with God the Word, by lifting the curse, has re-established all nature in full force, thus making inexcusable for us the yielding of our will to passions. The Divinity of the Word, being, through grace, always present in those who believe in Him, stifles the law of sin which is in the flesh. (Rom. viii. 2). (5, 46)

185. Knowledge, uncurbed by the fear of God, brings arrogance, which makes a man regard as his own what has been a gift. But doing, which increases together with love of God, receiving no knowledge above what a man should do, renders the doer humble. (5, 48)

187. The first passionlessness is refraining completely from evil actions, such as is to be seen in beginners; the second, is totally renouncing all thoughts of mental consent to evil; this can be found in those who follow the path of virtue with understanding; the third, is utter stillness of passionate desire; this is found in those who from visible things ascend to mental contemplations; the fourth passsionlessness is complete purification from

even the barest and simplest images, the state of those who, through knowledge and contemplation, have made their mind a clear and pure mirror of God. Thus a man who has cleansed himself of passionate actions, who has become free from mental consent to them and has cut off impulses of lust towards them, who has cleansed his mind of even a simple representation of them —a man who possesses these four degrees of passionlessness leaves the domain of material creation and enters the degree of immaterial beings, which is Divine and all at peace. (5, 51)

188. The first passionlessness is when the body does not move in response to an impulse of the flesh to sin by action; the second —a complete rejection of passionate thoughts in the soul, by which any movement possible in the first passionlessness is stifled, since there are no passionate thoughts to incite it to action; the third—complete stillness of all desire for passions, which also implies the second, that is, purity of thought; the fourth passionlessness is a total rejection in thought of all sensory images, which also originates the third, since there are no sensory images, which would paint pictures of passions. (5, 52)

189. The beginning and end of salvation for every man is wisdom, which begins by producing fear, but later becomes more perfect, to end by bringing love. Or rather, in the beginning wisdom itself is prudent fear, restraining its lover from harm, but later, towards the end, it naturally and of itself proves to be love, filling with spiritual rejoicing those who have taken it as companion in place of possessing all visible blessings. (5, 60)

190. Every confession brings humility to the soul, whether it teaches it to recognise that it is justified by grace, or forces it to admit that it is itself guilty in its trespasses, through negligence. (5, 62)

191. The content of confession can be of two kinds: one comes with the feeling of thankfulness for gifts received; the other with feelings of self-accusation and realisation of evil done. For we call confession both the grateful memory of God's favours, deeply felt, and a sincere consciousness of evil deeds, for which we are to blame. Both one and the other engender humility. For both he who renders thanks for gifts, and he who tortures himself for his trespasses, humbles himself; one because he counts himself as

unworthy of the gifts received, the other by imploring forgiveness of his sins. (5, 63)

192. The passion of pride consists of two kinds of ignorance or lack of realisation, which, merging together, produce one compound attitude. For only he is proud who recognises neither God's help nor human weakness. Thus pride is lack of knowledge of God and of man. (5, 64)

193. Vanity is to abandon an aim, which is according to God, and to shift to another aim, which is not according to God. For he is vain who strives after virtue for his own glory instead of the glory of God, and who aims by his labours to buy only the inconstant praises of men. (5, 65)

194. He who seeks to please men is only concerned to make his external conduct appear good and to earn a good word from a flatterer. In one case, he bribes the sight and in another the hearing of those, who take pleasure or who marvel merely at what they see and hear, and who judge virtue only by what is shown by the senses. Therefore pleasing men means displaying good behaviour and words before men and for the sake of men. (5, 66)

196. The cause of all creatures and of all the good that is in them is God. Therefore a man who prides himself on his virtue or knowledge and who does not combine awareness of his weakness with the measure of his virtue, that is, his progress in it by the help of grace, has obviously not escaped the evil spirit of pride. For a man who does good for his own glory prefers himself to God, since he is pierced by the thorn of vanity; and he who practises virtue or speaks of it merely 'to be seen of men' (Matt. xxiii. 5) places men's approval above that of God, being possessed by the passion of pleasing men; and he who has merely clothed his behaviour in a semblance of virtue with evil intent to deceive, and who covers by an outer appearance of righteousness the evil disposition of his heart, is bartering virtue with the slyness of hypocrisy. Is it not clear that each of them has as his aim not the Cause of all, but something else? (5, 68)

200. 'The effectual fervent prayer of a righteous man availeth much', as is said (James v. 16). It availeth much in two ways: first (when the man who prays is himself righteous) and he brings to

God a prayer accompanied by deeds in accordance with commandments, so that it does not consist merely of words and is not an empty sound, idle and having no firm foundation, but is given life and soul by the practice of commandments. For the power and efficacy of prayer depend on fulfilling the commandments through practice of virtues, as a result of which the righteous man's prayer is powerful and avails much, since it is rendered effectual by commandments. The second way is when a man, who asks a righteous man to pray for him, himself practises the works of prayer, promising to mend his former ways and actually mending them, and thus by his conversion making the prayer of the righteous man powerful and of much avail. (5, 80)

203. A sign of great ignorance, not to say foolishness, is to seek salvation through prayers of the Saints, when in his heart the man takes pleasure in harmful deeds and asks forgiveness for the very things, by which in actual fact he complacently pollutes himself in thought and feeling. He who asks a righteous man for prayer must not render it ineffectual and fruitless for himself, if he truly abhors evil; but he should give it wings by his virtues and make it effectual and strong enough to reach Him, Who has power to remit sins. (5, 83)

205. The word of truth knows two kinds of suffering, the first of which arises in the soul invisibly, while the second is visible and belongs to the sensory order. The first embraces the whole depth of the soul, being produced by the scourge of conscience, and the second affects our sensory part, restraining it from its natural dispersion by the weight of painful tribulations. (5, 86)

206. Just as the word of truth knows two kinds of suffering, so also it knows two kinds of temptations, some of which arise within, in the realm of the will, by the stimulation of evil desires, while others come from without, independently of the will, in the form of involuntary troubles, sorrows and afflictions. The first is the cause of suffering for the soul, the second—of suffering for the senses. (5, 90)

207. A temptation arising in the realm of the will causes sorrow to the soul, and gives pleasure to the senses; conversely, involuntary temptation comforts the soul (which meets it with understanding) while it wearies the flesh with grief. (5, 91)

208. I think that when our Lord and God taught His disciples how they should pray, by the words 'Lead us not into temptation' (Matt. vi. 13) He taught them to pray to be spared temptations arising in the realm of the will, that is, stimulations of lust, which undermine good disposition and intentions. The great James, known as the Lord's brother, teaching those who fought for truth not to be overcome by temptations which assail them, had in mind involuntary temptations, since he said, 'Count it all joy when ye fall into divers temptations' (James. i. 2), that is, involuntary, coming independently of our will and causing hardships and sorrows. This is clearly shown in the words which follow the first and the second sayings, for in the first the Lord adds, 'but deliver us from evil,' and in the second the great James says, 'Knowing this, that the trying of your faith worketh patience. But let patience have her perfect work, that ye may be perfect and entire, wanting nothing' (James i. 3, 4). (5, 92)

209. *Perfect* is he who fights against voluntary temptations by self-mastery and who endures the involuntary with patience; and *entire* is he who in his actions acts with knowledge and who does not leave contemplation inactive. (5, 94)

210. Mind and senses have natural activities opposed to one another, owing to the extreme dissimilarity and difference between their objects. The one has as its object immaterial and incorporeal realities which it apprehends incorporeally; the other—sensory and carnal beings, which they apprehend sensorily. (6, 2)

211. The mind, as soon as it begins to regard the senses as its own natural power, becomes entangled in the visible aspect of sensory things and begins to devise carnal pleasures, having no strength to rise above the nature of visible things, owing to its passionate attachment to the senses. (6, 5)

213. As the eye cannot perceive sensory objects without the light of the sun, so without the light of the spirit the human mind can never apprehend spiritual contemplation. For sensory light naturally illumines the senses for their perception of sensory objects; whereas spiritual light illumines the mind for its contemplative understanding of the suprasensory. (6, 17)

218. God, by a single infinitely powerful act of His will, with

His goodness encompasses and holds all, whether they be angels or men, good or wicked. But though God passes freely through them all, they participate in Him not equally but according to what they are. (6, 53)

222. As a lamp cannot burn without oil, so a man cannot preserve the light of spiritual gifts unless a good disposition becomes habitual and feeds inner goodness by corresponding words, deeds and morals, as well as by appropriate thoughts and feelings. For each spiritual gift requires a corresponding habitual disposition, which constantly pours into it, like oil, a certain mental substance to keep it safe through the good disposition of its receiver. (6, 81)

223. God is and is called Father by grace only in the case of those who testify their spiritual birth from God through grace by their virtuous temper. This temper mirrors as it were the face of the soul, clearly reflecting in virtues the features of its begetter —God. Those who possess them dispose onlookers to glorify God by offering their life for imitation as a true pattern of virtue. For God is glorified not by bare words, but by deeds of righteousness, which proclaim much better than words the splendour of God. (6, 86)

224. He who manifests in himself knowledge, which has acquired a body through activity, and activity which has gained a soul through knowledge, has found the precise method by which in truth God acts in us. But if a man has one of these features separated from the other, he has either made of knowledge an empty phantasy, or has transformed activity into a soulless idol. For inactive (ἄπρακτος) knowledge in no way differs from the dreams of phantasy since it is not confirmed by activity, and unintelligent (ἀλόγιστος) activity is the same as an idol, since it has no knowledge to give it a soul. (6, 88)

225. A truly accursed passion is arrogance, composed of a combination of two evils, pride and vanity; of these, pride denies the Creator of virtue and nature, while vanity counterfeits nature and virtue itself. For with a proud man nothing is done according to God, and with a vain man nothing happens according to nature. (7, 5)

226. The written law, restraining by fear from unrighteousness,

schools a man in righteousness. With time this schooling engenders a truth-loving disposition, preserving firmly established a disposition towards good, which makes man forget his former depravity. (7 , 11)

227. Circumcision, in its spiritual sense, is a complete cutting off of inclination towards physical lusts. (7, 41)

228. Sabbath is the quietening of the movement of passions, or their complete inaction. (7, 43)

229. God ordained the honouring of the Sabbath, the months and festivals, not because he wanted these days to be honoured by men as days, for that would mean serving 'the creature more than the Creator' (Rom. i. 25), implying that days are naturally worthy of honour and therefore of worship in themselves. But through the ordinance to honour the days, He symbolically ordained the honouring of Himself. For He Himself is the Sabbath, as being rest from the cares and sweats of life and from labours in the way of righteousness. He is also the Passover, as the Liberator of those held in the bitter servitude of sin; and He is the Pentecost, as the beginning and end of all. (7, 46)

230. We recognise as spiritual sacrifice not only the killing of passions put to death by 'the sword of the Spirit, which is the word of God' (Eph. vi. 17), but also the dedication to God of all natural powers and bringing them as a burnt offering to God, to be burnt in the fire of the grace of God. (7, 51)

235. The end of the present life is wrongly, I think, called death, but rather is it liberation from death, escape from the realm of corruption, freedom from slavery, cessation of tribulations, end of battles, way out of darkness, rest from labours, the calming of agitation, protection from shame, escape from passions and, generally speaking, the end of all evils; the saints gained all these things, making themselves strangers and pilgrims on earth by refashioning themselves through freely self-inflicted death. For they fought valiantly against the world and the flesh and their uprisings, and having overcome in both the attraction born of the sympathy of the senses with the objects of sense, they kept from slavery the dignity of their soul. (7, 76)

THE BLESSED THEODORE

THE BLESSED THEODORE[38]

This 'Theoretikon' deserves a place among other ascetic writings, both for its wise interpretation of the inner phenomena of our spiritual life and as a source of instruction for those engaged in spiritual work.

Who was the author of this writing is unknown. In the heading he is called the blessed Theodore, but it does not indicate who he was. The compilers of the Greek Philokalia, seeing that this writing contained thoughts similar to those found in the Century of St. Theodore of Edessa, have ascribed it to the latter and have placed it immediately after his Century. But Bishop Philaret of Chernigov ('On the Fathers', par. 277) writes that it can only tentatively be attributed to St. Theodore of Edessa. And indeed the writing itself gives no clear indication.

[38] Introductory note in the Russian edition.

THE BLESSED THEODORE
Theoretikon

1. What a great task it is to sever these strong bonds of attachment to things, to free oneself from serving it and to acquire a firm practice of right activity! Truly must a soul be valiant and courageous, to free itself from all material things.

2. After this, what has to be sought is not only purification from passions; for by itself purification is not yet virtue, but merely preparation for virtue; to purification from wrong habits must be added acquisition of virtues.

3. Purification of the soul consists in the following—for *the thinking part*—changing and completely abandoning our low 39 deluded habits and dispositions, that is the worries and cares of life, wrong tendencies and misplaced surmises and conjectures; for *the desiring part*—not to strive after anything sensory and not to be guided by the senses, but to be obedient to reason; for *the excitable part*—not to be troubled by anything that may happen.

4. And after such purification and elimination of everything that makes our powers impure and after putting them in good order, there should follow ascent to spiritual perfections and to deification; for he who has turned away from evil must do good (Ps. xxxiii. 14). Moreover, the first thing of all is to renounce oneself and thus, taking up one's cross, to follow the Lord in order to reach the highest state of deification.

5. What then is this ascent to perfection and deification? For *the mind*—it is the most perfect knowledge of what is and of Him Who is above all that is, as far as such knowledge is accessible to human nature; for *the desires*—an unending and continuous desire and striving for the first good; for *the excitable part*—the most

---

39 Literally, 'of the valley'. (Translators' note.)

energetic and active movement towards the object of desire, never ceasing and never weakening, which no tribulations met with on the way can arrest in its advance and which progresses irresistibly, never turning back.

6. The movement of the soul towards good should be as much stronger than its movement towards evil, as intelligible[40] beauties surpass sensory ones. So that the soul's care for the flesh should be allowed so far as is necessary to satisfy its needs and to maintain life, lest our physical organism be brought into forcible disorder. Though this is easy to establish for oneself, yet it is extremely difficult to put into practice, for it is impossible to eradicate without struggle the old-established habits of the soul.

7. Just as training in any art is not achieved without sweat, so intense raising of the eyes towards the blessed Being—God—and stretching out one's attention towards Him is achieved with much labour over a long time, until the desiring power becomes conversant with the results of this striving, and tastes its fruits. In this process our mind must manifest much opposition to the senses, which pull it valley-wards; hence our battle and struggle with the flesh never ceases till death, although at times it seems to diminish when anger and lust are tamed and the senses brought into subjection to a mind enriched by practical knowledge and skill in the art of warfare.

8. It should be borne in mind, however, that an unillumined[41] soul, since as a rule it has no help from God, can neither be truly purified nor ascend to the Divine light as was described, for what was said should be regarded as concerning the faithful. To make this more clear, it should be briefly explained what differences exist in our knowledge. Of the kinds of knowledge existing here on earth, one is natural and the other supernatural. What the second is will be clear from the first.

9. We call natural the knowledge the soul can receive by using natural methods and powers to investigate and examine the creation and the Cause of the creation, as far as this is possible, of course, for a soul tied to matter. For the energy of the mind is

[40] Intelligible. There are beauties apprehended by the intellect, as there are beauties apprehended by the senses. (Translators' note.)
[41] See below paras. 12, 13, 26. (Translators' note.)

weakened by its closeness to and fusion with the body, as a result of which it cannot have direct contact with intelligible things but needs to form images for thinking of them. And the natural function of imagination is to create images, which have extension and volume. Thus, since the mind is in the flesh, it requires corresponding images of things for forming judgments about them and understanding them. Now, the knowledge that the mind, being such, acquires by this natural method we call natural.

10. But supernatural knowledge is knowledge which enters the mind by a way which transcends its natural means and powers, or in which the object of knowledge is transcendant in relation to the mind tied to the flesh, so that such knowledge is clearly the attribute of incorporeal mind. It comes from God alone when He finds the mind purified of all material attachment and filled with Divine love.

11. Moreover, not only knowledge is divided thus, but also virtue; for some virtue is such as does not transcend nature and so is justly called natural; while other is made active by the prime Source of good and should fittingly be called supernatural, as transcending our natural powers and state.

12. Having explained this, we assume that natural knowledge and natural virtue can belong even to an unillumined man, but he can never possess the supernatural. For how could he have them without being a participant in the supreme Cause which acts here? But an illumined man can have them both.

13. I shall add to this but one more distinction: supernatural virtue cannot be acquired without first acquiring natural virtue; but there is nothing to prevent a man from participating in supernatural knowledge, without natural knowledge. However, we must know that both man and animals have senses and imagination, but in man these powers are much better and higher. In the same way, both an illumined and an unillumined man can have natural knowledge and virtues, but in an illumined man they are much better and higher than in the unillumined.

14. There is one more thing to add: of the knowledge called natural, that which is concerned with virtues and the tendencies opposed to them can be of two kinds—one, bare knowledge, when the man philosophising about these dispositions has not

experienced them in practice—and this kind of knowledge is at times shaken by doubts; and the other practical, engaging all parts of the soul, when it is confirmed by actual experience of such dispositions; and this latter knowledge is self-evident and true, never wavering nor admitting of doubt.

15. Together with realising that this is so, we learn also of the existence of four things which hinder the mind in its acquisition of virtue: *first*—the predisposition to practices opposed to it which, through long habit, draw it towards the earthly; *second*—the effect of the senses which, carried away by sensory beauties, draw the mind with them; *third*—the weakening of mental energy which the mind suffers from being interwoven with the body. For the relationship between the mind and intelligible things is not the same as that between sight and its objects, and generally between the senses and their objects.—I speak here of the mind of a soul which is still in the body. For incorporeal minds are in more active contact with intelligibles than is sight with its objects.—But as when sight is clouded the forms of things it reflects are not clear, not exact and, above all, blurred; so also our mind, although aware of intelligible things, yet cannot in practice see intelligible beauties. Moreover, it cannot desire any of them, since the degree of inclination depends on the degree of knowledge. And so it is immediately pulled down once more towards sensory beauties, which are represented to it more clearly, since it is necessarily drawn towards what appears before it as being good, whether this good be true or not true. In addition to all this there is (*the fourth*)—attacks of inhuman unclean spirits. Words cannot express the number and variety of nets which they spread to catch souls—everywhere on the way, in a great diversity of manner and form—in the senses, in words, in the mind, in everything that exists. No soul could ever escape them by itself, if He Who carried the lost sheep on His shoulder did not, in His infinite care, lift above them those who turn their eyes to Him.

16. To escape all this we need three means, of which the *first* and greatest is turning our eyes to God with our whole soul and asking for help from His hand, putting all our trust in Him in the sincere conviction that if He does not intercede, we shall inevitably be made captive by those who draw us to them. *The*

second which, I believe, is also the cause of the first, is constantly feeding the mind with knowledge. By this knowledge I mean knowledge of all that is, both sensory and intelligible, as it is in itself and in its relationship to the First Cause, since it has its being from It and for It; and contemplation, as far as is accessible to us, of the Source of all that is, by induction from that which comes from It. For investigation of the nature of creatures purifies from passionate attachment to them, gives freedom from their beguilement and leads to their origin, making one see, as in a mirror, in the beautiful, great and marvellous the most beautiful, greatest and most marvellous, or rather, that which is above all beauty, greatness or marvel. Constantly revolving in such thoughts how can mind not conceive a desire for the real good? For if at times it is drawn to what is alien to it, would it not be drawn more strongly to its own kin? And if the soul is enraptured by this vision, to what thing existing below would it allow itself to be attached, if this thing tends to draw it away from Him Who loves it and is beloved by it? Indeed, it will even dislike life in the flesh itself, since it hinders it in attaining and partaking of true blessings. For if, as is said, the mind sees but darkly the intelligible beauty in material things, intelligible blessings are such that even a small stream from the sea of this beauty and a faint radiance of its rays can persuade the mind to fly over all that is not intelligible and to ascend to those blessings alone, nor ever let itself fall away from their sweetness, even though this should mean some bitter suffering. And the *third,* which must accompany it, is mortification of our companion, the flesh; for otherwise it is impossible to see, clearly and distinctly, such heavenly blessings when they come. Flesh is mortified by fasting, vigil, sleeping on bare earth, rough garments as far as they are needed and exhausting labours. This is how the flesh is mortified or rather crucified to Christ. Becoming thus refined and purified, light and harmonious, it follows the movements of the mind readily without opposition and ascends with it on high. Without this all our efforts prove in vain.

17. This excellent trinity, when harmonious within itself, gives birth to a choir of blessed virtues in the soul. No trace of sin nor absence of any virtue is possible in those adorned with this

trinity. The mind of such men is no longer troubled by acquisitiveness, for this is already abandoned, nor by glory, for this is despised—two passions which make a soul, that is strongly attached to them, vulnerable to many others. And just as I assert that it is impossible for a soul attached to riches and glory to rise on high, so I deny that a soul could care for them if it has practised these three spiritual activities for long enough to have acquired experience in them. For if, with this disposition, it counts as truly good nothing except the Supreme Good, and among other good things counts as the best what, in its persuasion, is most like the former, then how can it love and welcome gold and silver or anything else of this vale? The same could be said of glory.

18. Even that most insatiable thing, care, does not then attack the mind from the side of the adversary. For what cares can a man have if he is attached to nothing and concerned with nothing over here? The cloud of cares is made up of evaporations from the principal passions—love of pleasures, love of money, and love of glory, so that a man free from them is a stranger, too, to cares.

19. Neither are people experienced in these three spiritual activities lacking in good judgment, which is regarded as a friend of wisdom and is the most powerful of all means leading on high. For the science of virtues includes an exact discrimination between good and what is opposed to good, and this requires sound judgment. With its guidance, experience and struggle with the flesh teach how it is best to do good and oppose evil.

20. Fear too is their attribute. For as love grows, so grows fear also; and the extent of one's hope to gain the good is the measure of one's fear of not receiving it. And this gnaws at the soul of those stung by love much more than the threat of innumerable tortures. For as to receive is the most blessed thing, so not to receive is the most accursed.

21. In order that reason may run before us on our way in yet another manner, we must begin with the end; for everything that happens derives from its end, both differentiation of parts and their harmonious co-ordination. The end of our life is bliss, or, what is the same, the kingdom of heaven or the kingdom of God. And in itself it means not only to contemplate the most mighty

Trinity but, with this, also to receive the influx of the Divine, to receive, as it were, deification and by this influx to fill in what is lacking in us and to make the imperfect perfect. And it is this that serves as food to spiritual beings—this filling in of what is lacking by means of this Divine influx. Here occurs a certain never ending circle, which begins where it ends. For the more a man understands the more he desires, the more he desires the more he draws nourishment, the more he draws nourishment the more he is incited to still greater understanding, and immediately resumes this unmoving movement or rather unmoving immobility.

22. So this is the end of our life, as far as it is accessible to our understanding. Now we must examine how to go towards it. For rational souls, which are immaterial entities endowed with minds only a little lower than the minds of the angels, life here is struggle and life in the flesh is given us as a task. And the reward for this struggle and effort is the state we have described —a gift worthy both of God's goodness and God's justice: justice, because these blessings are attained not without our own sweat and labour; goodness, because the gift immeasurably exceeds all labour of our own, and also because the very possibility of doing good is a gift of God.

23. And wherein lies the task here? The rational soul is conjoined with the animal body, which has its being from the earth and which gravitates valleywards. It is fused with this body in such a manner that these two—soul and body—totally opposed to one another, form one creature, without these parts becoming transformed into one another or mixed with one another—may this never be!—but in such a way that the two, each containing what is appropriate to it by nature, compose one person with two complete natures. This composite animal—man—this dual-natured being manifests also in action what belongs to each particular nature. It is natural for the body to desire what is of its kind—the physical. This desire of kindred things is natural to all creatures, for their very existence depends on absorbing into themselves what is of their own kind. It is natural for the body to take pleasure in kindred things by the senses; and it welcomes rest when weary. This is what is natural and desirable to our

animal nature.—For the intelligent soul, as an entity possessing mind, what is natural and desirable is similarly the intelligible, and its enjoyment in a corresponding way. But before all and above all it is natural for it to have an inherent love for God. So it is natural for it to desire enjoyment of this and of other intelligible things, but it cannot do so without hindrance.

24. The first man could unhindered perceive and enjoy the sensory by the senses and the intelligible by the mind. But he should have been pre-eminently occupied with the better rather than the worse, although by nature he could enter into communication with the intelligible through the mind and with the sensory through the senses. I do not say that Adam ought not to have used the senses, for it was not for nothing that he was clothed in the body; what I mean is that he should not have taken pleasure pre-eminently in the sensory and for the sake of the sensory; but perceiving through sensory impressions the beauty of creatures, he should have ascended to their Cause and taken joy in Him with wonder; for he had greater cause to wonder at the Creator than to cleave to the sensory and marvel at it, forsaking the intelligible beauty of the Creator. This is how Adam should have acted.

25. But since he used the senses wrongly and began to marvel at sensory beauty, he saw that the fruit was beautiful to behold and good to eat, and so tasted it, forsaking the enjoyment of intelligible things. Therefore the just Judge, considering him unworthy of contemplating God and all that is—things that he disdained— banished him and 'made darkness his secret place' for Himself (Ps. xvii. 11) and for all immaterial objects. For it was not fitting to give what is holy to one who was impure; but what he had conceived a love for, that God allowed him to enjoy, leaving him to live by the senses, with slight traces of the life of the mind.

26. This is why the effort of attaining communion with intelligible things has become so hard for us. For it is not in our power to enjoy with the mind what is intelligible in the same way as we enjoy the sensory with the senses, although we receive great help towards it through baptism, being purified and exalted thereby. However, to the extent that we can, we must exercise ourselves in the intelligible, and not in the sensory. We must marvel at it and desire it, and not marvel at anything sensory or

desire to enjoy it in itself (as being sensory and to indulge our sensory nature), for indeed it can have no comparison with the intelligible. We see that as one entity can in essence be more wonderful than another, so one beauty is more marvellous than another; but our attitude to them should be in accordance with what they are. To love the shameful more than the splendid and the base more than the praiseworthy is the height of madness! And if this be so concerning creatures, whether intelligible or sensory, what can be said of our attitude to Him Who is above all things, when even to Him we prefer ugly and worthless matter?

27. So this is what our task must now be—to pay diligent attention to ourselves in order always to take joy in the intelligible, stretching thither our mind and our desire, and never let ourselves be robbed by the sensory, beguiled by the senses to marvel at it for its own sake. If we have to use the senses, we should use them to know the Creator through His creatures, seeing Him in them as we see the sun reflected in the waters, for in the measure of its capacity all that is reflects the image of the First Cause of all.

28. Such is the work that lies before us. But how to put it into practice needs thought. For, as has been said, the body desires to enjoy its own kindred things through the senses and the more this desire is satisfied the more it grows. And this is opposed to the aspirations of the soul. So let the *first* care of the soul be to put a curb on all the senses that they may not enjoy the sensory, as has been said. But, since the stronger the body the more strongly it is drawn to what is its own, and the more strongly it is drawn the more irresistible the impetus, the *second* care of the soul should be diligently to mortify the flesh by fasting, vigil, standing at prayer, sleeping on bare earth and all other privations in order, by exhausting its strength, to render it humble and obedient in the spiritual activities of the soul. This is the principal thing it must achieve. But since it is easy to wish but hard to achieve, and in doing it many omissions occur contrary to what one ought to do, because the senses steal the attention, a *third* wise remedy has been devised—prayer and tears. Prayer gives thanks for the gifts received and asks for remission of sins and for the sending down of strength for further progress; for without God's help the soul

can do nothing rightly by itself, as has been said. Moreover, prayer unites the soul with Him Whom the soul seeks, gives joy in Him and makes the desiring power strive wholly towards Him —which is the most important thing in living as we should, namely, this inclining of the will to have such desire with all possible force. Tears also have great power: they obtain the Lord's mercy in our trespasses, purify the defilement we suffer from sensory pleasures and give wings to desire of what is on high.

29. So the whole thing is in this: first and most important— contemplation of intelligible or spiritual blessings and a total desire for them; for this reason, subjugation of the flesh, consisting of fasting, chastity and so on, all undertaken to help one another; for the same purpose and together with them—prayer. Each of these activities is divided into many parts, though they are all connected, so that one is required by another and does not exist without it.

30. No one should think that love of money and love of glory belong to bodily passions. The only bodily passion is love of physical pleasures, which finds a suitable remedy in mortification of the flesh. The two passions mentioned are the offspring of ignorance. Having no knowledge or experience of true blessings, intelligible or spiritual, the soul has invented false ones, thinking to find consolation in riches for its dearth of spiritual gifts. It also strives after wealth in order to satisfy lust for pleasures and love of glory, as well as for its own sake, regarding it as a bliss in itself. Of this we will say that it is all the result of ignorance of true blessings. Love of glory does not come from lack of physical necessities, for it satisfies something that is not physical. Its cause lies in lack of knowledge and of experience of the prime good and true glory.

31. Not only love of glory, but, in short, all evils have their roots in ignorance. For it is impossible for a man to know, as he should, the true nature of things and the origin and purpose of each, and then forget about his own final end and strive after things of the earth. The soul will not desire a blessing of which it knows for certain that it is a blessing only in appearance. Even if habit tyrannically draws it towards something, it can overcome habit itself if it understands the position clearly and exactly. But

even before habit was formed, it was beguiled through ignorance. So above all, and as soon as possible, one has to try to acquire right knowledge about all existing things and then, in accordance with it, to give wings to one's will by striving after the First Good. And to despise all present blessings is not hard for him who has rightly realised their total vanity.

APPENDICES

APPENDIX I

ST. GREGORY PALAMAS

Archbishop of Thessalonica (c. 1296–1359 A.D.)

1. *On the Blessed Hesychasts*

Question

Some say that we do wrong to try and confine the mind within the body; for, they say, it is much more necessary and useful to do our best to direct it away from the body. Moreover they severely criticise some of our people, and write against them for advising beginners to look into themselves and, through breathing, to lead their minds within, for they say that mind is not separated from soul. So, if mind is not separated from soul, but is joined with it, how can it be reintroduced within? They also accuse them of teaching people to breathe in Divine grace through the nostrils. But, knowing that this is pure calumny (for I never heard any of our people speak like this), I have come to the conclusion that their other accusations are also malignant slander; for it is usual for them to invent against people what does not exist, and to distort maliciously what does exist. Yet I beg you, my father, to teach me how and why we take special care to try and lead the mind within and do not think it wrong to confine it in the body.

St. Gregory's answer

For those who keep attention in themselves in silence it is not unprofitable to try to hold their mind within the body.

1. Brother! Do you not hear the Apostle saying that 'your body is the temple of the Holy Ghost which is in you' (1 Cor. vi. 19), and again, that 'ye are the temple of God' (1 Cor. iii. 16), as God also says, 'I will dwell in them, and walk in them; and I

will be their God.' (2 Cor. vi. 16)? Who then, possessing a mind, will deem it unseemly to introduce his mind into that which has been granted the honour of being the dwelling of God? How is it that God Himself in the beginning put the mind into the body? Has He too done wrong? Such words, brother, properly belong to heretics, who say that the body is evil and the creation of an evil principle. But we regard it as evil for the mind to be concerned with mindings of the flesh, and not wrong for the mind to be in the body—for the body is not evil. Therefore all those who cleave to God by their life cry to Him with David, 'My soul has thirsted for thee: how often has my flesh longed after thee' (Ps. lxii. 1), and 'My heart and my flesh have exulted in the living God' (Ps. lxxxiii. 2); and with Isaiah, 'My belly shall sound as a harp for Moab, and thou hast repaired my inward parts as a wall' (Isaiah xvi. 11). 'We have conceived, O Lord, because of thy fear . . . the breath of thy salvation . . . we shall not fall' (Isaiah xxvi. 18). When the Apostle calls the body death, saying, 'Who shall deliver me from the body of this death?' (Rom. vii. 24), he means by this the minding of the senses and the flesh. In relation to the spiritual he was right to call it body, and not simply body, but the body of this death. Thus, pointing out a little earlier that it is not the flesh that condemns but the tendency to sin that followed the fall, he says, 'I am . . . sold under sin' (Rom. vii. 14). And he who is sold is not a slave by nature. And again, 'For I know that in me (that is, in my flesh) dwelleth no good thing' (Rom. vii. 18). You see that it is not flesh that he calls evil, but what dwells in it. So evil is not that which is mind, but that which is the 'law in my members, warring against the law of my mind' (Rom. vii. 23). Therefore we fight against this law of sin, banish it from the body and establish there the mind as a bishop; and thereby we lay down laws for every power of the soul and for every member of the body as is appropriate for it. To the senses we prescribe what they have to receive and in what measure—this practice of the spiritual law is called self-mastery; the desiring part of the soul we bring to that most excellent state, whose name is love; the mental part we improve by banishing all that prevents the mind from soaring to God—and this part of the spiritual law we call sobriety.

2. He who purifies his body by self-mastery, who by love makes anger and lust an occasion for virtue, and who teaches the mind, cleansed by prayer, to stand before God, will receive and see in himself the grace promised to the pure in heart. Then can he say with Paul, 'For God, who commanded the light to shine out of darkness, hath shined in our hearts, to give the light of the knowledge of the glory of God in the face of Jesus Christ. But we have this treasure in earthen vessels' that is, in bodies (2 Cor. iv. 6, 7). So if we too hold our mind within the body, shall we be doing something unworthy of the greatness of the mind? Who would assert this, except perhaps a man who is completely unspiritual and whose mind, though otherwise human, is stripped of Divine grace?

3. Our soul is endowed with many powers, and it uses the body as an instrument, to which it gives life. What is the organ used as an instrument for its activity by that power which we call mind? No one ever thought that mind resided in nails or eyelashes, in nostrils or cheeks. But all agree that it is inside us— they disagree only as to which inner organ it uses as an instrument. For some place it in the brain as in some citadel; others say its seat is in the innermost part of the heart. We agree with the latter, adding only that it is not as in a vessel that our mental power is so confined in the heart, for it is incorporeal; nor is it outside it, as though something connected with the heart; but it is in the heart as in its organ, as we surely know, being so taught not of men but of man's Creator Himself, Who says in the Gospels, 'Not that which goeth into the mouth defileth a man; but that which cometh out of the mouth, this defileth a man. . . . For out of the heart proceed . . . thoughts' (Matt. xv. 11, 19). Macarius the Great says the same, 'The heart governs the whole organism, and when grace occupies all the divisions of the heart, it rules over all thoughts and members, for therein is the mind and all the thoughts of the soul.' Thus the heart is the secret chamber of the mind and the prime physical organ of the mental power.

4. Therefore, striving with diligent sobriety to keep watch over our mental power, to govern and correct it rightly, how can we succeed in this except by collecting the mind, which is

dispersed outside by the senses, and introducing it within, into that very heart which is the storehouse of thoughts? Thus the blessed Macarius says a little after the words I have quoted, 'It is there that we must look to see whether grace has inscribed the laws of the spirit.' There—where?—In the chief organ, where stands the throne of grace, and where are the mind and all the thoughts of the soul, that is, in the heart.

5. You see how essential it is for those, who have decided to keep attention in themselves in silence, to turn the mind back and confine it in the body, especially in that part, which is the innermost body within the body and which we call the heart? For if according to the Singer of Psalms 'The king's daughter is all glorious within' (Ps. xlv. 13) [42], why should we seek her anywhere outside? If, according to the Apostle, 'God hath sent forth the Spirit of his Son into your hearts, crying, Abba, Father' (Gal. iv. 6), how can we pray with this Spirit, if not in our hearts? If, according to the words of the Lord, of Prophets and of Apostles, 'The kingdom of God is within you' (Luke xvii. 21), would not the man who so zealously tries to chase his mind out from within, find himself also outside the kingdom of heaven?

7. The essence of the mind is one thing and its activity another. . . . The mind is not like the eye, which sees all visible things but does not see itself. The mind exerts itself in examining also all else that it needs, which, as the great Dionysius says, is the direct motion of the mind, and thereafter it returns into itself by a reverse motion, and sees itself. The same father calls it a circular motion.

8. But the action of the mind, which is best and most natural to it, is that in which it is sometimes raised above itself and unites with God. Because, as Basil the Great says, a mind which is not dispersed among external things, returns to itself, and from itself it ascends to God by an unerring path. For, as that infallible seer of spiritual things, St. Dionysius, says, this movement of the mind is incapable of any error. . . . John,[43] who made us a Ladder leading to heaven, definitely and decisively said that 'the hesychast is an incorporeal being who strives to keep his soul within the

[42] Authorised Version. (Translators' note.)
[43] John Climacus. (Translators' note.)

limits of its bodily home' (Ch. 27, 6). And all our spiritual fathers have taught the same. For, if we do not confine the mind within the body, how can we concentrate it within itself?

9. You see, brother, that not only spiritual, but general human reasoning shows the need to recognise it as imperative that those who wish to belong to themselves, and to be truly monks in their inner man, should lead the mind inside the body and hold it there. It is not out of place to teach even beginners to keep attention in themselves and to accustom themselves to introduce the mind within through breathing. For no one who thinks rightly would dissuade those, who have not yet attained contemplation, from using certain methods to lead the mind into itself. In those who have not long undertaken this work the mind, when collected within, often jumps out, so that, just as often, they have at once to bring it back; but in those who are not practised in this work, the mind again slips away, since it is extremely mobile and hard to hold by attention to singleness of contemplation. Hence some advise them to refrain from breathing fast, but to restrain their breath somewhat, so that, together with their breath, they may also hold the mind inside, until, with God's help, through training, they accustom the mind not to go out into its surroundings and mingle with them, and make it strong enough to concentrate upon one thing. However, this (restraining of the breath) naturally follows attention of mind (or accompanies it) as anyone can see; for if one meditates deeply on something, the breath goes in and out slowly, especially in those who are silent in body and spirit. For these, keeping spiritual Sabbath and resting from all their activities, as far as is fitting, suspend the diversified movements of the powers of the soul, especially in relation to collecting information, to all sensory receptivity and, in general, to all movements of the body, which are in our control.

10. All this is natural to those who are advanced in silence; for when the soul enters completely into itself, this all comes naturally of necessity, without effort or special care. But to beginners nothing of this is possible without strenuous work. Although patience naturally follows love, for love 'endureth all things' (1 Cor. xiii. 7), we learn to do the work of patience through forcing ourselves, in order thereby to gain love. This

is how things happen, and why say much about it? All those who have experience in it laugh at men who, without experience, write formal instructions to the contrary. For such things are learnt not from words but from active work and from the experience of work, which brings profitable fruit, turning men away from the barren words of people who love arguments and display.

11. One of the great teachers says that since the fall the inner man usually accords with the outer (with outer movements and postures). If this be so, why not accept it that a man who strives to turn his mind within is greatly helped in this if, instead of letting his eyes wander hither and thither, he turns them inwards and fixes them in his breast? When the eyes wander outside, the mind becomes dispersed among things through seeing them. In the same way, if the eyes are turned inwards, this movement of theirs will naturally lead the mind too inside the heart in a man who strives to reverse the movement of his mind, that is, to recall it from outside and lead it inwards.

12. 'Take heed to thyself' says Moses, 'that there be not a secret thing in thine heart, an iniquity' (Deut. xv. 9). Take heed to yourself, that is, the whole of yourself; not so that you heed one thing and not another—you must heed the whole. With what do we take heed? Of course with the mind, for nothing else can take heed of the whole of oneself. Therefore set it as guardian over soul and body, and you will easily be delivered from evil passions of the soul and the body. Thus stand on guard before yourself, stand over yourself, observe yourself, or rather watch, examine and judge. For in this way you will subjugate the unruly flesh to the spirit, and your heart will never harbour a secret word of iniquity.

13. 'If the spirit of the ruler' (that is, evil spirits and passions) 'rise up against thee,' says Ecclesiastes, 'leave not thy place' (Eccles. x. 4)—that is, do not leave unguarded a single part of your soul, a single member of your body. For in this way you will be victorious over the spirits which tempt from below, and unafraid of trial will stand with daring before Him, Who tries the heart and the reins from above, having previously tried them yourself. 'For if we would judge ourselves, we should not be judged' says St. Paul (1 Cor. xi. 31); so, having experienced

David's blessed apprehension (of God's omnipresence: 'Whither shall I go from thy Spirit?' [Ps. cxxxviii. 7]), you too will say to God, 'For darkness will not be darkness with thee; but night will be light as day: . . . For thou, O Lord, hast possessed my reins' (Ps. cxxxviii. 12, 13). Not only, will you say, shall I make Thine the desiring power of my soul, but if there be found in my body a spark of such desire, it too will fly to Thee, will strive to Thee, will cling to Thee. As in those devoted to sensory lusts the whole desire of the soul is given up to the flesh, so that thereby they become nothing but flesh, and God's 'Spirit shall certainly not remain among these men' (Gen. vi. 4); so too in those who direct their mind towards God and devote their soul to desire of the Divine, even their flesh, being transformed, rises up with them and takes part in Divine communion, whereby it too becomes a possession of God and His house and ceases to harbour 'enmity against God' and to lust 'against the Spirit' (Rom. viii. 7; Gal. v. 17).

14. Which is the most favourable place for the spirit which attacks us from below—the flesh or the mind? Is it not the flesh where, as the Apostle says, 'dwelleth no good thing' (Rom. vii. 18) until man has received 'the law of the Spirit of life' (Rom. viii. 2)? Therefore it is all the more needful not to leave it without attention. Otherwise how will it be ours? How shall we keep it for ourselves? How can we repulse the attacks of the evil one, especially when we learn how to oppose the spirits of wickedness spiritually, if we do not learn to keep attention in ourselves by external methods also? And I say this not only of beginners, since even among the perfect there were those who used such methods during prayer, and were heard by God, not only after Christ, but also before His coming to us. For even the most perfect seer of God, Elijah, 'stooped to the ground, and put his face between his knees' (3 Kings xviii. 42), and thus collecting his mind within and cleaving with it to God, he broke the drought of many years.

15. It seems to me, brother, that those from whom you have heard the opposite are sick with the sickness of the pharisees, and so do not want to guard and cleanse 'that which is within the cup' (Matt. xxiii. 26), that is, their heart, and not conforming with the tradition of the fathers, they attempt arbitrarily to

dominate everybody as new teachers, not admitting the external humble posture adopted during prayer by the publican, who was justified, and persuading others not to assume it when they pray. Since, as the Lord said in the Gospels, 'the publican, standing afar off, would not lift up so much as his eyes unto heaven' (Luke xviii. 13), those who keep attention in themselves during prayer try to imitate him externally. People who call them omphalo-psyches (those whose soul is in their navel) evidently so call them to ridicule that of which they wrongly accuse them. For who among the latter asserts that the soul is in the navel? By this the former show that they are clearly malicious slanderers. . . .

16. Of course you know the life of Simeon the New Theo-logian; he was a marvel to all men and was famed for supernatural miracles. And to call his writings writings of life would not be sinning against truth. You know too Nicephorus, this holy man who passed many years in quiet and silence, and then went to dwell in the wildest part of the Holy Mountain and undertook the work of extracting from the writings of the holy fathers and transmitting to us their rule of holy sobriety. There the work of sobriety is clearly expounded for the benefit of those who wish to learn it—that work to which, as you say, some people object.

17. And why quote ancient fathers? Men who have lived shortly before us and who bore witness to and manifested the power of the Holy Spirit, have transmitted it all to us verbally. Such were Theoleptus, the much revered head of the Church of Philadelphia, who was indeed a true theologian and a sure seer of the truth of the mysteries of God and who, from his church, as from a lamp, shed light for all the world. There was Athanasius, who occupied the patriarchal see for many years and whose relics were glorified by God; there was Nilus who came from Italy, the follower of the great Nilus; Seliotes and Elias who were in no way second to him; Gabriel and Athanasius who were granted the gift of prophecy. All these and many others who lived before them, with them and after them, praise this tradition and advise those, who so wish, to adopt it, despite the fact that new teachers of silence, who know not a trace of silence, and teach not from experience but from their own theories, or rather prattle about it, strive to refute and depreciate it, with no kind of profit for

their listeners. But we have talked personally with some of these saints and had them as our teachers. How can we presume to disregard these men, taught by grace and experience, and give way to those who dare to teach by means of an intricate and artful tangle of words, inspired by arrogance?

18. So do you too turn away from them, mentally repeating with David: 'Bless the Lord, O my soul; and all that is within me, bless his holy name' (Ps. cii. 1). And surrendering yourself as an obedient pupil to the fathers, listen how persistently they advise men always to lead the mind within and hold it there.

2. On Prayer and Purity of Heart: three Chapters

1. Since God is goodness itself, mercy itself and a limitless deep of benevolence, he who enters into union with Him, partakes in every way of His mercy. And union with Him is achieved by acquiring godlike virtues, as far as this is possible, and by communion with Him through prayer and supplication. However, communion through godlike virtues renders the diligent doer capable of receiving the Divine union, but does not effect it; it is intense prayer by its holy action that accomplishes the soaring of man to God and union with Him; for in its essence prayer is the union of intelligent beings with their Creator, when its action transcends passions and passionate thoughts through piercing of the heart and contrition. For while the mind is passionate, it cannot unite with God. Therefore so long as it remains such, it does not receive God's mercy in prayer. But to the extent that it drives away passionate thoughts, it acquires mourning and contrition. And in proportion to contrition and the piercing of the heart it is granted merciful comfort, and, after long remaining in these feelings with humility, it at last transforms the desiring part of the soul.

2. When the single mind is threefold, while yet remaining single, it is united with the Divine Threefold Oneness, closes the door to all prelest, sin and error and becomes above flesh, above the world and above the prince of this world. Having thus escaped their snares, it remains wholly

enclosed in itself and in God, tasting the spiritual joy which flows from within. And the single mind is threefold, while yet remaining single, when it returns to itself and rises through itself to God. The mind's return to itself is its guarding of itself, and its rising to God comes of prayer. When a man abides in this collected state of mind and in this soaring to God, then, curbing his volatile thoughts by intense effort of self-constraint, he mentally approaches God, meets with the ineffable, tastes of the life to come and knows by spiritual apprehension how good is the Lord, as the Singer of Psalms says, ' Taste and see that the Lord is good' (Ps. xxxiii. 8). To bring the mind to a threefold state so that, while being one and the same, it guards, is guarded, and performs prayer is perhaps not so difficult, but to remain long in this state, which gives birth to something indescribable, is exceedingly difficult. The work on any other virtue is small and very easy compared with it. This is why many, by refusing the straitness of the virtue of prayer, fail to acquire the spaciousness of the gifts; while those who endure it are granted the greatest Divine intercessions, which give them strength to undertake and endure all things, and joyfully to strive forward, since it makes the difficult easy and gives our nature angelic power, as it were, to do what is above nature; in the words of the Prophet, 'But they that wait on God shall renew their strength; they shall put forth new feathers like eagles; they shall run, and not be weary; they shall walk, and not hunger' (Isaiah xl. 31).

3. What is called mind is also activity of mind, consisting of thoughts and understandings; and mind is the power, too, which produces this, and which in the Scriptures is also called heart. Through this power of the mind, the most important of our powers, the soul within us thinks. In those who practise prayer, the action of mind, consisting of thoughts, is easily purified; but the soul which gives birth to these thoughts will not become pure unless at the same time all its other powers are purified. For the soul is one, although it has many powers; therefore the whole of it is defiled, if evil has crept into any one of its powers; for since the soul is one and single, all its other powers are in communication with that one. Since each of the powers is manifested in different actions, it may be that, through special attention and

diligence, one of these actions temporarily proves pure. But it cannot be concluded from this that the whole power is pure, since, being in communication with others, it may be more impure than pure. In this way, if, through special attention and diligence during prayer, the action of a man's mind proves pure and he acquires, within measure, either enlightenment of understanding or mental illumination (contemplation), and if in consequence he considers himself purified, he will delude himself and, falling into a lie, will in his conceit open wide the doors to him who is ever trying to seduce us. But if, knowing the uncleanness of his heart, he does not puff himself up at a measure of, as it were, accidental purity, then with its help he will see more clearly the uncleanness of the other powers of his soul, will progress in humility, increase his mourning and contrition, and will try to find effective remedies for each power of the soul, cleansing his active part by deeds, his mental part by knowledge, the contemplative part by prayer and, through them, reaching the true, perfect and stable purity of heart and mind, which no one ever gains except by perfection in actions, constant contrition, contemplation and prayer in contemplation.

APPENDIX II

From the life of St. Gregory Palamas, Archbishop, miracle-worker of Thessalonica[44]

How all Christians in general must pray without ceasing

Let no one think, my brother-Christians, that it is the duty only of priests and monks to pray without ceasing, and not of laymen. No, no; it is the duty of all of us Christians to remain always in prayer. For look what the most holy Patriarch of Constantinople, Philotheus, writes in his life of St. Gregory of Thessalonica. This saint had a beloved friend by the name of Job, a very simple but most virtuous man. Once, while conversing with him, His Eminence said of prayer that every Christian in general should strive to pray always, and to pray without ceasing, as Apostle Paul commands all Christians, 'Pray without ceasing' (1 Thess. v. 17), and as the prophet David says of himself, although he was a king and had to concern himself with his whole kingdom: 'I foresaw the Lord always before my face' (Ps. xv. 8), that is, in my prayer I always mentally see the Lord before me. Gregory the Theologian also teaches all Christians to say God's name in prayer more often than to breathe. . . .

So, my Christian brethren, I too implore you, together also with St. Chrysostom, for the sake of saving your souls, do not neglect the practice of this prayer. Imitate those I have mentioned and follow in their footsteps as far as you can. At first it may appear very difficult to you, but be assured, as it were from Almighty God, that this very name of our Lord Jesus Christ, constantly

[44] This text, considerably abridged here, terminates both the Greek and Russian versions. A section of it draws on Philotheus' Life of Palamas; the remainder appears to have been written by one of the compilers of the Greek Philokalia. (Translators' note.)

412

invoked by you, will help you to overcome all difficulties, and in the course of time you will become used to this practice and will taste how sweet is the name of the Lord. Then you will learn by experience that this practice is not impossible and not difficult, but both possible and easy. This is why St. Paul, who knew better than we the great good which such prayer would bring, commanded us to pray without ceasing. He would not have imposed this obligation upon us if it were extremely difficult and impossible, for he knew beforehand that in such case, having no possibility of fulfilling it, we would inevitably prove to be disobedient and would transgress his commandment, thus incurring blame and condemnation. The Apostle could have had no such intention.

Moreover, bear in mind the method of prayer—how it is possible to pray without ceasing, namely by praying in the mind. And this we can always do if we so wish. For when we sit down to work with our hands, when we walk, when we eat, when we drink we can always pray mentally and practise this mental prayer—the true prayer pleasing to God. Let us work with the body and pray with the soul. Let our outer man perform his bodily tasks, and let the inner man be entirely dedicated to the service of God, never abandoning this spiritual practice of mental prayer, as Jesus, God and Man, commanded us, saying: 'But thou, when thou prayest, enter into thy closet, and when thou hast shut thy door, pray to thy Father which is in secret' (Matt. vi. 6). The closet of the soul is the body; our doors are the five bodily senses. The soul enters its closet when the mind does not wander hither and thither, roaming among things and affairs of the world, but stays within, in our heart. Our senses become closed and remain closed when we do not let them be attached to external sensory things, and in this way our mind remains free from every worldly attachment, and by secret mental prayer unites with God its Father.

'And thy Father which seeth in secret shall reward thee openly,' adds the Lord. God who knows all secret things sees mental prayer and rewards it openly with great gifts. For that prayer is true and perfect which fills the soul with Divine grace and spiritual gifts. As chrism perfumes the jar the more strongly the tighter it is closed, so prayer, the more fast it is imprisoned in the heart, abounds the more in Divine grace.

Blessed are those who acquire the habit of this heavenly practice, for by it they overcome every temptation of the evil demons, as David overcame the proud Goliath. It extinguishes the unruly lusts of the flesh, as the three men extinguished the flames of the furnace. This practice of inner prayer tames passions as Daniel tamed the wild beasts. By it the dew of the Holy Spirit is brought down upon the heart, as Elijah brought down rain on Mount Carmel. This mental prayer reaches to the very throne of God and is preserved in golden vials, sending forth their odours before the Lord, as John the Divine saw in the Revelation, 'Four and twenty elders fell down before the Lamb, having every one of them harps, and golden vials full of odours, which are the prayers of the saints' (Rev. v. 8). This mental prayer is the light which illumines man's soul and inflames his heart with the fire of love of God. It is the chain linking God with man and man with God. Oh the incomparable blessing of mental prayer! It allows a man constantly to converse with God. Oh truly wonderful and more than wonderful—to be with one's body among men while in one's mind conversing with God.

Angels have no physical voice, but mentally never cease to sing glory to God. This is their sole occupation and all their life is dedicated to this. So, brother, when you enter your closet and close your door, that is, when your mind is not darting hither and thither but enters within your heart, and your senses are confined and barred against things of this world, and when you pray thus always, you too are then like the holy angels, and your Father, Who sees your prayer in secret, which you bring Him in the hidden depths of your heart, will reward you openly by great spiritual gifts.

But what other and greater rewards can you wish from this when, as I said, you are mentally always before the face of God and are constantly conversing with Him—conversing with God, without Whom no man can ever be blessed either here or in another life?

Finally, my brother, whoever you may be, when you take up this book and, having read it, wish to test in practice the profit which mental prayer brings to the soul, I beg you, when you begin to pray thus, pray God with one invocation, 'Lord have mercy', for the soul of him who has worked on compiling this book and of him who helped to give it to the public. For they have great need of your prayer to receive God's mercy for their soul, as you for yours. May it be so! May it be so!

APPENDIX III

List of Writers in the Greek Philokalia, compiled by Macarius of Corinth and Nicodemus of the Holy Mountain. Venice, 1792

PART I

St. Antony the Great
St. Abba Isaiah
Abba Evagrius the Monk
St. John Cassian
St. Mark the Ascetic
Hesychius of Jerusalem
St. Nilus of Sinai
Diadoch of Photikos
John of Carpathos
St. Theodore of Edessa
St. Maximus the Confessor
Abba Thalassius
St. John Damascene
Abba Philemon
Theognostus
Philotheus of Sinai
Elias Ekdikos
St. John Climacus (of the Ladder)

PART II

Peter Damascene
Simeon Metaphrastes

St. Simeon the New Theologian
Nicetas Stethatos
Theoleptus of Philadelphia
Nicephorus the Solitary
St. Gregory of Sinai
St. Gregory of Thessalonica (Palamas)
Hagiorite Tome
Callistus and Ignatius of Xanthopoulos
Callistus, Patriarch
Callistus Telecudes
Selection from the Holy Fathers on Prayer and Attention
Callistus Cataphygiotes
Simeon, Archbishop of Thessalonica
Anonymous Treatise on the Jesus Prayer
Interpretation of the words 'Lord have mercy'
Maximus Kapsokalivitos
Macarius of Corinth or Nicodemus the Hagiorite

List of Writers in the Slavonic Dobrotolubiye, translated by Paissy Velichkovsky. Moscow, 1793

PART I

St. Antony the Great
St. Mark the Ascetic
St. Simeon the New Theologian
St. Gregory of Sinai
Theophan, a Monk

Nicephorus the Solitary
Theoleptus of Philadelphia
Callistus, Patriarch
Callistus and Ignatius of Xantho-
poulos
Abba Evagrius the Monk

PART II

Hesychius of Jerusalem
Philotheus of Sinai

PART III

St. Abba Isaiah
Peter Damascene

List of Writers in the Russian Dobrotolubiye, translated by Theophan the Recluse. 1877, et seq.

VOL. I

St. Antony the Great
St. Macarius the Great
St. Abba Isaiah
St. Mark the Ascetic
Abba Evagrius the Monk

VOL. II

St. John Cassian
Hesychius of Jerusalem
St. Nilus of Sinai
St. Ephraim of Syria
St. John Climacus (of the Ladder)
Sts. Barsanuphius and John
St. Abba Dorotheus
St. Isaac of Syria (Nineveh)

VOL. III

Diadoch of Photikos
John of Carpathos
Abba Zossima
St. Maximus the Confessor
Abba Thalassius
St. Theodore of Edessa
The Blessed Theodore
Abba Philemon
Theognostus
Philotheus of Sinai
Elias Ekdikos

VOL. IV

St. Theodore the Studite

VOL. V

St. Simeon the New Theologian

APPENDICES

Simeon the Devout
Nicetas Stethatos
Theoleptus of Philadelphia
St. Gregory of Sinai
Nicephorus the Solitary
St. Gregory of Thessalonica
  (Palamas)
Callistus and Ignatius of Xantho-
  poulos
Callistus, Patriarch

Callistus Telecudes
Selection from the Holy Fathers
  on Prayer and Attention
Simeon, Archbishop of Thessa-
  lonica
Interpretation of the prayer
  'Lord have mercy'
Maximus Kapsokalivitos
Macarius of Corinth or Nico-
  demus the Hagiorite

INDEX OF PROPER NAMES

INDEX OF PROPER NAMES